Good Citizenship in America

Good Citizenship in America describes the history in America of a civic ideal of who enjoys membership in the state and what obligations that entails. Before 1865, the ideal called for virtuous political behavior by some people (republicanism) but gradually extended the franchise beyond early republican expectations to many people (democracy). Democracy continued to expand after 1865, to women and people of color. At the same time, republicanism was challenged when economic development fostered serious disparities of property and income. In the twentieth century the civic ideal was somewhat displaced by consumer aspirations and satisfactions, which flowered especially after World War II. More recently, however, environmental problems and the creative destruction generated by globalization suggest that good citizens should instruct government to rein in consumerism by promoting public policies inspired by "economic conscience." *Good Citizenship in America* is an easily accessible analysis of civic trends in America, and it recommends strengthening much that is decent in American life.

David M. Ricci, professor and former chairman in the departments of Political Science and American Studies at the Hebrew University in Jerusalem, is also the author of *Community Power and Democratic Theory*, *The Tragedy of Political Science*, and *The Transformation of American Politics*. He is a frequent visitor to the United States and has taught at Pennsylvania State University, the University of Pennsylvania, American University, the University of Tulsa, the University of Wisconsin in Milwaukee, and the Johns Hopkins University. He has been a visiting scholar at the Woodrow Wilson International Center for Scholars in Washington, D.C., at the Institute for Advanced Study at Princeton University, and at the Brookings Institution.

Good Citizenship in America

DAVID M. RICCI

The Hebrew University

CAMBRIDGE
UNIVERSITY PRESS

PUBLISHED BY THE PRESS SYNDICATE OF THE UNIVERSITY OF CAMBRIDGE
The Pitt Building, Trumpington Street, Cambridge, United Kingdom

CAMBRIDGE UNIVERSITY PRESS
The Edinburgh Building, Cambridge CB2 2RU, UK
40 West 20th Street, New York, NY 10011-4211, USA
477 Williamstown Road, Port Melbourne, VIC 3207, Australia
Ruiz de Alarcón 13, 28014 Madrid, Spain
Dock House, The Waterfront, Cape Town 8001, South Africa

http://www.cambridge.org

First published 2004

Printed in the United States of America

Typeface Sabon 10/13 pt.   *System* LATEX 2$_\varepsilon$ [TB]

A catalog record for this book is available from the British Library.

Library of Congress Cataloging in Publication Data
Ricci, David M.
Good citizenship in America / David M. Ricci.
    p.   cm.
Includes bibliographical references and index.
ISBN 0-521-83580-1 – ISBN 0-521-54370-3 (pbk.)
    1. Citizenship – United States – History.   2. Political participation – United States –
History.   1. Title.

JK1759.R45   2004
323.6′0973 – dc22

2003063547

ISBN 0 521 83580 1 hardback
ISBN 0 521 54370 3 paperback

Contents

Tables

PART I

ORIGINS

The Concept of Citizenship

Some features of American politics stand out clearly. There are fifty states, which exercise substantial powers according to the Constitution. Congress has two houses, one with 435 members, the other with 100, and both must agree before bills can become national laws. The president serves a four-year term, and perhaps another, is charged with administering various government agencies, and has a commanding role in foreign affairs. The federal courts work through districts and circuits, and the Supreme Court sits in a marble palace in Washington. The details are endless, but one knows more or less what to look for and where.

Good citizenship is less tangible, more difficult to study, and sometimes overlooked in the national roster of political institutions. Americans admire good citizenship. But they are not always sure what citizens should do on behalf of the communities in which they live. This is so even though many people believe that, when civic practice does not measure up to its ideal, a vital element is missing from the national landscape.

In truth, the concern for good citizenship, no matter how imprecisely defined, takes aim at something very important. That is, Americans understand not only that government officials should work properly but also that citizens must help assure the quality of public life. The point is self-evident: In a democracy citizens rule, yet if they rule badly, all will suffer. Thus it is no exaggeration to say that not just constitutional checks and balances but also the practice of good citizenship has helped the nation to establish justice, insure domestic tranquility, provide for the common defense, promote the general welfare, and secure liberty.

A General Concern

Many Americans worry about how they and their neighbors do, or do not, practice good citizenship. This anxiety appears in newspaper editorials, in political speeches, in sermons, and so forth, with formal expressions such as the report of the National Commission on Civic Renewal entitled *A Nation of Spectators: How Civic Disengagement Weakens America and What We Can Do About It.*[1]

The commission, for example, strove to examine citizenship impartially, in the belief that concern for that subject cuts across party affiliations and is therefore an all-American impulse. Co-chaired by former Democratic Senator Sam Nunn of Georgia and former Republican Chairman of the National Endowment for the Humanities William Bennett, the commission worried, in a nonpartisan way, over symptoms of political disengagement such as a rate of national voter turnout that declined in presidential elections from 62.8 percent in 1960 to 48.9 percent in 1996, even while turnout in state and local elections hovered around 10 to 20 percent.[2]

Commission members were aware, no doubt, that the right to vote is shared today by most citizens, although this was not always the case in American history. But the will to vote together with friends, neighbors, countrymen, and countrywomen, and thereby to take part in producing election results capable of desirably shaping public life, seemed to the commission, and to many other observers, quite weak.[3]

---

[1] The report was funded by the Pew Trusts and published at the University of Maryland in 1998.

[2] Many political scientists believe that low voter turnout indicates a serious shortfall in civic behavior. This is because election results conclusively put candidates into office or keep them out, whereas lobbying is an uncertain business that may or may not persuade elected officials to respond to constituent preferences. Furthermore, most adult Americans, of whatever means, have the right to vote, whereas various forms of lobbying are practiced by people who possess resources of time, energy, money, ethnicity, gender, location, talent, and more, that are not distributed equally among America's citizens. Thomas E. Patterson, *The Vanishing Voter: Public Involvement in an Age of Uncertainty* (New York: Knopf, 2002); and Marvin P. Wattenberg, *Where Have All the Voters Gone?* (Cambridge: Harvard Univ. Press, 2002), are both troubled by low voter turnout. Less concern on that score appears in Michael Schudson, *The Good Citizen: A History of American Civic Life* (Cambridge: Harvard Univ. Press, 1998), esp. pp. 294–314.

[3] One reason for civic disengagement is that many citizens believe government ignores what they want. See National Issues Forums Research, *Governing America: Our Choices, Our Challenge: How People Are Thinking About Democratic Government in the U.S.* (Englewood Cliffs, N.J.: John Doble Research Associates, 1998). This report was sponsored by the Kettering Foundation of Dayton, Ohio. See also Joseph S. Nye, Jr., Philip D. Zelikow, and David C. King (eds.), *Why People Don't Trust Government* (Cambridge: Harvard Univ. Press, 1997).

From this reality we may deduce that nonvoters are, in a sense, bad citizens. They do not intend their abstention to harm public life and institutions. But neither do they regard themselves as obliged to fill what may be called *the office of citizenship*, which is nowhere formally defined but constitutes a vital calling in any democratic society. Of that office, more in a moment.

The Public and Hidden Transcripts

From frequent usage, citizenship is a tangled concept with many connotations. Americans have talked about citizenship for more than two hundred years, and many millions of them have practiced it, for better or worse, during the same time as voters, candidates, officeholders, civic activists, and, when necessary, soldiers.[4] The subject is so large, then, that no one can analyze it by consulting more than a representative sample of documents and studies indicating what Americans have thought about citizenship in the past and what they think about it today. Unfortunately, to survey only some sources and not others means that, inevitably, some opinions and the people who express them will be slighted. I cannot avoid this result, but I can explain the reasoning that guided my choice of source materials for this book.

To make a long story short, I decided that the best place to locate a representative sample of documents and studies bearing on American citizenship is in what James C. Scott calls *the public transcript*. This is Scott's term for the visible part of any nation's conversation with itself, with its founders and their descendants.[5] In America, the public transcript includes official documents such as the Mayflower Compact (1620), the Declaration of Independence (1776), and the Constitution (1789); political speeches such as George Washington's Farewell Address (1796), Abraham Lincoln's Gettysburg Address (1863), and John F. Kennedy's inaugural address (1961); and Supreme Court decisions such as *Dred Scott v. Sandford* (1857), *Lochner v. New York* (1905), and *Brown v. Board of Education* (1954). The American public transcript also includes widely publicized expressions of opinion such as *The Federalist* (1787–1788),

---

4 Stephen E. Ambrose, *Citizen Soldiers: The U.S. Army from the Normandy Beaches to the Bulge to the Surrender of Germany, June 7, 1944–May 7, 1945* (New York: Touchstone, 1998), expresses enormous respect for ordinary Americans who took up arms and risked all to preserve the commonweal.

5 On public and hidden transcripts, see James C. Scott, *Domination and the Arts of Resistance: Hidden Transcripts* (New Haven: Yale Univ. Press, 1990), esp. pp. 1–16.

"The Seneca Falls Declaration" (1848), and Martin Luther King's "Letter from Birmingham Jail" (1963).[6]

When Scott analyzed nondemocratic societies, he regarded their public transcripts as expressing the values of dominant elites. Less powerful members of the same societies, he observed, who might be slaves, serfs, women, or religious and ethnic minorities, are often afraid to speak openly about what they believe. They therefore express their opinions and ideas, if at all, mostly in a *hidden transcript*, whose sometimes bitter messages, perhaps via diaries, letters, protest songs, and folktales, run through underground channels of communication.

To consult a substantial part of America's public transcript, even without citing the country's hidden transcript, requires considerable effort. It is a feasible effort, however, as compared with trying to study both. Moreover, in the case of considering America's devotion to citizenship, one may regard this feasible effort as adequate, if not perfect. In a democracy where frequent elections determine who will hold public office, we can reasonably assume that political people, even elites, will mostly refrain from expressing opinions that contradict what large numbers of citizens believe.

In fact, democratic candidates usually affirm principles and preferences that match what voters hold to be true. To do otherwise would cause the mavericks to lose electorally. It follows, in a free society, that we can look at what political winners say and assume that it approximately represents what many, or most, citizens believe. This is so even though, as we shall see, many Americans, and especially women and many African Americans, were prevented from voting and being elected until fairly recently.

Three Kinds of Citizenship

Considering mainly the public transcript, it would appear that for Americans there are three parts to the concept of citizenship. Popular talk does not refer to these aspects of the subject separately and distinctly,

---

[6] Anthologies are helpful for providing representative selections of American thinking on public affairs. For example, Richard Hofstadter (ed.), *Great Issues in American History*, 3 vols. (New York: Vintage, 1958); Alpheus T. Mason (ed.), *Free Government in the Making: Readings in American Political Thought*, 4th ed. (New York: Oxford Univ. Press, 1985); and Diane Ravitch (ed.), *The American Reader: Words That Moved a Nation* (New York: Harper, 1991).

but to keep them clear in our minds it will be convenient here to call them Citizenship I, Citizenship II, and Citizenship III.[7]

Citizenship I refers to a person's legal status, to whether or not, for example, one is entitled to reside in a specific country and, in modern times, carry its passport. Many regimes furnish their members with this status, which can exist today in places as diverse as Canada, Iran, and Japan. Citizenship I may entail little social interaction, as when Daniel Boone is reputed to have moved his homestead further into the primeval forest when he saw smoke from his neighbor's log cabin. For such people, as de jure citizens, good citizenship is mainly a matter of obeying their country's laws, which defend and preserve the local populace. The range of obedience will vary, of course, from country to country, from stopping at red lights, to serving on juries, to enlisting in the armed forces, to paying taxes.

Citizenship II appears when, in some cases, there exists an active sort of belonging, with political participation as its hallmark. Here, some de jure members of the community (Citizenship I) are entitled to participate in making decisions concerning matters of public interest. In most modern states, and especially in republics and democracies, Citizenship II has become a common condition of political life. In America, Abraham Lincoln praised this sort of politics when he described it in the Gettysburg Address as "government of the people, by the people, and for the people."[8] For such people, good citizenship means obeying their country's laws *and* helping to make them, say, by voting or being elected to a public office.

---

[7] A qualifying note is in order here. Some colleagues have advised me, in a spirit of constructive criticism, to call these elements of the subject "legal citizenship," "political citizenship," and "moral citizenship." I understand their concern, but I prefer not to do that. The danger is that talking in this book about citizenship via familiar words might suggest to readers connotations and consequences beyond those conveyed by the novel, and somewhat inelegant, terms of Citizenship I, Citizenship II, and Citizenship III. That is, telling my story in terms used elsewhere might evoke reminders of other stories, other considerations, other problems, other aspirations, and other expectations. These may be legitimate for other purposes but they may also divert attention from the messages I hope my story will convey. It is for the same reason that I make few references in this book to some very profound academic thinkers such as Charles Taylor, Jurgen Habermas, and Hannah Arendt, who have written often and compellingly about citizenship. Citing the ideas of such thinkers would suggest, at least to scholarly readers, implications far beyond those I wish to convey in the more popular story I tell. Thus citing, for example, Taylor, Habermas, and Arendt would bring us into an academic conversation, both interesting and important, which is, nevertheless, not the one I set out to analyze.

[8] This speech, from 1863, is analyzed at length in Garry Wills, *Lincoln at Gettysburg: The Words That Remade America* (New York: Simon and Schuster, 1992).

Citizenship III is more difficult to define than its companions. Unconditional civil obedience and routine political participation can produce bad social results, as in cases where citizens like Germany's Adolf Eichmann collaborated calmly, or even enthusiastically, in legalized genocide.[9] Consequently, it seems advisable to promote an active practice of citizenship that is sometimes better than ordinary. In this third sense of the subject, good citizenship requires more than just obeying a country's laws and perhaps helping to make them. Citizenship III requires, in addition, virtuous behavior. It obliges citizens to use their political resources and skills to participate well, that is, to maintain not just effective laws but also a decent state.[10]

Good Citizens and Good People

Although each sort of citizenship may be admirable in its own way, they can be separately and jointly problematical. For example, between Citizenship I and Citizenship III, there is an implication that individuals can practice a commendable form of citizenship only by combining the demands of two different social roles. On this score, the right sort of citizenship, for Americans at least, sometimes requires a good citizen to also be a good person.

Yet between these two roles, and therefore between Citizenship I and Citizenship III, there arises a moral dilemma that may be traced back at least to the life of Socrates. One of the great teachers in Western history, Socrates left no written works to tell his story. But commentators like Plato, who admired Socrates as a good man, say he insisted on challenging the traditions of Athens to the point where his neighbors, assembled in an Athenian jury, convicted him in 399 B.C. of corrupting young people by leading them away from routine obedience to Athenian laws (Citizenship I).

Acting publicly in his role as a good person (Citizenship III), Socrates apparently argued that, under certain circumstances, citizens should not contribute to injustice by obeying an immoral state. With examples such as the Socratic life in mind, men and women in Western society for more than two thousand years have envisioned the social role of a good person

---

9 See Hannah Arendt, *Eichmann in Jerusalem: A Report on the Banality of Evil* (New York: Viking, 1963).

10 Edmund Burke is credited with expressing this point succinctly: "The only thing necessary for the triumph of evil is for good men to do nothing." However, no one has found this exact quotation in his writings. See Antony Jay (ed.), *The Oxford Dictionary of Political Quotations* (New York: Oxford Univ. Press, 1997), p. 68.

as being sometimes, and occasionally severely, at odds with the social role of being a good citizen. After all, obedience provides predictability and stability in public affairs, whereas civil disobedience, no matter how virtuous, may undermine the routine conditions of law and order that enable members of a community to prosper together.

This point is highly significant. Because the role of good citizen (who sustains law, order, and security) and the role of good person (who pursues curiosity, knowledge, and virtue) may point toward different ends and call for different kinds of behavior, people may not know for sure how to act out Citizenship III. In truth, to combine law and virtue can be difficult and even dangerous.[11] Thus Allied judges at the Nuremburg Trials after World War II assumed that, on behalf of natural justice, good Germans in the law-abiding sense (Citizenship I) should have disobeyed Nazi laws (Citizenship III). But how could Germans have known this before they lost the war? Where, for example, as the storm raged, could most Germans have found the courage to risk losing their loved ones by hiding Jews or Gypsies if death for entire families was the punishment for helping enemies of the state according to laws enforced by implacable Nazi police?

In an example closer to home, many Americans admired Martin Luther King, Jr. Here was a man who led thousands of demonstrators to disobey segregation laws but seemed praiseworthy for serving the highest interests of a country that had, shamefully, enacted such laws in many states and enforced them even in Washington, D.C. King reminded his followers of legalized racism in Nazi Germany and insisted that decent men and women must strongly oppose America's homegrown brand of the same evil.[12] The principle seems clear, but where should one draw the line? Are antiabortionists who defy the Supreme Court as laudable as Martin Luther King, Jr.?

---

[11] Literature offers classic cases of this dilemma. For example, in Herman Melville's *Billy Budd*, introd. by Cyrus R. K. Patell (orig., 1924; New York: Washington Square Press, 1999), the British government charged Captain Edward Vere with upholding naval orders aboard his warship in order to maintain crew discipline in defense of the realm. Consequently, Vere felt obliged to pronounce a death sentence against Billy Budd, the simpleminded but decent sailor who, intensely provoked, impulsively struck and accidentally killed his cruel petty officer, John Claggert. Must all government officials, as obedient servants of the state (Citizenship I), enforce their country's laws so mercilessly to uphold public order?

[12] See Martin Luther King, Jr., "Letter from Birmingham Jail," in King, *Why We Can't Wait* (New York: Signet, 1964), pp. 76–95, on why laws should be tested by higher standards of virtue.

Inclusion and Empowerment

In American history, Citizenship II is doubly problematic. First, we know the country did not extend participation rights to all its early residents, for example, not to Native Americans, not to slaves, not to most free African Americans later, not for a long time to women, and very slowly to Asian immigrants.[13] Only gradually, then, did such people overcome what is called today *exclusion*.

Modern scholars have extensively explored the history of political exclusion.[14] I will not refer much to their research, though. I will comment a little on who gained *inclusion*, who got Citizenship II, when they received it, and why they seemed worthy of possessing it. But mainly I will ask what they were supposed to do with Citizenship II once it entitled them to participate. I assume that although many Americans were long left out of political life, most of them were eventually brought in. Accordingly, I am concerned less with what happened on the way to that end and more with what people believe they should do upon arriving.

Second, even when, as today, political inclusion is widely authorized by law, there remains a question of whether or not to assure to each citizen enough resources so that he or she will be able to exercise the rights of Citizenship II effectively.[15] In this regard, we sometimes speak of empowerment, which may flow from entitlements.

Thus most Americans now possess the rights of Citizenship II. These include the rights to vote, to speak freely, to organize interest groups, to petition government officials, to run for office, to be elected, and so forth. However, social conditions enable some Americans to exercise these rights more powerfully than others, on the basis of health, wealth, ethnicity, gender, race, or other potent resources. Where this is so, it may seem reasonable to redress, perhaps by affirmative action, various imbalances

---

[13] On the long struggle for Asian inclusion, see Hyung-Chan Kim (ed.), *Asian Americans and the Supreme Court: A Documentary History* (New York: Greenwood, 1992); and Hyung-Chan Kim (ed.), *Asian Americans and Congress: A Documentary History* (Westport, Conn.: Greenwood, 1996).

[14] For example, see Rogers M. Smith, *Civic Ideals: Conflicting Visions of Citizenship in U.S. History* (New Haven: Yale Univ. Press, 1997).

[15] Resource questions are explored in Judith Shklar, *American Citizenship: The Quest for Inclusion* (Cambridge: Harvard Univ. Press, 1991); Jeff Spinner, *The Boundaries of Citizenship: Race, Ethnicity and Nationality in the Liberal State* (Baltimore: Johns Hopkins Univ. Press, 1994); and Timothy J. Gaffaney, *Freedom for the Poor: Welfare and the Foundations of Democratic Citizenship* (Boulder, Colo.: Westview, 2000).

of political outcome that will exist even after almost everyone enjoys the status of Citizenship II.[16]

Some scholars focus mainly on how inequality of resources may affect Citizenship II. I have chosen, instead, to write about citizens who are not particularly weak. I hope those who suffer on this score will eventually overcome resource deprivation, for example, when immigrant children join the mainstream of American life, or as women gradually surmount various forms of gender discrimination.[17] I agree then, and very strongly, with those who say that the struggle for entitlement and empowerment must continue. But this struggle is more a project for marginal groups than for the great majority of people in America today.

In short, the problem I wish to address, without suggesting that other problems are less urgent, is not a matter of who has what but what should be done by those who, in large numbers, are already positioned to practice citizenship properly. Here are citizens who command democratic rights and economic resources beyond the reach of most men and women in previous eras and other societies. Here, I think, are the people who, in an important sense, collectively constitute America.[18]

The Office of Citizenship

The people I have in mind are especially obligated, as we shall see in later chapters as the tale of citizenship unfolds. Thus where Citizenship II is widely available to Americans, and when Citizenship III calls upon them to use their civic rights virtuously, then, in effect, to *do* citizenship properly is to fulfill *the office of citizenship*. On this score, where a combination of

---

[16] For example, see the feminist arguments advanced by Iris Marion Young in *Justice and the Politics of Difference* (Princeton: Princeton Univ. Press, 1990), and see the racial arguments advanced by Lani Guinier in *The Tyranny of the Majority: Fundamental Fairness in Representative Democracy* (New York: Free Press, 1994).

[17] As a group, African Americans seem most likely *not* to overcome the difficulties of unequal resource distribution. I will have more to say on that probability later.

[18] In short, my point of departure is the plight of those Americans who possess the resources needed for practicing citizenship but do not know how to use them properly. Robert Bellah, Richard Madsen, William M. Sullivan, Ann Swidler, and Steven M. Tipton, in *Habits of the Heart: Individualism and Commitment in American Life* (New York: Harper and Row, 1986), describes various hardworking and moderately successful Americans who want to be good persons and good citizens. Although not wealthy, these people have the means to do whatever they should to that end. The trouble is that they do not know what to do in order to fulfill their citizenship ideals, and there is the problem I intend to address.

implications flowing from Citizenship II and Citizenship III speaks to well-meaning men and women, it is not enough to ignore political campaigns, to stay home on election day, or to vote solely on behalf of one's own interest.

Instead, there is something in the American political tradition that calls upon men and women not just to take their places as members of the community but to serve it faithfully, to respect its needs, to reflect on the public interest, and to act on behalf of that end, all this so that friends and neighbors may live effectively and prosper together. In the language of citizenship, I will call this sort of behavior "republicanism" and eventually analyze many of its implications. Most importantly, for the moment, let us note that if rights and right are to be blended properly, then elected officials are not the only people who must give shape to public life. Citizens too have this responsibility, even if they exercise it less frequently than politicians whose careers lead them, or so they say, to practice good citizenship at work every day. Thus Americans tend to believe that education is not just for acquiring vocational skills but should prepare "the people" both morally and intellectually to exercise their sovereignty.[19]

Does endorsement of this ideal translate into practice? Not necessarily, because those who admire republicanism do not always abide by its requirements. Similarly, churchgoers, and even ministers, do not always abstain from sin. No matter. Many Americans feel that citizenship entails some degree of social responsibility and therefore requires them to make at least some effort to fulfill the obligations of a small but significant public office. Here is the reason today for popular concern over voter fatigue, over indifference to public affairs, and over distrust of public institutions, all being indications that, deplorably, many citizens are

---

[19] See Chief Justice Earl Warren, writing for a unanimous Supreme Court in *Brown v. Board of Education of Topeka* (1954) 347 U.S. 483, forbidding segregated and hence unequal access to grade school education because "education is perhaps the most important function of state and local governments.... It is required in the performance of our most basic public responsibilities.... It is the very foundation of good citizenship." The same is true for young adults in higher education. Thus a regent of the University of California, speaking in 1872: "The University is founded primarily on that essential principle of free republican government which affirms that the state is bound to furnish the citizen the means of discharging the duties it imposes on him: if the state imposes duties that require intelligence, it is the office of the state to furnish the means of intelligence." Quoted in Frederick Rudolph, *The American College and University: A History* (New York: Vintage, 1962), p. 278. For earlier indications of this view, see Richard D. Brown, *The Strength of a People: The Idea of an Informed Citizenry in America, 1650–1870* (Chapel Hill: Univ. of North Carolina Press, 1996).

unwilling to do what they must in order to serve a democratic society as they should.[20]

Exceptionalism

To focus on citizenship is to shed light on what sets America apart from other countries, a matter of variation which scholars refer to as American *exceptionalism*. On this score, America may be regarded as politically special, or even exceptional, in several ways. For example, when George Washington and his comrades rebelled against Great Britain, the country had neither strong feudal institutions nor much enthusiasm for aristocratic political ideas. Thus Americans could devise and maintain democratic practices without interference from powerful local forces still committed to an older regime.[21] Moreover, until the late 1800s, moving west encouraged many Americans to continue the process of democratic invention. Thus frontier life instilled among pioneers a sense of individual worth and the need for voluntary participation in community affairs.[22] And, finally, Americans inhabited a country blessed with great quantities of untapped natural resources such as fertile land. Thus they could create economic abundance without, for the most part, fighting among themselves to divide up a fairly static economic pie.[23]

Historians and other scholars who first underscored such qualities in American life recognized their significance by comparing what happened

---

[20] Some scholars have usefully described the imperatives that inform Citizenship III although, of course, they do not use that term. Thus Joseph Tussman has argued that citizens who enjoy participation rights should use them to fulfill the requirements of a public office where citizens so acting constitute *the sovereign tribunal*. Moreover, he has pointed out that in that office citizens must go beyond *bargaining* to *deliberating*, which is less a matter of determining the momentary price of a policy than of recognizing its intrinsic value. See Joseph Tussman, *Obligation and the Body Politic* (New York: Oxford Univ. Press, 1960), pp. 104–121. See also David Shelbourne, *The Principle of Duty: An Essay on the Foundations of the Civic Order* (London: Sinclair-Stevenson, 1994), passim. Shelbourne claims that when citizens enjoy the safety and comfort of living within a civic order, they are morally obliged to foster policies which help to maintain that order rather than just extract benefits from it. In other words, as citizens are entitled to rights, so also they must fulfill the duty of using those rights to do what is right.

[21] Louis Hartz, *The Liberal Tradition in America* (New York: Harcourt, Brace and World, 1955). Some historians today feel that Hartz praised American politics too highly. For example, see James T. Kloppenberg, "In Retrospect: Louis Hartz and *The Liberal Tradition in America*," *Reviews in American History* (September 2001), pp. 460–478.

[22] Frederick Jackson Turner, *The Frontier in American History* (New York: Holt, Rinehart and Winston, 1920).

[23] David M. Potter, *People of Plenty: Economic Abundance and the American Character* (Chicago: Univ. of Chicago Press, 1954).

in the United States with what happened elsewhere. The comparative technique has therefore long been valuable for suggesting useful generalizations about America as a wide-ranging and populous society even though it is composed mainly of small-scale acts and aspirations. More recently, making comparisons suggests that, after the Soviet Union collapsed, after more than a decade of political turmoil and reconstruction in Eastern and Central Europe, after fierce bloodletting in Bosnia, Kosovo, and Chechnya, and after frightful ethnic violence in Central Africa and Southeast Asia, we should look for additional comparative insights into American exceptionalism. For example, what caused, or permitted, public life to collapse in those places but not in America?

Citizenship and Nationalism

The answer to this question is, I think, that Americans over many generations fashioned a distinctive ideal of citizenship which, for the most part, eased or prevented at least some civic tensions that earlier political thinkers had recognized but not resolved. Apologies, and regrets, are certainly in order for the fact that America's voting majority did not always honor this ideal but long discriminated politically against women and various minorities. However, the ideal did inspire, from the outset, some admirable practices in American public life, and it was, as enshrined in documents like the Declaration of Independence, available for extension when, as time passed, citizens increasingly discarded timeworn prejudices in favor of more equality and democracy.[24]

Now comparatively speaking, two great organizing principles – of *citizenship* and *nationalism* – animated most political leaders in the late eighteenth and nineteenth centuries. This was the time when Western countries struggled to replace the assemblage of emperors, kings, princes, aristocrats, established churches, estates, and other feudal relics that Alexis de Tocqueville called "the old regime" in European civilization.[25] Real world solutions to the challenge mixed and combined the two major principles in varying proportions from one place to another, and some Marxian experiments that eventually failed, such as in the Soviet Union, seemed to avoid both entirely. Nevertheless, it is clear that, in this time of challenge, America established a government rooted mainly in the concept

[24] Two great exceptions are the relations between mainstream Americans and African Americans and between mainstream Americans and Native Americans. I will say something about these exceptions in later chapters.

[25] Alexis de Tocqueville, *The Old Regime and the Revolution*, trans. Alan S. Kahan (orig., 1856; Chicago: Univ. of Chicago Press, 1998).

of *citizenship*,[26] while many other Western countries, such as France, Germany, and Italy, developed governments which drew their legitimacy more from *nationalism* or some other form of ethnic solidarity.[27]

Here lies a civic dividing line that may be described in legal terms. In many countries, and in America today, most people acquire citizenship rights either by being born in their state's territory (jus soli) or by being born into a family that already enjoys those rights (jus sanguinis).[28] In America, however, an additional factor has long been at work, because millions of people acquired such rights in the past, and millions continue to acquire them today, by coming to the United States from abroad and committing themselves to uphold America's political ideals.[29]

In fact, it is a vision of America as a land of conscious and committed citizenship that characterizes the American experience[30] to the point of forestalling a considerable measure, but not all, of ethnic exclusion and some, but not all, large-scale social violence. To that end American citizenship, which from the Revolution has been republican in *mode*, became during the nineteenth and twentieth centuries democratic in *scale*. As we shall see, this amalgamation was a remarkable accomplishment in the history of Western political thought that had, until Americans

---

[26] See Michael Walzer, *What It Means to Be an American: Essays on the American Experience* (New York: Marsilio, 1992), p. 27:

> The United States is not a literal "nation of nationalities" or a "social union of social unions." At least, the singular nation or union is not constituted by, it is not a combination or fastening together of, the plural nationalities or unions. In some sense, it includes them; it provides a framework for their coexistence; but they are not its parts.... The parts are individual men and women. The United States is an association of citizens.

[27] On nationalism as a principle for organizing governments, or for justifying existing governmental arrangements, see Elie Kedourie, *Nationalism*, 4th ed. (Oxford: Blackwell, 1993); E. J. Hobsbawm, *Nations and Nationalism Since 1780: Programme, Myth, and Reality*, 2nd ed. (New York: Cambridge Univ. Press, 1992); and William Pfaff, *The Wrath of Nations: Civilization and the Furies of Nationalism* (New York: Simon and Schuster, 1993).

[28] For a discussion of these legal principles and how they have influenced acquiring citizenship in two European countries, see Rogers Brubaker, *Citizenship and Nationhood in France and Germany* (Cambridge: Harvard Univ. Press, 1992), pp. 81–82, 86–125, and passim.

[29] The point is not that, after the original establishment of colonial settlements, immigrants were ever a majority but that they were always a visible and significant presence.

[30] An indication of America's indifference to nationalism as a theory of community appears by omission in Richard Wightman Fox and James T. Kloppenberg, *A Companion to American Thought* (Oxford: Blackwell, 1995). This book is an encyclopedia of articles dealing mainly with social concepts that have concerned American thinkers over several centuries. It contains articles on "democracy," "liberalism," "republicanism," and "citizenship," but it has none on "nationalism."

fashioned their distinctive vision of political belonging and behavior, regarded republicanism and democracy as quite different and somewhat incompatible.

Prologue

In the chapters that follow, we will see where the American concept of citizenship came from and how the roles of good citizen and good person began their tense, but constructive, journey into the modern world. On the way, I will describe how citizenship as an ideal evolved and what devotion to it in America has achieved. I will then explain, starting in Chapter 6, how a passion for acquiring economic goods, especially in the twentieth century, via consumerism, has impaired the ability of Americans to practice citizenship as originally envisioned. And finally, in Chapters 7–9, I will suggest that if citizens would more widely recognize the debilitating effects of consumerism, they might work together toward striking a better balance than exists today between material comforts and civic decency.

A Caveat

Political theorists like Ronald Beiner note that people learn how to behave civically from stories they hear about public life and how they should contribute to it.[31] On that score, I believe the evolution of citizenship as a concept is an inspiring chronicle based largely on what Americans have told each other about who they are and what they should be.[32] It may seem like a fairy tale, however, to historians and political scientists who pride themselves on being realists, on hewing to the unvarnished truth, on being suspicious of superlatives and wary of the worst in human affairs.

Let me stipulate, then, that in what follows I do not intend to highlight the warts in American history. Surely there are many. I am, however, more

---

[31] See Ronald Beiner, *What's the Matter with Liberalism?* (Berkeley: Univ. of California Press, 1992), pp. 10–14: "Prologue: The Theorist as Storyteller." See also Rogers M. Smith, *Stories of Peoplehood: The Politics and Morals of Political Membership* (Cambridge: Cambridge Univ. Press, 2003). Part of Smith's approach appeared earlier in his "Citizenship and the Politics of People Building," *Citizenship Studies* (February 2001), pp. 73–96, which describes civic stories as "political," "economic," "constitutive," or a mixture of all three.

[32] Every historical narrative relies on a selection of facts that supports the author's view of what happened. My selection highlights an ideal of republican citizenship not because that ideal has inspired all civic practices in America but because I believe that it has been expressed frequently and that it is worth remembering as a potential inspiration. This strategy of highlighting positive aspects of the past is similar, I think, to what David Harlan, in his *The Degradation of American History* (Chicago: Univ. of Chicago Press, 1997), recommends that historians do at least occasionally.

2

Early Civic Ideas

Ideas they inherited from the past strongly influenced America's Founders.[1] Paradoxically, then, we must begin the tale of good citizenship in America by using this chapter to take a quick look elsewhere, into the background to American political thought. We do not need to search there for new evidence of revolutionary intentions but to touch base with a vocabulary familiar to literate Europeans several centuries ago. That vocabulary was especially important to the Founders because, whenever political crises erupt, people will communicate with one another, and perhaps act together, via whatever terms are available to them.[2]

Our starting point is this: Early Americans did not invent an entirely novel understanding of citizenship. Rather, they came on the historical

---

[1] John Maynard Keynes commented famously on this reality. See Keynes, *The General Theory of Employment, Interest, and Money* (London: Macmillan, 1936), p. 383:

> The ideas of economists and political philosophers, both when they are right and when they are wrong, are more powerful than is commonly understood. Indeed the world is ruled by little else. Practical men, who believe themselves to be quite exempt from any intellectual influences, are usually the slaves of some defunct economist. Madmen in authority, who hear voices in the air, are distilling their frenzy from some academic scribbler of a few years back.

[2] For a modern example, see Michael Walzer, *Just and Unjust Wars* (New York: Basic, 1977), p. xi:

> Our anger and indignation [over the Vietnam War] were shaped by the words available to express them.... [and when] we talked about aggression and neutrality ... atrocities and war crimes, we were drawing upon the work of many generations of men and women.... Without this vocabulary, we could not have thought about the Vietnam war as we did, let alone have communicated our thoughts to other people.

stage at a moment when Western talk about public affairs permitted them to think about their situation in ways that were partly old and partly new. More specifically, when the Founders decided to break away from Great Britain, they knew they would have to construct in America an alternative to the "old order" of empires, monarchies, nobility, established churches, guilds, corporations, and other feudal relics that reigned in England and other European countries. To that end, they looked for instruction to what Europeans, including themselves, already knew about governments that had existed in various forms and disparate eras.

Thus on behalf of their fateful project, men such as Thomas Jefferson, John Adams, James Madison, Alexander Hamilton, and their colleagues ransacked the store of political wisdom that had accumulated over centuries. In the process, colonial leaders considered how important ideas about citizenship had evolved for two thousand years. Consequently, as we shall see in Chapter 3, during the Founding they created a special sort of government based, at least partly, on civic ideas first expounded by men such as Plato and Aristotle, St. Augustine and Martin Luther, Thomas Hobbes and John Locke.

Greece

To begin with, many of the Founders admired Greek and Roman writings.[3] Thus their thinking grew out of a tradition of Western political thought that began in the ancient world of more than one hundred Greek city states. The typical such state, or *polis*, centered upon some sort of urban settlement, perhaps walled, surrounded by rough hamlets and primitive farms in the countryside, with populations ranging from a few thousand to more than two hundred thousand in Athens around 425 B.C.

By modern standards, Greeks were very poor. They had no stoves, no bed sheets, no public transit, no newspapers, no televisions, no computers, no antibiotics, no indoor plumbing, no stockings, no watches, no orange juice, no pizza, no glass windows, no armchairs, no toothbrushes, and none of a thousand and one other things familiar to modern life. The lack of such amenities would be remedied over more than two thousand years, making us far more comfortable than Greeks were. But they already had a remarkable ability to think constructively about public life. And some of the concepts they developed on that score, which emerged from what we

---

[3] Carl Richard, *The Founders and the Classics: Greece, Rome, and the American Enlightenment* (Cambridge: Harvard Univ. Press, 1994).

would regard as grinding poverty, came eventually to influence American political thinking.

The Polis

The setting for these concepts, the polis, was small, ethnically homogeneous, and discriminatory.[4] As such, it was smaller than modern Greece no less America; it disdained cultural pluralism at home, although Herodotus occasionally admired it abroad;[5] it accepted the subordination of women and the brutality of slavery; and it refused to let significant numbers of strangers join the local community. Except for visitors and foreign residents, the people of a polis like Athens, Sparta, Thebes, Melos, Argos, or Corcyra were somewhat or entirely knowledgeable about their small country and those who dwelt in it; they shared language, religion, laws, family customs, epic poems, and public holidays; and they reserved membership in the community, which we have called Citizenship I, mainly to those born into it.[6]

Each polis thought of itself as ethically special, as distinguished from even its Greek neighbors by a particularly commendable combination of gods, rites, traditions, ordinances, heroes, local clans, and governmental institutions. Under the circumstances, education was crucial to maintaining civic distinctions, such as those between Athens and Sparta, over time. Such education – in schools, in religious ceremonies, in drama festivals, in athletic competitions – stressed that even as membership in the community would benefit many individuals, so also it would impose serious and sometimes onerous duties on some of them.

For example, because Greeks lived under constant threat of raiding and war, defense of the realm superseded other social and political aspirations. Accordingly, it was logical that being a citizen required most free men to serve their polis as soldiers when necessary. This dangerous aspect of citizenship, and the pride Greeks took in exercising it, accounts for the epitaph on Aeschylus's tombstone. The lines engraved there said nothing about the extraordinary *Orestian Trilogy* that Aeschylus wrote but recalled

---

[4] Peter Riesenberg, *Citizenship in the Western Tradition: Plato to Rousseau* (Chapel Hill: Univ. of North Carolina Press, 1992), p. xviii.

[5] See what he had to say about foreign lands in Walter Blanco and Jennifer Tolbert Roberts (eds.), *Herodotus: The Histories* (New York: Norton, 1992).

[6] In Athens, for example, a law passed in 450/451 B.C. stipulated that a child would enjoy citizenship only if both of its parents were Athenian citizens. See Robert K. Sinclair, *Democracy and Participation in Athens* (Cambridge: Cambridge Univ. Press, 1988), pp. 24–27, for the evolution of criteria for granting Athenian citizenship.

that he fought bravely against Persians at the Battle of Marathon in
490 B.C.

Good States and Bad States

Although the courage of citizens was clearly necessary to maintain the polis, Greek philosophers knew that, beyond battle, citizenship was a complex and problematical affair. Consequently, they approached it within
the framework of several related concepts, starting with the good state
and the bad state.[7]

The *good state* provided for defense; it facilitated prosperity; it honored
the gods; it educated local children; and it commended virtue. This is not
to say that every good state resembled every other good state, because
safety, order, and human well-being could be achieved by different sorts
of regimes. This happened, for example, when Athens fostered patriotism
based on pride in cultural projects while Sparta encouraged communal
discipline by regimenting schooling so as to turn male children into hard-
ened soldiers. Here were two different societies, taking alternative roads
to success, whereby each achieved civic results worthy of respect.

Bad states fell into two classes. The first, of no particular structure,
included those that made serious errors of judgment, perhaps evoked by
some flaw of a particular regime in power.[8] The second, crucial to political thought in the long run, contained those ruled on behalf of their rulers
rather than the citizenry as a whole. On this score, writers like Aristotle
described a dangerous sequence of regimes, where monarchy would deteriorate into tyranny, where aristocracy would deteriorate into oligarchy,
and where a government of several social ranks would deteriorate into

---

[7] I am using the term *state* here even though it came into widespread use only after
Machiavelli wrote about states in the sixteenth century. Greek philosophers would have
spoken of *regimes* rather than *states*, but the latter term will help us keep in mind some
aspects of those regimes which later thinkers, also concerned about citizenship, singled
out for emphasis.

[8] For example, Thucydides criticized Athens for heeding the demagoguery of Alcibiades and
sending its fleet and army to be defeated at Syracuse in 413 B.C.; Plato blamed Athens for
permitting a jury of citizens to sentence Socrates to death in 399 B.C.; and Isocrates condemned Spartan imperialism for being notably brutal during the fourth century B.C., as if
the Spartans, who displayed great integrity at home, could not resist moral corruption when abroad. See Thucydides, *The History of the Peloponnesian War*, ed. Richard
Livingstone (New York: Oxford Univ. Press, 1960), Bks. VI–VII, pp. 274–388; Plato,
"Apology" and "Crito," in Thomas G. West (ed.), *Four Texts on Socrates: Plato's Euthyphro,
Apology, and Crito and Aristophanes' Clouds* (Ithaca: Cornell Univ. Press, 1998), pp. 63–
114; and Isocrates, "Panegyricus," in George Norlin (ed.), *Isocrates*, Vol. I (Cambridge:
Harvard Univ. Press, 1928), esp. pp. 195–201.

democracy. In each case, the bad regime ignored the interests of those out of power and enacted laws to benefit whoever ruled the rest.

Citizenship

Beyond good and bad states lay the concept of citizenship. Men, women, and children might be citizens by birth, in which case they enjoyed the status of Citizenship I although, of course, they knew nothing of that term. What is more important is that, on behalf of Greek political thought, Aristotle defined Citizenship II although, again, he did not use that term. As he put it, the citizen is "a man who shares in the administration of justice and in the holding of office."[9] For Athens, this entailed voting on juries and in assemblies and holding offices pertaining to defense, public construction, religious ceremonies, tax collecting, record keeping, and more.[10]

In the Aristotelian sense, to be a citizen defines who one *is*. But beyond that, the Greeks spoke of what citizens should *do*, whereupon an aspiration to practicing citizenship properly, rather than just possessing it, defined the social role of *good citizen*. On this score, the Greeks assigned two sorts of good citizenship practices differently, but not incompatibly, to Citizenship I and II.

Citizenship I

Those Greeks who possessed Citizenship I were morally required, almost without exception, to exercise good citizenship by obeying their city's laws. Experience showed that when people routinely did so, the ensuing public order led to well-being. Barring unforeseen setbacks, that well-being encouraged members of the community to live together peacefully rather than to try violently to overthrow existing governments in the hope of improving the quality of city life.

Plato wrote about men acting as good citizens in this sense when he described Socrates as refusing the advice of friends to go into exile rather than commit suicide in fulfillment of the death sentence passed upon him by an Athenian jury. According to Plato, Socrates insisted that every man should carry out "his just agreements." It followed that Socrates should not flee from Athens because doing so would mock the city's laws which,

---

[9] Aristotle, *The Politics of Aristotle*, trans. and ed. Ernest Barker (New York: Oxford Univ. Press, 1946), Bk. III, Ch. 1, p. 94.

[10] For a description of public offices in Athens during the fourth century B.C., see "The Constitution of Athens," in Jonathan Barnes (ed.), *The Complete Works of Aristotle*, 2 vols. (Princeton: Princeton Univ. Press, 1984), Vol. II, pp. 2367–2383.

before empowering the errant jury, had brought Socrates into the world, educated him, and given him "and every other citizen a share of all the good things" that a city can provide.[11]

In a common form, essential but not especially celebrated in Plato's dialogues, military service expressed obedience to the city's laws. Violence from abroad always lurked in the fiercely contested world of Greek city states. When it threatened, the citizen who obeyed a civic call to arms deserved high praise from those who, consequently, lived in safety.[12] This reality prompted Pericles to eulogize fallen Athenian soldiers early in the Peloponnesian War, saying that their "greatness was won . . . with courage, with knowledge of their duty, and with a sense of honor in action, [by men] . . . who sacrificed their lives as the best offerings on . . . [Athens's] behalf." Therefore, he continued, "the whole earth is the sepulcher of famous men; and their story is not graven only on stone over their native earth, but lives on far away, without visible symbol, woven into the stuff of other men's lives."[13]

Citizenship II

Some Greeks who possessed Citizenship I, which required legal obedience, were also citizens in the sense of Citizenship II, which imposed upon them a duty to participate in their city's public life. For more than 150 years, starting with the reforms of Cleisthenes in 509 B.C., most freemen in Athens were citizens in this second sense, and Pericles had them in mind when he claimed that, as compared with Sparta, Athens stood as an inspiration to all of Greece.

Thus, said Pericles, Athenian citizens were bold and imaginative; they acted only after open debate and careful reflection; and the city could afford to befriend those whom she favored not out of self-interest but because her freedoms inspired wise policies and strong loyalties. Under the circumstances, Pericles ridiculed those who, even though empowered in other cities, contributed nothing there to the sort of civic intercourse which

---

[11] See Plato's "Crito" in Plato and Xenophon, *Socratic Discourses*, ed. A. D. Lindsay (New York: Dutton, 1910), pp. 350–364.

[12] Man-to-man combat in Greek warfare called for great courage. For a description of Greek battlefield activity, see John Keegan, *A History of Warfare* (New York: Vintage, 1993), pp. 237–263.

[13] Pericles, "Funeral Oration," in Thucydides, *History of the Peloponnesian War*, pp. 115–116. Similar praise appeared in the epitaph written by Simonides for three hundred Spartans who died fighting under the command of Leonidas against the Persians at the Battle of Thermopylae in 480 B.C.: "Go tell the city, stranger, that here we lie, obedient to her decrees." Quoted in Elizabeth Rawson, *The Spartan Tradition in European Thought* (Oxford: Clarendon, 1969), p. 15.

made Athens great. A citizen who was politically passive or indifferent to public affairs, said Pericles, was not just "quiet but useless."[14]

Good People Versus Good Citizens

When Greeks thought about the matrix of good states, bad states, civic obedience, and civic participation, they realized that relations among these political factors could become complicated and even dangerous. This was especially so when people who were expected to act as *good citizens* might feel obliged to act also as *good persons*.

Aristotle noted the tension that could arise, within the same citizen, between these two social roles.[15] Every citizen, he said, belongs to his polis as to an association, which is analogous to a sailor belonging to a boat crew. That being the case, one can say that to be a good citizen, like being a proper member of any other association, requires one to serve a collective goal, in this case helping the polis to fulfill its mission of, say, protecting the city's residents just as sailors bring cargo safely from one port to another. It follows, however, that the excellence of good citizens will vary from place to place as the kind of regime varies from polis to polis. For example, the good Athenian citizen will behave differently from the good Spartan citizen, depending on the way in which each obeys laws that are specific to his city.

Citizenship III

But what of absolute good or true excellence? Greek philosophers said that people should try to live justly, should try to do good, should refuse to lead an unexamined life. Yet there were scores of Greek states, with many different regimes and laws, into which anyone might be born by chance. And when that happened, what should a person seeking justice do if a local law required behavior that seemed to him patently bad? What, for example, should one do to try to change such a law?

Here were grounds for Citizenship III, but the dangers of civil disobedience made these questions difficult to answer. After all, if everyone were entitled to decide which laws to obey and which to ignore, public order would collapse and with it would vanish the safety and well-being afforded by life in the polis.[16]

---

[14] Thucydides, *History of the Peloponnesian War*, Bk. II, Secs. 37–40, pp. 111–114.

[15] Aristotle, *The Politics*, Bk. III, Ch. 4, pp. 101–106.

[16] To use a twentieth-century example, if the local dictator runs trains on time, should good citizens *not* rebel against fascism and concentration camps?

Plato and Aristotle

With such large questions in mind, Plato suggested in *The Republic*, around
375 B.C., creating a polis ruled by philosopher kings whose laws, on behalf
of defense and prosperity, would conform to men's natural character so
precisely that they would be entirely just.[17] Under the circumstances, tension between being a good citizen and a good person would not arise,
because even good people would find no reason for disobedience. Furthermore, because such a polis would maintain a proper balance of classes
over time, between rulers and ruled, it would not deteriorate into a *bad
state*, make bad laws, and thereby become unacceptable to virtuous men.

But around 335 B.C., in *The Politics*, Aristotle dismissed Plato's suggestion by saying that if men were as perfect as Plato described them in *The
Republic*, no one would need government or laws to begin with. Instead,
Aristotle argued that a good state must not just promote defense and
prosperity but also seek to achieve what Aristotle called a *good life*, to
which all good men could assent.[18] The obstacle to easily fostering such a
life, he said, was that different classes of real men, as opposed to those in
Plato's imagined city, will disagree on how to define goodness, depending
on their social and economic circumstances.

And so Aristotle suggested that the best, but not necessarily the perfect,
regime would draw upon the talents and contributions of several classes
of men in public life. To this end he recommended a bit of monarchy, a bit
of aristocracy, and a bit of democracy, the whole mixture tilted toward
moderation and sobriety by a large middle class that would stand constructively between the upper class which did not know how to obey and
the lower class which did not know how to rule.[19] Like Plato, Aristotle
in effect recommended a stable regime that would not deteriorate and
therefore become so bad as to forfeit the allegiance of virtuous men.

Sophocles

No one knows how many Greeks read the works or heard the lectures of
Thucydides, Plato, and Aristotle. It is clear, though, that many Athenians
attended their city's drama festivals, where some of what Greek historians
and philosophers said about cities, citizens, laws, obedience, and virtue
appeared on stage. This was especially so in Sophocles' powerful tragedy
Antigone, which first played in 442 B.C. and then entered the corpus of
classical writings that strongly impressed America's Founders.

---

[17] See Allan Bloom (ed.), *The Republic of Plato* (New York: Basic, 1968).
[18] *The Politics*, Bk. III, Ch. 9, pp. 119–120.   [19] Ibid., Bk. IV, Ch. 11, pp. 180–181.

Antigone recounts what happens after Polynices died leading an unsuc-
cessful revolt against Creon, king of Thebes. As punishment for violating
public order, Creon declares that Polynices' body must be left unburied
outside the city's walls so that, because it will be eaten by scavengers,
the rebel's soul will be unable to enter the underworld. Antigone buries
Polynices anyway, and later tells Creon, her uncle, that because the rebel
was her brother, she was religiously obliged to bury him. Creon explains
to her that, under pain of death, she should have obeyed his ruling. After
all, he is responsible for public safety and well-being; he pursues those
ends by upholding law and order; without obedience to his commands,
anarchy and discord will kill the city's inhabitants.

Antigone insists that she was right to bury Polynices, whereupon Creon
insists on punishing her for doing so. Later, Creon realizes that his ruling was too harsh and must be softened. But Antigone dies before she
can be released from the cave where Creon's soldiers have imprisoned
her; Creon's anguished son Haemon, her betrothed, commits suicide; and
Haemon's grieving mother Eurydice, the queen, kills herself as well.

The tragedy of *Antigone* highlighted the potential conflict between what
Greeks demanded of a good citizen and what a good person might feel
compelled to do instead. Creon said that whoever disobeys the city's laws
must be punished for endangering "the ship that bears us all."[20] Antigone
said that, come what may, she had to bury her brother because secular
laws are inferior to moral commands laid down by Zeus.[21] Antigone
was, in short, a good person who could not be a good citizen if being so
required obedience to bad laws.[22]

A Matrix of Civic Factors

Today, Athens, Sparta, and their neighbors seem far away in time and
place. Still, it is worth remembering how Plato, Aristotle, and Sophocles
approached issues of citizenship because, along with other Greeks, these
men invented some of the fundamental elements of our story. Later
European thinkers took the Greek concepts we have just reviewed,

[20] Sophocles, *Antigone*, in L. R. Lind (ed.), *Ten Greek Plays* (Boston: Houghton Mifflin,
1957), p. 87.
[21] Ibid., p. 92.
[22] Sophocles offered no clear guidelines for practicing Citizenship III. However, he did offer
the warning of *Antigone*'s chorus that, if men would be happy, they must seek wisdom.
See ibid., p. 109. In other words, members of the polis must compromise between the
conflicting ideals of obedience and flexibility, order and equity, prudence and justice.

TABLE 2.1. *Basic Concepts of Citizenship*

	Citizenship	Roles	Standards
State	I	Good citizen	Obey laws
	II	Good citizen	Participate
Society	III	Good person	Exercise virtue

discussed them at length, and adapted them to fit changing times.[23] Those concepts then inspired a tradition of talk about citizenship that unfolded, century after century, to reach America two thousand years later. There, as we saw in Chapter 1, they remain a template for how Americans think about civic practices even today.

Now because we will meet these concepts again and again, it is important to keep them analytically distinct in our minds. To that end, they may be portrayed graphically as shown in Table 2.1. This table shows how basic concepts of citizenship are logically and analytically related. In that sense, it is abstractly useful. However, we will have to fine-tune Table 2.1 later in this chapter, and we will have to repeat the exercise several times in subsequent chapters, because some very serious problems arose from one era to another concerning, especially, Citizenship II and III.

For example, in some Western states people disagreed, and violently so, on who should participate in public life. That is, sometimes they quarreled over who deserved what we today call political *inclusion*, or the possession of rights associated with Citizenship II. Furthermore, as we shall see, problems did not stop there, for Table 2.1 shows, via Citizenship III, that good people should serve society by exercising virtue.[24] Yet from time to time, even after *Antigone* warned men that civil disobedience can be dangerous, public order in some Western states wavered or collapsed because various people insisted on practicing this special sort of virtue, however it might be defined momentarily. That is, there were times when routine elements of Citizenship I and II were challenged, and dangerously

---

[23] Thus the adaptation of *Antigone* by French playwright Jean Anouilh, which was staged in German-occupied Paris in 1942, sympathized more with the civil disobedience of Antigone than with the realpolitik of Creon. See Jean Anouilh, *Antigone*, trans. Barbara Bray (London: Methuen, 2001).

[24] I am using the term *society* here for simplicity's sake. Just as Greeks did not think of the "state" but of "regimes," so also they did not speak of a "society" as standing against even the "regime," which itself created and maintained a way of life. Nevertheless, to the modern ear, *society* is the term that best helps us keep in mind the setting within which "good persons," as in Aristotle's conundrum, might feel obliged to disobey a bad law of the polis.

so, within *states* by forceful manifestations of Citizenship III which arose, sometimes without regard for political order, in *society*.

The Empires

America's Founders knew that ancient Greece invented citizenship. But they also knew that Aristotle's student Alexander the Great made the world of city states obsolete forever. First, he and his father, Philip of Macedonia, conquered Greece at the battle of Chaeronea in 338 B.C. Next, in constant campaigning from 335 to 323 B.C., Alexander went on to establish a Hellenistic Empire that stretched east to India and south to Egypt.

Under the circumstances, people could see that public life in an independent polis was no longer feasible. The polis regimes, of whatever constitution, had failed to defend themselves from being swallowed up in the cosmopolis created by Alexander. Furthermore, in the empire only a few people could hold public offices and perform political functions. Accordingly, active Greek citizenship, in the sense of Citizenship II, could not survive.

The Philosophical Schools

As the polis ideal retreated, Greek philosophers created new schools of thought, including Epicureanism, Cynicism, Skepticism, and Stoicism. These focused mainly on the nature of men in their private life wherever that might be. Against the backdrop of cultural differences from one place to another in far-flung empires, the new ideas, which passed on into Roman and Christian thinking, included a tendency to regard men as, in some sense, morally equal. The polis, in contrast, had been so provincial as to speculate mostly about what set men apart and very little about universal qualities.

By modern standards, the new schools promoted social progress. But the notion that men shared a spark of common humanity did not lead philosophers, in centuries dominated first by Hellenistic and later by Roman imperialism, to conclude that most men should wield the powers of Citizenship II. True, Rome granted citizenship to many slaves and foreigners who helped wage her wars of conquest, and their numbers increased while the empire grew.[25] But such men enjoyed legal rights that rarely extended to political participation, and when the Edict of Caracalla eventually granted citizenship to most imperial freemen in A.D. 212, the

---

[25] See Arthur Boak and William Sinnigen, *A History of Rome to A.D. 565*, 5th ed. (New York: Macmillan, 1965), pp. 277–278.

act aimed mainly to identify members of the empire within the framework of Citizenship I in order to facilitate more efficient tax collecting.[26]

Cicero

In this age of limited political participation, Stoics redefined the concepts of good state, good citizen, and good person in ways that would strongly impress later thinkers. Marcus Tullius Cicero, for example, writing in the first century B.C., praised what remained of the Roman Republic before Julius Caesar set in motion the events that led to Augustus's becoming emperor in 27 B.C. Cicero described the republic as a *mixed government* based on some monarchy in the Consuls, some aristocracy in the Senate, and some democracy in the elected Tribunes.[27]

With his enthusiasm for such arrangements, Cicero kept alive the Greek notion of stabilizing government by building into it a balance of worthy contributions from different social groups. Just as importantly, with Rome's mixed government as his example, Cicero defined for all time the ideal of a *republic*, which is sometimes translated into English as a *commonwealth*. As Cicero described it, a republic is the people's affair.[28] Yet the people is not just a collection of human beings but a large group "associated in an agreement with respect to justice and a partnership for the common good."[29]

By defining the republic in this way, Cicero aspired to resolve the potential for conflict between good citizens and good people. Thus in his terms, every society must balance the goals of prudence and justice.[30] That is, it must enforce obedience to laws that secure survival and well-being for the community, even while it should permit virtuous behavior which causes no harm to other people. The point is that, in a republic united by shared chords of justice, those who make laws must take what is right as their guideline. If they will do so, their laws will serve the community rather

---

[26] Ibid., pp. 343–344.

[27] Marcus Tullius Cicero, *On the Commonwealth*, trans. and introd. George Sabine and Stanley Smith (orig., 51 B.C.; Indianapolis: Bobbs-Merrill, 1960), "Introduction," pp. 62–64; Bk. I, Secs. 29–46, pp. 134, 140, 151.

[28] *Res publica*, or the republic in Latin, means the thing that belongs to the public.

[29] The point is made by Scipio in *On the Commonwealth*, Bk. I, Sec. 25, p. 129. It meant that Syracuse under Dionysius may have been beautiful and powerful. Syracuse was not a republic, though, because Dionysius was a tyrant and ruled for his own benefit rather than to promote justice for all Syracuseans. See also *On The Commonwealth*, Bk. III, Sec. 31, p. 224.

[30] This is a main theme in *Cicero on Moral Obligation*, trans. and introd. John Higginbotham (Berkeley: Univ. of California Press, 1967), esp. Bk. III, pp. 137–183.

than private interests. In which case good people will be able to obey such laws in good conscience.[31] For one tradition in Western political philosophy, and especially for America's Founders, here was the epitome of a *good state*.

Marcus Aurelius

Of course, a passion for justice did not always animate Roman rulers. For example, we still remember the emperor Caligula, who apparently intended to appoint his horse to the office of Consul, and the emperor Nero, who reputedly torched the imperial capital.[32] On the other hand, the Stoic ideal of good government and just laws was present even when corruption plagued the empire. Thus Stoicism was occasionally remembered and even praised by Romans such as the emperor Marcus Aurelius (A.D. 121–180). In *The Meditations*, Marcus insisted that every man has a duty to do good. For him this meant that, even when beset by adversity, every man should seek to promote social well-being in order to preserve the society in which he and other men may prosper.[33] Marcus wrote the book, but his ideas came from predecessors who infused Stoicism with connotations of duty and responsibility that command respect even today.

Christianity

While Stoicism dominated Roman thinking, Christianity began to promote a new sense of who people are and what their communities are about. It was inevitable, then, that Christians would redefine Western political concepts as their theology superseded paganism within the Roman Empire after the emperor Constantine converted to Christianity in 312, and especially once Theodosius I made Christianity the empire's official religion in 391.

Sin and Virtue

Early Christianity confronted a Roman Empire that, in the West, collapsed in the fifth century but whose nature, while it lasted, Christians could not

---

[31] See *On the Commonwealth*, Bk. III, pp. 143–145ff., about how, as a matter of self-interest, everyone who helps make the laws should do so to benefit the community because, without a strong community, even lawmakers will perish.

[32] On Caligula and Nero, see Suetonius, *The Lives of the Twelve Caesars* (New York: Modern Library, 1931), pp. 200, 268.

[33] Marcus Aurelius Antoninus, *The Meditations* (Harmondsworth: Penguin, 1964).

TABLE 2.2. *Citizenship for the Universal Church*

	Citizenship	Roles	Standards
State	I	Good citizen	Obey laws
	II	Good citizen	Participate
Society	III	Good person	Exercise Christian virtue

easily explain. The state – be it a polis or a republic or an empire – was clearly capable of doing some good for its people, especially in the realms of defense and commerce. At the same time, the state must be somewhat bad since, according to Christian theology, both rulers and subjects inevitably sin. St. Paul emphasized this limiting factor in human affairs when he wrote that, because Adam sinned in the Garden of Eden by eating an apple from the Tree of Knowledge, all his descendants would also sin, after which Jesus would save only some of them by His grace.[34]

Yet if all people sin, where could Christians find the fairness and moderation necessary for creating and running a good state? Here was the virtue which good people must practice if they are to make the sort of laws that will enable their communities to live well. On this score, as paganism gave way to Christianity, Christian virtue, as set forth in scripture, became the standard to which a good person should aspire, as we see in Table 2.2. It was not clear, though, for followers of Jesus who assumed that the doctrine of original sin was true, that a Christian *could* behave virtuously.

The dilemma was at first mostly moot because, as virtue became more Christian in scope, Citizenship II largely disappeared. Thus in the third century, Rome abandoned even the legal fiction which stipulated that the emperor, who in truth dominated lawmaking, was simply the first citizen among all others, primus inter pares.[35] Most people were now subjects and would remain so after the empire collapsed and feudalism arose on its ruins in Western Europe.

Under the circumstances, most Christians were not expected to make laws well or at all. Yet there remained, for every Christian, a potential conflict between obeying a state's laws, whatever they might be, and refusing, in the name of Christian morality, to obey bad laws. Here was the old counterpoint between Citizenship I and Citizenship III, because

---

[34] Romans 5:12–18. [35] Boak and Sinnigen, *A History of Rome*, p. 448.

if theology seemed to say that rulers are sinful and will make evil laws, some Christians might feel that Heaven required them to ignore those same laws. But if they did so, the perennial danger, which even devout Christians could not ignore, was that social order might collapse.

To forestall chaos, the Church noted that Jesus had declared that Christians should "render unto Caesar the things that are Caesar's, and to God the things that are God's."[36] But Jesus never said exactly which things were which, or how Christians should respond to an evil Caesar. To rectify the oversight, the Church under Pope Gelasius (492–496) adopted a *two-sword theory*, which said that God placed Christendom under the authority of two swords, one secular and the other spiritual. According to this dispensation the Pope, as head of the Church, was entitled to discipline any Christian ruler who, within the pastoral flock, behaved badly. As vague as when Jesus had earlier enunciated a similar concept in different terms, it was, as we shall see, a doctrine that would eventually fail to prevent severe friction between some popes and assorted kings.

St. Augustine

Early Christian thought received much of its shape when St. Augustine (354–430) addressed various issues raised by the intersection of Western Christianity with public life. Most important for our purposes, Augustine, bishop of Hippo in North Africa, started writing *The City of God* in 413, after the Visigoths led by Alaric sacked Rome in 410.[37] His aim was to show how something so shocking could happen, to explain how the world's richest and most powerful city, whose inhabitants had enjoyed centuries of safety and prosperity, could be reduced to wretchedness and misery by a band of primitive people.[38]

In *The City of God* Augustine claimed that Rome fell because of pagan sin, because what looked like "civilization" in Rome entailed the worship of false gods, who could not save the city in its hour of need.[39] Thus Rome fell not because many of its citizens had become Christians over the years and were therefore, as pagan critics charged, too unworldly to

---

[36] Mark, 12:17.   [37] *The City of God* was written from 413 to 426.

[38] Analogies are never entirely persuasive, but perhaps an instructive comparison may be drawn between the horror triggered by the terrorist attack against New York and Washington on September 11, 2001, and the dread caused by barbarians sacking Rome in 410.

[39] Augustine, *The City of God*, trans. Marcus Dods, introd. by Thomas Merton (New York: Modern Library, 1950), Bk. I, Sec. 3, pp. 5–7.

fight fiercely enough to defend Rome successfully. The city fell, instead, because its citizens were too pagan and not Christian enough.

Technically, Augustine indicted paganism within the framework of Cicero's concept of a republic, where the good state represents a people united by a shared sense of justice. Rome, said Augustine, was never a republic in this sense even though Cicero had claimed it to be so. This was because justice requires that men will give what is due to both God and man, whereas Rome could not have been a republic because the city was so pagan as never to have loved Jesus enough to be truly just.[40] In short, whatever the apparent accomplishments of Roman government, Rome was never really republican and never really good, in which case her fall should surprise no one.

From such premises, Augustine went on to offer a Christian vision of human life in what he called the *city of God* and the *city of Earth*. Both exist in this world, although we see around us only the city of Earth. Most importantly, some Christians are only sojourners in the city of Earth, for they live there by the love of God and are actually on their way to Heaven. Theirs is thus the mystical city of God, invisible in everyday surroundings, but present and awaiting those who, by the grace of God, will be saved. Other Christians and their pagan neighbors live for the city of Earth, which is animated by self-love rather than the love of God, and which in public affairs is ruled by the lust for rule. Theirs is the city of Earth now, and they will suffer eternal damnation in Hell afterward.[41]

In the largest scheme of things, Augustine knew that government in the earthly city can provide men with a considerable measure of security and well-being, and that it did so at times while Rome reigned. For such achievements, Augustine observed, God had already rewarded in this life various civic-minded and law-abiding Romans. Indeed, since their lust for rule, although itself an injustice, had led them to desire and maintain earthly peace, Augustine said we should concede that government is not necessarily evil. However, because peace is only a temporary and lesser good, not inherently imbued with the love of God, Christians should seek to join the city of God in order to try to attain there the greater good of everlasting life in Heaven.

---

[40] Ibid., Bk. II, Sec. 21, p. 63; Bk. IV, Sec. 4, pp. 112–113; Bk. XIX, Sec. 21, pp. 699–700, and Sec. 24, p. 706.
[41] For such aspects of the two cities, see ibid., Bk. XIV, Sec. 28, p. 477; Bk. XV, Secs. 1–8, pp. 480–489; and Bk. XIX, Sec. 28, p. 709.

The vision of two cities touched on crucial aspects of citizenship because, if the city of Earth can provide security, it can preserve human lives from day to day. That being so, Augustine would not deny that good citizens, as Greeks had insisted, should obey secular laws.[42] However, since according to Augustine even Christian cities are governed by men who sin from lusting to rule, it would appear that some laws made by those men may be so immoral as to require resistance by virtuous people. Furthermore, resistance may be justified by Augustine's notion that Christians should aspire to join the city of God. Presumably they may gain entrance there, and perhaps eternal life, by practicing Christian virtue.[43] But doing so may, once again, require such citizens to disobey any secular law that offends their religious sensibilities.

In principle, then, Augustinian Christianity implied that citizens may criticize and sometimes disobey their country's laws. But Augustine was not enthusiastic about government by consent (Citizenship II), and he was not, in his day and age, about to encourage individual Christians to decide which laws to obey or not (Citizenship III). Accordingly, he argued that God sometimes tests His children by sending bad men to rule over them, in which case Christian citizens (Citizenship I) should heed His will by obeying whatever laws such men make.[44]

The point conformed to one of St. Paul's injunctions: "Let every soul be subject to the higher powers. For there is no power but of God.... Whoever therefore resisteth the power, resisteth the ordinance of God."[45] Yet if men must submit to any rulers they find in power, the implicit corollary is that political activity, which forms the substance of Citizenship II and III, is not worth studying enough to do well. Thus Augustine did not advise men to try to improve on their fate which was, after all, ordained by God. And thus Augustine, in effect, devalued public life and the concepts that surrounded it.

Thomas Aquinas
If Christianity had stopped there, America's Founders would have lacked some of the terms they needed for their vision of a political community.

---

[42] Ibid., Bk. XIX, Sec. 26, p. 707.

[43] The Augustinian doctrine of predestination did not absolve Christians from behaving virtuously. But it did claim, paradoxically, that God has decided before we act who will receive a place in Heaven, in which case He/She will not dispense salvation according to how well we behave.

[44] *The City of God*, Bk. IV, Sec. 3, p. 112; Bk. XIX, Sec. 15, p. 694.

[45] Romans 13:1–2.

But from 1256 to 1274, while he was teaching at universities in Paris, Rome, and Naples, the Dominican monk St. Thomas Aquinas restored to European political life some of the optimism that Augustine had taken from it.[46] This he did by helping to reincorporate Aristotelian philosophy into the corpus of Western thinking.[47]

Thus Aquinas agreed with Aristotle that there is a natural law which God creates and which men can know by their God-given ability to reason. He further agreed with Aristotle that if men will examine this law rationally, they will see that it tells them to live together politically, in cities or states, in order to attain security, trade, comfort, art, and so forth. Most importantly, Aquinas accepted the Aristotelian notion that political life permits men to exercise a significant measure of virtue or to achieve what Aristotle called the good life.[48]

So far, Aquinas held that reason and politics can help people to achieve commendable ends. However, beyond this point there lies a higher good, said Aquinas, which is salvation, and to know of this good, which requires faith in Jesus Christ the Messiah, he argued that revelation and grace must supplement reason.[49] That is, there are truths that reason cannot discover and that Aristotle did not know. These truths, which appear in the Bible and are interpreted by the Church, do not contradict natural law but complete it. The good Christian, it follows, will heed natural philosophy as far as it goes and will round out his or her understanding of life and virtue by consulting with Christian theology for those guidelines which reason cannot supply.

In this synthesis of Aristotelianism and Christianity, Aquinas revived for Western thinkers the concept of a potentially *good state*, growing

---

[46] Aquinas offered no major work specifically about politics. But his writings on that subject are conveniently collected in A. P. D'Entreves (ed.), *Aquinas: Selected Political Writings* (Oxford: Blackwell, 1959).

[47] One defining characteristic of late Middle Age philosophy and then the Renaissance was the way European intellectuals interpreted classical texts, some long lost or destroyed but recently brought into their world from libraries and monasteries around the Mediterranean and in the Middle East. Among these texts were works by Aristotle, such as *The Politics*, whose sweep and brilliance led many medieval Christians to call him "The Philosopher." The problem with Aristotle was that he had been a pagan, untouched and uninspired by Christ. How, then, could Christians incorporate his shrewd and attractive insights on human life into their worldview? Part of the answer was supplied by Aquinas. Some of the difficulty is illuminated by Umberto Ecco's *The Name of the Rose* (New York: Warner, 1984). In Ecco's story, a medieval monk who is committed to piety and sobriety in Christian life, destroys Aristotle's distracting book on comedy which, in truth, did not survive into the modern era.

[48] For these points, see *Aquinas: Selected Political Writings*, pp. 3–9, 79–83, 103–113.

[49] Ibid., pp. 113–117.

naturally toward praiseworthy ends, and not founded in sin by Cain for the lust of rule as Augustine had believed.[50] Furthermore, because real states do not necessarily attain their full potential but can be better or worse, as the Greeks knew, men should work at making them as good as possible. On this score, Aquinas followed Aristotle and wrote, as Augustine had not, about various regimes, among which he recommended monarchy as best.[51]

To classify states is to judge them, of course, and Aquinas judged both regimes and their rulers. Accordingly, he addressed the issue of obedience which, as we saw, links long-standing notions of states, citizens, and proper civic behavior. To this end, Aquinas accepted the Greek notion that bad rulers serve their own ends rather than the public interest, in which case a monarch may become a tyrant and deserve to be overthrown.[52] He also accepted the basic Christian notion that a bad ruler might command his subjects to trespass against Christian virtue, in which case such a ruler may be removed from temporal power in the name of spiritual values.[53]

Like Augustine, though, Aquinas assumed that men should ordinarily obey secular laws in order to maintain public order and the security it can provide. That is, he favored mostly the role of Citizenship I and was little inclined to recommend that good Christians, via Citizenship III, should feel free to decide when and where to obey laws they considered bad. And so he straddled this issue by citing Jesus's injunction to give unto Caesar that which is Caesar's and to God that which is God's.[54] The problem, as we have seen, was that Jesus never said exactly which was which. This problem Aquinas approached with great caution. Therefore he argued that a state which seems bad should only be overthrown upon advice from some "public authority." This entity presumably consisted of feudal notables, either secular or spiritual or both combined, rather than "the private judgment of individuals."[55]

The Two Swords

Aquinas offered Christians an acceptable way of overcoming Augustine's bleak view of politics, to the point where pursuing civic improvement seemed, as in classical times, a praiseworthy goal. But that pursuit would

---

[50] On Cain, see *The City of God*, Bk. XV, Sec. 1, pp. 478–479.

[51] *Aquinas: Selected Political Writings*, pp. 11–13. This recommendation precluded a revival of Citizenship II.

[52] Ibid., pp. 15–19.   [53] Ibid., pp. 167, 187.

[54] Ibid., p. 187. The reference is to *Matthew*, 22:21.

[55] *Aquinas: Selected Political Writings*, p. 31.

not produce efficient states and modern citizenship until men of the Renaissance and the Reformation would give new meaning to the Christian assumption, endorsed by both Augustine and Aquinas, that temporal and spiritual powers should rule men simultaneously. In a medieval world dominated by this assumption, popes, cardinals, and bishops had a right to meddle in what we call affairs of state. But their doing so encouraged emperors, kings, and princes to interfere with affairs of the Church, if only to defend secular prerogatives. The result was that powerful men found that an effective mixture of temporal and spiritual rule was difficult to achieve because no one could define precisely its boundaries. For example, one signal event where the two powers interacted unsatisfactorily was the tangled web of political infighting between feudal rulers that accompanied the selection of new popes, which led between 1378 and 1417 to the Great Schism, a demoralizing snafu where as many as three popes – Alexander V, Benedict XIII, and Gregory XII – reigned simultaneously.

What Western Europe required, in fact, was for men to decide how they could serve the needs of life in this world while doing what they must to reach salvation in the next. Arguments about which route led to Heaven could not be settled conclusively, since no traveler had returned to describe the way. We should not be surprised, then, that relief of the tension between secular and spiritual swords came not from agreement on religious principles but from a growing perception, new at the time, of what we now call *the autonomy of politics*. Here was the idea that, while not disparaging religion, politics should put men's house on Earth in order without much reference to theology. The Founders would eventually enshrine this idea in America's Constitution.

The Divine Right of Kings

The new understanding gathered strength when some monarchs claimed the divine right of kingship as an answer to what they regarded as unwarranted papal interference in political affairs. Their argument relied on the notion of a world whose largest and smallest details are created and maintained by an all-powerful and all-knowledgeable God. Assuming that such a deity exists, one could also assume that He, rather than any pope, placed kings on their thrones, in which case the king's mandate to rule came from Heaven and should not be challenged from anywhere else.[56]

---

[56] See the *Trew Law of Free Monarchies* (1598), reprinted in *The Political Works of James I*, introd. by Charles H. McIlwain (Cambridge: Harvard Univ. Press, 1918), pp. 53–70.

Armed with elements of this argument, and after Pope Leo X refused to let Henry VIII of England divorce Catherine of Aragon and marry Anne Boleyn, Parliament in the Act of Supremacy (1534) declared Henry to be England's "sovereign." In the new circumstances, Henry placed himself at the head of the Church in England, transformed it into the Anglican Church of England, executed the recalcitrant Sir Thomas More, appointed clergymen friendly to the Crown, seized hundreds of monasteries, and gave large tracts of church property to his supporters.[57]

The divine right of kings was designed to strengthen princes in their struggles against popes by opposing the sanctity of temporal rule to the holiness of spiritual authority.[58] Of course, claims by themselves do not always secure power in the real world, therefore kings were most successful in establishing their independence from Rome when, for whatever reason, local nobles and commoners supported them against the Church. Here, the collapse of theological consensus in Western Christianity during the Reformation helped kings to enlist allies against the Church, but it did so with disastrous results across Europe.

Martin Luther

Martin Luther epitomized the shift in religious thinking that would fatefully affect politics. In 1517, he posted his ninety-five theses at the Castle Church in Wittenberg. These denounced long-standing Catholic practices like the sale of indulgences, the emphasis in many monasteries on praying rather than working, and the administration of various sacraments which, if necessary, cast priests as powerful middlemen between Christians and their God. Luther believed that such practices led to moral and material corruption, as unchaste popes sat on the throne of St. Peter, and as money raised from lay people in Germany flowed to local prelates and Roman coffers.[59]

In the face-off against papal authority, Luther sought and obtained support from German princes, who protected him and his "protestants" for reasons ranging from piety to avarice, reverence to ambition. Whatever their reasons, the conceptual die was cast. Luther and his followers

---

57 See G. R. Elton, *Reform and Reformation: England, 1509–1558* (London: Edward Arnold, 1977); and D. G. Newcombe, *Henry VIII and the English Reformation* (London: Routledge, 1995).

58 Edmund S. Morgan, *Inventing the People: The Rise of Popular Sovereignty in England and America* (New York: Norton, 1988), p. 18.

59 See the stories of papal corruption described in William Manchester, *A World Lit Only by Fire: The Medieval Mind: Portrait of an Age* (Boston: Little, Brown, 1992), pp. 76–85, 131–136.

supported the German princes because they sheltered Protestants, and this support endorsed the divine right of kings to promulgate secular laws which promoted Protestantism even if, at the same time, they offended principles of faith dear to Catholic subjects. After fierce fighting between Catholics and Protestants within the Holy Roman Empire, the principle of permitting kings to establish state churches of their choice, even unto Protestantism, was ratified by the Peace of Augsburg in 1555.[60]

Virtue as Sectarianism

Luther and other Protestants, such as John Calvin in Geneva, advanced different, although sometimes overlapping, theological arguments against Rome. These differences were insignificant, however, with regard to how rejection of Rome per se recast a major concept bearing on politics and citizenship. On that score, the rise of Protestantism changed the Western European definition of what it meant to exercise Christian virtue, which was the standard according to which a good person should behave. Henceforth, each Christian denomination, or sect, would describe its own members as virtuous and would regard other Christians as misled.

The point is worth restating: As the Reformation got under way, virtue became a function of sectarianism, as shown in Table 2.3. The outcome was disastrous, for defining virtue according to competing versions of Christianity led inexorably to war. Kings who regarded themselves as good Christians believed they had a divine right, and even a duty, to maintain laws that would oblige their subjects to practice the true faith. But if that were so, could a good Protestant obey laws made by the king to impose Catholic behavior if, in the Protestant's understanding of God's will, obedience assured that he would go to Hell? The answer was that, as a matter of Citizenship III, violent rebellion against a Catholic king was, for Protestants, justified as resistance to tyranny.[61] Catholics would use

---

[60] The principle was *cuius regio, eius religio*, which means that whoever is entitled to rule the state is also entitled to regulate religion.

[61] The classic work was Philippe Du Plessis-Mornay, *The Defence of Liberty Against Tyrants*, or *Vindiciae Contra Tyrannos* (1579). See this work discussed in Quentin Skinner, *The Foundations of Modern Political Thought*, Vol. 2: *The Age of Reformation* (Cambridge: Cambridge Univ. Press, 1978), pp. 305–338. See also Robert M. Kingdon, "Calvinism and Resistance Theory, 1550–1580," in J. H. Burns (ed.), with Mark Goldie, *Cambridge History of Political Thought, 1450–1700* (Cambridge: Cambridge Univ. Press, 1991), pp. 194–218.

cannot be imposed by force, however adamantly the sovereign may try to do so.[68]

The Treaty of Westphalia

Bodin and Hobbes advocated a concept of sovereignty that Europeans eventually accepted because a century of carnage persuaded them to seek some new rationale for living together. Thus in a time that seemed like almost recent history to America's Founders, the realm of theory became the crucible of practice in terms laid down in 1648 by the Treaty of Westphalia, which ended the Thirty Years War. Mainly French, Spanish, German, Swedish, Dutch, and Austrian armies fought that war in and around what is now Germany. It was the last and worst paroxysm of continental religious conflict. Played out by Catholics, Lutherans, and Calvinists against a complicated tangle of religious and dynastic impulses swirling around the Holy Roman Empire, the slaughter ground on between 1618 and 1648 to the point where historians have estimated that as many as one third of the populace died in areas directly affected by the war.[69]

Apart from territorial annexations, the treaty endorsed two principles that ultimately affected citizenship.[70] First, in accordance with the new concept of sovereignty, it stipulated that rulers of states in the Holy Roman Empire, who might be princes, electors, kings, emperors, or whatever else, would be regarded as sovereign within their legal borders. Here the aim was to foster domestic peace. To this end, the concept of sovereignty authorized those rulers to set up state churches, which meant it forbid local subjects from challenging the sovereign's choice of religion. But, also in order to foster domestic peace, the insistence on sovereignty aimed at eliminating a foreign cause of previous wars. From now on, movers and shakers such as the Pope or the Holy Roman Emperor or the Catholic king of Spain, or Protestant rulers from Sweden or Saxony, were enjoined to refrain from meddling in the affairs of states not their own on behalf of people living there but linked to outside powers by some bond of principle or affection.

---

[68] Ibid., Pt. 3, Ch. XLII, pp. 326–327. See the parallel arguments in Bodin, *Six Books of the Commonwealth*, Bk. IV, Ch. 7, pp. 138–144.

[69] On the war, see C. V. Wedgewood, *The Thirty Years War* (London: Jonathan Cape, 1961); David Maland, *Europe at War, 1600–1650* (London: Macmillan, 1980); Gerhard Benecke (ed.), *Germany in the Thirty Years War* (New York: St. Martin's, 1979); and Geoffrey Parker, *The Thirty Years' War* (London: Routledge and Kegan Paul, 1984).

[70] See the treaty's major points in Maland, *Europe at War*, pp. 183–187.

Second, the treaty sought to soften the potential arbitrariness of sovereignty with a principle we might call prudential toleration. Thus sovereign rulers could establish state churches, but they were admonished not to require attendance at those churches and instead to permit subjects to worship privately. Even this mild degree of toleration, which permitted the use of general taxes to support particular religions, was only partially realized by the Treaty of Westphalia, for the deal struck there extended toleration mainly to Calvinists, Lutherans, and Catholics. But those who negotiated an end to the war recognized the need for restraint even while they were devout because, as Bodin and Hobbes noted, trying to enforce outward conformity could not assure inner conviction, in which case compulsion would produce only unrest rather than salvation.

Renewing the Civic Dialogue

The seventeenth century's lesson on religious toleration was not lost on America's Founders, who wove it into the Constitution's provisions for separation of church and state.[71] But the Reformation move to discuss politics in terms of sovereignty was also important to our story in a wider sense, because it encouraged Europeans – including those who had moved to America – even when they had not planned on doing so, to resume a dialogue on Greek and Roman concepts relating to the nature of states and citizenship.

Since Augustine, Europeans had thought little about the state in and of itself. Rather, they had usually assumed that politics should be studied via theology, as if the rights and duties of rulers and their subjects could be understood only by reference to considerations that arose outside the boundaries, sometimes physical and sometimes spiritual, of temporal rule. It was as if Europeans had long regarded their world as composed of laymen and clerics, where the clerics, sometimes led from Rome, were entitled to define the parameters of public order.[72]

Endorsing the concept of sovereignty changed all that. Now rulers and their states were seen as entities possessing an intrinsic justification, not

---

[71] Seventeenth-century toleration was pragmatic rather than ecumenical. Nevertheless, it was a crucial step forward in the evolution of statecraft. For example, it would have helped Creon to avoid the tragedy that engulfed his family.

[72] The point on laymen and clerics is made by Walter Ullmann in *Principles of Government and Politics in the Middle Ages* (New York: Barnes and Noble, 1961), p. 25. He explains why Machiavelli's writings on the autonomy of politics, as if laymen are entitled to define and judge the state, were so unacceptable to the Church.

subject to theological interpretation, for existing and for performing governmental functions. It followed, logically, that men would begin asking questions about what relations should exist between those entities and the people who resided within their boundaries. Hobbes called each such entity a *civitas*. And in the *civitas*, it was the *civis* or citizen whose standing, apart from his religious status, had now to be explained.[73]

The Right to Rebel
One thing was clear as the new debate got under way: During the religious wars most leaders, Protestant or Catholic, were themselves royalty, noblemen, clergy, or members of the gentry. It followed that social revolution was not their goal. Consequently, they opposed giving to people of lesser rank the kinds of power that, as Citizenship II, some had enjoyed in antiquity.[74] Christianity seemed to justify rebellion against evil kings. But like Aquinas, those who advanced this claim proceeded cautiously. Usually, therefore, they assigned the right of deciding to rebel to social notables sometimes called "magistrates." These men, mainly unelected in Tocqueville's "old order," were regarded by leading writers for every side in conflict as legitimate representatives of "the people." Thus the Protestant tract *Vindiciae Contra Tyrannos* (1579) sanctioned rebellion against a tyrannical French king but identified those entitled to propose and lead the revolt as "electors, palatines, patricians" or "the assembly of the estates."[75] Such people might declare some ruler to be a tyrant, after which they would enlist lower-class support to fill in their fighting ranks.

Notwithstanding this original elitism, ideas about who would be civically active began to change with the times, and especially was this so in

---

[73] Ibid. See also John N. Figgis, *The Divine Right of Kings* (New York: Harper and Row, 1965), p. 162.

[74] Leading Reformation partisans distinguished between what we have called Citizenship I and II although, of course, they did not use those terms. Thus a citizen, said Bodin, is "a subject since his liberty is limited by the sovereign power to which he owes obedience." Here was Citizenship I. Bodin acknowledged that, along with Aristotle, one might regard as a citizen someone who "is eligible for public office, and has a voice in the popular estates, either in a judicial or a deliberative capacity." Here was what we have called Citizenship II. But Aristotle was mistaken, according to Bodin, because it is "the submission and obedience of a free subject to his prince, and the tuition, protection, and jurisdiction exercised by the prince over his subject, that makes the citizen." See Bodin, *Six Books of the Commonwealth*, Bk. I, Chs. 6–7, pp. 18–24.

[75] See Harold J. Laski, *A Defence of Liberty Against Tyrants: A Translation of the Vindiciae Contra Tyrannos* (London: G. Bell, 1924), pp. 97–99, 109–112. For a similar Catholic qualification on the people's right to decide for themselves when and where to rebel, see Figgis, *The Divine Right of Kings*, pp. 101–102.

England, which was America's political forerunner. There Hobbes, in his *Leviathan* (1651), and John Locke, in his *Second Treatise of Government* (1689), used the metaphor of a social contract to show how sovereigns had definite responsibilities to their communities.[76] Of course, neither Hobbes nor Locke was democratic enough to suggest that any community at large had a right to decide if its rulers were upholding their side of the contract. At best, Locke may be interpreted as desiring some extension of English franchise rights to additional property owners, although exactly how many of those he favored including no one can know for sure.

As debate over religion unfolded in England, many men got drawn into the conflict between Parliament and Charles I. Consequently, and perhaps unintentionally, they began to transform thinking about sovereignty. For no matter how much early social contract theorists may have wanted to limit the practical content of their favorite concept, in the real world what came to be understood as compact and covenant situations were evoking ever wider participation, whereby more people than before, among them some previously passive, took part in deconstructing and reconstructing English public life.[77]

The Putney Debate
In a recapitulation of Greek and Roman experiences, military service was one activity which encouraged some unenfranchised Englishmen to demand at least some of the political rights that belong to Citizenship II. During the Reformation, religiously inspired "magistrates," such as Oliver Cromwell of England, found that circumstances required them to enlist into their armies men who had never taken part in public life, men who no one had ever consulted about the shape of government, men who had never been regarded as part of the social contract which might be violated by an evil king. It was only natural, however, that some of these men, serving their sects out of passionate conviction, would make the argument that if they were righteous enough to fight on behalf of a better social order, they were entitled to membership in the limited group authorized to maintain that same social order.[78]

---

[76] See also John Milton, *The Tenure of Kings and Magistrates* (1649), which Milton published just after Charles I was executed by Cromwell, and in which Milton argued against the theory of divine right and in favor of a natural liberty which permitted subjects to depose a tyrant.

[77] This story is told by Michael Walzer in *The Revolution of the Saints: A Study in the Origins of Radical Politics* (New York: Atheneum, 1968).

[78] Ibid., pp. 276–277.

And so, at Putney near London in 1647, members of the Parliamentary Army, commanded by Cromwell, discussed the question of who should be permitted political privileges in the new England they hoped to build. The general lineup was between those who supported historic and property rights, under which mainly freeholders of land worth at least forty shillings a year were enfranchised, and those who argued in favor of natural rights and empowerment for men who at least served the community militarily. This argument, if accepted, would have justified doubling the number of English voters to over four hundred thousand.[79]

Ireton spoke for the former when he argued that "no person hath a right to an interest or share in the disposing of the affairs of the kingdom, and in determining or choosing those that shall determine what laws we shall be ruled by here...that hath not a permanent fixed interest [property] in this kingdom, and those persons together are properly the represented of this kingdom."[80] Rainborough spoke for the latter, sometimes called Levelers, when he said that, if the franchise would not be widened, he wanted to know "what the soldier hath fought for all this while. He hath fought to enslave himself, to give power to men of riches, men of estates, to make him a perpetual slave."[81] Continued disenfranchisement, said Rainborough, was offensive to the ideal of natural rights, for "the poorest he that is in England hath a life to live, as the greatest he; and therefore...I think it's clear, that every man that is to live under a government ought first by his own consent to put himself under that government."[82] In this view, government without consent is tyranny.

The American Connection

The Putney debates changed little in England. Cromwell agreed with Ireton about the special rights of real estate; the incipient democrats therefore did not win concessions; Cromwell's army defeated King Charles I's supporters at Preston in 1648; the army then deposed and executed the king; Parliament brought back the monarchy in 1660 and limited it by a series of acts including the Bill of Rights in 1689; voting for Parliament went unreformed; and the English franchise was liberalized, though not by much, only in 1832.[83]

---

[79] C. B. MacPherson, *The Political Theory of Possessive Individualism, Hobbes to Locke* (Oxford: Oxford Univ. Press, 1964), pp. 114–115.

[80] A. S. P. Woodhouse (ed.), *Puritanism and Liberty, Being the Army Debates (1647–9)* (Chicago: Univ. of Chicago Press, 1951), pp. 53–54.

[81] Ibid., p. 71.   [82] Ibid., p. 53.

[83] In 1831, 12.7 percent of adult English men were permitted to vote. In 1866, after the liberalization of 1832 but before the Reform Act of 1867, the rate had risen to no more

But when American colonists in 1776 demanded, under the slogan "No taxation without representation," what had been denied to common soldiers at Putney, they could not be put off so easily. In truth, the arguments of men like Ireton and Cromwell were less persuasive than they were backed up by force, which English property owners could exercise decisively in England. It was fitting, then, that the case for widespread Citizenship II was eventually restated by an immigrant in Philadelphia who had lived under government without consent in England and was determined to banish it from America. Far from the arm of British law, Thomas Paine encouraged his new countrymen to demand citizenship in terms that permitted no compromise.[84] Of his ideas, more in a moment.

> than 20 percent. No salaries were paid to Members of Parliament and, until 1858, candidates for Parliament had to have at least three hundred English pounds of annual private income. These figures come from Eric J. Evans, *The Great Reform Act of 1832*, 2nd ed. (London: Routledge, 1994), pp. 75, 78.
>
> [84] On Paine, see Eric Foner, *Tom Paine and Revolutionary America* (New York: Oxford Univ. Press, 1976); Jerome D. Wilson, *Thomas Paine* (Boston: Twayne, 1989); A. J. Ayer, *Thomas Paine* (Chicago: Univ. of Chicago Press, 1990); and Jack Fruchtman, Jr., *Thomas Paine: Apostle of Freedom* (New York: Four Walls Eight Windows, 1994).

PART II

AMERICAN EXCEPTIONALISM

3

The Republican Moment

Keeping the historical backdrop in mind, let us turn now to America's experience. From previous writers and events, the colonists knew something about civic life. However, this knowledge did not inspire all of them equally. Therefore some remained loyal to King George III and his Parliament even as others sought independence. Furthermore, the Revolution that finally came was so complex an event that historians attribute it to various causes. Still, insofar as rebellion established a special sort of American citizenship, based partly on terms such as those we just explored briefly, the British policy of mercantilism provides an instructive starting point for understanding what happened.

Mercantilism

Mercantilism was a collection of institutional arrangements sanctioned by royal or parliamentary charters and decrees. Via such arrangements, European countries like Portugal, Holland, Spain, France, and Britain, starting even before Columbus reached America in 1492 but continuing afterward, established overseas colonies that were expected to send raw materials, such as silver and naval stores, and agricultural staples, such as tea and tobacco, to their home country. Some of these materials were converted there into finished goods and some of those were then exported for sale to customers abroad, including the colonists.

When working smoothly, the system was supposed to cause gold and silver to accumulate in imperial centers. This was because a colony's exports would sell for less in London or Paris than the same colony's imports would cost in Philadelphia or Martinique. As a result, the colonists would pay out for purchases more than they would collect on sales. And that meant, for some economic thinkers, that the home country would grow stronger and safer vis-à-vis its neighbors to the extent it could afford, from the proceeds of a trade surplus, to pay for armies and navies which cost a great deal to field. In this light, mercantilism looked like a policy designed to serve the national interest.

Economists later argued that the rationale for mercantilism was more plausible than true. For example, Adam Smith criticized its central ideas in 1776 when he claimed that national wealth would grow most quickly if governments would regulate manufacturing and commerce very little and would instead promote efficiency by fostering specialized labor and free trade.[1] Moreover, what fueled British power and security in the colonial era more than anything else was probably not so much hard currency profits from mercantilism as the system of paper credit and government borrowing made possible by the Bank of England, founded in 1694.[2]

True or false, the official explanations for mercantilism helped to explain why, when the American colonies were growing, the politically strong in England felt entitled to seek government regulations favorable to themselves. Thus great chartered monopolies like the East India Company and smaller industrialists like the Manchester textile merchants lobbied successfully in London for imperial legislation that may have been good for the British Isles but surely aimed at keeping trade and technology out of colonial hands so that well-heeled and well-connected Englishmen could profit from protected business enterprises.

Here were the economic circumstances that encouraged Americans to rebel. For example, colonists felt exploited by restrictive legislation such as the Hat Act of 1732. This act, designed to protect British businessmen from colonial competitors, stipulated that "no person residing in any of his Majesty's plantations in America," except for those who served a seven-year apprenticeship in "the same art or mystery of felt-making," should make felt hats either for domestic consumption or for export.[3]

---

[1] *An Inquiry into the Nature and Causes of the Wealth of Nations*, ed. Edwin Cannan (orig., 1776; New York: Modern Library, 1937).

[2] The bank and other financial innovations for sustaining public debt permitted England to make war effectively and enlarge commerce successfully in the eighteenth and nineteenth centuries. See Niall Ferguson, *The Cash Nexus: Money and Power in the Modern World, 1700–2000* (New York: Basic Books, 2001), esp. pp. 105–136.

[3] "The Hat Act (1732)," in Jack P. Greene (ed.), *Settlements to Society, 1607–1763: A Documentary History of Colonial America* (New York: Norton, 1975), pp. 233–234.

In other words, to avoid criminal prosecution by agents of the Crown, Americans were told to buy most of their hats from abroad rather than make them more cheaply at home.

A year later, King George II and Parliament again favored British businessmen over their American counterparts with the Molasses Act. If left alone, Americans would buy molasses, rum, and sugar not from places like British Jamaica but more cheaply from Spanish and French competitors in the Caribbean Sea. To remove this danger to sales by British sugar plantations, many of them owned by absentee English landlords, the Molasses Act imposed an import tax on sugar products coming into the American colonies from non-British sources, assuming that "the welfare and prosperity" of British sugar colonies were vital to "the trade, navigation and strength of this kingdom."[4]

As usual, colonial consumers were required to subsidize Englishmen who enjoyed parliamentary clout. Furthermore, the Molasses Act insisted that bargain-hunting colonists must pay the new tax in hard currency, which was wanted in London but scarce in North America.[5] The empire accorded similar treatment to items such as iron, whose manufacture in America was forbidden and which as raw material had to be shipped to Great Britain so it might be fashioned there into implements which were then sent back to America, with colonists paying both freight and fabrication charges.[6]

Paying for Imperialism

Scofflaws and smugglers helped America to avoid many expenses of mercantilism. Nevertheless, the concept accustomed London to think of British welfare first and colonial well-being last. In that context, relations between London and her Atlantic seaboard colonies worsened after the Treaty of Paris in 1763, which ended what Americans called the French and Indian War and what Europeans called the Seven Years War. According to this treaty, France ceded to England control over Canada, various islands in the West Indies, and North American territories west of the Appalachian Mountains. The result was more British colonies around the world and especially in the New World.

---

[4] "The Molasses Act (1733)," in ibid., p. 234.   [5] Ibid., p. 235.

[6] Thomas Jefferson, "A Summary View," in Jefferson, *The Political Writings of Thomas Jefferson: Representative Selections*, ed. Edward Dumbauld (Indianapolis: Bobbs-Merrill, 1955), p. 21.

Somehow money had to be found for paying the war debt and for administering and defending the enlarged empire. English property owners who dominated Parliament, and who were accustomed to having it legislate on their behalf, preferred not to pay this money themselves but to collect it from colonists who could not vote against the burden. To this end, London argued that the colonies gained shelter from a secure empire, say, by having British soldiers protect them from hostile Indians. And if that were so they should, like it or not, contribute money to help run that empire.

Accordingly, Parliament enacted the Sugar Act of 1764, whose preamble stipulated that "new provisions and regulations [should] be established for improving the revenue of this kingdom, and for extending and securing the navigation and commerce between Great Britain and your Majesty's dominions in America."[7] The Sugar Act imposed or increased imperial taxes on colonial imports and exports, or external trade. But in 1765, Parliament followed up this law with the Stamp Act, which required colonists to purchase tax stamps and place them on colonial newspapers, legal documents, pamphlets, playing cards, and so forth, all clearly matters of internal trade.

Taxed from without and from within, American colonists persuaded Parliament to repeal the Stamp Act in 1766. But London promptly passed the Townshend Acts in 1767, which included new import duties on many British products. The colonists responded by boycotting British imports, which declined by 50 percent in two years. Consequently, the North ministry in 1770 repealed all the Townshend duties except that on tea. Then in 1773, Parliament approved an act in effect granting the East India Company a monopoly on selling that commodity in America. In December of the same year, irate colonists in Massachusetts staged the Boston Tea Party. Disguising themselves as Indians, they boarded English merchant vessels at anchor in Boston and threw 9,000 pounds sterling worth of tea into the city's harbor.

Parliament responded with the Coercive Acts in early 1774, closing the port of Boston to trade, authorizing the king rather than the colonial legislature to appoint the Massachusetts Council, shifting trials in certain capital offense cases out of the colony, say, to Canada or England, and requiring families in all the colonies, under certain circumstances, to quarter British soldiers in their homes. Twelve colonies sent delegates in protest

---

[7] "The Sugar Act of April 5, 1764," in Jack P. Greene (ed.), *Colonies to Nation, 1763–1789: A Documentary History of the American Revolution* (New York: Norton, 1975), p. 19.

to the First Continental Congress in September of 1774. Fighting broke out in April of 1775 at Concord and Lexington, after which the Congress adopted Boston's militia as the Continental Army and appointed George Washington to be its commander in chief.

Resuming a Previous Conversation

When the quarrel began after 1763, most people on both sides did not foresee a violent outcome. Consequently, early complaints from America were usually deferential, as if colonists there hoped that small policy corrections in London would permit old ways of governing to survive fairly intact.[8] But as time passed, some of the dissidents turned defiant, and they compressed their anger over many grievances into what became, in effect, a single but nonnegotiable demand, that free men have a natural right to representation in any government that taxes them.

Consciously or not, this demand recapitulated arguments voiced more than a century earlier in the Putney debate. Then, unenfranchised Englishmen had challenged the existing power structure in terms that became timely once the concept of sovereignty, as in the Treaty of Westphalia, had sealed off each state from outside interference and left room for men to try out new ideas about relations that should obtain among people who lived inside those states, within the *civitas*. Then, Rainborough had claimed that the "poorest he" is as much entitled as the "richest he" to live under government by consent.

At Putney, the radicals failed to acquire political rights. Consequently, when war broke out in America, only two hundred thousand Englishmen out of 9 million of their countrymen were entitled to vote, while fewer than three thousand owned enough property to run for a seat in the House of Commons.[9] However, the colonists were farther from London than

---

[8] For example, see "The Petition to the King" sent to George III by the Stamp Act Congress in October, 1765, and excerpted in Henry Steele Commager (ed.), *Documents of American History*, 7th ed. (New York: Appleton-Century-Crofts, 1963), Vol. 1, p. 66:

> With Hearts therefore impressed with the most indelible Characters of Gratitude to your Majesty ... and convinced by the most affecting Proofs of your Majesty's Paternal Love to all your People, however distant, and your unceasing and benevolent Desires to promote their Happiness, We most humbly beseech your Majesty, that you will be graciously pleased to take into your Royal Consideration, the Distresses of your faithful Subjects on this Continent. ... [etc., etc., etc.] *And your Petitioners as in Duty bound will pray.*

[9] Henry Steele Commager, *The Empire of Reason: How Europe Imagined and America Realized the Enlightenment* (Garden City, N.Y.: Anchor Doubleday, 1977), pp. 135–137.

Putney was; they were therefore more difficult to silence than the Levelers; and their rebellion, with considerable help from France, eventually succeeded.[10]

The Founding

In terms used by Tocqueville later to describe the French Revolution, the men who protested against imperial injustice in America sought to replace the "old regime" which, in their case, was the British Empire. America's rejection and then replacement of that regime passed through three stages. First, the colonists made up their minds that, whatever the cost, they would no longer endure rule by George III and Parliament. Thus as individuals, but also mutually, Americans crossed a political Rubicon in 1775 and 1776.

After deciding against England, colonial representatives resolved that they deserved a new government aimed at safeguarding natural rights. On this score, Jefferson and his colleagues in the Continental Congress wrote the Declaration of Independence in 1776. And finally, the Americans concluded that only a limited federal government embodying ancient principles of *republicanism* could serve the radical aspirations expressed in their Declaration. To this end, George Washington, James Madison, Benjamin Franklin, John Adams, and other members of the Constitutional Convention, meeting in Philadelphia during the summer of 1787, fashioned the Constitution as a blueprint for that government.

Common Sense

To decide to throw off English rule was to pave the way for creating a country run by and for its residents via a considerable measure of what I have called Citizenship II. Thomas Paine made the case for this decision most powerfully and famously in his *Common Sense*, published early in 1776.[11] When Paine's call to arms appeared, many colonists still hoped to resolve peacefully the conflict that started in Concord and Lexington in 1775. At that time, British soldiers had marched out of Boston to disarm colonial militiamen whom the British commander, General William Howe, thought might resist imperial decrees designed to punish

---

[10] On French help, see Barbara Tuchman, *The First Salute* (New York: Knopf, 1988).

[11] On Paine, see Howard Fast, *The Selected Work of Tom Paine and Citizen Tom Paine* (New York: Modern Library, 1945), and the works cited in Chapter 2, n. 84, above.

Massachusetts for the Boston Tea Party of 1773. Paine, however, rejected temporizing and compromise.

Common Sense stood out among other pamphlets of the day for two reasons. One was Paine's trip-hammer prose, without a trace of deference to those legally in power throughout the empire. Because he had recently arrived from England and had suffered there from what he regarded as British tyranny, Paine was ready to attack the old regime more graphically and persuasively than most homegrown American radicals could.[12] With surpassing clarity and undaunting consistency, then, the Philadelphian told his new countrymen that their situation was intolerable and unlikely to improve.

As he put it, "There is something exceedingly ridiculous in the composition of Monarchy; it first excludes [by social isolation] a man from the means of information, yet empowers him to act in cases where the highest judgment is required."[13] Moreover, better information could not change the fact that, in a sense, kings are perfectly useless, since they do nothing but "make war and give away places [sinecures]," both of which yield no benefit to ordinary men yet must be underwritten by taxing their hard-earned income.[14] And what possible purpose could the empire serve? "To be always running three or four thousand miles with a tale or petition, waiting for four or five months for an answer, which, when obtained, requires five or six more to explain it in, will in a few years be looked upon as folly and childishness."[15] On every count, Paine thought the old regime had nothing to recommend it.

The second noteworthy property of *Common Sense* was its strategy of appealing to common sense. As Paine wrote from the outset, "I offer nothing more than simple facts, plain arguments, and common sense, and have no other preliminaries to settle with the reader than that he will divest himself of prejudice and prepossession, and suffer his reason and his feelings to determine for themselves."[16] From this unpretentious starting point, significant, and even drastic, political conclusions followed. For example, to Paine and his readers it seemed reasonable to believe that, if Americans must be governed like all people in order to control their occasional vices, they should create their government in a "cool deliberate manner" rather than "trust such an interesting event to time and chance."[17] So much for the British argument that if a government

---

[12] This point is made in Bernard Bailyn, *Faces of Revolution: Personalities and Themes in the Struggle for American Independence* (New York: Vintage, 1992), pp. 82–84.

[13] *Common Sense*, in Fast, *The Selected Work of Tom Paine*, p. 9.

[14] Ibid., p. 18.   [15] Ibid., p. 24.   [16] Ibid., p. 18.   [17] Ibid., p. 30.

has endured for generations, men should support it because, in this field, longevity proves worthiness.[18]

Most important, however, was no particular conclusion that Paine drew from common sense but that he recommended this sometimes underrated way of reasoning to his audience. Unlike most earlier writers in America and in Europe, Paine offered his arguments in *Common Sense* without certifying them by reference to authority. He did point out, to buttress his disdain for monarchy, that ancient Israelites insisted on having a king even though the prophet Samuel rebuked them for it. But mainly he ignored historical precedents, social traditions, long-dead philosophers, Church fathers, holy books, and legal injunctions.[19] Instead he assumed that if people have a right to judge their own governments, then no one but "the people" should decide, as a matter of common sense, why and when this should be done.

Here Paine rejected the social caution that had long animated most European political thinkers, who sometimes entertained competing opinions but usually shared a class interest as members of the gentry, clergy, or nobility. Like Augustine and Aquinas, and like most pamphleteers during the Reformation, such men had argued, in principle, that bad laws can be disobeyed. But because they feared that evoking this principle might lead to social chaos, they reined in what I have called Citizenship III by insisting that civil disobedience should be authorized only by a "public authority," or by "magistrates," or by "the estates," or by other social notables.

Now Paine, a former tutor and corset maker, came from exactly those walks of life that genteel reformers preferred to exclude from their political universe. Accordingly, when he praised the efficacy of common sense he was, in effect, suggesting that all men, and not just those belonging to some sort of social elite, are capable of deciding for themselves if and when the government that taxes and conscripts them has become intolerable.

---

[18] Edmund Burke advised against the British effort to subdue America's rebels. But when radicalism threatened Britain, he expressed the conservative political philosophy of that country's rulers. See his *Reflections on the Revolution in France*, ed. Thomas H. D. Mahoney (orig., 1790; New York: Liberal Arts, 1955), p. 70: "It is with infinite caution that any man ought to venture upon pulling down an edifice which has answered in any tolerable degree for ages the common purposes of society, or on building it up again without having models and patterns of approved utility before his eyes."

[19] In this sense, Paine's approach to politics resembled that of Greek authors who, before their writings became Great Books to be quoted by later thinkers, assumed that the measure of man is more man than authority.

The Declaration of Independence

Paine assumed that ordinary people are politically competent. But *Common Sense* went further than expressing his point of view, for it called on Americans to authorize an official manifesto declaring that they would no longer live under "the cruel disposition of the British Court."[20] As representatives of "the people" in thirteen colonies, the Continental Congress resolved in June of 1776 to issue such a manifesto; it declared independence on July 2; and it adopted the Declaration of Independence on July 4 to explain why the colonies were breaking away from England.

The Declaration followed Paine in making common sense the key to political principles when it alluded to "self-evident" truths of a case which, presumably, anyone could understand. Lest that point be overlooked, Jefferson later wrote to Henry Lee that he had intended in the Declaration "to place before mankind the common sense of the subject" in terms both "plain and firm."[21] Indeed, Jefferson's emphasis on common sense rather than authority left the Declaration's text so bare of citations that some historians have argued that its central ideas, such as its Lockean-style claim that men have rights to "life, liberty, and the pursuit of happiness," were not derived from John Locke because, after all, the text did not mention his name.[22]

We can best understand the Declaration as emerging from a European political conversation that had readopted the Greek and Roman concern for relations between rulers and ruled, regimes and residents, states and citizens.[23] Sovereignty, we have seen, was justified in sixteenth-century Europe by the divine right of kings. Then it was qualified, and kings were somewhat restrained, by the seventeenth-century notion that sovereigns should enter into a covenant, or compact, or social contract, with their subjects. For English thinkers, this covenant idea approximated the proper nature of government particularly well because it conveyed implications of a Protestant vision whereby communities agreed that rulers and ruled are together constrained to serve God by obeying His laws. Here was the setting for New World covenants like the Mayflower

---

[20] *Common Sense*, p. 39.

[21] Thomas Jefferson, "Letter to Henry Lee, May 8, 1825," in *The Political Writings of Thomas Jefferson*, p. 8.

[22] For example, see Garry Wills, *Inventing America: Jefferson's Declaration of Independence* (Garden City, New York: Doubleday, 1978), pp. 167–180.

[23] Thus Louis Hartz argues that Americans expressed mainly the "liberal" part of that conversation in *The Liberal Tradition in America* (New York: Harcourt, Brace, and World, 1955).

Compact signed by the Plymouth settlers in 1620 and the Massachusetts Bay Colony charter described in John Winthrop's sermon on the *Arabella* in 1630.[24]

Many American colonists, who were mostly Protestants, continued to admire the ideal of a covenanted community by whatever name. But the mutual obligations imposed by that community became for them increasingly secular when, like people in Europe, the colonists had to neutralize potentially dangerous differences of religious conviction. This happened in New England, for example, when Puritans in what had been religiously homogeneous towns and villages, such as in Massachusetts, eventually had to deal with stubborn local dissenters such as Anne Hutchinson and Roger Williams. It also happened when especially devout Puritan colonists raised children who, in disappointing numbers, never underwent conversion experiences to become born-again Christians like their parents.[25] Furthermore, as time passed, the seaboard colonies received an influx of immigrants from various lands who shared a passion for freedom rather than a blueprint for salvation.[26] Many of these people, along with some of the earlier arrivals, while looking for new and affordable land, moved deeper into America's forests and prairies, where they combined and recombined in frequently heterogeneous towns and villages.

Under these circumstances, and far from Europe's great centers of tradition and precedent, it was probably inevitable that America's colonists came to expect that relations between rulers and ruled would flow from pragmatic consent between neighbors rather than principles worked out in advance by people who claimed to know what was best for everyone. It was not that ultimate principles became unimportant.[27] But for lack of agreement on which ones to follow, churches became increasingly

---

[24] See the "Mayflower Compact" in Clarence L. Ver Steeg and Richard Hofstadter (eds.), *Great Issues in American History: From Settlement to Revolution, 1584–1776* (New York: Vintage, 1969), pp. 73–74. See the sermon on the *Arabella*, entitled "Christian Charitie: A Model Hereof," in Edmund S. Morgan (ed.), *Puritan Political Ideas: 1558–1794* (Indianapolis: Bobbs-Merrill, 1965), pp. 76–93.

[25] Starting in 1662, such children were baptized and brought into Puritan churches according to a "half-way covenant." On that covenant, see Perry Miller, *The New England Mind: From Colony to Province* (Cambridge: Harvard Univ. Press, 1953), pp. 93–104.

[26] The fact of religious pluralism in America was noted and praised by J. Hector St. John de Crèvecoeur in "What Is an American," in his *Letters from an American Farmer* (orig., 1782; New York: Dutton, 1957), pp. 44–47.

[27] Thus Roger Williams founded Rhode Island in 1644 to promote religious tolerance not because he regarded faith as trivial but because devout Christians did not always agree on basic points of theology. See Perry Miller, *Roger Williams: His Contribution to the American Tradition* (New York: Atheneum, 1970).

private,[28] and both ordinary people and local magistrates tended to apply secular rather than spiritual standards to the business of living together.

Here, then, was the social context within which America's Founders rejected the old order and began to construct a new one. To use a term that had gained currency since the writings of John Locke, it was as if several generations of colonists had grown accustomed, apart from strictures imposed by faraway London, to living in a *state of nature*.[29] Here was a society of largely self-made men, who assumed they could deliberately organize their public affairs, taking care of practical needs without reference to Truth and History and Prerogative but in keeping with important interests they could identify and promote together.

The Theory of Independence

So what did the Declaration say? It said that all men are "created equal," and then it stipulated that they are "endowed by their Creator with certain inalienable rights." On both counts, the Declaration assumed a state of nature, since it referred first to men who, to begin with at least, are not ranked by social distinctions and second to men who, for their entire lives, enjoy rights that originate in natural law rather than the legislative history of any particular country.

Next, the Declaration described the rights relevant to independence as those of "life, liberty, and the pursuit of happiness," whereas Locke, who remained uncited, had spoken of life, liberty, and property.[30] Governments, said the Declaration, legitimately exist by the "consent of the governed" in order "to secure these rights." It followed that, if a government fails to uphold its obligation to safeguard those rights, "the people" may "alter or abolish" that government and replace it with another, designed to assure their "safety and happiness."

Here, quite plainly, was a notion that, whatever new regime might emerge from the act of rebellion, it would enjoy the qualities of a compact, or covenant. Thus the Declaration argued, in effect, that Americans were entitled to build a state in which they would authorize their government

---

[28] That is, even though Catholics and what we now call Anglicans (disciples of the Church of England) deferred to central theological authorities, other colonists increasingly struck out on their own, tending to maintain congregationalism rather than presbyterianism.

[29] As Locke said, "In the beginning all the World was America." See John Locke, *Two Treatises of Government*, ed. Peter Laslett (Cambridge: Cambridge Univ. Press, 1960), *Second Treatise*, Ch. V, "Of Property," p. 319.

[30] Ibid., Ch. IX, "Of the Ends of Political Society and Government," p. 368.

to do exactly this and that, and in which "the people" may rightfully replace the same government if they decide it has failed to carry out their instructions. And why should "the people," and not Europe's familiar "magistrates," make this decision? Because, like Paine, the Declaration assumed that ordinary men can draw on common sense. After all, the Declaration cited truths that were "self-evident," in which case "the people" are as capable as anyone else of seeing those truths and deciding if and when an existing government needs abolishing.

Finally, the Declaration argued that British rule in America should end because George III had persistently "injured" the colonists. Examples of such injuries included his quartering of soldiers in American homes, cutting off foreign trade, suspending trials by jury, taking away royal charters, impressing men into naval service, and imposing taxes without colonial consent. All this added up to establishing "an absolute tyranny over these States," in accordance with the idea, going back to classical Greece, that *tyranny* exists when a ruler makes laws to his benefit rather than for the community as a whole. The Declaration then complained that "our repeated Petitions have been answered only by repeated injury. A Prince whose character is thus marked by every act which may define a Tyrant, is unfit to be the ruler of a free people." In which case the Continental Congress, elected by such people to serve their common interests, was entirely justified in severing their relationship with George III.

Basic Concepts

The American rebels would eventually create a republican regime characterized by relatively widespread Citizenship II and by government exercising only limited control over citizens' lives. Technical arrangements were yet to come, but clues to what the Founders would establish were present in the Declaration, for example, with regard to guiding concepts such as natural rights, individualism, and civil society.

Natural Rights

Thus the Declaration claimed that men have *natural rights*, which include the right to government by consent. On this score, Americans abandoned earlier arguments according to which they had portrayed themselves as oppressed Englishmen petitioning for recognition of their historical rights as members of that nation. The truth is that, by 1776, history had given Englishmen too few rights to justify creating government by widespread consent either in England or in America. Consequently, the Founders realized that arguments from precedent were not radical enough to bring them to where they wanted to go.[31]

Not surprisingly, English spokesmen for the old order also recognized the subversive appeal of colonial claims to natural rights. Therefore even those who, like Edmund Burke, sought peacefully to accommodate American grievances, praised the British constitution for embodying the wisdom gained by many generations of political trial and error, from at least the Magna Carta in 1215 to the Glorious Revolution of 1688. Accordingly, they condemned far-reaching political innovations, such as the Declaration, by praising a specific, familiar, and limited stock of historical rights, as if men's store of common sense, used to interpret the consequences of their natural rights at any particular moment, was insufficient for the task of constructing so complex and delicate a thing as government.[32]

Individualism

Such arguments did not impress America's Founders, and their enthusiasm for a natural right to government by consent would eventually lead to more Citizenship II in America than in England. It also indicated that the Declaration assumed a society based on what Tocqueville later called *individualism*.[33] The Declaration moved in this direction by arguing that all men are in some sense morally equal for being entitled to the same natural rights. Of course, even in the Age of Reason prejudice excluded many people from this equal possession of rights, and so Native Americans,

---

[31] On the move to natural rights arguments, via writings by James Wilson, Thomas Jefferson, and John Adams, see Max Beloff (ed.), *The Debate on the American Revolution, 1761–1783: A Sourcebook* (New York: Harper Torchbooks, 1960), pp. 34–35, 157–179, 186–188.

[32] Burke recommended to Parliament that England should, for the sake of prudence, accept some colonial demands. But he never conceded that Americans possessed a natural right to more freedom than existing English laws allotted them. See his "Speech on American Taxation" (1774) in Ross Hoffman and Paul Levack (eds.), *Burke's Politics: Selected Writings and Speeches of Edmund Burke on Reform, Revolution, and War* (New York: Knopf, 1959), p. 58:

> I am not here going into the distinctions of rights, nor attempting to mark their boundaries. I do not enter into these metaphysical distinctions; I hate the very sound of them. Leave the Americans as they anciently stood, and these distinctions, born of our unhappy context, will die along with it.... Do not burden them by taxes; you were not used to do so from the beginning. Let this be your reason for not taxing. Leave the rest to the [philosophical] schools; for there only they may be discussed with safety.

[33] Alexis de Tocqueville, *Democracy in America*, 2 vols. (orig., 1835, 1840; New York: Vintage, 1954), Vol. II, Bk. II, Chs. II, III, IV, VIII, pp. 104–113, 129–132.

most African Americans, and American women would become empowered citizens only as time passed.

Although early Americans honored it less than we would today, the principle of moral equality was important for rejecting conventional European thinking. In America it was the individual rather than any existing or potential group who became the basis for aspirations, expectations, and political demands. Thus the Declaration described society as composed simply of men rather than as a conglomeration of social groups – including clergy, aristocracy, guilds, corporations, peasants, and burghers – that began in feudalism and that continued to exist, although not unchanged, in European states of the eighteenth century.[34]

In Europe, a host of groups had a variety of rights and obligations, and spokesmen for the old regime assumed that the proper balance of all these sustained a necessary public order. In America, on the other hand, the Declaration assumed that no one should be bound by legal and social restrictions of the sort attaching to Europeans born into different stations of life. In American politics the Declaration envisioned a society where groups could form and petition and vote to promote their shared interests. However, such groups would emerge from voluntary association rather than, as in Europe, a social constellation fixed in advance. It was as if each American were like Adam, unencumbered by previous ties and commitments.[35]

Civil Society

Individualism rested on an optimistic view of *civil society*. Here is the sphere of human life and achievement that, in theory, precedes the

---

[34] Some historians have emphasized how a great many colonists and their descendants belonged to Calvinist-inspired denominations whose principles powerfully influenced the content of American politics during the late eighteenth and early nineteenth centuries. For example, see Barry Alan Shain, *The Myth of American Individualism: The Protestant Origins of American Political Thought* (Princeton: Princeton Univ. Press, 1994). I agree that Protestants in those early years were committed to living in communities, often networked, to use a recent term, to other communities inhabited largely by like-minded Protestants. In that respect, these Americans did not promote what Shain, p. xiv, calls "the modern concept of individual freedom – freedom to do what one wishes." Nevertheless, even those Protestant communities accepted, by and large, a great secular concept of *individualism* in the sense that Tocqueville used that term to describe an American rejection of long-standing European notions which justified holding people in fairly static social ranks and allocating to them differential obligations and privileges.

[35] Terrance Ball, "The Myth of Adam and American Identity," in Ball, *Reappraising Political Theory: Revisionist Studies in the History of Political Thought* (Oxford: Clarendon, 1995), pp. 273–296.

establishment of government. Or, as Paine described the sequence, society is formed to supply men's wants, while government becomes necessary to restrain their wickedness.[36] Here also, analytically speaking, one finds men who are not limited to acting on the basis of rights certified by government but are free to use natural talents and abilities to promote individual and shared interests.

In Europe, civil society was known for producing severe ethnic and religious divisions. These could be terribly dangerous, as sects were during the wars of the Reformation. Consequently, European thinkers such as Thomas Hobbes and Jean Bodin, and later Georg Hegel, advocated maintaining powerful, and not especially democratic, governments capable of resisting popular passions and preserving public order.[37]

But in America, millions of individuals were setting up new towns and taming the wilderness. In light of their accomplishments, civil society seemed an arena where, when people act freely, the results are good for them and safe for other people, if not for slaves and Native Americans. Consequently, government need not be autocratic in order to suppress popular impulses. On the contrary, government could rest upon Citizenship II, since ordinary people seemed unlikely to export dangerous sentiments from civil society into public life. In particular, their religious beliefs could be regarded as benign. The Constitution eventually recognized that point, as we shall see.

The Constitutional Solution

The Declaration announced that Americans would no longer live under the old regime. It even said why this was so. Then the colonies adopted the Articles of Confederation, which created an alliance of new states that won the war. But the Articles did not establish a true government, and some of the Founders feared that the alliance would fail in the long run. Consequently the Congress of the United States, elected under the Articles but prodded by skeptics, authorized a convention to reconsider those Articles. In May of 1787, delegates appointed by the states convened in Philadelphia to that end. However, they chose not to suggest amendments to the Articles but to offer instead a new scheme of government for ratification by the American people.

[36] *Common Sense*, p. 6.
[37] Hobbes and Bodin we have seen. On Hegel (1770–1831), see Shlomo Avineri, *Hegel's Theory of the Modern State* (Cambridge: Cambridge Univ. Press, 1972).

What became known as the Constitutional Convention marked a historic moment, when men from Western Europe first established a viable substitute for the old order of government. Unfortunately, the Founders never explained the precise character of their invention clearly and consistently.[38] They spoke in many voices, they quoted many sources, they used materials old and new, and they worried about principles but also about making compromises that would satisfy various interests already present in their lives. That is, rather than neatly turning some philosophical theory into a political reality, the Founders simply did what they did, hopefully with good sense. Then some of them, as in *The Federalist*, by James Madison, Alexander Hamilton, and John Jay, tried to explain what they had done. And later, men like George Washington, John Adams, Thomas Jefferson, Andrew Jackson, and Abraham Lincoln explained still further what it all meant.

Points of Agreement

Some points of consensus did emerge. For example, the Founders agreed that there should be a constitution. Echoing Paine, Hamilton wrote in *The Federalist*, No. 1, that men should create their government "from reflection and choice" instead of leaving its shape to be determined by "accident and force."[39] For the Founders, this meant that "the people" were entitled to make a constitution which would lay down terms under which their government would take shape.

And so the Preamble cites "the people" as authors of the Constitution.[40] Here was a point of principle which contradicted those Englishmen who claimed their government had fashioned a constitution composed of political acts and decrees going back to the Magna Carta of 1215. The

---

[38] See the frustration of Justice Robert Jackson in *Youngstown Sheet and Tube Company v. Sawyer* (1952) 343 U.S. 579 (pp. 634–635): "Just what our forefathers did envision... must be divined from materials almost as enigmatic as the dreams Joseph was called upon to interpret for Pharoh. A century and a half of partisan debate... only supplies more or less apt quotations from respected sources on each side of any question. They largely cancel each other." Historian Gordon Wood was more optimistic. See his *The Creation of the American Republic, 1776–1787* (New York: Norton, 1972), p. 615: "[The vision of the Founders] was diffusive and open-ended; it was not delineated in a single book; it was peculiarly the product of a democratic society, without a precise beginning or an ending. It was not political theory in the grand manner, but it was political theory worthy of a prominent place in the history of Western thought."

[39] Alexander Hamilton, John Jay, and James Madison, *The Federalist* (orig., 1787–1788; New York: Modern Library, 1937), p. 3.

[40] Thus "We the People of the United States... do ordain and establish this Constitution for the United States of America."

Americans assumed that their constitution would make the government, rather than vice versa, and that the same document, designed and ratified for its singular purpose, would be amended only by the people's will, if at all.

The Founders additionally agreed that they did not consider confederation to be a form of true government. It was, of course, an alliance of states, or a league of states. But history suggested that such combinations were fragile because they relied too much on voluntary cooperation among their members. And so the Founders opted for federalism, that is, for a division of powers between the national and state governments, where the national government would have direct powers to tax citizens, to regulate commerce, and to muster soldiers, to the point where it would control enough resources to maintain itself against enemies and adversity.[41]

The Founders further agreed that the Constitution would establish a government that could not, under most circumstances, focus its power so sharply as to become tyrannical. To this end, the Founders devised a central government that separated the executive, the legislature, and the judiciary. Here, they implemented the classical understanding of a republic based on divided powers, as formulated by men such as Cicero, and as updated by Baron Charles de Montesquieu's more modern view of constitutional arrangements for establishing political liberty advanced in *The Spirit of the Laws* (1748).[42] Most of the American states already enjoyed such arrangements, which the Constitution sought to assure in Article IV, Section 4: "The United States shall guarantee to every state in this Union a republican form of government" In their first inaugural addresses, both Washington and Jefferson referred to this republican quality as the outstanding characteristic of American government.[43]

Extending Individualism

The Constitution extended the concept of individualism inherent in the Declaration. For example, it provided that Americans would be directly

---

[41] Commager, *The Empire of Reason*, p. 191.

[42] Montesquieu, *The Spirit of the Laws* (orig., 1748; New York: Hafner, 1949). See esp. Bk. XI, "Of the Laws Which Establish Political Liberty with Regard to the Constitution," pp. 149–182.

[43] George Washington, "First Inaugural Address" (April 30, 1789), in James D. Richardson (ed.), *Messages and Papers of the Presidents, 1789–1902*, Vol. I (Washington, D.C.: Bureau of National Literature and Art, 1905), p. 53; and Thomas Jefferson, "First Inaugural Address" (March 4, 1801), ibid., p. 322.

represented by number in the lower house of Congress, where one representative was allocated for up to thirty thousand "free persons."[44] Most
important, these persons were not to be represented by kind, or interest, or region, or class, or wealth, or occupation, or any other criterion
shared involuntarily with other people. That is, the Constitution regarded
citizens as individuals and not as members of a traditional, feudal-like
society.

This emphasis on *direct representation* contrasted with how Britain
treated individuals politically. There, spokesmen for the old order justified a very limited franchise by claiming that those who did not vote
were nonetheless *virtually represented* in Parliament because the officials
elected to serve there were morally obliged to take into account the great
and permanent interests of England as a whole rather than just the immediate desires of those relatively few Englishmen who voted.[45] The same
spokesmen even worked out a rough list of which interests those were,
including land, commerce, the armed services, and the professions.[46]

The Founders rejected such ideas on representation. But they also expressed their enthusiasm for individualism in the Bill of Rights, which
consisted of ten amendments that were attached to the Constitution as
part of an understanding with voters who feared creating too strong a

---

[44] Article I, Section 2, clause 3.

[45] The basic concept already held for sixteenth-century England. See Sir Thomas Smith, *De Republica Anglorum*, ed. Mary Dewar (orig., 1583; Cambridge: Cambridge Univ. Press, 1982), p. 79:

> [Parliament] hath the power of the whole realme both the head and the bodie.
> For everie Englishman is entended to bee there present, either in person or by
> procuration and attornies, of what preheminence, state dignitie, or qualitie soever
> he be, from the Prince (be he King or Queene) to the lowest person of Englande.
> And the consent of the Parliament is taken to be everie man's consent.

> Thomas Whately, the principal author of the Stamp Act, restated this concept to the
> colonists. See Whately, "The Regulations Lately Made..." (1765), in Greene (ed.),
> *Colonies to Nation*, pp. 48–50, but esp. 49:

> All *British* Subjects [including colonists] are really in the same [situation]; none
> are actually, all are virtually represented in Parliament; for every Member of
> Parliament sits in the House, not as Representative of his own Constituents, but
> as one of that august Assembly by which all the Commons of *Great Britain* are
> represented. Their Rights and their Interests, however his own Borough may be
> affected by general Dispositions, ought to be the great Objects of his Attention,
> and the only Rules for his Conduct; to sacrifice these to a partial Advantage in
> favour of the Place where he was chosen, would be a Departure from his Duty.

[46] J. R. Pole, *Political Representation in England and the Origins of the American Republic*
(New York: St. Martin's, 1966), pp. 442–443.

central government. The Bill of Rights was designed to prevent congressional encroachment on freedom of religion, freedom of expression, the right to petition, the right in serious cases to trial by jury, the ban on self-incrimination, the ban on cruel and unusual punishments, and so forth.[47] Safeguarding these rights assured that an electorate of free individuals would always be able to exercise control over that national government which, of necessity, the Constitution authorized.[48]

Elements of Caution

To establish a republic was to check the power of government. But the Founders also wished to check, at least somewhat, the power of the people. To this end, they mandated indirect voting for senators, who would be chosen by state legislatures rather than elected at large, and who would serve a six-year term so as to be somewhat free of popular pressures.[49] They also created the Electoral College, whereby voters cast ballots for electors in their states, who were authorized to vote for whoever they regarded as the best candidate for president, with the runner-up becoming vice president.[50] In both cases, voters would choose people to act in their name, but those who made policy would be a step removed from the voters themselves.

Moreover, in *The Federalist*, Madison explained an additional constitutional factor that limited popular power. As he observed, political thinkers had long believed that republics should be small and intimate in order to preserve the integrity and patriotism of their citizens. Such was the opinion, for example, of Montesquieu.[51] Madison argued, instead, that small republics were dangerous for being too easily taken over by tyrannical groups of citizens. It was fortunate, then, that the American republic would be so large, with so many states and with more to come, that any

---

[47] After World War I, Supreme Court justices increasingly argued that passage of the fourteenth Amendment in 1866, which obliged the states to abide by "due process of law," in effect forbid them from infringing on various freedoms protected in the Bill of Rights. The chronology of Supreme Court decisions that bear on this point is described in Henry J. Abraham and Barbara A. Perry, *Freedom and the Court: Civil Rights and Liberties in the United States*, 4th ed. (New York: Oxford Univ. Press, 1998), Ch. 3, "The Bill of Rights and Its Applicability to the States," pp. 29–91. See also Akhil Reed Amar, *The Bill of Rights: Creation and Reconstruction* (New Haven: Yale Univ. Press, 1998).

[48] Michael Walzer, *What It Means to Be an American: Essays on the American Experience* (New York: Marsilio, 1992), pp. 105–106.

[49] Article I, Section 3, clause 1.

[50] Article II, Section 2, superseded by the Twelfth Amendment.

[51] See his *Spirit of the Laws*, Bk. VIII, Sec. 16, pp. 120–121.

potentially tyrannical group would be unlikely to gain control of enough resources and powers to threaten the rest.[52]

Citizenship

The Constitution said little about citizenship, which became a complex and difficult subject.[53] The Founders generally assumed that, except for slaves and Native Americans, people born in the United States would be citizens in the sense of what I have called Citizenship I. Beyond that point of agreement, serious problems lurked. For example, one immediate question was who else could join the existing body of citizens. The Constitution authorized the national government to "establish a uniform rule of naturalization" for immigrants.[54] It did so in 1790, and it amended that law several times until 1802, when several basic requirements became fairly stable: five years of residence in the United States, an oath of loyalty to the Constitution, and a renunciation of foreign titles and allegiances.

But this law did not address the issue, never resolved before the Civil War, of the relationship between national and state naturalization. The Constitution did not forbid the states to continue, as they were already doing, to accept immigrants and grant them citizenship rights with regard to local law and politics. Therefore many immigrants continued to reach the states at various entry ports. They then settled in places where officials and neighbors came to regard them as members of the community. In which case, for all practical purposes, they were sooner or later recognized as state citizens at least in the sense of Citizenship I.

Citizenship II, however, was a different matter. The Constitution authorized each state to decide which of its residents would be permitted to vote for state and federal officers.[55] Yet setting the qualifications was not a simple matter, as we shall soon see. Most of the states, for example, withheld the franchise from unpopular groups, such as Native Americans and free African Americans. And women, of course, were usually excluded from the electorate.

Furthermore, there was considerable confusion concerning the constitutional stipulation that "the citizens of each State shall be entitled to all privileges and immunities of citizens in the several States."[56] This

---

[52] *The Federalist*, No. 10, pp. 60–61.

[53] For an overview of ideas on citizenship in and around the Constitution, see Richard C. Sinopoli, *The Foundations of American Citizenship: Liberalism, the Constitution, and Civic Virtue* (New York: Oxford Univ. Press, 1992).

[54] Article I, Section 8, clause 4.   [55] Article I, Section 2, clause 1.

[56] Article IV, Section 2, clause 1.

concept made sense logically, for the Founders assumed that Americans might move from one state to another, and if one was, for example, married in Massachusetts, it seemed reasonable to expect that Georgia would recognize the marriage as valid. Furthermore, the Founders knew that interstate trade would take place, in which case some sort of reciprocity in commercial law was necessary if the Union were to prosper.

Unfortunately, no clear rule explained what laws in one state owed to citizens of another. Yet since, as part of the liberty which Americans sought by rebelling in the first place, the states were free to enact laws reflecting local and regional differences of culture and preference, it was inevitable that legislators and judges would occasionally have difficulty reconciling the outcome of such differences. For example, how should South Carolina, a slave state, deal with a free black citizen of New York who happened to be traveling in South Carolina? And what should Alabama do with a Northern visitor who violated Alabama speech laws by advocating abolition? And how should St. Louis judges treat a black man who was a slave in Missouri but who had resided for a time with his owner in the free state of Illinois and the federal territory of Minnesota? This last question eventually produced the Supreme Court decision of *Dred Scott v. Sandford* (1857),[57] which failed to avert the Civil War.

Finally, there was no definitive answer to the crucial question of what citizens of one state owed to other states. That is, what were the responsibilities of citizenship in the United States as a whole? Here, too, matters came to a head with the Civil War, when men found themselves torn between fidelity to the states where they lived and loyalty to the Union. Robert E. Lee, for example, refused to serve as commander of the Union Army, resigned his commission, and went home to lead Confederate forces in his beloved Virginia.[58] And Jefferson Davis, later president of the Confederacy, proclaimed as he resigned from the Senate that even if the state of Mississippi had seceded from the Union without "sufficient provocation," he, as a Mississippi citizen, was "bound by her action."[59]

---

[57] *Dred Scott v. Sandford* (1857), 19 Howard 393.

[58] Thus on April 20, 1861, he wrote to his sister: "With all my devotion to the Union, and the feeling of loyalty and duty of an American citizen, I have not been able to make up my mind to raise my hand against my relatives, my children, my home. I have therefore resigned my commission in the Army, and save in defence of my native state ... I hope I may never be called on to draw my sword." Excerpts from the letter are reprinted in Douglas Southall Freeman, *R. E. Lee, A Biography*, 6 vols. (New York: Charles Scribner's Sons, 1951), Vol. I, p. 443.

[59] "Farewell Address" (January 21, 1861), in Lynda Lasswell Crist (ed.), *The Papers of Jefferson Davis* (Baton Rouge: Louisiana State Univ. Press, 1971–1999), Vol. 7, p. 19.

The Republican Moment

The years in which America produced the Declaration and the Constitution may be described as a *republican moment*. Americans of many persuasions, from Federalists to anti-Federalists, from Hamiltonians to Jeffersonians, thought they were founding a republic even though they did not define that term exactly and regarded republicanism mainly as an absence of monarchy and aristocracy.[60] For example, in *The Federalist*, Madison argued that a republic is "a government which derives all its powers directly or indirectly from the body of the people."[61] His lack of precision reflected the tendency of Americans not to frame their thoughts theoretically. Still, there were important points of agreement which characterized this republican moment, which later evolved into a democratic moment.

Citizens and Equality

For one thing, the republican moment embraced a turning point in political self-perception. At this time, Americans stopped thinking of themselves as *subjects* and began to call themselves *citizens*.[62] The former were ruled by some sort of master, as the king in England; the latter were free and independent people.[63]

---

[60] See Linda K. Kerber, "The Republican Ideology of the Revolutionary Generation," *American Quarterly* 4 (Fall 1985), pp. 475–476.

[61] *The Federalist*, No. 39, p. 243. See also "Thoughts on Government" (1776), in *The Works of John Adams, Second President of the United States*, 10 vols. (Boston: Little, Brown, 1850–1856), Vol. IV, pp. 193–200, but esp. p. 194: "There is no good government but what is republican.... because the very definition of a republic is 'an empire of laws, and not men'.... Of republics there is an inexhaustible variety, because the possible combinations of the powers of society are capable of innumerable variations."

[62] For example, the preamble to the Massachusetts Constitution of 1780, drafted by John Adams, reads: "The body politic is...a social compact by which the whole people covenants with each citizen and each citizen with the whole people, that all shall be governed by certain laws for the common good." See George A. Peek (ed.), *The Political Writings of John Adams* (New York: Macmillan, 1985), p. 95.

[63] Historians cite David Ramsey, a South Carolina doctor, on this point, which in our terms means that the colonists rejected Bodin's definition of citizens as subservient to a sovereign. (On Bodin, see Chapter 2, n. 74, above.) On Ramsey, see Gordon S. Wood, *The Radicalism of the American Revolution* (New York: Vintage, 1993), p. 169: "Subject [said Ramsey] is derived from the latin words, *sub* and *jacio*, and means one who is under the power of another; but a citizen is an unit of a mass of free people, who, collectively, possess sovereignty."

Most important, Americans thought of citizens as being, in some sense, equal, as if the designation "citizen" indicated a person standing apart from any sort of permanent social hierarchy.[64] Americans knew that people of larger and smaller talents in their country would acquire more or less resources and status. However, so long as such inequality flowed from natural abilities and personal efforts, it could be regarded as morally justified and useful to the community. Someone, after all, had to lead, and it might as well be the truly best.[65]

On the other hand, for "free inhabitants" at least, America would not permit hereditary and permanent inequalities of class like those that had existed for so long in Europe. That is why the Constitution both assumes that government will grant no titles of nobility and specifically forbids Americans to accept such titles from foreign governments.[66] It is also why George Washington, a useful barometer of the national mood in his day, insisted that people call him "Mr. President" rather than "Your Excellency." After all, anyone in the new order could be a "mister."[67]

The Rejection of Mixed Government

The egalitarian assumption helps to explain how the American republic was significantly different from those republics recommended by writers like Cicero and Montesquieu. Such political thinkers, keeping the nature of European society in mind, had assumed that a republic contains within itself several social classes. Each of these makes some valuable contribution to public policy, and the balance of all classes prevents any one of them from behaving tyrannically toward the others. Such a regime was sometimes known as a "mixed government," or a "balanced

---

[64] Michael Walzer, *Spheres of Justice: A Defense of Pluralism and Equality* (New York: Basic, 1983), pp. 276–277. Later generations would say that even someone born in a log cabin could become president. In his Farewell Address (1796), George Washington implied the same absence of fixed social ranks in the language of republicanism. Thus his opening statement: "Friends, and Fellow Citizens: The period for a new election of a Citizen, to Administer the Executive government of the United States, being not far distant...." See the entire Address in Matthew Spalding and Patrick J. Garrity, *A Sacred Union of Citizens: George Washington's Farewell Address and the American Character*, introd. by Daniel Boorstin (London: Rowman and Littlefield, 1996), pp. 175–188.

[65] Thus Jefferson hoped that a life of freedom in America would encourage the emergence of a "natural" aristocracy of achievement. See his letter to John Adams, October 28, 1813, in Jefferson, *The Political Writings of Thomas Jefferson*, p. 91.

[66] Article I, Section 9, clause 8.

[67] Wood, *The Radicalism of the American Revolution*, p. 233.

constitution,"[68] and it was recommended by conservatives such as Edmund Burke.[69] It was, however, emphatically not what Americans sought or produced.

America had no European-style classes and therefore felt no need to balance them against one another to prevent tyranny. Furthermore, Americans rejected the idea that classes made special contributions to the welfare of society, an idea which in Europe supported chiefly the assumption that virtue flowed mainly from membership in the hereditary upper classes. Americans ridiculed the notion that virtue could be hereditary.[70] Instead, they regarded their society as fairly open and fluid, with opportunities for many people to prosper via their efforts and to promote social welfare via their talents.

True, the Constitution restrained the new government from acting tyrannically, as Cicero and Montesquieu recommended. But the structure of that government, which superficially resembled a European-style division of powers, did not divide men of one rank against men of another. Instead, it divided the government against itself, where each part of that government was, directly or indirectly, elected by the same people rather than by different classes.[71]

And thus Madison, in *The Federalist*, did not regard unchecked *classes* as dangerous in America, because there were none.[72] Instead, he warned against *factions*, which could form on the basis of interests momentarily shared among men who themselves belong to "the people" rather than to any permanent part of the body politic. Madison argued that factions could become *tyrannical* in the traditional sense of that term, because they might seek a public policy adverse to the interests of other men. But factions would be checked by the nature of the new republic, whose size

[68] On the balanced constitution, see Robert J. Morgan, "Madison's Theory of Representation in the Tenth Federalist," *Journal of Politics* (November 1974), p. 881.

[69] Thus Burke, in *Reflections on the Revolution in France*, p. 58, described property owners, who dominated Parliament, as the "ballast" in the "vessel of the commonwealth," and he assumed that the lords and the commons preserved liberty by restraining the king.

[70] See the examples in Wood, *The Radicalism of the American Revolution*, p. 181.

[71] Commager, *The Empire of Reason*, pp. 207–209.

[72] Certainly there were "classes" in the sense of people more or less affluent. But that was not the same as European classes which were sometimes defined by law and sometimes legally characterized by different rights and obligations. As always, the great American exception was the class of slaves, mostly in the South, which simply did not figure in *The Federalist*, No. 10, since that essay was directed at New York voters.

and complexity would divide up power among so many governmental units as to make it highly unlikely that any faction would gain control of a commanding number of the same units.[73]

Citizenship II

Natural rights, civil society, individualism, the people, constitutionalism, republicanism, citizens, and egalitarianism – the Founders employed concepts that helped them create a regime very different from what Westerners had seen before. In the realm of Citizenship II, though, the Constitution said little. Mainly, it stipulated that the right to vote in federal elections, for the House of Representatives and for the Electoral College, would go to citizens authorized by their states to vote for the lower house of state legislatures.[74] Amendments would later enforce some uniformity on voting rights, as, for example, when race and sex were eventually forbidden as grounds for exclusion in state politics.[75] But apart from such strictures, America's states have always been free to decide who would become citizens in the Aristotelian sense.

Property and Virtue

How did the states originally decide? When they ratified the Constitution, a republican outlook limited the number of those entitled to vote. That is, the Founders believed that a republic is the best possible regime, and they thought that republics can only survive and prosper when their officials are elected by voters who understand the public interest and act virtuously to promote it. The ability to reach this understanding flowed from owning some quantity of property because, or so many of the Founders thought, property assured economic self-reliance which, in turn, permitted independence of mind and will.[76] Most women could be excluded, in contemporary terms, as dependent on husbands or fathers, sons or brothers.[77] Moreover, men of color could be excluded, again in contemporary

---

[73] *The Federalist*, No. 10, pp. 61–62.   [74] Article I, Section 2, clause 1.

[75] Amendments XIV (1865), XV (1868), XVI (1870), and XIX (1920).

[76] Wood, *The Radicalism of the American Revolution*, pp. 104–105.

[77] Single women, as heads of household, may not have been "dependent" on any male kinfolk. Nevertheless, they were excluded from political life on various grounds that we now recognize as inspired by gender bias. For an introduction to this subject, see Linda K. Kerber, "The Paradox of Women's Citizenship in the Early Republic," *American Historical Review* (April 1992), pp. 349–378.

terms, as racially inferior. In practice, then, the pool of potential voters was limited almost entirely to white men.

Against the backdrop of Europe's political conversation, the idea of linking virtue to property was not new.[78] What surpassed expectations was an American society where property holding became more widespread than ever. Consequently, even though white men held most of the franchise, it embraced a larger portion of the population than anywhere else. From 60 to 70 percent of America's adult white males were probably entitled to vote,[79] since about two-thirds of them owned land compared with perhaps 20 percent of Englishmen.[80] Most states maintained a higher property qualification for office holding, but there too the proportion of potential candidates was surely greater than elsewhere.[81]

Moreover, Americans assumed that a growing number of men would acquire property and become open-minded and virtuous citizens. As Native Americans were displaced, arable land in quantities unimaginable by European standards became available for white settlement. Founders like Jefferson were determined that government should promote access to this property, so that more and more Americans could become independent farmers, that is, hardworking, prosperous, and virtuous citizens.[82] Jefferson showed his preference in this regard with a proposal that any "person of full age neither owning nor having owned fifty acres of land" would be entitled to receive such a tract from Virginia.[83] Nothing came of this proposal, but land was cheap anyway, and later, when Jefferson became America's third president, he and the Congress doubled the country's acreage when they paid Napoleon fifteen million dollars for the Louisiana Purchase.

---

[78] See the British jurist William Blackstone, *Commentaries on the Laws of England*, 4 vols. (orig., 1765–1769; Chicago: Univ. of Chicago Press, 1979), Vol. I, p. 156:

> The true reason of requiring any qualification, with regard to property, in voters, is to exclude such persons as are in so mean a situation as to be esteemed to have no will of their own. If these persons had votes, they would be tempted to dispose of them under some undue influence or other. This would give a great, an artful, or a wealthy man, a larger share in elections than is consistent with general liberty.

[79] Alexander Keyssar, *The Right to Vote: The Contested History of Democracy in the United States* (New York: Basic Books, 2000), p. 24.

[80] Wood, *The Radicalism of the American Revolution*, p. 123.   [81] Ibid., pp. 106–107.

[82] See Joyce Appleby, *Liberalism and Republicanism in the Historical Imagination* (Cambridge: Harvard Univ. Press, 1992), p. 304.

[83] From "A Draft Constitution for Virginia," in Jefferson, *Political Writings*, pp. 14–15.

Citizenship III and Religion

To say that only virtuous citizens should vote, and to allocate voting rights mainly according to that principle, was to minimize the likelihood that civil disobedience would disturb the new country. After all, if voters were virtuous, they were likely to enact laws which people could obey in good conscience. That being so logically, we may regard the original distribution of voting rights in America via property ownership as designed, analytically speaking, to produce a state so good that no significant number of people in it would find cause to exercise Citizenship III as dangerously as many dissenters had in Europe during the sixteenth and seventeenth centuries.

On this score, however, we should add that the Founders hoped to neutralize even more directly the sort of religious impulses that had strained public life in earlier generations. Most of the colonies started out with established churches. But many of their inhabitants gradually came to believe that churches are rightfully voluntary organizations, arising harmlessly in civil society for important but limited reasons. Thus J. Hector St. John de Crèvecoeur, writing in the 1780s, noted that Catholic and Lutheran and Low Dutch farmers lived side by side in America, each tending to his own fields, each believing what he wished without offending or persecuting others. Why, then, should it concern "the welfare of the country, or of the province at large," what any such person believes, so long as it harms no one else?[84] Jefferson put the matter even more bluntly. "The legitimate powers of government," he said, "extend to such acts only as are injurious to others. But it does me no injury for my neighbor to say there are twenty gods, or no God. It neither picks my pocket nor breaks my leg."[85]

In short, why should voters instruct government to make any law concerning the practice of religion? Trying to intervene between men and God can only turn a benign realm of civil society into an arena for embitterment and probable disobedience. This piece of commonsense wisdom would be enshrined twice in the Constitution, in the First Amendment forbidding Congress from supporting any particular religion and in Article VI's insistence that there would be no religious tests for holding federal office.[86]

---

[84] Crèvecoeur, *Letters from an American Farmer*, p. 45.

[85] Jefferson, *Notes on the State of Virginia*, introd. by Thomas P. Abernathy (orig., 1785; New York: Harper Torchbooks, 1964), p. 152.

[86] See Amendment I and Article VI, Section 3.

This is not to say that the Founders belittled the positive contribution that religious morality could make to public life. When they praised such morality, however, they often assumed it could emerge from a sort of nonsectarian Christianity which some called *deism*.[87] Benjamin Franklin wrote of this view when he described his own creed by saying: "I believe in one God, creator of the Universe. That he governs it by his providence. That he ought to be worshiped. That the most acceptable service we render to him is doing good to his other children.... These I take to be the fundamental principles of all sound religion."[88] Such beliefs Franklin associated with Jesus of Nazareth, but he was more certain that they worked than that they were, in some theological or metaphysical sense, objectively true.

The Republican Paragon

The new republic was fortunate that George Washington led its founding generation.[89] Here was the quintessential man of property, living close to the soil, comfortable and independent but neither as rich nor as haughty as a British aristocrat. A man who left home and hearth behind, like the Roman hero, Cincinnatus, to lead the national army in his country's struggle for freedom. A man who, after victory, returned home quietly, without seeking prizes or titles. A man who, by the consent of his peers, chaired the Constitutional Convention. A man who agreed to serve his country again, as its first president, twice chosen unanimously by the Electoral College. A man who insisted on being called no more than Mr. President. A man of quiet religious convictions, who honored those of others.[90] And a man who, by accepting only two terms of office, set an example for how

---

[87] On deism, see William H. Marnell, *Man-Made Morals: Four Philosophies That Shaped America* (Garden City, N.Y.: Doubleday Anchor, 1968), pp. 1–174.

[88] Benjamin Franklin, letter to Ezra Stiles, March 9, 1790, in *The Writings of Benjamin Franklin*, ed. Albert Henry Smyth, 10 vols. (New York: Macmillan, 1905–1907), Vol. X, p. 84.

[89] On Washington as a man of republican virtue, see Garry Wills, *Cincinnatus: George Washington and the Enlightenment* (New York: Doubleday, 1984).

[90] For Washington's tolerance of religious minorities, see his reassuring letter "To the Hebrew Congregation of Newport, Rhode Island" (August 18, 1790), in Dorothy Twohig (ed.), *The Papers of George Washington, Presidential Series*, 8 vols. (Charlottesville: Univ. of Virginia Press, 1987–), Vol. 6, pp. 284–285: "Happily the government of the United States, which gives to bigotry no sanction – to persecution no assistance, requires only that they who live under its protection should demean themselves as good citizens, in giving it on all occasions their effectual support."

republican leaders should curb their political ambitions.[91] Revolutionary America got Washington; revolutionary France got Napoleon. The difference spoke volumes.

[91] Today, when presidential oratory is inspired mainly by political consultants, speech writers, and television coaches, some Americans might like Washington's political heirs to accept as republican precedent the intrinsic modesty of his second Inaugural Address, which was four sentences long. See Washington, "Second Inaugural Address" (March 4, 1793), in Richardson (ed.), *Messages and Papers of the Presidents*, Vol. I, p. 138.

4

The Democratic Moment

To his contemporaries, the man from Mount Vernon was enormously impressive. True, the Founders enfranchised neither women nor most men of color, and some of the Founders, such as Jefferson and Washington, owned slaves.[1] By their lights, however, the immediate problem was not so much modern expectations as that republicanism, which predicated political inclusion mainly on land ownership, or what was called *freeholding*, justified leaving many white men without the rights of Citizenship II.

This problem intensified because ordinary men had more economic opportunities in America than in Europe. From these opportunities, there evolved a thriving society no longer dominated by landed citizens. Country squires remained, but new circumstances challenged their traditional leading role in what had been envisioned as a classical republican

---

[1] Surely the Revolutionary generation's main failing was its perpetuation of slavery. However, in the republic's early years, antislavery statesmen, including many of the Founders, knew that white Southerners were mostly in favor of slavery and would prevent the fragile Union from taking root if serious steps were taken to end the evil practice. The Constitution therefore protected slavery, the day of reckoning was postponed indefinitely, and when the Civil War broke out, the price paid for emancipation was enormous (as was the price paid for slavery all along by those who suffered it). Quakers and other abolitionists like John Brown knew that slavery was a sin, against which people of conscience must act regardless of cost calculations. We should recall, though, that even Abraham Lincoln went to war against the Confederacy only because its forces attacked the Union at Fort Sumter. If Southern whites had not made that enormous strategic blunder, he was planning, and his Republican Party recommended, to keep slavery out of new western states in the hope that human bondage in America would gradually fade away by itself. For some of the early, tragic maneuverings on this issue in Congress, played out against Southern threats to secede even in 1790, see Joseph J. Ellis, *Founding Brothers: The Revolutionary Generation* (New York: Vintage, 2002), "The Silence," pp. 81–119.

society.[2] Those who competed with the squires were men pursuing dynamic livelihoods based on exploitation of natural resources, new techniques of production, expanding networks of trade, improvements in transportation, and innovations in finance.[3] These men often prospered not so much from work on the land as from their ability to contribute to, and profit from, what we now call a cash economy, centered on manufacturing, services, and professions, and housed on relatively small land lots in towns and cities.

Then too, American society was constantly changing, with immigrants arriving from abroad, and with local residents moving from one place to another to get ahead. By one estimate, for example, 70 percent of those who lived in the old Northwest Territories in 1810 had not been there in 1800, even while many of the people living in those territories had changed residence in the same region, some many times.[4] Under the circumstances, social hierarchies were fluid rather than stable, and non-freeholders argued that the franchise should apply at least to men who possessed tangible assets and paid taxes even if they owned little land.[5] Their insistence on being politically included created, in effect, a demand for democratizing the franchise.

The New Virtue

Consideration of that demand centered on how virtue should be defined. Men of republican outlook assumed that virtue was a public-regarding value which appeared in civic engagement based on ethical detachment. That is, a man should care about what happens in his community, and he should be able to act there without reference to his private interests. For republicans, of course, property provided both an incentive for concern and the means for detachment, and therefore property should be a qualification for voting.

---

[2] Joyce Appleby, *Liberalism and Republicanism in the Historical Imagination* (Cambridge: Harvard Univ. Press, 1992), p. 216, notes that purely republican assumptions were no longer appropriate to explain how to conduct public affairs in a New World society so economically different from the classical model.

[3] Sean Wilentz, "Property and Power: Suffrage Reform in the United States, 1787–1860," in Donald W. Rogers (ed.), *Voting and the Spirit of American Democracy: Essays on the History of Voting and Voting Rights in America* (Urbana: Univ. of Illinois Press, 1992), p. 35.

[4] Robert Wiebe, *The Opening of American Society* (New York: Vintage, 1985), p. 132.

[5] See the examples of substituting the value rather than the size of land lots as a qualification for voting in Chilton Williamson, *American Suffrage: From Property to Democracy, 1760–1860* (Princeton: Princeton Univ. Press, 1960), pp. 212–213.

The economy, however, moved in unexpected directions. Many Americans were getting ahead constructively. But their private success, which sometimes led away from landholding, did not always seem designed, in a republican sense, to evoke virtuous public behavior. The need, then, was to see that what those men were doing did not just promote their private interest but also served the community. Accordingly, Americans would have to learn to regard industry, frugality, sobriety, and prudence as qualities of character that justify calling the man who practices them virtuous.[6] In which case, even if he is short on real estate, why not let him vote?

Work as Demeaning

The problem was that work, or some kinds of it, had long been disparaged. Thus no less an authority than Aristotle introduced Westerners to the notion that much work is demeaning. If that were so, those who depend upon it for daily bread are incapable of virtue, which for Aristotle flowed from a regard for public values that can only be appreciated by men of leisure who enjoy independence of mind. He therefore argued that men such as mechanics and tradesmen and agricultural workers, although residing in the polis, should not be citizens in the sense of being entitled to participate in public affairs.[7]

For Christians, St. Augustine updated the animus against work by linking labor to sin. He argued that there are three major sins: lust for power, lust for sex, and lust to acquire boundless money and possessions.[8] Work in this context may be necessary for attaining sufficient money and possessions to maintain human life. But Augustine lived in a static economic world, where one man's gain might be wrong for causing another man's loss. And so, for him, work remained a matter of unwelcome drudgery rather than a positive force capable of promoting steady and commendable increases in health and material well-being.

European spokesmen for the "old order" combined the themes of dependence and grinding toil to assume that a good life was free of both, that such a life permitted civic virtue in the sense of detachment and

---

[6] On the shift from property-based virtue to commercially inspired virtue, see Isaac Kramnick, "The 'Great National Discussion': The Discourse of Politics in 1787," *William and Mary Quarterly* (January 1988), pp. 15–23.

[7] Aristotle, *The Politics of Aristotle*, trans. and ed. Ernest Barker (New York: Oxford Univ. Press, 1946), Bk. VII, Ch. 9, pp. 300–303.

[8] Herbert A. Deane, *The Political and Social Ideas of St. Augustine* (New York: Columbia Univ. Press, 1963), pp. 45–56.

contemplation, that there was a natural hierarchy of men which embraced some who were capable of virtue and others who were not, that virtue in this hierarchy belonged mostly to a hereditary aristocracy, and that people expressed it in a life of *honor*. Thus Edmund Burke charged French revolutionaries with seeking to level the natural order of society, with regarding all occupations as honorable, with therefore mistakenly assuming that a hairdresser or a candlemaker can act honorably. Not so, said Burke, in which case men of such occupations should not share in ruling the state.[9]

Work as Virtuous

So far, it was common knowledge that virtue accompanied leisure, contemplation, and honor, in which case only those who fit the bill should receive Citizenship II. Little by little, however, men sensed the possibility that virtue might be linked to labor, productivity, and the generation of earned rather than inherited wealth. A few examples of the new outlook will suffice here to establish its pedigree.

The Puritans contributed the notion that God gives every man a "vocation, or calling . . . [which] is a certain kind of life, ordained and imposed on man by God, for the common good."[10] In other words, different sorts of work, no matter how high or low, are ordained by God and maintain human communities. It follows that those who do not work, such as rogues, beggars, vagabonds, monks, friars, and the idle rich, are guilty of contributing to what William Perkins, around 1600, called a "foule disorder" of the "Commonwealth."[11]

This concept of callings did not at first undermine existing hierarchies. Thus early Puritans assumed that every community rests upon various callings which add up to a balance of different social ranks, such as when John Winthrop, governor of the Massachusetts Bay colony noted that he had been "called" to be a magistrate.[12] Still, a certain spiritual equality obtained among callings, because all of them were ordained by God. And in that case, via the concept of callings, what came to be known as the

---

9 Edmund Burke, *Reflections on the Revolution in France*, ed. Thomas H. D. Mahoney (orig., 1790; New York: Liberal Arts, 1955), pp. 55–56.

10 William Perkins, "William Perkins on Callings (1603)," in Edmund S. Morgan (ed.), *Puritan Political Ideas: 1558–1794* (Indianapolis: Bobbs-Merrill, 1965), p. 36.

11 Ibid., p. 54.

12 "The Journal of John Winthrop," in Morgan, ibid., p. 137. The reference here is to Winthrop's "little speech," delivered before the General Court of Massachusetts in May 1645.

social contract could increasingly be viewed somewhat radically, as an arrangement between, in a sense, moral equals, with many men entitled to enforce its terms.[13]

In his *Second Treatise of Government*, in 1689, John Locke suggested another concept that would foster respect for work and those who perform it. In his argument concerning a state of nature, which seemed so descriptive of life in America that Jefferson wrote part of it into the Declaration of Independence, Locke said that, even before government is created, men mix their labor with natural resources in order to create property.[14] That is, the very property which Europeans saw as commendable for assuring life, liberty, comfort, and leisure, was defined by Locke as the product of work, in which case, he concluded, it is work that creates things of value, thereby sustaining men and their communities.[15] Assuming that labor creates value can justify a social contract wherein all working men are entitled to some say in how government will protect and preserve the fruit of their efforts. However, Locke did not recommend such a widespread distribution of Citizenship II rights.

In Scotland, Adam Smith updated the labor theory of value when he published *The Wealth of Nations* in 1776. Offering a qualified but influential recommendation for what would later be called capitalism, Smith shifted attention from Locke's property to the category of wealth, a more modern and comprehensive repository of what should be valued as the source of communal well-being. Smith claimed that wealth increases when men labor effectively by dividing up different sorts of work to those most able and willing to do it.[16] Furthermore, he challenged the notion, as old as Aristotle, that men should live with each other according to some disembodied standard of value and virtue. Work creates both, said Smith, in the sense that "it is not from the benevolence of the butcher, the brewer, or the baker, that we expect our dinner, but from their regard to their own interest. We address ourselves, not to their humanity but to their self-love."[17] In fact, it is the marketplace which, as if by an invisible hand, combines the efforts of butchers, brewers, bakers, and other

---

[13] Michael Walzer, *The Revolution of the Saints: A Study in the Origins of Radical Politics* (New York: Atheneum, 1968), p. 214.

[14] John Locke, *Two Treatises on Government*, ed. Peter Laslett (Cambridge: Cambridge Univ. Press, 1960), Second Treatise, Ch. V, Secs. 26–28, pp. 304–307f.

[15] Ibid., p. 314.

[16] Adam Smith, *An Inquiry into the Nature and Causes of the Wealth of Nations*, ed. Edwin Cannan (orig., 1776; New York: Modern Library, 1937), pp. 3–12.

[17] Ibid., p. 14.

private workers to serve most fruitfully the welfare of the community as a whole.[18]

Work in Civil Society

During the republican moment, such ideas encouraged Americans to regard work as a constructive and praiseworthy part of civil society. Here, work stood alongside the realm of religious activity, where it equally deserved protection from undue government interference. Work not only created value. When disciplined by marketplace forces it was, as Smith pointed out, largely benign. So why not commend the realm of work as an inherently moral domain, where men do what they can and get what they deserve, more or less, and where life may proceed without much need for what Paine had called the necessary evil of government?[19] Here, in fact, was the Jeffersonian ideal of civil society working so well that government need barely act at all and therefore could remain so small as never, or rarely, to realize its potential for tyranny.

Observers like Crèvecoeur saw, even during the Revolution, that work rather than rank had become the social cement of American society, which had "no aristocratical families, no courts, no kings, no bishops, no ecclesiastical dominion...no great refinements of luxury."[20] Instead, said Crèvecoeur, most people in America, unlike in Europe, were free to work productively, which enabled them to accumulate money to buy property, to become freeholders, and to achieve the rank of citizen.[21] It remained only to recognize that, as the economy grew and cash proliferated, other forms of ownership and success, less linked to landed property, flowed from virtuous effort and warranted full-fledged citizenship.

Franklin and the Visitors

The growing regard for work rather than social standing did not imply that Americans preferred to be poor rather than rich. It did mean, though, that they came to see work and its results as respectable, and that belief was a considerable contrast to how work had long been regarded by Europeans as ignoble. Benjamin Franklin captured the new mood when he remarked that when Americans meet a stranger, they do not ask "*What is he?* but *what can he do?* If he has an useful Art, he is welcome; and if he exercises it, and behaves well, he will be respected by all that know

---

[18] Ibid., p. 423.   [19] Appleby, *Liberalism and Republicanism*, p. 337.
[20] J. Hector St. John de Crèvecoeur, *Letters from an American Farmer* (orig., 1782; New York: Dutton, 1957), pp. 35–36.
[21] Ibid., pp. 37–39.

him." After all, "God Almighty is himself a Mechanic, the greatest in the Universe; and he is respected and admired more for the Variety, Ingenuity, and Utility of his Handyworks, than for the Antiquity of his Family."[22] Franklin also wrote, in the pithy maxims of *Poor Richard's Almanac*, about how work would produce enviable rewards if it were done well, that is, by practicing virtues such as thrift, punctuality, sobriety, honesty, and persistence.[23]

This sort of outlook became so common in America that it impressed visitors who highlighted work when they explained to European readers the special qualities of American life. Thus in *Democracy in America* (1834, 1840), Alexis de Tocqueville marveled at the way work had transformed America and at how many large and small undertakings sustained the new country.[24] He also observed that in the New World almost everyone worked, including wealthy men who would have been embarrassed if other men were to see them idle.[25]

Michel Chevalier, in *Society, Manners, and Politics in the United States* (1839), formed much the same impression and pointed out that an energetic combination of capital and industry in America had permitted New York to grow tenfold in fifty years.[26] Like Tocqueville, he noted that Americans admired those who worked and enhanced their nation's prosperity. Indeed, Americans were educated to believe, he said, that none should be idle, that each will have some occupation, and that "if he is active and intelligent, he will make his fortune."[27]

Harriet Martineau, in *Society in America* (1837), deployed this line of observation to use attitudes toward work as a basis for comparing regional cultures in America. In the North, she noticed, children learned to respect work and study hard to succeed in whatever occupation they chose to pursue. "Many a great man in Congress," she wrote, when young guided his father's horses in plowing and brought them to water. In the South,

---

[22] "Information to Those Who Would Remove to America" (1782), in *The Writings of Benjamin Franklin*, ed. Albert Henry Smyth, 10 vols. (New York: Macmillan, 1905–1907), Vol. VIII, p. 606.

[23] Benjamin Franklin, *Poor Richard, An Almanack* (orig., 1733–1758; New York: David McKay, 1976), p. 108: "Early to bed, and early to rise, makes a man healthy, wealthy, and wise." See additional maxims in Franklin, "The Way to Wealth," which first appeared as a preface to the *Almanack* in 1758. Reprinted in Smyth (ed.), *The Writings of Benjamin Franklin*, Vol. III, pp. 407–418.

[24] Alexis de Tocqueville, *Democracy in America*, 2 vols. (orig., 1834, 1840; New York: Vintage, 1954), Vol. II, p. 166.

[25] Ibid., p. 250.

[26] Michel Chevalier, *Society, Manners, and Politics in the United States* (orig., 1839; New York: Augustus M. Kelley, 1966), p. 78.

[27] Ibid., p. 283.

by contrast, the "servile class" worked with no hope of reward, while the "imperious class" taught its children the "vicious fundamental principle of morals in a slave country, that labour is disgraceful."[28] In the long run, this principle could not endure in America.

The Democratic Moment

So appreciation grew for the virtues of work and those who did it.[29] Meanwhile, demands for more democracy gathered strength even while republican aspirations limited the number of white men regarded as worthy of Citizenship II. These demands arose in every region of the country but especially in northwestern and southwestern states such as Ohio, Indiana, and Kentucky, where everyone participated in the new and dynamic economy, with its social leveling effects.

Progress came unevenly, because it involved many states with different vectors of local power and interest. In general, however, and as a halfway step away from classic republicanism, some states permitted taxpaying to count for property owning. And so by 1824, twenty-one out of twenty-four states had given almost all adult white males the right to vote, based on property or taxpaying or some other equivalency test.[30] People at the time called this "universal suffrage."[31] Yet the demand for an even wider franchise was so strong that, after Mississippi in 1817, not a single new state joined the Union with property or taxpaying qualifications.[32]

Massachusetts, New York, and Virginia
In original states like Massachusetts, New York, and Virginia, formal debates over widening the franchise employed the sort of arguments made

---

[28] Harriet Martineau, *Society in America*, ed., abr., and introd. by S. M. Lipset (orig., 1837; New Brunswick: Transaction, 1981), pp. 216–218.

[29] Modern historians would note that this growing regard was mainly for work done by free white men rather than by slaves or women.

[30] Kirk H. Porter, *A History of Suffrage in the United States* (New York: Greenwood, 1977), p. 60, notes that in 1821 New York adopted a tax qualification which provided that electors "must have paid a state or county tax, or have performed military service, or worked on the highway, or have lived three years in the state instead of the one year prescribed ordinarily."

[31] Christopher Collier, "The American People as Christian White Men of Property: Suffrage and Elections in Colonial and Early National America," in Rogers (ed.), *Voting and the Spirit of American Democracy*, p. 26.

[32] Porter, *A History of Suffrage*, p. 110, offers a chart which shows the duration of property and taxpaying qualifications for twenty American states in the first decades of the nineteenth century. A state-by-state list of such qualifications between 1790 and 1855 appears in Alexander Keyssar, *The Right to Vote: The Contested History of Democracy in the United States* (New York: Basic Books, 2000), pp. 342–347.

for and against property qualifications. No new principles appeared in these debates. Rather, they constituted a dialogue aimed at stretching the egalitarianism of the Declaration to apply to more men than it had covered at first. Women were still excluded, of course. Moreover, only later would Abraham Lincoln insist that the Declaration was true for men of color.

In Massachusetts, a constitutional convention addressed the suffrage question in 1820. On behalf of property, Daniel Webster argued that life and liberty should be protected by law but that property also should be safeguarded, for it is "the fund out of which the means for protecting life and liberty are usually furnished."[33] Josiah Quincy concurred, and he suggested that "the provision of a pecuniary qualification" for membership in the state senate should be regarded along with the separation of governmental powers as one of the checks and balances built into the Bay State's constitution in order to preserve liberty.[34]

In reply, Thomas Lincoln insisted that government is for people rather than property, and that it will succeed on the basis of their intelligence rather than their belongings. At most, he said, if property is to be represented in Massachusetts, it should not be in proportion to the size of a man's holdings but according to his taxes regardless of how much he pays.[35] Josiah Quincy, who supported a property qualification for state senators, at this point echoed the Putney radicals and complained that, with regard to voting, Massachusetts unjustly excluded "the laboring parts of society" even though they had fought in the Revolution and would be called upon to fight again in case of invasion.[36]

Delegates voiced similar arguments in the New York constitutional convention of 1821 and the Virginia constitutional convention of 1830. Thus in New York, Chancellor James Kent rejected a proposal for universal adult white male suffrage by saying that such a degree of democracy "has been regarded with terror, by the wise men of every age, because in every European republic, ancient and modern, in which it has been tried, it has ... been productive of corruption, injustice, violence and tyranny."[37] So much for America's faith in civil society and the basic decency of men who might emerge from there into public life.

---

[33] Daniel Webster, "Political Power Naturally Goes ...," in Alpheus Thomas Mason (ed.), *Free Government in the Making: Readings in American Political Thought*, 1st ed. (New York: Oxford Univ. Press, 1949), p. 396.

[34] Josiah Quincy, "The Spirit of Our Constitution ...," ibid., p. 386.

[35] Thomas Lincoln, "A System of Checks and Balances ...," ibid., p. 388.

[36] Quincy, "The Spirit of Our Constitution ...," ibid., p. 387.

[37] Chancellor James Kent, "The Tendency of Univeral Suffrage ...," ibid., p. 399.

P. R. Livingston, on the other hand, made New York's case for the little man when he argued that, although wealth may support civilization, it is labor which creates wealth in the first place. Furthermore, said Livingston, since the days of Greece and Rome, it is the laboring man who joins the militia and defends his country in time of war.[38] These men, added John Cramer, may have little property. But they have as much integrity and patriotism as any other class.[39]

And finally, John Marshall, chief justice of the Supreme Court of the United States, asked the Virginia convention in 1830 to revisit its first principles. The Revolution, he said, was fought not because English taxes were too high for America, but because their imposition on men without representation robbed those men of their freedom. And there, said Marshall, was the reason why excluding such men should cease.[40]

As a result of such discussions, all three of these states decided to ease their voting qualifications, although not to the same extent.[41] In the process, changing attitudes toward work and work-related values influenced the outcome. In Virginia, for example, a typical petition in 1829 from those demanding inclusion, from the "Non-Freeholders of the City of Richmond," argued that urban workers were neither lacking in civic interest nor unworthy of a voice in public affairs. They practiced occupations useful to the community, said the petition; they exercised integrity and intelligence; and they loved their towns or cities as firmly as men attached to real estate. Indeed, mere property ownership might, in the wrong hands, encourage "sordid sentiments," whereas non-freeholders were as patriotic as any man.[42]

Jacksonianism

Across the nation, voters clearly favored Andrew Jackson, and their support for him was another indication of respect for men who work. In 1829, Jackson delivered his first "Annual Message to Congress," wherein

[38] P. R. Livingston, "Character Does Not Spring...," ibid., p. 402.

[39] John Cramer, "Let Us Not Brand the Constitution...," ibid., p. 404.

[40] John Marshall, "They Alone Deserve to Be Called...," ibid., p. 411.

[41] In 1821, Massachusetts dropped property qualifications and instituted a small tax requirement; between 1821 and 1826, New York set aside property and tax requirements for whites but retained both for "men of color"; in 1830, Virginia reduced property qualifications and permitted a tax payment substitute but cancelled both only in 1850. For these details, see Keyssar, *The Right to Vote*, pp. 342–346.

[42] Cited by Rowland Berthoff, "Independence and Attachment, Virtue and Interest: From Republican Citizen to Free Enterprise, 1787–1837," in Richard L. Bushman, Neil Harris, David Rothman, Barbara Miller Solomon, and Stephan Thernstrom, *Uprooted Americans: Essays in Honor of Oscar Handlin* (Boston: Little, Brown, 1979), pp. 118–119.

he declared that no person is more entitled to public office than another. First, because the purpose of government is to serve the people, in which case offices should not be reserved to some citizens who might exploit their positions to serve private rather than public interests. And second because, despite what someone like Burke might have argued, no special talent is required for executing public work. After all, as Jackson put it, "The duties of all public offices are, or at least admit of being made, so plain and simple that men of intelligence may readily qualify themselves for their performance."[43]

So anyone might be sufficiently able and virtuous enough to do public work. But Jackson was also instructive about what sort of that work should be done and who should benefit from it. Thus, in 1832, he vetoed a congressional bill intended to renew the national charter of the Bank of the United States. The bank deserved to die, said Jackson, because, favored by government, it provided unmerited profits to wealthy shareholders who created nothing of value. In this sense, the bank was an unwarranted burden that should not be borne by truly productive members of society, who were "farmers, mechanics, and laborers."[44]

Rights and Interests

A certain logic concerning interests infused the eventual American willingness to include working men in public life. We know that a society which proclaims that men have natural rights will eventually have to concede that all people have political rights, even if women and men of color are at first excluded. One way this happens starts when the concept of *rights* suggests that if a person has rights, he will exercise them in order to advance his *interests*, that is, to stay alive, to prosper economically, to seek happiness.

Yet if everyone may pursue his or her interests as a matter of right, and if, as the Declaration says, government exists to protect men in the exercise of their rights, then Americans would eventually conclude that all men, and not just some special group, were justified in overseeing the process by which government is held accountable for safeguarding whichever rights it must serve. In other words, to begin with natural rights was to recognize,

---

[43] Andrew Jackson, "First Annual Message" (December 8, 1829), in James D. Richardson (ed.), *Messages and Papers of the Presidents, 1789–1902*, Vol. II (Washington, D.C.: Bureau of National Literature and Art, 1905), p. 449.

[44] Andrew Jackson, "Veto Message" (July 10, 1832), ibid., p. 590. On Jackson's regard for productive people, see Marvin Meyers, *The Jacksonian Persuasion: Politics and Belief* (Stanford: Stanford Univ. Press, 1957), pp. 21–23.

although not immediately, that society is composed of people who all have interests, who all are entitled to pursue those interests, and who all should therefore be empowered to participate in public life exactly as Aristotle had defined citizenship in our sense of Citizenship II.[45]

To extend the franchise with this sort of reasoning in mind was significantly to reject, once again, the European notion of a *mixed government*. The separation of powers that Montesquieu and Burke saw in English government balanced each social class against the others, assuming that such classes represented the great and permanent interests of English society. But Americans eventually widened the franchise to give Citizenship II to individuals rather than to classes so that, via elections, they might instruct government to take into account an ever-changing kaleidoscope of interests which form and reform, arise and disappear. There was no suggestion that these interests were great and permanent. Indeed, the fact that they were not lent flexibility to American politics, which stumbled into civil war precisely when that flexibility vanished and an intractable confrontation between long-term regional interests almost destroyed the Union.

Factions, Parties, and Spoils

Legitimate interests based on individual needs eventually justified the growth of political parties in America. Eighteenth-century Europeans assumed that parties arise from dangerous conspiracies against the public interest. Thus in the absence of truly representative elections, they regarded parties as tyrannical cliques of men seeking to gain control of the government, or parts of it, in order to use public means to advance private ends.[46]

---

[45] The element of inevitability suggested here – moving from natural rights to widespread rights – is based on my reading of Albert O. Hirschman, *The Passions and the Interests: Political Arguments for Capitalism Before Its Triumph* (Princeton: Princeton Univ. Press, 1977); and Judith Shklar, *American Citizenship: The Quest for Inclusion* (Cambridge: Harvard Univ. Press, 1991), esp. pp. 37–38. Shklar's book as a whole focuses on the long struggle to establish civil rights for African Americans and women.

[46] Bernard Bailyn, *The Origins of American Politics* (New York: Vintage, 1968), pp. 36–37. For an American example of this view, see Robert A. Gross, *The Minutemen and Their World* (New York: Hill and Wang, 1976), p. 14:

> In [colonial] Concord [Massachusetts]...a potential leader neither sought nor clung to office; were he to campaign openly, he would simply demonstrate his unfitness for public trust. Once elected, he would continue on the same conscientious course for the public good.... The ordinary citizen in this vision of politics had an equally virtuous code of conduct. When he joined in a town meeting, he would set the needs of the group before his own.... Never would he concert his opposition with others; such action was universally condemned as the work of "faction," of men in league against the common good.

It was in this sense that, in *The Federalist*, Madison defined "faction" as "a number of citizens ... who are united ... by some ... interest, adverse to the rights of other citizens, or to the ... interests of the community."[47] Washington feared the same phenomenon when he warned, in his "Farewell Address," of the "baneful effects of the Spirit of Party."[48]

But the truth was that America conducted many elections, in which voters were free to express their interests and anyone elected to office was constrained to heed popular mandates or risk losing the next election. It was therefore natural that citizens of different outlooks would band together and seek to capture, at least temporarily, part of the government in order to tell it how to protect their interests. It was equally natural that this process would eventually seem more legitimate than a contest between eighteenth-century cliques, parties, factions, or cabals by any other name.

Getting citizens organized began when the Federalists coalesced around Adams and Marshall, while the anti-Federalists rallied to Jefferson and Madison, at that time called Republicans. Within a generation, the Jeffersonians became so popular that the Federalists disappeared, and the second great two-party confrontation arose between Jefferson's heir, Andrew Jackson, and his Whig opponents only in the 1830s. Jackson's people eventually produced the Democratic Party of Woodrow Wilson and Bill Clinton, and the Whigs combined with Lincoln's forerunners to produce the Republican Party of Calvin Coolidge and Ronald Reagan.

Most importantly, the growth of parties, although unforeseen, could be recognized as making good sense in the American context.[49] Seeking out an increasing number of voters who were legitimately pursuing their interests, parties between 1800 and 1860 became a new sort of business, consisting of large organizations led by career politicians, designed to recruit candidates, mobilize voters, win elections, and compete against other parties on a regular basis. The political business paid handsomely, and democratic principles justified that, too. As Jackson explained, no

---

[47] Alexander Hamilton, John Jay, and James Madison, *The Federalist* (orig., 1787–1788; New York: Modern Library, 1937), No. 10, p. 54.

[48] See the "Farewell Address" reprinted in Matthew Spalding and Patrick J. Garrity, *A Sacred Union of Citizens: George Washington's Farewell Address and the American Character* (Lanham, Md.: Rowman and Littlefield, 1996), pp. 175–188. On party, see p. 181. See also the lingering fear of parties in James Fenimore Cooper, *The American Democrat* (orig., 1838; New York: Vintage, 1956), pp. 177–178.

[49] On the logic of early parties in America, see Richard Hofstadter, *The Idea of a Party System in America: The Rise of Legitimate Opposition in the United States, 1780–1840* (Berkeley: Univ. of California Press, 1970).

person possessed a right to public office but had to compete to acquire one. That being the case, when a winning party went to carry out an electoral mandate, there was no reason why it should not replace old officials appointed on the basis of previous mandates with new officials loyal to the winning party.[50] The spoils system, in other words, was a legitimate, if sometimes unseemly, manifestation of the way in which rights innocently turned into interests, interests turned electorally into mandates, and mandates justified parties, within the law, handing out patronage to their supporters.

It is worth noting that the new national parties were acceptable not because they displayed charm in office but because they were seen to endorse the Constitution and to abide, more or less, by the rules of America's political game. Or, as Jefferson said, both the Federalists and the Jeffersonian Republicans, even while they competed, were similar for believing in the Republic and acting accordingly.[51] In this sense, as in many others, America was different from Europe, where rival parties in a single country sometimes endorsed different ideas about what regime should be installed, perhaps by violence, in place of the existing regime, from monarchy to democratic socialism, from liberal democracy to communism, from anarchism to fascism.

American voters and elected officials, by contrast, were almost entirely liberal with regard to regimes, in the sense of favoring natural rights, individualism, limited government, private property, and popular sovereignty.[52] That being the case, Federalists, Republicans, Whigs, and Democrats were able to alternate back and forth in office without rending the fabric of public life. Sadly for America, but fortunately for African Americans, this consensus, which had excluded them, would temporarily unravel in the years leading up to the Confederate attack on Fort Sumter.

The Republican Party Vision

The Republican Party of Abraham Lincoln, founded in 1854, formulated the last pre–Civil War version of America's mainstream civic ideals by

---

[50] Jackson, "First Annual Message," p. 449.

[51] Thomas Jefferson, "First Inaugural Address" (March 4, 1801), in Richardson (ed.), *Messages and Papers of the Presidents*, Vol. I, p. 322.

[52] On liberalism in this sense, see Louis Hartz, *The Liberal Tradition in America* (New York: Harcourt, Brace, and World, 1955). For a recent discussion of some undemocratic aspects of the liberal tradition identified by Hartz, see Robert A. Dahl, *How Democratic Is the American Constitution?* (New Haven: Yale Univ. Press, 2001).

weaving together several political concepts developed since the Revolution. Like Jeffersonians in a previous generation, the Republicans aimed at achieving middling economic independence rather than great riches. Like Jacksonians, they held that laboring occupations of all kinds could furnish the means of this independence. Accordingly, their platform called for land grant colleges, which they established in 1862, where energetic and enterprising young people could acquire an education and use it to succeed in life. They were, though, also like Jeffersonians and Jacksonians, especially enthusiastic about farming in an age when most Americans still lived in rural areas. Hence the Republican Party enlisted former members of the Free Soil Party, established in 1848,[53] and enacted the Homestead Act of 1862, designed to provide frontier land to small farmers at reasonable prices.

The Republican vision offered a harmony of interests theory to men who increasingly recognized the importance of private interests. On this score, Lincoln himself expressed Republican, and republican, optimism when he argued that, in America, even hired laborers, whose numbers were growing especially in urban areas, could achieve economic independence. As the onetime rail-splitter put it, a laborer can live frugally, save some of his wages, use the money to buy tools or land, and set himself up in farming or business.[54] In this sense, the Republicans assumed a harmony of interests between workers and capitalists – that both are free to succeed in America, and that the success of capitalists should not foster envy but encourage laborers to work hard and better themselves in a land of opportunity.[55]

In short, Republicans offered an upbeat interpretation of life in America, closely linked to mainstream ideals of economic independence, hard work, fruitful enterprise, and the civic virtues encouraged by freedom. Unfortunately, as we shall see, there were more wage workers than Lincoln thought there were even before the war,[56] and their chances of achieving economic independence were worse than he and his political

---

[53] Eric Foner, *Free Soil, Free Labor, Free Men: The Ideology of the Republican Party Before the Civil War* (New York: Oxford Univ. Press, 1970), pp. 124–126.

[54] Abraham Lincoln, "Address Before the Wisconsin State Agricultural Society, Milwaukee, Wisconsin," in Roy P. Basler (ed.), *The Collected Works of Abraham Lincoln*, 8 vols. (New Brunswick, N.J.: Rutgers Univ. Press, 1953), Vol. III, pp. 478–479.

[55] Foner, *Free Soil, Free Labor, Free Men*, p. 20.

[56] Ibid., p. 32, points out that in 1859 Lincoln thought that only an eighth of Americans worked for wages, whereas the true figure for 1860 was closer to 60 percent.

associates imagined.[57] Of more immediate concern, the free soil idea helped to precipitate the Civil War because, in pursuit of cheap land and economic independence, the Republican Party platform of 1860 insisted that Congress should not permit slavery to expand into United States' territories in the West. Land there, the party said, must go to men determined to be their own masters and committed to the values of thrift, industry, sobriety, prudence, and perseverance encouraged by free farming.

Democratic Republicanism

More than fifty thousand Northerners and Southerners were killed, wounded, or listed as missing at the battle of Gettysburg from July 1 to July 3, 1863. In November of the same year, Abraham Lincoln eulogized those who fell and were buried near that Pennsylvania town. In this Gettysburg Address, Lincoln explained what he thought was the political meaning of America. First he recalled that the Founders had established a very particular sort of new nation four score and seven years earlier. Then he described the special character of that nation as emanating from the Declaration of Independence, with its proposition that all men are born equal and endowed with inalienable rights.

By so framing his remarks, Lincoln invited listeners to understand that, while the Union their men were fighting to preserve may have emerged technically from the Constitution in 1789, that same Constitution incorporated within itself the moral principles proclaimed in the Declaration from 1776. It was an inspiring insight. Other observers have tried to explain what made the country special in those early years, although none ever did so as concisely as when Lincoln described the Founders' invention, of the Declaration plus the Constitution, as "government of the people, by the people, and for the people."[58]

The American Persuasion

In the eighty-seven years that Lincoln cited, America went through a "republican moment" and then a "democratic moment." Together, these two

---

[57] Manual workers were unlikely to become farmers, professionals, or businessmen in the second half of the nineteenth century. See the study of Newburyport, Massachusetts, in Stephan Thernstrom, *Poverty and Progress: Social Mobility in a Nineteenth Century City* (New York: Atheneum, 1975).

[58] On the "Gettysburg Address," see Garry Wills, *Lincoln at Gettysburg: The Words That Remade America* (New York: Simon and Schuster, 1992).

eras produced the government that Lincoln described so beautifully. Together, although he did not explain it in such terms, they also assured that the new government would rest upon a distinctive concept of citizenship. It was, in fact, an amalgam of citizenship in a *republican mode* that was, at the same time, citizenship on a *democratic scale*.

In the history of Western political thought, combining republicanism with democracy was a remarkable accomplishment. Conventional wisdom regarded the two as quite different.[59] After all, going back to Cicero, republics were never expected to enroll the largest part of their residents as citizens.[60] And, going back to Aristotle, democracies based on widespread political participation were usually considered capricious and unstable.[61]

In America, on the other hand, enthusiasm for the new amalgam appeared at least as early as the Age of Jackson, when widening the franchise became less a bone of contention than a source of national pride. Thus in the *Democratic Review*, editor John O'Sullivan wrote in 1837 in favor of democracy and against class distinctions.[62] Then Sullivan added that his magazine espoused "the principle of *democratic republicanism.*... We have an abiding confidence in the virtue, intelligence, and full capacity for self-government, of the great mass of our people, our industrious, honest, manly, intelligent millions of freemen."[63] In other words, with the automatic contemporary exception of women and most men of color, Sullivan

---

[59] Today, these terms are sometimes used interchangeably, as if they denote much the same thing. But for most of Western history, political thinkers understood them to describe significantly different regimes. See Sanford Lakoff, *Democracy: History, Theory, Practice* (Boulder, Colo.: Westview, 1996), pp. 37–98, but esp. the first paragraph on p. 65.

[60] For example, William Blackstone (who did not use the term *republic*) praised England's eighteenth-century government because it fostered freedom by dividing up legislative and executive powers among the king, the nobility in the House of Lords, and the people in the House of Commons. Within that amalgam, which Montesquieu defined as republican, Blackstone assumed that only some people should vote. See Blackstone, *Commentaries on the Laws of England*, 4 vols. (orig., 1765–1769; Chicago: Univ. of Chicago Press, 1979), Vol. I, p. 156: "It is of the utmost importance to regulate by whom, and in what manner, the suffrages are given." In fact, "the suffrages" should exclude those owning so little property that "they are esteemed to have no will of their own" (p. 156).

[61] See Madison in *The Federalist*, No. 10, p. 58: "Democracies have ever been spectacles of turbulence and contention; have ever been found incompatible with personal security or the rights of property; and have in general been as short in their lives as they have been violent in their deaths."

[62] See his "Introduction," in the *United States Magazine and Democratic Review*, Vol. I, No. 1 (October 1837), pp. 1–15. Reprinted in Joseph L. Blau (ed.), *Social Theories of Jacksonian Democracy* (New York: Liberal Arts Press, 1954), pp. 21–37.

[63] Ibid., p. 22.

TABLE 4.1. *Jacksonian Citizenship*

	Citizenship	Roles	Standards
State	I	Good citizen	Obey laws
	II	Good citizen	Participate
Society	III	Good person	Exercise virtue via deism, property, work

believed that the great majority of American citizens were virtuous, in which case their behavior was *republican*, even while more of those citizens were empowered in America than ever before, in which case their participation was *democratic*.[64]

The Components of Citizenship

By combining elements of republicanism and democracy, Americans resolved some of the role tensions which earlier thinkers, starting in classical Greece, were afraid would arise between rulers and ruled, states and their residents. We can see how this was so by updating the chart of citizenship to take into account America's version of its basic components (see Table 4.1).

This chart represents an ideal realized only imperfectly in practice. Still, ideals count for something, and in the American scheme of civic things, Citizenship I and II were mainly unproblematic. Both of these stations in life required good citizens to obey their country's laws under most circumstances, if only to maintain public order. But civil obedience would not normally be seen as an unacceptable imposition on American citizens, because their laws flowed from institutions more balanced and accountable than those in previous eras and other countries. As for Citizenship II, historical resentment over exclusion from this status was largely relieved in America because, again, in comparison to other times and places, participation rights were widely conferred, at least for adult white males, first via property and then on the basis of work.

Where the role of *good citizen* became mainly unproblematic, so too the role of *good person*, responsible for Citizenship III, was less likely

---

[64] The darker side of democratic republicanism in the Age of Jackson is reviewed in Rogers M. Smith, *Civic Ideals: Conflicting Visions of Citizenship in U.S. History* (New Haven: Yale Univ. Press, 1997), pp. 196–242, in a chapter entitled "High Noon of the White Republic."

to cause friction in America than it had elsewhere. Most of America's laws were presumably good and worth obeying because they emerged from widespread representation rather than the exclusive will, possibly tyrannical, of a faction or ruling class. Beyond that, however, men seeking to live virtuously knew that, due to the constitutional separation of church and state, government was forbidden to impose religious standards in public life. That being the case, men of good conscience had no cause to resist draconian statutes which, in the spiritual sphere, did not exist.[65]

As for secular values which good men might pursue, America's faith in common sense meant that all citizens, in principle at least, could decide for themselves what those values were and how to realize them in everyday life. No one, that is, expected to hand over initiative in this realm to some elite group of supposedly wiser men, like aristocrats, theologians, or philosophers.[66] Moreover, secular values were often linked to work, to the notion that individual enterprise fostered reason and evoked good character. It followed that any ordinary person, who worked like everyone else, could gain respect for thereby performing a virtuous act. In fact, when the sober performance of one's occupation took into account the needs of other people in the community, such self-interest would, hopefully, evoke the moral understanding necessary to inspire Citizenship III and its support for good laws.

Even though they were more likely than Europeans to regard their state as *good*, many Americans believed they should resist its decisions if those were *bad*. Here was one setting for exercising Citizenship III. Here was what Ralph Waldo Emerson meant when, in the spirit of Thomas Paine, he said that "every actual State is corrupt." Therefore, "Good men must not obey the laws too well."[67] Here was what Henry David Thoreau had

---

[65] The First Amendment restrained Congress but left the states more free to act in religious affairs. Some of them did meddle. On church-state relations during American history, see Robert L. Maddox, *Separation of Church and State: Guarantor of Religious Freedom* (New York: Crossroad, 1987), passim but esp. pp. 49–96 on colonial and nineteenth-century variations. See also John F. Wilson and Donald L. Drakeman (eds.), *Church and State in American History*, 2nd ed. (Boston: Beacon, 1987), which includes, for example, documents relating to nineteenth- and twentieth-century cases of Protestant influence on public schools and Prohibition.

[66] Tocqueville began the second volume of his famous commentary on American life by pointing out how little use Americans had for philosophers. See his *Democracy in America*, Vol. II (1840), Ch. 1, "Philosophical Method of the Americans," p. 3: "I think that in no country in the civilized world is less attention paid to philosophy than in the United States."

[67] Emerson, "Politics," in Mark Van Doren (ed.), *The Portable Emerson* (New York: Viking, 1946), p. 195.

in mind when he insisted that, because one must resist bad laws, every man is entitled, and sometimes obliged, to regard himself as "a majority of one."[68] And here was what troubled Lincoln when, speaking for the North, he focused on the Civil War's closing days in his great Second Inaugural Address. There, after deploring two hundred years of human bondage in America, he acknowledged that slavery was so sinful that it could only be redeemed by the terrible losses which both sides suffered in battle.

Colonialism and Nationalism

In short, early Americans established an ideal of citizenship combining republicanism with democracy. Although practice has always fallen short of that ideal, we will see that it still informs American politics. Meanwhile, let us note several vital aspects of public life in early America which hinged on concepts that surrounded citizenship. Here were commissions and omissions that, very importantly, spoke of roads not taken.

The Colonial Issue

For one thing, the original states moved to avoid creating a colonial problem when they enacted the Northwest Ordinance in 1787, permitting new states like Ohio, Illinois, and Indiana to form in the Northwest Territory as soon as each had sixty thousand "free inhabitants." This willingness to enable new states to join the Union meant that settlers on the American frontier would acquire representation in Congress and thereby avoid living under conditions of exclusion similar to those suffered by America's eighteenth-century colonists as subjects in the British Empire.

We may describe the accomplishment on this score more precisely: The principle of an ever-expanding Union assured that America, for free white men to begin with, would not consist of one class of citizens enjoying the status of Citizenship II and ruling over another class of citizens having, at best, only the status of Citizenship I.

In the Constitution, the Founders affirmed this willingness to accept new states into the Union.[69] Later, Congress extended the principle to additional federal territories, so that eventually the United States came to consist of fifty states. After the Civil War, America acquired overseas

---

[68] Thoreau, "Civil Disobedience (1849)," in Carl Bode (ed.), *The Portable Thoreau* (New York: Viking, 1947), p. 121.

[69] Article IV, Section 1.

territories such as Hawaii, Puerto Rico, Cuba, and the Philippine Islands, thus creating a colonial situation. Fortunately, most of these places eventually became independent or acquired statehood.[70] The process was sometimes painful and often prolonged. But it did not massively disturb public life on the mainland.

Nationalism

The early aversion to potential colonialism was a triumph for America's positive attitude to citizenship. So, too, was the avoidance of nationalism as an organizing principle for government.[71] As we noted in Chapter 1, eighteenth- and nineteenth-century Europeans tried to sort through the debris of old regimes and establish government upon new principles. Taking their cue from the French Declaration of the Rights of Man, which proclaimed in 1789 that the nation and not its king was sovereign on French soil, Europeans tended to espouse what they called the right to *self-determination.*

Self-determination, which is the idea that every nation is entitled to form a government to carry out its national will, did provide some social cohesion as an alternative to old regimes. But it also provoked violence between some ethnic groups and others. This happened where circumstances placed one nation in control of another, or where historical developments, such as in the Austro-Hungarian Empire, left various groups so intertwined that state boundaries, as in the Balkans today, could not easily be redrawn so as to coincide with national populations and therefore grant each nation the independence to which it aspired.

In America there was, of course, social discrimination between early and late arrivals, between Protestants and Catholics, between this ethnic or racial group and that, between the nineteenth-century Irish and Chinese

---

[70] Fortunately, because colonies are incompatible with American ideals. For example, on Washington's sometimes brutal administration of the Philippine Islands, seized by America during the Spanish-American War, see Elihu Root, secretary of war from 1899 to 1904 and secretary of state from 1905 to 1909, quoted in William Pfaff, *The Wrath of Nations: Civilization and the Furies of Nationalism* (New York: Simon and Schuster, 1993), p. 179: "*Government does not depend on consent.* The immutable laws of justice and humanity require that a people shall have government, that the weak shall be protected, that cruelty and lust shall be restrained, whether there be consent or not" (emphasis supplied).

[71] On nationalism as an organizing principle of government, see Pfaff, ibid.; Hans Kohn, *The Idea of Nationalism: A Study in Its Origins and Background* (New York: Macmillan, 1944); E. J. Hobsbawm, *Nations and Nationalism Since 1780: Programme, Myth, and Reality*, 2nd ed. (New York: Cambridge Univ. Press, 1992); and Elie Kedourie, *Nationalism*, 4th ed. (Oxford: Blackwell, 1993).

and almost everyone else. But this tension was not rooted in a European-style national principle,[72] although some immigration, for example, that of black Africans and Asians, was restricted even before Washington incorporated national quotas into the 1924 Immigration Act.[73]

Instead, Americans built their regime on the classical ideal of citizenship, on the idea that no one, unlike in a regime of strict nationalism, should automatically be excluded from membership in the community because of ethnic origin. In theory at least, what counted was not immutable character but deliberate commitment to principles established by the Founders.[74] As one scholar noted of America, "Citizenship [rather than origin] was the only criterion which made the individual a member of the national community: and national loyalty meant loyalty to the Constitution."[75] Or, as another observed, "What is distinctive about the nationality of... Americans is... its nonexclusive character.... America is not a jealous nation. In this sense, at least, it is different from most of the others."[76]

In other words, Americans came to the New World as, analytically speaking, individuals. Of course they moved into ethnic neighborhoods,

---

[72] This does not mean that nationalism as a sense of social solidarity did not evolve among people who immigrated to America and who, over the years, came to share many sentiments, expectations, and aspirations. Thus Liah Greenfeld, *Nationalism: Five Roads to Modernity* (Cambridge: Harvard Univ. Press, 1992), Ch. 5, "In Pursuit of the Ideal Nation: The Unfolding of Nationality in America," pp. 397–484, argues that American "nationalism" originated in New England, whose people admired English patterns of behavior. Greenfeld's analysis differs from that in the text above in that she regards dedication to "liberty and equality" as a form of "nationalism," whereas I regard such dedication as a manifestation of "democratic republicanism."

[73] The severity of this act, and its violation of the antinationalism ideal in America, were mitigated by the fact that, even as some ethnic groups were being almost entirely excluded, they were still permitted to enter in small numbers. Furthermore, people from those groups who had already gained citizenship were not expelled.

[74] A strong caveat is in order here. What follows in the text describes how Americans welcomed newcomers who, like themselves, would become good citizens. However, there is also a darker side to this story. Within the framework of republican thinking, one may argue in favor of excluding some potential immigrants on the grounds that they are incapable of behaving as virtuously as republicanism requires. Accordingly, there were always some Americans who promoted this point of view. Their thinking and political activism, both consciously republican, are described in Dale T. Knobel, "*America for the Americans*": *The Nativist Movement in the United States* (New York: Twayne, 1996). See especially Ch. 1, "Citizens and Brethren: The Ideological and Organizational Roots of American Nativism," pp. 1–40.

[75] Yehoshua Arieli, *Individualism and Nationalism in American Ideology* (Baltimore: Penguin, 1966), p. 22.

[76] Michael Walzer, "What Does It Mean to Be an 'American'?" in Walzer, *What It Means to Be an American: Essays on the American Experience* (New York: Marsilio, 1992), p. 42.

maybe into Little Italy, which was perhaps next door to Chinatown.[77] But they did not come to America in social groups, to re-create "home and country" in their new land.[78] They came to give up their past willingly, to get along successfully with new neighbors by joining themselves to something unknown in their past. This is what Theodore Roosevelt had in mind when he said, "A man has got to be an American and nothing else... [and he has] no business to try to perpetuate [British or Irish, German or French] language and customs in the land of complete religious toleration and equality." But, "If... he does become honestly and in good faith an American, then he is entitled to stand precisely as all other Americans stand, and it is the height of unAmericanism to discriminate against him in any way because of creed or birthplace."[79] The same convictions still resonated in President George W. Bush's inaugural address:

America has never been united by blood or birth or soil. We are bound by ideals that move us beyond our backgrounds, lift us above our interests and teach us what it means to be citizens. Every child must be taught these principles. Every citizen must uphold them. And every immigrant, by embracing these ideals, makes our country more, not less, American.[80]

Tragedies

While enjoying two civic triumphs by rejecting colonialism and nationalism, America experienced three civic tragedies involving Native Americans, African Americans, and women. In the long run, the ideal of citizenship would compel white male voters to endorse Citizenship II for these groups, even if that required enacting constitutional amendments to correct biases which Washington, Franklin, Madison, and the other Founders had permitted to infect their invention.

Exactly how this happened is not our main concern, for now that inclusion in America is virtually universal, the problem is not how people

---

[77] To this day, my family eats shitaki mushrooms on Christmas Eve because my Italian grandparents before World War I came from the Abruzzi Mountains to live in Little Italy next to Chinatown in Manhattan. From there, my grandfather bought the mushrooms in a Chinese grocery store and used them to flavor a special spaghetti sauce which, according to Southern Italian Catholic tradition at that time, could not include meat on Christmas Eve.

[78] Geoffrey Gorer, *The American People: A Study in National Character*, rev. ed. (orig., 1948; New York: Norton, 1964), p. 25.

[79] Theodore Roosevelt, "The Duties of American Citizenship," address before the Liberal Club, Buffalo, New York, January 26, 1893, in *The Works of Theodore Roosevelt*, 24 vols. (New York: Charles Scribner's Sons, 1923–1925), Vol. XV, pp. 79–80.

[80] "President: 'I Ask You to Be Citizens,'" *New York Times* (January 21, 2001), pp. A14–15.

"get in" but how they should relate to public life once their rights to active citizenship are acquired. Whatever the larger aim, however, we should not pass lightly over the fact that in early American politics, at least three groups did not possess political rights. Once more, but in these cases bitterly, their condition spoke of roads not taken.

Native Americans

Native Americans paid for the triumph on the issue of colonialism when their way of life was almost destroyed in the process by which white people seized from them widespread lands and extensive resources that enabled the newcomers to build what they regarded as a great society. State and federal officials signed treaty after treaty with Native Americans and then violated those pacts so that former Europeans and their descendants could ceaselessly enlarge the Union. Mostly, what happened came about because many white people regarded Native Americans as barbaric and ungodly creatures who deserved no political rights, and whose lands and lives were forfeit to men who called themselves civilized.[81]

Some principles were evoked by the invaders in this saga. For example, white judges regarded Native Americans as foreign nationals whose rights were embodied in treaties rather than as citizens who were protected by state or federal laws. Yet if those treaties were ignored, it was not clear how these "foreigners," who were not citizens, could defend themselves in court.[82] That was one problem. A second concerned the tribal lifestyle of most Native Americans. White men who professed to believe in a Lockean-style theory of labor value tended to argue that Native Americans did not correctly use the land which God gave mankind, did not mix their labor with natural resources to make property.[83] Accordingly, even though they inherited America's great mountains, broad prairies, and fertile valleys from their forefathers, Native Americans had no right to that land and should give way to men who, ostensibly, lived according to God's will.[84]

---

[81] Many Americans today probably do not realize that Native Americans are disparaged even in the Declaration of Independence, where they are described as "merciless Indian Savages, whose known rule of warfare is an undistinguished destruction of all ages, sexes and conditions."

[82] The anomalous status of Native Americans before the Civil War is discussed in James H. Kettner, *The Development of American Citizenship, 1608–1870* (Chapel Hill: Univ. of North Carolina Press, 1978), pp. 288–300.

[83] John P. Diggins, *The Lost Soul of American Politics: Virtue, Self-Interest, and the Foundations of Liberalism* (Chicago: Univ. of Chicago Press, 1984), esp. pp. 106, 117–118.

[84] Like the British theory of virtual representation, early American reasoning against Native Americans seems today to have been designed mainly to persuade people who were

These two problems appeared in the case of lands coveted by whites but belonging to the Cherokee nation in western Georgia. Many of the Cherokee lived in orderly villages on tribal land, where they practiced modern agriculture, where they had created an alphabet for reading and writing their native language, where they had translated the Bible into that language, and where many of them had converted to Christianity. On Lockean grounds, then, the Cherokee were clearly civilized. Nevertheless, Georgia decided to sell their lands to white settlers and speculators.

Tribal leaders went to the Supreme Court and argued that, as a sovereign nation and signatory to treaties going back as far as 1732, first with King George II, but later amended and updated with Senate approval many times between 1791 and 1819, the Cherokee were not subject to the laws of Georgia where, of course, they had no electoral power because they were not citizens of that state. Chief Justice John Marshall,[85] writing the majority opinion in *Cherokee Nation v. Georgia* (1831), refused to address the merits of the case. He ruled instead that the tribe had no standing in court. If it were a "foreign nation," it could sue under Article III, Section 2, of the Constitution, where cases may arise in federal courts between an American state and foreign states. But Marshall decided that the Cherokee were not a "foreign nation" but only a "domestic dependent nation" and "in a state of pupilage. Their relation to the United States resembles that of a ward to his guardian."[86]

With this reasoning, Cherokee Indians were denied the right to apply for judicial redress against legislative theft. In truth, Congress had already passed the Indian Removal Act in 1830, which during the 1830s and 1840s would justify, in the eyes of many white Americans, forcibly uprooting almost all Native Americans, north and south, including the Cherokee of Georgia, from the eastern United States and exiling them across the Mississippi River into the Indian Territory which later became Oklahoma. Andrew Jackson, president at the time and himself a

---

already convinced. Thus the Supreme Court decided in 1823 that Native Americans held their land by a "right of occupancy" which was subordinate to the "right of discovery" that the United States had inherited from the British. The judges did not believe it was necessary to explain how the British could "discover" a land which was already "occupied." See *Johnson and Graham's Lessee v. William McIntosh* (1823) 8 Wheaton 543.

[85] Many wealthy American families before the Civil War were heavily engaged in land speculation, which involved chiefly frontier lands taken from Native American tribes one way or another. In 1800, for example, the Marshall family, including the chief justice, held four hundred thousand acres in Kentucky. See Michael Paul Rogin, *Fathers and Children: Andrew Jackson and the Subjugation of the American Indian* (New York: Knopf, 1975), p. 81.

[86] *Cherokee Nation v. Georgia* (1831) 5 Peters 1.

land speculator, spoke for most Americans of his day when he asked rhetorically: "What good man would prefer a country covered with forests and ranged by a few thousand savages to our extensive Republic, studded with cities, towns, and prosperous farms, embellished with all the improvements which art can devise or industry execute, occupied by more than 12,000,000 happy people, and filled with all the blessings of liberty, civilization, and religion?"[87]

After the Civil War, Washington transported many western tribes to Oklahoma. Then the Dawes Act of 1887 offered 160 acres there to heads of Native American households and left some of the other lands for tribal reservations,[88] after which, in 1889, much of Oklahoma's remaining lands were opened to pioneer settlers. Here, however, Indian citizenship finally became possible, after it had been explicitly denied by the Supreme Court in *Elk v. Wilkins* (1884) on the grounds that Native Americans, even if born in the United States, were no more citizens than the children born in America to foreign ambassadors.[89] The Dawes Act stipulated that Native Americans who accepted land grants in Oklahoma, and who thereby undermined tribal solidarity, could become citizens, and in 1924, all Indians born in the United States were admitted to citizenship by the Immigration Act of that year.

Slavery

Slavery was the great early exception to America's faith in civil society, for slavery arose in that realm and eventually engendered a culture clash based on regions but as deadly as the ethnic and religious tensions that occasionally rended European states. Fortunately for African Americans, the theory of natural rights underlying the Declaration enabled some white Americans to define slavery as a moral flaw unconscionably endorsed by the Constitution. And so the abolitionists before 1861 were exercising Citizenship III when they called on the federal government to abolish slavery. On this score, having the right sort of ideals available was important even if they could not, for the moment, guarantee impeccable practice.

Material gains and cultural convenience drove the South to perpetuate slavery. But some Southerners claimed that human bondage was also

---

[87] Quoted in Ronald N. Satz, *American Indian Policy in the Jacksonian Era* (Lincoln: Univ. of Nebraska Press, 1975), p. 44.

[88] On the historical background to the Dawes Act, see Robert W. Mardock, *The Reformers and the American Indian* (Columbia: Univ. of Missouri Press, 1971), pp. 211–228. See also excerpts of the law in "The General Allotment Act (Dawes Act)," in Francis Paul Prucha (ed.), *Documents of United States Indian Policy*, 2nd ed. (Lincoln: Univ. of Nebraska Press, 1990), pp. 171–174.

[89] *Elk v. Wilkins* (1884) 112 U.S. 94.

justified in principle. Thus George Fitzhugh argued that some men are naturally servile and that Northern wage workers were no freer than Southern slaves because both groups were, and properly so, subordinate to others.[90] The argument made no sense to Republicans because it clashed with their belief that many laborers were competent men who, by exercising frugality and prudence, could save enough money to become businessmen and farmers.

Similarly John C. Calhoun insisted that, in principle, because the Constitution designated states as sovereign elements of the Union, Congress must ask their permission rather than try, even by majority vote, to prevent individual states from maintaining a particular way of life.[91] Non-Southerners rejected this theory of a concurrent rather than numerical majority because, in effect, it recommended treating America as a "mixed society" of great and permanent interests, all entitled to veto power over national policies. Instead, as we have seen, most Northerners and Westerners advocated a society based on individualism, for example, as summed up in the Free Soil aspiration to independent farming and small business. In such a society the rule was, roughly speaking, one white man, one vote.

The Supreme Court tried to defuse the slavery issue in *Dred Scott v. Sandford* (1857) and ran aground on the Constitution's lack of precision concerning citizenship. Scott had traveled with his owner, John Emerson, to Illinois and Minnesota in 1834 before returning to Missouri in 1838. After Emerson died in 1843, Scott sued for freedom in federal court on the grounds that he had been free when out of Missouri. Speaking for the Court, Chief Justice Taney did not rule on whether or not Missouri had to honor the antislavery laws of Illinois or Minnesota. Instead, he said that Scott could not sue Missouri within the constitutional provision of Article III, Section 2 – according to which citizens may sue states – because Scott was not a citizen. The argument held that, when the Founders established the Constitution, African Americans were not citizens of the several states. It followed that their descendants, including Dred Scott, were also not citizens. In which case, Scott remained a slave.[92]

Like Native Americans, slaves without citizenship could hardly defend themselves in court. But Taney's decision did not persuade abolitionists

---

[90] George Fitzhugh, *Sociology for the South, or the Failure of Free Society* (orig., 1854; New York: Burt Franklin, 1965).

[91] Calhoun, *A Disquisition on Government* (1851), in John C. Calhoun, *A Disquisition on Government and Selections from the Discourse* (Indianapolis: Bobbs-Merrill, 1953), pp. 3–81.

[92] *Dred Scott v. Sandford* (1857) 19 Howard 393.

to accept slavery, and Southerners, rather than relying on judicial protection, chose secession four years later. Afterward, Union politicians enacted Amendments XIII (1865), XIV (1868), and XV (1870), which stipulated that former slaves were in fact citizens and should possess the "privileges and immunities" of all other United States citizens.[93]

Southern resistance to these amendments was, of course, a long story, starting with state franchise laws making African American voting impossible or extremely difficult. Unfortunately, the Supreme Court long condoned this strategy by accepting at face value exclusionary gimmicks such as poll taxes, literacy tests, grandfather clauses, white primaries, and more. The war did lead to African American suffrage in most non-Southern states, though, and public protests led by men such as A. Philip Randolph and Martin Luther King, Jr., in the 1950s and 1960s eventually brought about new Court decisions and federal regulations which established color-blind elections, but not always color-blind voters, even in the South.

Citizenship II for Women

Before the Civil War, no states gave women the rights of Citizenship II. Therefore women like Elizabeth Cady Stanton and Susan B. Anthony agitated in order to gain them. In their eyes, the exclusion of women from civic affairs violated the principle that women, like men, are created equal and endowed with natural rights. And thus the Seneca Falls Declaration of Sentiments and Resolutions, written and proclaimed by Stanton in 1848, announced, "We hold these truths to be self-evident: that all men and women are created equal; that they are endowed by their Creator with certain inalienable rights; that to secure these rights governments are instituted." The Seneca Falls Declaration held men to be analogous to King George III, in that "the history of mankind is a history of repeated injuries and usurpations on the part of man toward woman, having in direct object the establishment of an absolute tyranny over her."[94] As the Declaration pointed out, where women could not vote, they were powerless to resist enactment by men of laws that discriminated against women,

---

[93] Thus Amendment XIV, Sec. 1, specifically overruled *Dred Scott v. Sandford* when it stipulated that "all persons born or naturalized in the United States, and subject to the jurisdiction thereof, are citizens of the the United States and of the State wherein they reside."

[94] The Seneca Falls Declaration is reprinted in Marjorie Spruill Wheeler (ed.), *One Woman, One Vote: Rediscovering the Woman Suffrage Movement* (Troutdale, Oregon: New Sage Press, 1995), pp. 40–42.

for example, that forbid married women from owning property, that assured in divorce cases child custody to husbands, that barred women from acquiring a college education or serving in the ministry, and more.

Because the Civil War diverted attention to the issue of slavery, political inclusion remained out of women's grasp. Furthermore, the suffragettes failed to persuade congressmen to assure voting for women in the Fourteenth Amendment of 1868. Instead, the amendment specifically stipulated that no *male* citizens shall be denied the right to vote "except for participation in rebellion, or other crime." Turning then to federal courts, women brought suit in *Minor v. Happersett* (1873).[95]

Reese Happersett, a registrar in Missouri, refused to register Virginia Minor, a white citizen of the United States and of Missouri. He told her, accurately, that the constitution of Missouri and Missouri's Registration Act conferred the right to vote only on every "male citizen" of that state. In response, Virginia Minor asked the Court to rule that Missouri's law violated the Fourteenth Amendment, in the sense that, as a citizen of the United States, she was entitled to all the "privileges and immunities" of citizenship, including the right to vote.

The Court stipulated that Minor was indeed an American citizen in the sense of being a member of the national community, with whatever privileges and immunities such people have. From this fact it did not follow, however, that women were entitled to vote because, as the Court observed, no states had extended that privilege to women. In which case, women could not rightfully claim they were being denied their right to vote, for the Fourteenth Amendment could not add privileges to citizenship but only guarantee those already in place.

Furthermore, in the opinion of the Court, women could not validly argue that their lack of suffrage under existing state laws constituted a denial of republican government, as guaranteed by the Constitution in Article IV, Section 4. On that score, the Court found that common practice defined existing state governments as republican, while no specific provision in the Constitution challenged that popular view.

In short, *Minor v. Happersett* demonstrated, although not by using our terms, that women were American citizens in the sense of Citizenship I but not Citizenship II. Erasing this disparity would require another half century of agitation before Congress and the states would in 1919 adopt the Nineteenth Amendment assuring that no citizen of the United States may be denied the right to vote or hold office on account of sex.

95 21 Wallace 162.

5

The Challenge to Good Citizenship

By 1865, Americans had rebelled against Britain, created a republic, established democracy, and preserved the Union. Along the way, they came to regard their state as based on natural rights, egalitarianism, individualism, constitutionalism, federalism, separation of church and state, admiration for civil society, and respect for work. Together, these concepts justified citizenship rather than nationalism as the organizing principle of public life. Serious cases of exclusion remained, but hard politicking and social progress would eventually produce new suffrage legislation and, if necessary, constitutional amendments to the point where almost every American who is sane, without criminal record, and at least eighteen years old may now vote and hold elective office.

Accordingly, most Americans today possess not only the status of Citizenship I but also the rights of Citizenship II. But to what end? Here, the relevant concepts are those of covenant, social contract, commonwealth, and the republic as a community sharing a sense of justice.[1] These concepts inform the notion of Citizenship III, of citizens using the rights of Citizenship II to maintain a good state that will foster well-being for its members.

Citizenship III is the hallmark of a decent society. It is not enough simply to vote; one should vote *well*. Yet Citizenship III calls upon men and women to act virtuously during changing circumstances and in

---

[1] Thus the Pledge of Allegiance: "I pledge allegiance, to the flag [not the nation], of the United States of America, and to the *republic*, for which it stands, one nation [defined by political commitment rather than ethnic origin], under God, with liberty and justice [Cicero's definition of a republic] for all" (emphasis supplied).

situations plagued by ethical uncertainty. Accordingly, Citizenship III is no easy matter. Furthermore, it is a part of overall citizenship which became increasingly problematic after Appomattox, when economic trends combined to prevent many Americans from achieving the material success necessary for a republican approach to public affairs.

Dilemmas of Individualism

What happened as the nineteenth century wore on is that, even though more Americans than Europeans could work freely, many failed to acquire the economic resources that republican virtue seemed to require. The shortfall was central to national identity, for if ordinary men could not maintain economic independence, what would become of good citizenship as the hallmark of this new sort of Western society? If men, and later women, would not be economically free, how could they be politically effective?

Antirepublican Economics

Difficulties arose within the practice of individualism. *Political individualism* emphasized the equal worth of citizens in public life. Here, Americans aimed to avoid re-creating the inherited ranks of feudalism and mixed government that had existed in Europe. On the other hand, *economic individualism* stressed the right of citizens to work at whatever they could and to pursue their private interests with dignity. Here, Americans assumed that separate achievements would fit together as harmoniously as if men were to act from a sense of virtue emerging not from work but from leisure and the detachment it affords to property owners.[2]

Unfortunately, tension arose between these two manifestations of individualism. For example, Jacksonians admired productive people and scorned speculators but themselves got caught up in a scramble for material success, for pursuing the main chance, for risky investment in lands, for rapid exploitation of natural resources, for careless banking practices, and more. Thus in a dynamic economy such as Europe had never seen, some Americans succeeded more than others. But this unequal achievement of self-interest threatened to overwhelm the ties of social restraint and mutual accommodation that defined community life.

---

[2] For relevant remarks, see Yehoshua Arieli, *Individualism and Nationalism in American Ideology* (Baltimore: Penguin, 1966), pp. 179–206.

The dilemma was simple: Americans wanted an economy of unlimited opportunities to produce a stable world of virtuous yeomen.[3] To this end, Jackson's supporters would praise his war against the Bank of the United States, which they despised as an agent of constant flux, speculative values, and inexorable corruption, and whose termination they thought would permit decent men to pursue a life of sober and conscientious industry. In truth, however, even while critics condemned the bank on such grounds, it enabled Washington to finance internal improvements, to open up frontier areas to settlement and profit, and to stabilize frenetic state banks. In short, it helped sustain the economy of endless opportunities.

Technically, the economic side of individualism was at odds with the political side of individualism. Thus the freedom to pursue self-interest clashed at least potentially with the cultivation of civic virtue. In the 1830s, Tocqueville saw that America, not united by ancient bonds and traditions, was particularly susceptible to this danger. He claimed, however, that her citizens believed that political and economic freedom could be synchronized by the concept of "self-interest rightly understood." By this phrase he meant that, in small towns across the country, where local government helped to shape the quality of common life, successful men understood that their interest should spur them to sacrifice somewhat on behalf of their communities, that consideration for what other men needed was useful to themselves.[4]

Where Tocqueville used social science to highlight the danger of success displacing virtue, literature followed close behind. For example, Nathaniel Hawthorne published "The Celestial Rail-Road" in 1843.[5] The story retold John Bunyan's Puritan allegory, *The Pilgrim's Progress* (1678), which itself restated St. Augustine's vision of two cities, one earthly and the other divine. In Hawthorne's version of this tale, a Christian traveler from the City of Destruction journeys to the Celestial City by train, which Hawthorne regarded as a metaphor for ruthless technology and modern depravity. The traveler is accompanied by Mr. Live-for-the-world, Mr. Hide-sin-in-the-heart, Mr. Take-it-easy, the Reverend Stumble-at-truth, the Reverend Wind-of-doctrine, and Mr. Smooth-it-away, a director

---

[3] Marvin Meyers, *The Jacksonian Persuasion: Politics and Belief* (Stanford: Stanford Univ. Press, 1957), pp. 11–13.

[4] Alexis de Tocqueville, *Democracy in America*, 2 vols. (orig., 1835, 1840; New York: Vintage, 1954), Vol. II, pp. 129–132.

[5] Nathaniel Hawthorne, "The Celestial Rail-Road," in *The Centenary Edition of the Works of Nathaniel Hawthorne* (Columbus: Ohio State Univ. Press, 1974), Vol. X, pp. 196–206. This story was originally published in the *Democratic Review* (May 1843), pp. 515–523.

of the railroad corporation. Apolyon, the Devil himself, drives the train.[6] When it arrives in Vanity Fair, the pilgrims do not quarrel with the townspeople, as in *Pilgrim's Progress*, but do a booming business with them, where a script called "Conscience" can purchase almost anything. From the Final Station, the traveler takes a steamboat to cross the river to the Celestial City. It was at this point that Bunyan's Christian saw the damned taken to Hell through an opening in the cliff just below Heaven. Hawthorne's traveler wakes up instead, just as, in his dream, the other passengers begin to scream.[7]

Incorporation

Economic individualism embodied in the rise of corporations fueled economic growth but also fostered disparities of outcome that threatened republican virtue. Corporate charters, which promised commercial advantage to their owners, had originally been granted in America by the Crown or Parliament in return for recipients agreeing to serve specific functions considered important to the community. American state governments started by duplicating this practice but also by giving out more charters than ever for banks, insurance companies, and manufacturing, and for canal, bridge, and road construction and operation. By 1830, the states of New England alone had chartered roughly two thousand corporations,[8] and Congress in 1781 chartered the national bank of North America, forerunner to the Bank of the United States that Andrew Jackson vetoed in 1832.

Incorporation could be more productive than traditional partnerships because it permitted joint stock ownership and limited liability. But corporations sometimes fostered corruption, since men might bribe government officials to assign them exclusive charters which conferred lucrative advantages over potential competitors.[9] Hoping to avoid this vice, but also to stimulate efficiency, states like New York (1811), Connecticut (1817), and Massachusetts (1830) began to issue charters under what were called "general incorporation" laws. The new arrangement quickly

---

[6] Apolyon is "the angel of the bottomless pit" in Revelation 12:11.

[7] Ralph Waldo Emerson compressed the same anxiety over runaway technology into a single sentence when he remarked that "things are in the saddle, and ride mankind." See his "Ode Inscribed to W. H. Channing," in Mark Van Doren (ed.), *The Portable Emerson* (New York: Viking, 1946), p. 323.

[8] Daniel J. Boorstin, *The Americans: The Democratic Experience* (New York: Vintage, 1974), p. 414.

[9] On the corruption of republican values caused by exclusive corporations, see Gordon S. Wood, *The Radicalism of the American Revolution* (New York: Vintage, 1993), pp. 319–321.

The Middle Class

For much of the nineteenth century, many Americans lived in *island communities*.[29] These were places where local economic activity combined subsistence agriculture with basic crafts and services that a small town or village could provide to its surrounding farms. The social ecology in such communities was largely parochial. Men and women shared common conceptions of who they were, although not entirely equal, and of how their traditional aspirations could be fulfilled close to home, in the same community. Relationships were based on long-term experience, with moral standards understood similarly if not always observed perfectly. These were, in a sense, Tocqueville's republican communities, where neighbors could know each other on sight and where citizens could understand how their prosperity depended on the well-being of others.

Such communities could not survive the evolution of large-scale transportation, communication, banking, manufacturing, and retailing, whereby goods and capital from far away reached into every corner of the country and confounded the assumptions of local men and women who found themselves assaulted by economic forces beyond their control. How to deal with interest rates set on Wall Street? How to sell grain at prices calibrated in distant commodity markets? How to ship cattle by railroads that frequently changed haulage fees? Why pay the village cobbler for his product when cheaper shoes, mass-produced in New England, could be mail ordered from Sears, Roebuck in Chicago?

Under these circumstances, a middle class started to grow in America, composed of men and women who took an analytical rather than a traditional view of the world.[30] Born perhaps in island villages, but seeking to fathom new forces of life in order to adapt profitably to the economy that produced them, these people sought to acquire expertise rather than old-time craft skills. To this end, middle-class people were animated by a *vertical vision*, by the aim of rising in status even if that required them to leave their original community. For such people, work became less a matter of finding one's niche in fairly static social surroundings and more the pursuit of a *career*, which could be defined as a coherent and

[29] The term *island communities* and the argument to this effect appear in Robert Wiebe, *The Search for Order, 1877–1920* (New York: Hill and Wang, 1967), passim, but esp. pp. xiii, 4.

[30] The argument to this effect comes from Burton Bledstein, *The Culture of Professionalism: The Middle Class and the Development of Higher Education in America* (New York: Norton, 1976).

"goal-oriented life" that might take one far from home, following the main chance.[31]

Here were the accountants, the doctors, the lawyers, the physicists, the social workers, the architects, the engineers, the corporate managers, the geologists, the professors, the nurses, the public relations men, and the stockbrokers. That is, here were the men and women who acquired new truths, who understood how things were related from one place to another, who knew how to make the system run smoothly and effectively.[32] And here, of course, were those who depended on higher education to equip them for success. In schools teaching the latest discoveries of scientific research, ambitious people learned what they needed to know to leave their communities and go elsewhere, providing valuable services on the way but straining the social fabric that had distinguished the earlier republican world of small towns and perhaps smaller minds. In 1870, there were 52,000 students enrolled in America's colleges and universities. In 1900, there were 238,000. By 1930, there were 1,101,000, and in 1970, there were 7,920,000.[33]

Capitalist Ideology

Not surprisingly, those who succeeded in the new economy tended to portray themselves as virtuous and their rewards as merited. Accordingly, Gilded Age capitalists were likely to select from social science those ideas and concepts that acclaimed their economic behavior. Obviously, Karl Marx was not a favorite, with his scornful presumption that the capitalist carries his heart in his purse. The economic titans preferred to recall that, in Scotland, Adam Smith had praised parsimony as leading to capital accumulation, as if the willingness of some people to live frugally, to save money, and to invest that money in factories is what permits industry to be applied and value to be created through organized work.[34] Nassau Senior, from Oxford, later said much the same thing when he commended

---

[31] Ibid., pp. 105–112.

[32] Thomas L. Haskell, *The Emergence of Professional Social Science: The American Social Science Association and the Nineteenth-Century Crisis of Authority* (Urbana: Univ. of Illinois Press, 1977), pp. 15–16, 18–23, 28–30, speaks of professional people understanding the ways in which places and realms of life were "interdependent."

[33] In 1990, there were 13,819,000, with 14,979,000 projected for 2000. See *Historical Statistics of the United States: Colonial Times to 1970*, Pt. 1 (Washington, D.C.: U.S. Census Bureau, 1975), p. 383, and *Statistical Abstract of the United States* (Washington, D.C.: U.S. Census Bureau, 2002), p. 134.

[34] Adam Smith, *An Inquiry into the Nature and Causes of the Wealth of Nations* (orig., 1776; New York: Modern Library, 1937), p. 321.

abstinence, which for him connoted "the conduct of a person who...
abstains from the unproductive use of what he can command," invests the
saving, and thereby enables the community to produce goods in capital-
intensive factories.[35]

The next round of concepts came from Herbert Spencer, writing in
England but popular in America, who combined ideas from biology,
physics, and sociology in books like *Social Statics* (1850) and *The Study
of Sociology* (1872–1873). Spencer argued that societies evolve naturally;
that the fittest of them will survive; and that survival, which constitutes
social progress, is based on competition via natural rights. This sort of
Social Darwinism justified a contention that corporate titans were simply those who competed best and, while doing so, propelled the society
in which they lived to a higher plane of efficiency and material comfort.
From Yale, sociologist William Graham Sumner incorporated such ideas
into his *What Social Classes Owe to Each Other* (1883). Sumner argued
that successful people owe their improvident neighbors not social welfare
and public works but courtesy and mutual respect.[36]

In his *Autobiography*, Andrew Carnegie recalled how, as a young man,
he had read Darwin and Spencer and how suddenly "all was clear...
[because] I had found the truth of evolution."[37] Once converted, he went
on to write "The Gospel of Wealth" (1889), an essay wherein he justified his ascent to riches by saying that "while the law [of competition]
may be sometimes hard for the individual [who fails], it is best for the
race, because it insures the survival of the fittest in every department."[38]
John D. Rockefeller was not far behind. As he put it, in a Sunday school
sermon, "The growth of a large business is merely a survival of the
fittest. The American Beauty rose can be produced... only by sacrific-
ing the early buds which grow around it. This is not an evil tendency in
business. It is merely the working out of a law of nature and a law of
God."[39]

---

[35] Nassau Senior, *An Outline of the Science of Political Economy* (orig., 1836; London:
G. Allen & Unwin, 1951), p. 58.

[36] William Graham Sumner, *What Social Classes Owe to Each Other* (orig., 1883; Caldwell,
Idaho: Caxton, 1961), p. 34, and passim.

[37] Carnegie, *Autobiography*, p. 339.

[38] Andrew Carnegie, *The Gospel of Wealth and Other Timely Essays* (Cambridge: Harvard
Univ. Press, 1962), p. 16. This essay was first published in the *North American Review*
(June 1889), pp. 653–664, and (December 1889), pp. 682–698.

[39] Quoted in Richard Hofstadter, *Social Darwinism in American Thought*, 2nd ed. (Boston:
Beacon, 1955), p. 45.

The Harmony of Interests

Capitalist ideology was persuasive on two grounds. First, because it apparently explained what everyone already saw, that modern industry could create a cornucopia of commodities which would eventually permit many Americans to achieve degrees of material comfort previously unimaginable. This point especially impressed American Progressives, as we shall see.

Second, capitalist ideology offered a harmony of interests theory which skirted the fact that the notion of "self-interest rightly understood" seemed increasingly unable to describe much of the behavior that accompanied modern economic production and ownership. Titans of the Gilded Age were ruthless entrepreneurs who crushed labor unions[40] and devised strong-arm tactics such as the rebates that Standard Oil forced railroads to pay for the privilege of shipping its oil. Such winners kept most of their profits and lived so luxuriously as to inspire Thorstein Veblen to invent the term *conspicuous consumption*.[41]

Relatively speaking, titans of this age gave little back to the communities where they made their money. But they could justify the apparent skimpiness of their sacrifice by arguing that unbridled self-interest was a law of God, designed to help even the least successful. Here was a new harmony of interests theory where everyone, through voluntary contracts, received from the market exactly what his contribution was worth. It followed that he who received an income hundreds or thousands of times larger than the income of another, was not obliged to display any particular measure of generosity because, in effect, his income showed that he was already providing great benefits to the community. Carnegie gave away most of his fortune, using it, among other things, to build more than 2,500 public libraries. But he had few imitators.[42]

---

[40] For example, see Almont Lindsay, *The Pullman Strike: The Story of a Unique Experiment and of a Great Labor Upheaval* (Chicago: Univ. of Chicago Press, 1942). See also George S. McGovern and Leonard F. Guttridge, *The Great Coalfield War* (Boston: Houghton Mifflin, 1972), on the "Ludlow Massacre" during the Colorado strike in 1913–1914 against Rockefeller mines.

[41] Thorstein Veblen, *The Theory of the Leisure Class* (orig., 1899; New York: Mentor, 1953), pp. 60–80. The term *conspicuous consumption* referred not just to lavish displays by the rich but to any sign that a person could afford something that someone less affluent could not. Thus a middle-class housewife could be regarded as proof that her husband could afford not to send her to work.

[42] Substantial gifts were made to higher education and art. See Merle Curti and Roderick Nash, *Philanthropy in the Shaping of American Higher Education* (New Brunswick, N.J.: Rutgers Univ. Press, 1965), and Daniel Fox, *Engines of Culture: Philanthropy and Art Museums* (Madison: Univ. of Wisconsin Press, 1963). But only a minority of the rich

Political Responses

After the Civil War, a lands boom swept across the Great Plains in states like North and South Dakota, Nebraska, Kansas, and Colorado, where farmers bought millions of acres from the government, from railroads, and from speculators, and where population in some states rose two, three, and even four times between 1870 and 1890.[43] Mainly, family farms were created, but the agriculture they practiced was modern, which meant that it centered not on subsistence but on marketable commodities, such as grain and livestock, shipped by rail to buyers via commercial elevators and stockyards. At the same time, many southern farmers entered the same modern orbit, leaning more to cotton and tobacco, but also shipping their products to faraway markets as commodities.

This sort of life, centered on small towns and villages, was vulnerable to outside forces. Drought, for example, was so severe in 1889 and 1890 as to end the western land boom. At the same time, in states like Kansas, 60 to 70 percent of rural acreage was mortgaged to banks often controlled from far away, and penniless farmers were harassed by men who did not suffer from local hardships. Rail rates fluctuated dramatically, such as when lines were consolidated by titans like Jay Gould and Cornelius Vanderbilt. And commodity prices set in places like Chicago declined steadily, from $1.19 per bushel of wheat in good times to $0.49 in 1890.

Populism

Men trying to overcome such facts of economic life founded the People's Party in Kansas in 1890. By 1891, this party was widely known as the Populist Party. Populists hoped to maintain economic independence and community life for little people. They had some success in 1892, mainly in elections to state and local offices. Then came the depression of 1893, causing thousands of business bankruptcies, and throwing 20 percent of America's industrial workers out of work. Hoping for a massive protest vote by the dispossessed, the Populists endorsed William Jennings Bryan, congressman from Nebraska and Democratic presidential candidate

contributed and even fewer created foundations as Carnegie did. See Judith Sealander, *Private Wealth, Public Life: Foundation Philanthropy and the Reshaping of American Social Policy from the Progressive Era to the New Deal* (Baltimore: Johns Hopkins Univ. Press, 1997), p. 9.

[43] The lands boom and its decline into Populism are described in Robert C. McMath, Jr., *American Populism: A Social History, 1877–1898* (New York: Hill and Wang, 1993). See also Lawrence Goodwyn, *The Populist Movement* (New York: Oxford Univ. Press, 1978), and Michael Kazin, *The Populist Persuasion* (New York: Basic Books, 1995).

in 1896. They went down with him to crushing defeat against William McKinley, and the People's Party disbanded in 1898.

Like Thomas Jefferson and Andrew Jackson, Populists believed that producers, often agrarian, create the real wealth of society and behave more virtuously than speculators, bankers, middlemen, and lobbyists. As Bryan said in 1896, while assuming that most social parasites lived in urban areas, "Burn down your cities and leave our farms, and your cities will spring up again as if by magic; but destroy our farms and the grass will grow in the streets of every city in the country."[44] Populists held that corporations turned the nation's producers, who included urban workers, into tenants forced to work for men who owned the land, machines, and credit that make labor possible.[45] Accordingly, for Populists, unemployment and poverty were not deserved but flowed from idleness created to produce profits for men who controlled factories, credit, transportation, and marketing.[46] Under such circumstances, nominally free contracts were shackles which working men could not afford to reject, but which employers imposed to press workers into a sort of "slavery" that "degrades their manhood, and that of the republic."[47]

From all of this, Populists saw no harmony of interests in the marketplace praised by Social Darwinism. According to that theory, financial success was proof of virtuous behavior toward other men. Yet by the law of competition, said Populists, profits for the capitalist rise not because of his efforts but as a function of the number of people unemployed, and "his fortune grows relatively as the poverty of the poor makes them powerless."[48] Furthermore, large corporations are not natural entities created by economic titans but "exist by law" and "are chartered by law." So why not control them by law? "A trust," said one Populist historian who favored government regulation, "is a conspiracy against legitimate trade. It is against the interests of the people and the welfare of the public."[49]

---

[44] "Cross of Gold Speech," in Richard Hofstadter (ed.), *Great Issues in American History: From Reconstruction to the Present Day, 1864–1969* (New York: Vintage, 1969), p. 172.

[45] Letter to the editor, *Farmers Alliance* (Lincoln), March 21, 1891, and Topeka editorial, 1894, in Norman Pollack (ed.), *The Populist Mind* (Indianapolis: Bobbs-Merrill, 1967), pp. 15–16, 349. On urban workers, see selections from William A. Peffer, *The Farmer's Side, His Troubles and Their Remedy* (1891), ibid., p. 83: "The man who was once an individual citizen among the farmers is now part of a great manufacturing establishment in the city, doing his work with the same precision, the same regularity, the same method that an inanimate implement does."

[46] Pollack (ed.), *The Populist Mind*, pp. 334–335, 342.

[47] Ibid., p. 422.   [48] Ibid., p. 20.   [49] Ibid., p. 31.

The Omaha Platform

In short, Populists believed that republican citizenship was impossible for individuals who earned little in an economy dominated by large corporations. Worse, from their point of view, those firms were artificial individuals who competed unfairly against natural people, who corrupted government officials, and who induced them to enact legislation which, as in classical tyrannies, permitted rulers to pursue their interests rather than those of other men. As one editorial writer observed, "The corporation has absorbed the community," in which case the community must reassert control over the corporation.[50]

The Omaha Platform of the People's Party appeared in this context in 1892.[51] It called for government ownership of railroads, telegraphs, and telephones, for a federal income tax, for postal savings banks, for restrictions on immigration, for direct election of senators, for a single term of office for president and vice president, and more. Beyond seeking to prevent corruption, these proposals aimed to protect economically weak individuals from powerful marketplace pressures. For example, Populists thought that government ownership of railroads would prevent exorbitant freight rates for commodities that must be shipped to market. They thought that restricting immigration would encourage employers to pay good wages to local workers rather than a pittance to newcomers desperate for work. And they thought that postal savings banks would provide steady and reasonable interest rates rather than what they regarded as fluctuating but miserly rates offered by private banks.

Much of the Omaha Platform represented an exercise of Citizenship III, calling for better laws in defiance of the capitalist belief that government had no right to intervene in economic markets. That is, Populists insisted that citizens are entitled to use the rights of Citizenship II to demand public policies that will maintain a good state. Corporation men countered with the doctrine of Social Darwinism, which defined a good state as one whose government pursued a policy of laissez-faire.

Carnegie, for example, praised private philanthropy and argued, in his "Gospel of Wealth," that a personal sense of Christian stewardship should inspire wealthy people to make charitable contributions. He thus rejected the notion that citizens at large were entitled to decide, via progressive income taxes and Citizenship III, what should be done with great fortunes

---

[50] Ibid., p. 19.
[51] The Omaha Platform is reprinted in Kirk H. Porter and Donald B. Johnson (eds.), *National Party Platforms, 1840–1956* (Urbana: Univ. of Illinois Press, 1956), pp. 104–106.

thrown up by modern science and technology. And William K. Vanderbilt, head of the New York Central Railroad, spoke very bluntly when asked why he did not run his trains "for the public benefit." In Vanderbilt's immortal words, "The public be damned. . . . Railroads are not run on sentiment, but on business principles, and to pay."[52]

Against such resolute expressions of self-interest, which critics might regard as less than "rightly understood," Populists insisted that republican citizenship and decent communities cannot survive unless economic activity will be regulated and, at some points, replaced or supplemented by government credit, price regulation, and unemployment relief. Here was the ideal. People of modern sensibilities might draw a distinction, however, between what Populists promoted as conditions for good citizenship and the ways in which some of the same people actually behaved as citizens because, especially in the South, many Populists and former Populists eventually helped to establish and maintain the scourge of segregation.[53]

The Progressives

Populists used republican terms similar to those that inspired supporters of Jackson and Lincoln.[54] But they failed electorally and were replaced by more ambiguous reformers called Progressives. The Progressives did not create a party of their own. They preferred to operate in the Republican and Democratic parties, and their ideas influenced both Theodore Roosevelt and Woodrow Wilson. The result was that Progressives never offered a statement of principles such as the Omaha Platform, to which all Progressives might attest. On this score, the Progressive Platform of 1912 was only a campaign device fashioned by Roosevelt to promote his third-party candidacy for president in that year. Moreover, because at the height of Progressive influence no party of that name existed to

---

[52] Quoted in James Oliver Robertson, *American Myth, American Reality* (New York: Hill and Wang, 1980), pp. 182–183. See also George F. Baer, owner of the Philadelphia and Reading Coal and Iron Company, who criticized striking coal miners in 1902 by arguing that mining is "a business . . . not a religious, sentimental, or academic proposition." Baer is quoted in Herbert Agar, *The Price of Union: The Influence of the American Temper on the Course of History* (Boston: Houghton Mifflin, 1966), p. 647.

[53] What happened over time is complicated by the fact that, before Populism failed electorally, some white Populists tried to join forces politically with African Americans in the South. Later, though, many white Populists closed ranks in favor of racism and segregation. The basic elements of this retreat from Reconstruction were written into modern historiography in C. Vann Woodward's classic *The Strange Career of Jim Crow* (orig., 1955; New York: Oxford Univ. Press, 2001). See also n. 66 below.

[54] On the "republicanism" of Populists, see McMath, *American Populism*, pp. 51–53.

enroll members formally, there were no party lists which could confirm exactly who these people were. The most that can be said conclusively of Progressivism, then, is that it constituted a mood rather than a movement.

Precision aside, historians have claimed that, in comparison with Populists, the Progressives were more middle-class than farmers,[55] and more educated than amateurs.[56] That is, many Progressives emerged from the ranks of those people who were leaving behind the standards of small town life, who were learning scientific skills, and who were practicing forward-looking occupations which enabled the new economy to run smoothly. These were the men and women who, in field after field, left their mark on American thinking so strongly that some of their names are still familiar today: Edward Ross, sociologist; Richard Ely, economist; John Commons, economist; Herbert Croly, journalist; Walter Lippmann, journalist; Lincoln Steffens, journalist; Sinclair Lewis, novelist; Charles Beard, historian; Jane Adams, social worker; John Dewey, philosopher; Louis Brandeis, lawyer; Walter Rauschenbusch, minister.

On the one hand, such men and women, using middle-class skills, collected facts and publicized them to demonstrate that unbridled capitalism produces dangerous results. Thus Lincoln Steffens dedicated his *Shame of the Cities* (1904) to "all of the citizens in all of the cities of the United States." He then described for them corruption in New York, Chicago, Philadelphia, and several other cities, including practices such as "macing," where an existing municipal transit company was forced to sell its trolley tracks cheaply to a new company, chartered by corrupt politicians with little capital investment.[57] Thus Louis Brandeis, in the case of *Muller v. Oregon* (1908),[58] argued before the Supreme Court in defense of an Oregon statute which limited women's work to ten hours per day. His brief consisted of 2 pages based on legal principles and 100 pages describing the destruction wrought on women by long working days.

Thus congressional investigations focused on economic concentration to show how, regardless of capitalist theories, competition had become both unnatural and unfair. Thus the Pujo Committee reported in 1913 that New York banks held assets worth $5,121,245,175, which constituted

---

[55] On middle-class outlooks in this era, see Wiebe, *Self-Rule*, esp. pp. 117–161.

[56] On educated Progressives, see Eldon Eisenach, *The Lost Promise of Progressivism* (Lawrence: Univ. of Kansas Press, 1994).

[57] Lincoln Steffens, *The Shame of the Cities* (orig., 1904; New York: Hill and Wang, 1957), pp. 156–158.

[58] 208 U.S. 412.

21 percent of the total banking resources of the country, and that the four leading banks there, three of which J. P. Morgan and Company controlled, held 341 directorships in 112 corporations having aggregate resources or capitalization of $22,245,000,000.[59] Thus the Commission on Industrial Relations reported to Congress in 1915 that a handful of enormously wealthy individuals and banks owned much of the industrial capacity of the country, focused solely on making the industries they controlled profitable, and knew nothing about how millions of their workers suffered miserable conditions which "are subject to great criticism and are a menace to the welfare of the Nation."[60]

Beyond publicizing the facts, Progressives also offered theories to explain how America no longer much resembled the nineteenth-century world of small communities and roughly equal men, where material conditions permitted republican virtue even if human nature did not assure it. One sort of theory, mostly secular, came from writers like Herbert Croly, who became editor of the *New Republic* in 1914. In *The Promise of American Life* (1909), Croly argued that during most of the nineteenth century, as Jefferson and Crevecoeur had hoped, American life had improved because of individual efforts, economic independence, small-scale democracy, and so on. Then economic conditions changed, said Croly, so that severe inequalities emerged. In which case a sense of national purpose should be established so that, working through the state, it might help America fulfill her original promise by assuring "a morally and socially desirable distribution of wealth."[61]

The chief problem in his day, according to Croly, was the rise of "business specialists," who were more effective economically than old-time farmers, artisans, and merchants, even while their success in many cases either caused or depended on poverty, exploitation, and corruption. No one could control such men locally, because they created nationwide systems of production and distribution that only Washington could curb.[62] To that end, however, federal agencies should not regulate the economy haphazardly. They should, instead, use middle-class experts to administer sophisticated government policies on behalf of mandates arising from concerned but less knowledgeable citizens.

[59] "The Concentration of Control of Money and Credit" (1913), in Commager (ed.), *Documents of American History*, Vol. 2, pp. 78–82.

[60] "The Concentration of Wealth" (1915), in ibid., p. 107.

[61] Herbert Croly, *The Promise of American Life* (orig., 1909; New York: Dutton, 1963), p. 20.

[62] Ibid., pp. 105–117.

Another sort of Progressive theory was more religious and came from Protestant ministers. In *A Theology for the Social Gospel* (1917), Walter Rauschenbusch explained that pure economic individualism, of the kind recommended by Social Darwinists when they praised relentless competition and survival of the fittest, cannot suffice as a moral guide to modern behavior. The poor are not necessarily lazy and irresponsible, said Rauschenbusch. Rather, economic trends beyond their control may create too few jobs for everyone willing to work. Analogously, the rich do not necessarily disdain the poor because they, the rich, are arrogant and haughty. Instead, they may ignore the plight of those who have little because indifference, like other sins, is "lodged in social customs and institutions and is absorbed by the individual from his social group."[63] Moral obligations, then, can be fulfilled only if we will stop thinking of the poor and the rich as individuals of defective character and will make new laws to change the circumstances within which both groups coexist uneasily.

In theological terms, Rauschenbusch rejected the notion that good will and charity can arise in sufficient measure from individual efforts or, as recommended by Carnegie, that wealthy men should voluntarily practice Christian stewardship toward the deserving poor. The Social Gospel was thus a creed that socialized Christianity and that aimed "to spread in society a sense of the solidarity of successive generations and a sense of responsibility for those who . . . we are now outfitting with the fundamental conditions of existence."[64] This call to collective arms, advocated chiefly by mainline churches, inspired a great deal of civic activism. For example, in 1908 the Methodist Episcopal Church adopted a statement announcing its support for industrial arbitration, workers' safety, the abolition of child labor, regulation of working conditions for women, shorter working hours, a day each week without labor, and a living wage in every industry.[65]

Citizenship III

Like Populists, Progressives asked Americans to use their rights of Citizenship II to exercise Citizenship III, in the sense that they called upon citizens to insist on new laws that would create a more virtuous community.

---

[63] Walter Rauschenbusch, *A Theology for the Social Gospel* (orig., 1917; Louisville, Kentucky: Westminster John Knox, 1997), p. 60.

[64] Ibid., p. 43.

[65] "The Social Creed of the Churches," in Commager (ed.), *Documents of American History*, Vol. 2, p. 52.

Some of these reforms aimed to give voters more power over potentially venal politicians. Here the intention was to use the referendum, the secret ballot, the recall, primary elections, city managers, nonpartisan elections, at-large voting districts, direct election of senators, women's suffrage, and other technical devices at every level of government to weaken political machines and reduce their ability to "buy" votes by dispensing patronage. These reforms assumed that if facts would be widely disseminated, voters would respond by supporting the right candidates and the best policies.[66]

At the national level, Progressives dismissed laissez-faire as the sole guideline to public policy and passed laws that authorized government activism. These included the Pure Food and Drug Act of 1906, providing federal inspection and regulation of foods and medicines; the Hepburn Act of 1906, regulating railroad rates and forbidding rebates; the sixteenth Amendment for income tax in 1913, redressing somewhat the imbalance of resources between rich and poor; the Underwood Tariff in 1913, enacting the largest reductions on import duties since 1865; the creation of a Department of Labor in 1913; the creation of a Department of Commerce in 1913; the Federal Reserve Act of 1913, stabilizing interest rates; the Clayton Anti-Trust Act in 1914, which forbid certain monopolies and provided some protection for unions; the Federal Trade Commission in 1914, authorizing some regulation of commerce; and the Child Labor Act in 1916.

Civic Dilemmas

Populists wanted to preserve small communities that would enable Americans to practice republican virtue.[67] Progressives also sought reform. However, they were more ambivalent than their predecessors about the

---

[66] That Progressives thought such reforms would promote public virtue does not mean we would entirely agree. For example, many Progressives, even while helping to broaden the franchise by supporting women's suffrage via Amendment XIX, also helped to limit suffrage by not opposing the Southern imposition of segregation and by advocating, in the name of "good government," widespread institution of voter registration laws, residency requirements, and literacy tests. In effect, such devices disenfranchised many African Americans and other "discordant social elements" before World War I. On how this was accomplished, see Frances Fox Piven and Richard A. Cloward, *Why Americans Still Don't Vote: And Why Politicans Want It That Way* (Boston: Beacon, 2000), Ch. 3: "The Mobilization and Demobilization of the Nineteenth-Century Electorate," pp. 45–71, and Ch. 4: "How Demobilization Was Accomplished," pp. 72–93.

[67] McMath, *American Populism*, p. 86:

> Every fall the cotton South experienced collectively what many thousands experienced individually: the humiliation of being unable to 'hold' the crop and bargain for a better price. That loss of control, for one farmer or for the whole South,

new world, seeking less to repress it than to make it more livable. But making Progressive accommodations with modernity left three aspects of republican citizenship still problematical.

First, the Progressives endorsed electoral techniques that failed to produce as many virtuous results as their sponsors hoped to achieve. Referendums, primary elections, nonpartisan campaigns, and so forth, would work well, they thought, because voters would weigh the facts of public life and vote accordingly. But even when such facts were available, electoral behavior did not change appreciably. For example, voter turnout was low, with only around 50 percent of eligible adults voting in the presidential election of 1920 and even fewer in the Chicago mayoralty election of 1923.[68] Furthermore, social science research, a hallmark of the new age, revealed that when citizens did vote they were no more rational than human beings in general. And psychologists like Sigmund Freud began to claim that that was not very rational at all.[69]

Walter Lippmann, a leading Progressive journalist, highlighted some of these findings in *Public Opinion* (1922)[70] and *The Phantom Public* (1925).[71] Society is so complex, said Lippmann, that men necessarily lack complete information about it and think in stereotypes. Furthermore, because people live in a complicated world, they often have no opinion on particular public issues, no matter how important. For both reasons, a society cannot simply count up votes cast on election day and discover in them a coherent mandate that elected representatives should serve. But if elections do not indicate mandates, what is the purpose of voting?

---

meant loss of income in an unforgiving world of commercial transactions, and what is more, the loss of *independence* in the republican sense of that word.

[68] Charles E. Merriam and Harold F. Gosnell, *Non-Voting: Causes and Methods of Control* (Chicago: Univ. of Chicago Press, 1924), pp. viii–x.

[69] Freud argued that people's behavior is animated by a mixture of impulses, some only partly rational. See his *The Ego and the Id* (orig., 1923; New York: Norton, 1989). Of course, one needed only to look at the commercial world to see how it exploited human irrationality in order to sell goods. In 1916, the Piggly-Wiggly grocery store chain initiated the practice of encouraging impulse buying by designing store aisles so that customers would have to traverse them all and thereby see every item of merchandise, including things they had not intended to buy, before reaching the checkout counter. Phil Patton, *Made in USA: The Secret Histories of the Things That Made America* (New York: Penguin, 1992), pp. 256–261, describes the creation of the Piggly-Wiggly system, which was patented in 1920 by Clarence Saunders and whose original store interior is on display in the Memphis Museum of History and Science. Patton describes customers being "pinballed" through the aisles until they arrived at the cashier.

[70] Walter Lippmann, *Public Opinion* (New York: Harcourt and Brace, 1922).

[71] Walter Lippmann, *The Phantom Public* (New York: Harcourt and Brace, 1925).

Second, Progressives tended to believe, in the light of such difficulties, that experts should run modern government much of the time, working in well-staffed offices capable of dealing competently with America's largest issues and actors. Here was Croly's recommendation. The problem was that experts and their agencies, constituting big government, would interact with representatives of big labor, big agriculture, big industry, and big business. These sectors of modern life were finding common interests and expressing them to government via associations such as the American Federation of Labor, the Farm Bureau, the American Association of University Professors, the National Association of Manufacturers, and the Chamber of Commerce. In other words, special sorts of work and commerce in America were organizing themselves into what Theodore Lowi would later call "interest group liberalism."[72] The Progressives planned to manage this world of large entities by getting government organized on the same scale. In which case, once again, it was not clear exactly what civic role republican citizens should play.

Third, Progressives never managed to decide how to rein in successful economic actors who dominated their fields. Woodrow Wilson and Theodore Roosevelt addressed this issue when both campaigned for the presidency. Wilson argued that government should break up the country's largest corporations, which he called trusts.[73] Roosevelt said that combinations in industry were inevitable, but that government should supervise them "in the interest of the public welfare."[74] The first policy, of dismantling great corporations, risked losing their economic efficiency. The second policy, of government regulation, was dangerous for requiring government agencies so powerful they might evade popular control.[75]

This third point may be restated. Progressives appreciated the outpouring of goods that only large corporations were capable of producing. They never fashioned, though, a consistent policy for dealing with those corporations but oscillated between trust-busting and bureaucratic

[72] Theodore Lowi, *The End of Liberalism: Ideology, Policy, and the Crisis of Public Authority* (New York: Norton, 1969), pp. 55–97.

[73] See the collection of his 1912 campaign speeches in Woodrow Wilson, *The New Freedom*, introd. by William E. Leuchtenburg (orig., 1913; Englewood Cliffs, N.J.: Prentice-Hall, 1961).

[74] See the collection of his 1910 speeches in Theodore Roosevelt, *The New Nationalism*, introd. by William E. Leuchtenburg (orig., 1910; Englewood Cliffs, N.J.: Prentice-Hall, 1961). The quotation is from p. 29.

[75] This point is made by Grant McConnell, *Private Power and American Democracy* (New York: Random House, 1966), p. 38.

oversight.[76] The result was that Progressives offered, in effect, a harmony of interests theory which assumed that government would act as society's ultimate arbiter, but without firm guidelines set in advance.

On this score, the aim was to foster large organizations or pressure groups that would represent many of society's great interests – from labor to agriculture, from industry to commerce, from consumers to retirees – and then use government to maintain a balance of power between them, sometimes helping the weak against the strong.[77] This was perhaps the best that Progressives could do in view of how they regarded bigness as inevitable in modern life. But as a vague recipe for what some people would later call *liberalism*, this sort of harmony theory had difficulty competing with the capitalist vision of a just and efficient marketplace created by God and sustained by Him without assistance from imperfect legislators and clumsy bureaucrats.

The Impasse

We should not interpret the past too generously. Thus we should not assume that Populists and Progressives who regarded themselves as republicans would relate virtuously, as we define virtue today, to issues such as race, gender, and ethnicity.[78] On the other hand, our story does not aim at reviewing defects. Instead, it focuses on ideals while hoping they will influence practices. And from the standpoint of ideals, there can be no doubt that, by around 1920, contemporary facts challenged America's vision of a democratic republic.

Here was the problem: As industrialization proceeded, Americans still admired various elements of a social order that, apparently, could not thrive in modern economic conditions. What obtained instead were great disparities of income and wealth[79] and a corporate world where most people worked for wages that, even when they rose from time to time, permitted recipients to control neither their own lives nor America's means

---

[76] New Dealers were no more consistent. See Ellis W. Hawley, *The New Deal and the Problem of Monopoly: A Study in Economic Ambivalence* (Princeton: Princeton Univ. Press, 1966).

[77] Carl Resek (ed.), *The Progressives* (Indianapolis: Bobbs-Merrill, 1967), p. xxx.

[78] Some of America's shocking defects in these realms during the Populist and Progressive eras are described in Rogers M. Smith, *Civic Ideals: Conflicting Visions of Citizenship in U.S. History* (New Haven: Yale Univ. Press, 1997), pp. 347–469.

[79] Trachtenberg, *The Incorporation of America*, p. 99, notes that in 1890, out of 12 million families in America, 11 million lived on incomes of less than $1,200, and the average income of this group was $380, below the accepted poverty line. At the same time, the richest 1 percent earned more than the lowest 50 percent.

of production.[80] The world of roughly equal and mainly independent economic actors seemed gone, never to return. And with it, or so some people feared, vanished the political republic they aspired to maintain.

In *The Broken Covenant* (1975), Robert Bellah analyzed what happened.[81] From sociology, Bellah argued that America's civil religion, which he described as a general notion of Americans living a life of reason that fulfilled God's will, had long assumed that individuals were embedded in communities and obliged to behave there with some sense of social responsibility. Here was the long-standing ideal of a covenanted people, where the *covenant* may have started with Puritanism but was reinforced by the classical notion, passed on by thinkers like Montesquieu, of a *republic* based upon virtue.

These two *community* themes, of covenant and republic, were eventually combined in the Constitution, itself a solemn compact, where concessions to interest were accompanied by aspirations to virtue. But times changed and, by the late nineteenth century, many Americans hoped to live out a "success story" version of *individualism*, where the balance between private achievement and community welfare was overwhelmed by apparently legitimate cupidity. At that point, Bellah concluded, "the economic system of late industrial America [generating inequality] . . . [could not] be reconciled with the fundamental American ideology of economic independence [requiring rough equality] as the basis of political order. That ideology [of republicanism] we have never abandoned though it has described our social reality less accurately with every passing decade."[82]

---

[80] Stuart Ewen, *Captains of Consciousness: Advertising and the Social Roots of the Consumer Culture* (New York: McGraw-Hill, 1976), pp. 8–9, explains how the wage process, rather than the wage itself, was regarded by nineteenth-century workmen as an inevitable source of "inequitable social relations."

[81] *The Broken Covenant: American Civil Religion in Time of Trial*, 2nd ed. (Chicago: Univ. of Chicago Press, 1992).

[82] Ibid., p. 121. Political scientist Charles E. Lindblom judged the imbalance between economic and civic realities even more harshly. See his *Politics and Markets: The World's Political-Economic Systems* (New York: Basic Books, 1977), p. 356:

> Enormously large, rich in resources, the big corporations . . . command more resources than do most government units. They can also, over a broad range, insist that government meet their demands, even if these demands run counter to those of citizens expressed through their polyarchal [i.e., democratic] controls. Moreover, they do not disqualify themselves from playing the partisan role of a citizen – for the corporation is legally a person. And they exercise unusual veto powers. They are on all these counts disproportionately powerful. . . . *The large private corporation fits oddly into democratic theory and vision. Indeed, it does not fit.* [emphasis supplied]

In short, early in the twentieth century, the ideal of Citizenship III, of a civic community maintaining good laws for all its members, could inspire the republic's people but no longer seemed tenable in practice. What that meant was that somewhere between, say, 1900 and 1920, Americans reached a point where they would be able to describe the national experiment as successful only if they could find a new criterion for success, beyond *democratic republicanism*. That new criterion did eventually appear, in the form of *consumerism*.

PART III

THE MODERN ECONOMY

6

The Rise of Consumerism

Consumerism was about practices and expectations. On the one hand, it praised industrial and commercial trends that evolved in America by World War I and would characterize the country afterward. In this sense, to endorse consumerism meant to validate a world of science, technology, and marketing, which sparked extraordinary productivity, and which offered great opportunities to hard-driving entrepreneurs and far-flung corporations. In everyday terms, to subscribe to consumerism was to believe in capitalism, or free enterprise, or private property as a positive force in American life.

On the other hand, once the right economic practices flourished, Americans expected them to generate substantial material rewards. Thus there emerged a notion that work is not so much a means by which people create and maintain political freedom but more an activity by which they earn enough to buy the endless supply of commodities that capitalism can produce. In other words, within the context of consumerism, labor is regarded less as an activity that enables people to be effective citizens and more as the effort that enables them to prosper as consumers.[1] From which it follows that America's greatest achievement may be not the

---

[1] This part of consumerism is described by James Oliver Robertson, *American Myth, American Reality* (New York: Hill and Wang, 1980), p. 187:

> For the past half century or more, increasing numbers of Americans have measured individual worth – their own and others' – by the goods and services they are able to consume.... In modern America, individual work makes money. That money is *used* in order to *consume* the goods and services (in order to acquire the products) the individual desires.... [Thus] American society has become, so we believe, a consumer society.

republicanism which Lincoln struggled to preserve but the health and comfort which America's free economy can provide for more hard-working people than ever in human history.

It is important to understand what happened here. Consumerism did not deny the American ideal of virtuous citizenship. It did not reject the belief that fairly equal circumstances would be desirable for promoting the independence of mind and means that would permit most citizens to exercise political virtue on behalf of public interests. But consumerism did imply that, if the practice of republican citizenship were to falter because modern conditions do not encourage it, Americans could hope for a revival of good citizenship but meanwhile take great satisfaction from having some share in the nation's affluence. That is, people continued to revere republican citizenship, but that ideal began to coexist with the ideal of consumerism. Here was an enormous, although not sudden, shift of national perspective.

Private Origins

Consumerism arose in what we have called civil society and only later gained public support in government policies. Businessmen were the first to realize how many things could be produced by America's factories, and they were also the first to talk enthusiastically about what it would mean to sell those things at reasonable prices. Henry Ford, for example, announced in 1907 that he would build "a motor car for the great multitude." It would be sturdy, inexpensive, and easy to maintain. Every man earning a decent wage could buy it and enjoy "hours of pleasure in God's great open spaces."[2] Here was a new and in some respects democratic philosophy of life, which promised that many ordinary men who work will thereby acquire the means to secure material comforts. What is more, Ford kept this promise, so that by 1920, half the cars in the world had been manufactured and sold by his company.[3]

Of course, government eventually got into the business of bringing producers and consumers together fruitfully. In 1912, for example, under pressure from farmers' groups, Washington instituted parcel post service. The post office's rates supplemented the facilities of private express companies like Wells, Fargo so substantially that, within a year, the new

---

[2] Ford is quoted in Warren Susman, *Culture as History: The Transformation of American Society in the Twentieth Century* (New York: Pantheon, 1984), p. 136.
[3] Ibid., p. 137.

service was transporting 300 million packages per year.[4] Other assistance to business included establishing the Department of Commerce in 1913. The activities of that department, including oversight of mines, fisheries, steamboats, aeronautics, patents, and foreign and domestic commerce, proliferated so greatly that when Congress in 1932 brought most of them together in Washington, they were housed in what was then the world's largest office building.[5]

Production and Distribution

The use of economic resources to create and promote consumer goods constituted consumerism in practice, and it advanced in both the production and distribution of commodities. As for production, increasing concentrations of capital and electrification made plants larger and more effective, which meant that employers confronted two imperatives. First, they had to sell the tremendous amount of goods they could produce, and second, they had to do so year after year because failure would be catastrophic after so much money had been invested in production facilities.

Ford was again a classic example.[6] In 1910, his company started making the famous Model T at Ford's Highland Park factory, which contained the largest building in Michigan under one roof, 865 feet long. Men produced the car on a moving assembly line where work came to them at waist height, and where tasks were so specific and limited that workers could do them repetitively and therefore efficiently. Constant assembly innovations followed, so that a chassis that took twelve hours and twenty-eight minutes to produce in 1910, required only one hour and thirty-three minutes in 1914. By 1920, one completed car left the line every minute; by 1925, a car left the line every ten seconds. Production rose from 39,640 units in 1911 to almost 750,000 in 1917. Industry after industry made similar gains, in which case, to avoid gluts, Americans had to buy more than ever.

Improvements in production were accompanied by breakthroughs in distribution. Shopping had traditionally taken place in small stores where bargaining was common, where most people saw only standard items, and where higher priced goods were either brought out only for special

---

[4] Daniel J. Boorstin, *The Americans: The Democratic Experience* (New York: Vintage, 1974), pp. 134–135.

[5] William Leach, *Land of Desire: Merchants, Power, and the Rise of a New American Culture* (New York: Vintage, 1994), p. 350. On Washington's role in promoting business both at home and abroad, see Emily S. Rosenberg, *Spreading the American Dream: American Economic and Cultural Expansion, 1890–1945* (New York: Hill and Wang, 1982).

[6] See Susman, *Culture as History*, pp. 135–137, and Boorstin, *The Americans*, pp. 548–551.

customers or were sold in stores unavailable to ordinary people. Department stores, spearheaded in the 1880s and 1890s by Macy's in New York, Marshall Fields in Chicago, Jordan Marsh in Boston, and Wanamaker's in Philadelphia, changed all that by selling according to new principles: fixed prices, open displays, many kinds of commodities under one roof, and quick turnover of stock. The result was enormous stores, with Macy's alone employing three thousand workers in 1898, and economies of scale which offered a wide range of items at reasonable prices to ordinary people. Daniel Boorstin described the new shopping as a "democracy of consumers," where everyone could come and see, to explore and perhaps to buy, as if all were, in some sense, equal regardless of how they might differ in income and social standing.[7]

Mail-order houses also did a booming business. Montgomery Ward was first, marketing its goods to the Grange and circulating by 1884 a 240-page catalog listing almost ten thousand items for sale.[8] Sears, Roebuck started in the mid-1880s and by 1900 outstripped Ward's. Its catalog offered more items than most department stores, and eventually, with government help, millions of customers received their orders by parcel post. By 1907 Sears shipped more than 3 million fall catalogs. As Boorstin described them, these catalogs became "the Bible of . . . rural consumption communities," a book to be pored over by parents and children and that told the entire family wherein material salvation lay.[9]

Chain stores offered another innovation in retail marketing. The Great Atlantic and Pacific Tea Company opened its first store in 1869 and was eventually followed by chains such as Kroger, Woolworth, McCrory, Kress, and Kresge.[10] Such stores bought in quantity and avoided using middlemen. Consequently they could post lower prices than those found at family owned stores that had long dominated American shopping. By 1930, seven thousand national, regional, and local chain organizations controlled more than 20 percent of America's retail business, with A&P alone operating almost sixteen thousand stores from coast to coast. Like department stores and mail-order houses, the chain stores offered friendly and reliable shopping to Americans who were becoming accustomed to making and preparing fewer items at home but buying more finished goods and processed foods outside.

---

[7] Boorstin, *The Americans*, p. 107

[8] Susan Strasser, *Satisfaction Guaranteed: The Making of the American Mass Market* (Washington, D.C.: Smithsonian Institution Press, 1989), pp. 212–213.

[9] Boorstin, *The Americans*, pp. 128–129.

[10] On chain stores, see Strasser, *Satisfaction Guaranteed*, pp. 222–227.

From Supply to Demand

Driving the details were large trends. Production expanded rapidly due to advances in science, technology, and management. Accordingly, attention came to focus on the need to match that expansion in the realm of consumption. That is, in terms of economic theory, *supply* was becoming less of a problem than *demand* in the modern world.

For countless generations, most people experienced poverty caused by scarcity. Their thinking therefore highlighted virtues such as frugality, temperance, moderation, and diligence. Luxury, under the circumstances, seemed dangerous because to pursue unnecessary items was to risk straining the social fabric by seeking to pile up possessions that could only come at the expense of people already in need. Thus the Stoics feared that luxury would corrupt a republic, St. Augustine preached against the lust for things, and sumptuary laws sought to instruct each feudal estate to consume only its proper share, sometimes very little, of a static economic pie. In America, this fear of superfluous consumption showed up, for example, in 1675, after King Philip's War, when the General Court of Massachusetts condemned luxury and blamed the war on "manifest pride openly appearing amongst us in that long haire, like weomens haire, is worne by some men, either their oune or others haire made into perewiggs, and by some weomen wearing borders of haire, and theire cutting, curling, & immodest laying out theire haire, which practise doeth prevayle & increase, especially amongst the younger sort."[11]

In the first decades of the twentieth century, some economists still worried about shortages. So Thorstein Veblen accused corporate monopolists of *sabotage* – that is, restricting output and creating scarcity – which enabled them to raise prices and increase profits, all the while flaunting their wealth in wasteful displays of *conspicuous consumption.*[12] But other economists began to take high output for granted and to praise the move to increased consumption. Simon Patten, for instance, argued in 1901 that to pursue wealth via reasonable market relations, to enlarge consumption and thereby raise people's material standard of living, leads men to civility, social stability, and peace.[13] Here was a modern update

---

[11] "Provoking Evils," in Edmund S. Morgan (ed.), *Puritan Political Ideas: 1558–1794* (Indianapolis: Bobbs-Merrill, 1965), p. 227.

[12] On the concept of sabotage, see Thorstein Veblen, *The Engineers and the Price System* (orig., 1921; New York: Harcourt, Brace and World, 1923), pp. 38–53. On conspicuous consumption, see Veblen, *The Theory of the Leisure Class: An Economic Study of Institutions* (orig., 1899; New York: Mentor, 1953), pp. 60–80.

[13] This is the general argument in Simon Patten, *The Consumption of Wealth*, 2nd ed. (New York: Ginn and Co., 1901).

of Samuel Johnson's eighteenth-century dictum that, compared to what happens in history when people quarrel over principles rather than profits, men are never so innocently employed as when they are making money.

Wesley Mitchell was one of the first economists in America to realize that if basic needs could easily be met by modern productivity, consumption would become a serious and complex matter requiring considerable effort and training for good performance. In 1912,[14] he recalled that families used to prepare much that they needed at home, for example, food and clothing. In the industrial age, however, workers go out to produce and wives must decide how to use their husbands' wages for shopping on behalf of the entire family. Such women, observed Mitchell, know little about commodity prices and performance. Furthermore, they usually lack a sense of which wants, beyond basic needs, should be satisfied before others.

Advertising

Even before World War I, advertising began to stimulate demand and help people make those choices that Mitchell regarded as problematic. Operating through newspapers and magazines like *Cosmopolitan*, *McClure's*, the *Saturday Evening Post*, the *Ladies Home Journal*, and *Comfort Magazine*, stores like Macy's and companies like Procter & Gamble advertised their wares both prominently and persistently.[15] Wanamaker's department stores, for example, pioneered full-page newspaper advertisements as early as 1879 and in 1909 began to run such ads daily in New York City.[16] Other companies followed suit, and so many new experts evolved around this effort that they founded the Advertising Federation of American in 1904.

Most important, both businessmen and advertising experts realized that their individual efforts affected the entire industrial system, that such efforts were, in fact, necessary to keep it running smoothly. On this score, people who specialized in commercial persuasion assumed that Americans had too few *needs* to impel them to buy enough goods to clear the market of what industry was now capable of producing. They therefore concluded

---

[14] See Wesley C. Mitchell, "The Backward Art of Spending Money," *American Economic Review* (June 1912), pp. 269–281.

[15] Government helped by offering cut-rate postage for magazines starting in 1879. See Neil Postman, *Technopoly: The Surrender of Culture to Technology* (New York: Vintage, 1993), p. 168.

[16] Boorstin, *The Americans*, p. 106; Leach, *Land of Desire*, p. 43.

that such needs must be supplemented by *wants*, by what Emily Fog Mead in 1901 called a diffusion of "desire" throughout the land. The wealthy and refined would always buy more than what they needed merely to hold life and limb together. But somehow, in this formulation, it became clear that, in order to enlarge the supply of demand, ordinary people, who far outnumbered the elite, would have to learn to desire more than they had ever dreamed of buying and possessing.[17]

In general, ads stimulated desire across the board when they depicted people as being happy while purchasing, possessing, and consuming material goods. The techniques of persuasion varied but also repeated themselves. Thus much of this advertising popularized products like Coca-Cola, Colgate toothpaste, Jell-O, Wrigley's chewing gum, Kellogg's cornflakes, Uneeda biscuits, Ivory soap, and so forth. The point was to enthrall customers so they would request that the specific products they now desired would be sold wherever they shopped. In this situation, storekeepers had to pay whatever the manufacturer demanded, in order to stock that item and not disappoint their clientele. And so, in the modern sequence of selling and buying, customers were increasingly animated by brand-name loyalties inspired by advertising images, to the point where price and objective quality, once calculated by skilled salesmen, wholesalers, jobbers, and other economic middlemen, became less important to American shoppers than they had been.[18]

The Therapy Factor

What became central, instead, was a *therapy factor*. In many cases, ads were designed to evoke emotional responses in consumers, to cause them to achieve psychic satisfaction from things they could buy, to displace unhappiness or frustration that any person might feel, from time to time, in various realms of life.

Some of this therapeutic impact encouraged people to feel good for belonging together with other people using the same product, like the "Pepsi Generation" today. In this sense, *consumption communities* might inspire sentiments of solidarity even while older communities, of neighborhood, of town, of religion, and of ethnicity, crumbled under the disruptive impact of modernization.[19] Some strategies of therapy were less wholesome, though, because many advertisements aimed at persuading people to buy products by causing them to feel bad about themselves.

[17] Leach, *Land of Desire*, p. 37.   [18] Strasser, *Satisfaction Guaranteed*, pp. 27–31.
[19] On consumption communities, see Boorstin, *The Americans*, pp. 89–164.

Variations on this theme were endless. Buy toothpaste to make your teeth white. Buy mouthwash to eliminate bad breath. Buy shampoo to remove dandruff. Smoke cigarettes to look sophisticated. Above all, leave last year's hat or dress at home, because wearing either would constitute embarrassing "evidence of inability to buy."[20] Advertisers were explicit about this strategy. Mark O'Dea, a successful New York ad man, claimed that fear of mediocrity drove leaders like Caesar, Luther, Napoleon, Lincoln, and Balzac to great achievements. "So what's a little fear in advertising?" asked O'Dea rhetorically. In fact, "We've a better world with a bit of the proper kind of fear in advertising...fear in women of being frumps, fear in men of being duds."[21]

The therapy factor signaled a change in economic reality that theory eventually recognized. Economists had long assumed that customers bought products because things had a meaning and significance which customers put into them. Thus a farmer buys a hoe because he knows he needs a hoe. But with modern advertising, manufacturers acquired a considerable, although not absolute, power to inject meaning into products, depending on how those products were described as useful or necessary to consumers.[22] And this meant that, to some extent, manufacturers could create a demand for products where no demand had existed before.

Yet if businessmen, rather than consumers, could shape the sum total of purchases even imprecisely, advertising could pump up demand almost endlessly, from one year to the next. This was surely what businessmen wanted, but it was also what modern industry required, for to permit demand to exert only its natural force, and sometimes decline, would have devastated an economy capable of producing enormous quantities of everything. It was a point we can infer from the competition that took place between the Ford Motor Company and General Motors in the 1920s.[23]

---

[20] The quotation is from a business editor in 1903. Cited in Leach, *Land of Desire*, p. 92.

[21] The quotation is from Mark O'Dea, *A Preface to Advertising* (New York: McGraw-Hill, 1937), p. 93. Quoted in Stuart Ewen, *Captains of Consciousness: Advertising and the Social Roots of the Consumer Culture* (New York: McGraw-Hill, 1976), p. 99.

[22] On advertising's ability to inject meaning into products, see Sut Jhally, "Advertising as Religion: The Dialectic of Technology and Magic," in Ian Angus and Sut Jhally (eds.), *Cultural Politics in America* (New York: Routledge, 1989), pp. 221–224.

[23] The general information for this case comes from Alfred P. Sloan, *My Years with General Motors* (Garden City, N.Y.: Doubleday, 1963); Arthur J. Kuhn, *GM Passes Ford, 1918–1938: Designing the General Motors Performance-Control System* (University Park: Pennsylvania State Univ. Press, 1986); Alfred D. Chandler, Jr. (ed.), *Giant Enterprise:*

Ford Versus General Motors

Between 1908 and 1927, Ford's best-selling Model T car was cheap, sturdy, simple, and usually black. The Model T was available in some variety, for example, with starter or without, with solid or balloon tires, with canvas top or enclosed, with room for two passengers or five. In 1925, its price ranged from $260 to $685. The Ford philosophy, as we have seen, was to use assembly line technology to offer an affordable car to all Americans who needed transportation.

The car was hugely successful. In 1921, Ford sold 55 percent of all cars purchased in America, while General Motors sold 12 percent. But in 1925, Ford fell to 40 percent of national sales while General Motors rose to 20 percent. In 1929, General Motors drew ahead, by 32 percent to Ford's 31 percent. And in 1933, the original positions had almost completely reversed, with General Motors up to 41 percent of sales while Ford eked out only 20 percent.

What happened was that General Motors invented a strategy for selling cars in a market saturated by people who already owned them. Henry Ford sold as if he intended to meet natural needs. But General Motors decided there was a limit to such needs, that many people had already satisfied theirs, and that customers must be enticed into buying to fulfill their wants. To this end, the managers at General Motors turned automobiles into a replaceable item, encouraging customers to get rid of their old cars and buy new ones.

This they did by portraying cars as objects of desire rather than of necessity. Accordingly, they introduced the annual model change, to make cars more like hats and dresses; they spruced up these models, like clothing, by offering them in many colors; they made a variety of sizes and models including Chevrolets, Pontiacs, Oldsmobiles, Buicks, and Cadillacs; they priced their cars for every pocketbook, from $525 to $4,485, so some customers could demonstrate, not always subtly, that they were superior to people of lower income; they offered trade-ins so an individual who already had transportation could buy something more desirable while General Motors would sell his or her old vehicle to someone less able to afford a new one; and they offered installment buying and credit arrangements to enable people to buy a more expensive car than they could afford on the spot.

Ford, General Motors, and the Automobile Industry (New York: Harcourt, Brace, and World, 1964); and Anne Jardin, *The First Henry Ford: A Study in Personality and Business Leadership* (Cambridge: MIT Press, 1970).

General Motors thus became the archetype of a modern company designed not just to make a product but also to market it successfully, not just to make things but also to move them out of the salesroom by provoking desire to the point where shoppers would discard what they owned even though it was still usable. The point, after all, was not to market objective value but to create subjective impulses in the minds of consumers through advertising images and trendy styling. Or, in an odd sort of way, the point was to make profits rather than cars.[24]

G.M.'s vice president Charles Kettering described how it all worked when he explained in 1928 that his company intended to persuade people to want things they did not need, to the point where what had once been wants would feel like needs that must be fulfilled.[25] Kettering summed up the new strategy in a story about a man who complained to him that every time General Motors changed its models, the company in effect depreciated the car he owned. Not true, said Kettering. General Motors did not depreciate the older car. "What we did do was to appreciate your mind. We…elevated your mental idea of what an automobile should be."[26]

In short, Henry Ford did not understand that much of modern production, in his case making cars, is not just about making a product but also about evoking the therapy factor.[27] His car was too plain to tempt many potential buyers into leaving their old cars. Yet if they would not do so, first-time buyers were too scarce to sustain the market. Large as they were, cars had to become disposable items, although not so obviously as when the Gillette Company, before World War I, started making disposable razor blades for continual profit when serviceable but long-lasting straight razors could perform the same function. The Sorcerer's Apprentice would have been overwhelmed by modern production. Via strategies like planned obsolescence, the twentieth century solved his problem by periodically throwing away some of the surplus.[28]

---

[24] Sloan, *My Years with General Motors*, p. 64.

[25] Thomas A. Boyd (ed.), *Prophet of Progress: Selections from the Speeches of Charles F. Kettering* (New York: Dutton, 1961), p. 142.

[26] Ibid., pp. 161–162.

[27] In the case of cars, the therapy factor seems obvious today. See Peter Marsh and Peter Collett, *Driving Passion: The Psychology of the Car* (Boston: Faber and Faber, 1987), which explains what our cars say about who we are and who we want to be. For example, p. 55, "the real reason for driving these otherwise irrelevant vehicles [SUV's] is to project an image of independence, freedom and a buccaneering disregard for the petty restrictions of city life."

[28] Boyd (ed.), *Prophet of Progress*, p. 141: "We have to indoctrinate ourselves with the belief that no article should be kept off the scrap pile longer than it takes to provide a

Consumerism as Inspiration

The Declaration of Independence said that men have a right to life, liberty, and the pursuit of happiness. The practice of republican citizenship would presumably maintain life and liberty; that was what Lincoln meant when he said the North fought the Civil War to fulfill the principles of the Declaration. And the pursuit of happiness, or so the Founders thought, would unfold moderately as individuals strove to achieve a reasonable amount of material comfort.

The New Happiness

Then came consumerism, with another vision of what American life was about. Consumerism did not reject the Declaration and its republican sentiments. But those who celebrated buying and selling linked happiness to the phenomenal outpouring of commodities which modern industry and agriculture could produce. Thus in countless advertisements and eventually in countless political speeches, Americans described happiness to each other as making money or, more technically, as the opportunity to earn the means to consume an endless supply of new commodities. In the Roaring Twenties, Calvin Coolidge immortalized this switch when he declared that the business of America is business.[29] Somewhat more obscurely, he sanctified the pursuit of wealth when he announced that "the man who builds a factory builds a temple ... [and] the man who works there worships there."[30]

The concept of happiness rooted in material success undoubtedly exhilarated many people. And why not? In some obvious respects, more *is* better, like when indoor toilets replace outdoor privies and when electric refrigerators replace ice boxes. On the other hand, abundance is so familiar to some Americans today that unqualified praise for it may strike them as naive. After all, as Neil Postman recently remarked, there is a sense in which one message of consumerism is that "whoever dies with the most toys, wins."[31]

better article. Obsolescence is not a dangerous thing. It is an economy. Prosperity and obsolesence are tied together, and obsolescence makes prosperity."

[29] William Allen White, *Calvin Coolidge: The Man Who Is President* (New York: Macmillan, 1925), p. 218. The quotation is from a speech to American editors in January 1925.

[30] Quoted in William E. Leuchtenburg, *The Perils of Prosperity, 1914–1932* (Chicago: Univ. of Chicago Press, 1958), p. 188.

[31] Neil Postman, *The End of Education: Redefining the Value of School* (New York: Knopf, 1996), p. 33. For an example of preposterous consumption, see Amy Barrett's interview

What annoyed Postman was that consumerism promises happiness but may not deliver it. After all, ads often encourage customers to feel bad about themselves so they will buy more products.[32] Still, once consumerism appeared, new commodities offered a sort of freedom which many people embraced quickly and enthusiastically, and that was the main point. The automobile, for example, liberated Americans from rural isolation, permitting them to travel far from home and experience unfamiliar places. Paradoxically, it also helped them to re-create rural tranquility in suburbs serviced more and more by automotive commuting. For young people, moreover, on farms or in cities, the car was radically liberating, isolating them occasionally from chaperones, and thereby permitting them to shed inhibitions and break old taboos.[33]

In fact, the happiness provided by commodities changing and proliferating may be regarded as a hallmark of modernity for undermining tradition continuously. In that sense, consumerism set Americans free in exciting and unpredictable ways that much of the world now seeks to emulate. How else, for example, should we explain the extraordinary popularity of American television shows such as *Sex and the City* and *Baywatch* and *Ricki Lake* wherever more traditional societies are willing to broadcast them?

The New Harmony

Beyond numerous possessions, consumerism promised Americans a measure of social harmony which helped to downplay the fact that, in an industrial society dominated by corporations and other large organizations, many citizens would not achieve the economic standing they needed to fulfill their republican aspirations. This harmony appeared in two dimensions.

with Ivana Trump entitled "She Stoops to Spend," in the *New York Times Magazine* (October 15, 2000), p. 26, where the following exchange appears:

> Q. [Barrett] So how much does a beautiful bra cost to make you think twice about buying it? A. [Trump] I really don't look. This is the time when I go to Bloomingdale's, to the fourth floor. I go there for two hours and I buy 2,000 of the black, 2,000 of the beige, 2,000 of the white. And I ship them around between the homes and the boat and that's the end of it for maybe a half a year when I have to do it all over again.

Perhaps this passage contains transcription errors; perhaps Trump meant $2000 worth of bras in each color. The bottom line would still be, for most people, greatly exaggerated.

[32] Flagrant examples come from the realm of women's products. See Naomi Wolf, *The Beauty Myth: How Images of Beauty Are Used Against Women* (orig., 1991; New York: Harper Perennial, 2002).

[33] Daniel Bell, *The Cultural Contradictions of Capitalism* (New York: Basic Books, 1976), pp. 66–67.

First was the promise of shopping, which suggested that men and women of different incomes did not inhabit seriously different stations in life. True, some people never acquired enough money to support a republican lifestyle. Yet many of the same people did earn enough to buy, in low-priced versions, commodities which the more successful could easily afford. It followed that, in this democracy of goods, class distinctions were somewhat blurred or, at least, not so painfully obvious as they would be if commodities were unavailable to more and more ordinary Americans.[34]

Second, business and labor might be regarded as forming a harmonious partnership for producing and consuming goods.[35] On this score, the more successful were certainly in charge. But, in a sense, they were in charge of a common project, wherein all would produce, all would profit, and all would consume. And hard as work might be for any particular individual, the trend was clear. Production under capitalism was rising, wages were improving, and consumption was expanding. The point, then, was not who controlled the process but how all who participated made possible the consumption that production enabled.

It helped, too, that, as time passed, economic titans learned from public relations advisors not to talk like William K. Vanderbilt.[36] Instead, they portrayed themselves inoffensively as serving the twentieth-century community by providing responsible leadership.[37] Eventually, Rockefeller's heirs would tell customers that each of them had "a friend at the Chase Manhattan Bank." If that were so, big corporations should be regarded as bulky but congenial neighbors.

The New Deal

Consumerism suffered a setback during the Great Depression. Business and political leaders failed to maintain an effective balance between

---

[34] On classlessness, see Ronald Edsforth, *Class Conflict and Cultural Consensus: The Making of a Mass Consumer Society in Flint, Michigan* (New Brunswick, N.J.: Rutgers Univ. Press, 1987), pp. 33–34; and Leach, *Land of Desire*, p. 6.

[35] On the partnership of all classes, see David Montgomery, *The Fall of the House of Labor: The Workplace, the State, and American Labor Activism, 1865–1925* (New York: Cambridge Univ. Press, 1987), pp. 252–255. See also Calvin Coolidge, quoted in Leuchtenburg, *The Perils of Prosperity*, pp. 202–203: "We are reaching and maintaining the position where the property class and the employed class are not separate but identical."

[36] Some of this story is told in Stuart Ewen, *PR! A Social History of Spin* (New York: Basic Books, 1996). According to Ewen, pp. 339–398, corporate America succeeded at image making only after World War II.

[37] On the concept of businessmen providing service, see Susman, *Culture as History*, p. 129; and Leach, *Land of Desire*, pp. 116–117.

output, wages, and profits; the stock market crashed in 1929; and purchasing power plunged as unemployment rose eventually to one quarter of the workforce. In response, Americans in 1932 elected Franklin D. Roosevelt to the White House and a Democratic majority to Congress. Major legislation quickly followed, including the Agricultural Adjustment Acts, the National Labor Relations Act, the Social Security Act, the Public Works Administration, the Works Progress Authority, the Securities Exchange Act, the National Industrial Recovery Act, the Civilian Conservation Corps, and more. Economic relief and constructive regulation were thereby provided for groups such as bankers, businessmen, farmers, industrial workers, and retirees.

As a political mood, Progressivism ebbed during the 1920s. But Roosevelt's practice of acting on behalf of major sectors of the national community extended the Progressive concept of using government as society's final arbiter. Some gains were made, some people saw justice being done, and without a federal expression of collective responsibility, social unrest might have escalated out of control. In that sense, the New Deal may have preserved the Union. It was World War II, however, and not the New Deal, which revived the economy by drafting many of the unemployed and putting the rest to work making guns and bombs.

For our purposes, it is noteworthy that, although the New Deal provided economic relief, it made no effort to restore the Jefferson-Jackson-Lincoln land of republican opportunities. In his Commonwealth Speech delivered during the campaign of 1932, Roosevelt conceded that equality of opportunity no longer existed in America.[38] The frontier was gone, he said, and the nation's industrial plant had been built. The task, then, was not to find more resources or produce more goods. It was to administer properly the economic capacity already existing and to find markets for what Americans were capable of making so that wealth and profits could be distributed more equally.

In this task, according to Roosevelt, statesmen should work with businessmen. Together, they should formulate an economic declaration of rights that would supplement the Declaration of Independence which Roosevelt described as America's original social contract. In the new contract, as in the old, every man would have a right to life. But that right would imply another, that he would have the "right to make a

---

[38] "Campaign Address on Progressive Government at the Commonwealth Club" (San Francisco, September 23, 1932), in Samuel I. Rosenman (ed.), *The Public Papers and Addresses of Franklin D. Roosevelt*, 13 vols. (New York: Random House, 1938–1950), Vol. 1, pp. 750–753.

comfortable living...sufficient for his needs."[39] That is, all men are entitled to a job, at decent wages, but they will not all acquire the material
resources that republicans like Jefferson assumed are necessary to political
independence.

Roosevelt reiterated this point in his Four Freedoms Speech, a state of
the nation address in 1941.[40] There the president spoke of freedom of
speech, freedom of religion, freedom from fear, and freedom from want.
The last included "jobs for those who can work." The same right to work
appeared in "The Economic Bill of Rights," which constituted Roosevelt's
annual message to Congress in 1944. Here, Roosevelt argued that the
original Bill of Rights was political and that it had "proved inadequate to
assure us equality in the pursuit of happiness." Accordingly, Americans
should fashion a second Bill of Rights which would assure, among other
things, a "useful and remunerative job in the industries or shops or farms
or mines of the nation." Once more the assumption was that, for most
people, wage labor is the normal form of modern work.[41]

The bottom line was that Roosevelt and his advisors did not believe
that conditions favorable to republicanism could be restored in modern
America. Economic concentration was inevitable, they thought, and government should oversee it to promote efficiency but avoid the corporate
world's tendency to generate more supply than demand.[42] Since productive capacity was already in place, the long-run goal was for government
to maintain a high rate of consumption.[43] Thus when Roosevelt talked
about jobs and the right to work, he also talked about things that decent
wages could buy, such as adequate housing, clothing, food, medical care,
and old age insurance.

In this way, and while they attended to immediate needs, New Dealers
accepted the notion that "continuous and widespread consumption"
would serve as a social cement in America.[44] Keeping consumption up

---

[39] Ibid., p. 754.

[40] "The Annual Message to the Congress" (January 6, 1941), in ibid., Vol. 9, pp. 663–678.

[41] "Message to the Congress on the State of the Union" (January 11, 1944), in ibid.,
Vol. 13, pp. 32–44.

[42] The argument in this paragraph is based on Russell Hanson, *The Democratic Imagination
in America: Conversations with Our Past* (Princeton: Princeton Univ. Press, 1985), pp. 257–
295.

[43] Restricting production was tried in some of the programs created by the National Recovery Act. They had mixed economic success and fared badly before the Supreme
Court. Thus the Court declared the National Industrial Recovery Act unconstitutional
in *Schechter v. United States* (1935) 295 U.S. 495.

[44] Hanson, *The Democratic Imagination*, p. 258.

would assure profitable production, which would assure stable wages, which would assure continued consumption, and all these in combination would ease potential tensions between capital and labor, even though most workers might never become independent in the civic republican sense.[45] With hindsight, this conclusion seems almost inevitable. But the strategy of fostering consumerism while letting republicanism take care of itself was probably not much noticed during the Depression and World War II, because bankruptcies and unemployment in the first reined in private consumption, and military production during the second left little industrial capacity for satisfying private wants.

Postwar Commitments

Political support for consumerism ran high after World War II. Democrats and Republicans alike assumed that hardships experienced during the Depression had convinced many Americans that Washington should guide the economy more successfully than Republican politicians there had done in the 1920s. The two parties responded somewhat differently to this challenge because they worked on behalf of different constituents. But both agreed that government should do *something* about the nation's economic problems, and that conviction usually translated into support for maintaining an economic system devoted chiefly to endless production and consumption, both mainly under private control.

Keynesianism

A preliminary order of business was to find a technical rationale for consumerism. On this score, a respectable theory justifying government projects such as those of the New Deal arrived with *The General Theory of Employment, Interest, and Money* by John Maynard Keynes in 1936.[46] There is no evidence that many New Dealers read the Englishman Keynes. But mainstream economists soon agreed that, as his book recommended, governments should stimulate consumption in order to break the cycle of boom and bust that had produced the Depression.[47] Here, finally, was a powerful economic theory whose centerpiece was consumption rather than production, demand rather than supply.

Keynes agreed with previous economists that national income is usually spent entirely on personal consumption and productive investment, that

---

[45] Ibid., p. 293.   [46] (London: Macmillan).

[47] Economists at Harvard led the way. See John K. Galbraith, "How Keynes Came to America," in Galbraith, *A Contemporary Guide to Economics, Peace and Laughter* (Boston: Beacon, 1971), pp. 43–59.

is, on commodities and services, on savings accounts, stocks, bonds, and more. But he argued, as most earlier economists had not, that there are times when some people, fearful of future economic difficulties, will hold back some of their income for safety's sake, hiding it under the proverbial mattress. Keynes called this occasional reluctance to spend and invest a *liquidity preference*.

When too many people prefer liquidity, the result is that some economic resources get removed from the system of production and distribution. Consequently, less money goes into profits and savings, the quantity of money available for business investment falls, some employees get discharged, their purchasing power drops, other business enterprises enjoy fewer sales, they in turn lay off workers, and the economy is on its way into a downward spiral that will end in an equilibrium between production and consumption that leaves many workers unemployed and many employers bankrupt.

The solution, according to Keynes, is for governments to keep track of economic indicators, to calculate from them when some people are likely to fear hard times ahead, and at crucial moments to spend enough public money to assure everyone that the economy will continue to thrive. In this way, governments can prop up personal expectations so that people will withhold little or no income from the system. Accordingly, over time, the system will maintain steady economic growth, fueled by science and technology, that will keep employment and profits up and raise everyone's standard of living from one year to the next. Indeed, if individuals will simply believe that government is determined to perpetuate economic growth, their confidence will encourage a low and economically healthy liquidity preference.

Preserving the System

Conservative economists after World War II argued that Keynes was wrong.[48] Robert Lekachman observed, more usefully, that the Keynesian recommendation, for government to actively encourage optimistic expectations of economic growth, is neither liberal nor conservative, since the requisite impetus can be provided by public or by private spending.[49]

[48] The argument was that government should manage the economy by a fiscal policy of "compensatory finance" rather than by funding public works. The move to this conclusion was traced by Herbert Stein, *The Fiscal Revolution in America* (Chicago: Univ. of Chicago Press, 1969). Stein argued that the federal tax cut of 1964 clinched the trend, and in an "Epilogue," pp. 454–468, he noted that fiscal policy based on tax adjustments is conservative because it maintains the social status quo.

[49] Robert Lekachman, *The Age of Keynes* (New York: Vintage, 1968), p. 285.

For example, during much of the New Deal, Congress knew little of Keynesian theory but funded large public programs and projects. At that time, Washington subsidized agriculture and put unemployed people to work in many ways, including the construction of dams sponsored by the Tennessee Valley Authority. A government decision to spend money on public works is therefore one way of stimulating the economy.

On the other hand, government can encourage bullish expectations by reducing taxes and leaving money in private hands, to be spent not according to government policy but as individuals wish. Stimulation aside, tax reduction has the virtue of appearing to increase personal freedom, since it provides citizens with resources they can spend as they choose on items which are anyway recommended by advertisements. The strategy of lowering taxes rather than expanding public works, Lekachman called *commercial Keynesianism*.[50] It was employed by President John F. Kennedy in 1963 and by President Ronald Reagan from 1981 to 1983.

In theory, and if timed properly, both forms of stimulation will produce the same result, which is to encourage prosperity and private confidence that it will continue. The strategies are vastly different, though, in respect of who will gain from which sort of stimulus. Some people will benefit more than others from a particular government project, and others will save inordinately from a tax cut. In this sense, to favor commercial Keynesianism, or tax reduction, rather than welfare or public education or environmental protection, is to abstain from addressing inequality and other difficulties that may arise from modern ownership and production. That is, commercial Keynesianism is partial to consumerism, to keeping the economy going but to not interfering much with the way it shapes work or social relations.

The Employment Act of 1946

Two events in 1946 exemplified America's postwar commitment to consumerism. The first was enactment of the Employment Act of 1946, when federal politicians endorsed only a limited government role in forestalling or overcoming future depressions. The second was a strike by the United Automobile Workers against General Motors, when corporate leaders successfully fended off an attempt by labor to influence production and distribution decisions in the modern economy.

In the first case, several senators proposed in January of 1945 a "Full Employment Bill" because they feared a return to economic hard times

---

[50] Ibid., pp. 285–287.

after military production would shut down and millions of able-bodied soldiers would return home.[51] This bill won Senate approval in September 1945. It stipulated that every American has a "right to work," and it obligated the federal government to guarantee that right by "assuring continuing full employment." It called upon Washington to provide funding for as many public jobs as might be necessary to reach full employment, and it said that federal money should also underwrite urban renewal, education, conservation, rural electrification, assistance to small business, health services, and more.

There was something Populistic about all of this. True, the bill accepted the inevitability of wage labor. But it insisted that every American has the right to a job, and it called for public projects that would provide resources especially to those who had few. On both planes, it aimed at increasing the economic security of ordinary people. And that is why, when the Senate bill had to be reconciled with the House "Employment and Production Act of 1946" in a conference committee in January of 1946, powerful conservative opposition, especially from the House, produced a substitute bill which removed such Populist challenges to consumerism as usual.

This substitute bill was called "The Employment Act of 1946." It passed the House and the Senate in early February and was signed into law by President Harry Truman on February 20, 1946. By removing the word "Full" from its title, the substitute bill indicated that Congress had rejected the idea that every person has a "right to work." Instead, the act promised only federal responsibility for promoting "maximum employment." Nobody knew how much that was, but it could easily include 5 or 6 percent unemployment, and having a steady supply of idle men and women would help employers keep wages down by fostering competition between those who had jobs and those who did not.

The new act also rejected the notion that government should spend money to create public jobs. It obligated Washington instead to "coordinate" government departments and to "stimulate" nonfederal investment and spending, whatever "coordinate" and "stimulate" might mean in this context. Moreover, it amended the original bill to remove its provisions for public works projects, which would have amounted to noncommercial Keynesianism. And finally, to mark a congressional commitment to private production and distribution as usual, the act provided that government

---

[51] The legislative history of this act is described in Stephen Kemp Bailey, *Congress Makes a Law: The Story Behind the Employment Act of 1946* (New York: Columbia Univ. Press, 1950).

action according to its provisions would be undertaken "in a manner calculated to foster and promote free competitive enterprise [a known entity] and the general welfare [an unknown quantity]."

Ultimately, the act's intentions were clear: It would not revamp the economic system. To this end, it would not revise the balance of existing powers by establishing new rights for the weak. True, with apparent respect for expertise and professionalism, the act created a Council of Economic Advisors to monitor economic conditions and inform the president about them. It also created a "Joint Committee on the Economic Report" within Congress to consider the Council's annual report to the president. But Congress did not authorize the Council to set economic policy, and the act did not require the Joint Committee to carry out recommendations the Council might make, so information could accumulate without policy consequences.

The United Auto Workers Versus General Motors

Corporate leaders came down twice on the side of consumerism in 1946, first during the legislative battle over the Employment Act and second during the United Automobile Workers' strike against General Motors.[52] The key issue underlying that strike was whether unions would bargain only for wages and other work conditions or whether they would also deal with social issues and economic policy. In the contest, the disparity of resources between business and labor indicated the sort of gap in incomes and power that would remain if consumerism would continue. Walter Reuther, who earned $7,000 a year, was head of the General Motors division of the UAW. Charles E. Wilson, whose annual salary was $459,000, conducted the negotiations for General Motors.

In the fall of 1945, Reuther began to argue publicly that, because accumulated demand was likely to drive up sales and profits after the war, General Motors could afford to raise assembly line wages without increasing prices on the cars it made. Furthermore, said Reuther, General Motors owed its workers such a gesture, because their weekly income

---

[52] The UAW strike is described in Frank Cormier and William J. Eaton, *Reuther* (Englewood Cliffs, N.J.: Prentice-Hall, 1970); Frederick H. Harbison and Robert Dubin, *Patterns of Union-Management Relations: United Automobile Workers, General Motors, Studebaker* (Chicago: Scientific Research Associates, 1947); Robert L. Tyler, *Walter Reuther* (Grand Rapids, Mich.: Eerdmans, 1973); William Serrin, *The Company and the Union* (New York: Vintage, 1974); Irving Howe and B. J. Widick, *The U.A.W. and Walter Reuther* (New York: Da Capo Press, 1973); and Nelson Lichtenstein, *The Most Dangerous Man in Detroit: Walter Reuther and the Fate of American Labor* (New York: Basic Books, 1995).

was falling as they lost overtime pay obtained during the war, even while prices had gone up more than the 15 percent which hourly wages were permitted to rise in wartime.

In November, General Motors offered a 10 percent wage increase to its workers. Reuther rejected this offer and called on the company to open its books so that everyone could see if a wage increase of 30 percent could be made without price increases to follow. General Motors refused to do so, arguing that access to such information was a private management function. UAW workers – 175,000 strong – then started the strike on November 21 and stayed out for 113 days.

During the strike, President Truman appointed a three-man committee to study the conflict, and the committee met to collect relevant information. General Motors refused to talk to the committee about pricing, arguing as before that how the company set prices was a management function not properly subject to outside control or inquiry.[53] In January, the committee recommended a nineteen and a half cents hourly raise without price increases. Reuther accepted this recommendation but General Motors rejected it. In February, the United Electrical Workers agreed to an eighteen and a half cents hourly raise from General Motors, and on March 13, 1946, Philip Murray, head of the CIO and Reuther's boss, settled with Wilson on the same raise for UAW workers. Two months later, General Motors hiked car prices by an average of eighty dollars per vehicle. In the economy as a whole, wartime price controls were lifted on June 30, 1946, and during the first two weeks of July, the average cost of consumer goods went up 28 percent.[54]

The moral of the story is that no change in principle disturbed the economy. The union won an hourly wage increase. But it did not gain access to the process by which corporate managers make policy decisions. General Motors executives reserved to themselves the power to decide, for example, about product prices, dividends, plant locations, types of products, schedules of production, planning, and research. A year later, management gained further protection in the Labor-Management Relations Act of 1947, known popularly as the Taft-Hartley Act. That act drew a distinction between supervisors and other workers, whose right

---

[53] Information about how General Motors set prices to maximize profits rather than production and sales emerged later. See Daniel Bell, "The Subversion of Collective Bargaining," *Commentary* (March 1960), pp. 186–188. The situation implicitly confirmed Thorstein Veblen's criticism of what he called industrial "sabotage."

[54] This figure is from William Chafe, *The Unfinished Journey: America Since World War II* (New York: Oxford Univ. Press, 1986), p. 93.

to join a union was secured by law. It therefore permitted employers to discharge supervisors for joining unions, presumably on the grounds that, since supervisors were members of the management team, they should not enroll in an organization which was, in practice, not privileged to receive management information.[55]

The National Bargain

The Employment Act of 1946 and the defense of management prerogatives in the General Motors strike testified to considerable corporate power in America. And power, after all, is not consent. Nevertheless, there are indications that these and other aspects of business as usual were somewhat accepted in principle, even by workers who knew they were unlikely ever to overcome the disparities in clout and income that marked the modern economy.

Such acceptance was embodied in what scholars have described as a *national bargain*.[56] This bargain, sometimes called "the new social contract,"[57] or a "labor-management partnership,"[58] or the "Keynesian accommodation,"[59] was a tacit understanding worked out with government sanction between organized labor and big business. It lasted until the 1970s, when rising oil prices, inflation, worldwide industrial competition, and massive federal deficits began to reshape the American economy.

Like Progressivism, the national bargain never appeared in a formal document. Still, it clearly embraced a number of principles. Corporations rather than governments were to plan and make most products. Thus there were only a few government factories, say, for making atomic bombs but not combat helicopters. Production was to be large-scale, as by the Big Three for automobiles, which permitted keeping unit costs down. Prices would not drop, since there were few companies in each

---

[55] Here is one reason why many unorganized workers today, in stores like Sears Roebuck and Wal-Mart, are not called "clerks" but "managers" of "departments" like men's clothing, cameras, housewares, and so on.

[56] See Robert B. Reich, *The Work of Nations: Preparing Ourselves for Twenty-First-Century Capitalism* (New York: Vintage, 1992), pp. 58–68.

[57] Barry Bluestone and Bennett Harrison, *The Deindustrialization of America: Plant Closings, Community Abandonment, and the Dismantling of Basic Industry* (New York: Basic Books, 1982), p. 138.

[58] Chafe, *The Unfinished Journey*, p. 92.

[59] Samuel Bowles and Herbert Gintis, *Democracy and Capitalism: Property, Community, and the Contradictions of Modern Social Thought* (London: Routledge and Kegan Paul, 1986), pp. 55–62.

field and little competition from abroad. Profits would therefore be high, and some of them would go into research, investment, retooling, annual model changes, advertising, and other company expenses. But some profits would be allocated to workers, to provide steady and well-paid industrial jobs. In return for receiving those jobs, unions would rarely strike, which helped keep production and profits up.

In all this, government would play a constructive role indirectly. It would not participate in arrangements worked out by management and labor. But it would help both by smoothing out the business cycle, as when President Kennedy sponsored a tax cut. In the domestic policy realm, government would spend mainly on popular programs, such as highway construction, and would provide an income tax exemption for interest on mortgage loans, both of which subsidized suburbia and encouraged consumers to buy cars and houses. Defense spending was also useful. It propped up profits and wages by purchasing a substantial part of corporate output, and it facilitated the development of spin-off commodities such as Corningware, personal computers, and Boeing's civilian passenger planes.

The national bargain confirmed that workers accepted wage labor as a normal condition of life and that they expected few promotions on the job but only occasional hourly pay increases. Apparently, while accepting what was, after all, an inferior position in the overall system, workers regarded their labor as the means to a happier side of life, which focused on consumerism. In this sense, assembly line boredom and economic dependence were prices a worker paid for a private house, two-car living, color television, regular vacations, and so forth. And material gains did come steadily.

Here, then, was a new *harmony of interests* scheme, wherein inequality of economic control was accepted because the system churned out commodities that workers could afford to buy. Basic satisfaction with such a status quo was expressed in 1955 by George Meany, president of the AFL-CIO, when he exchanged views with Charles Sligh, chairman of the board of the National Association of Manufacturers. Speaking of what he called a "mutuality of interests," Meany stated labor's support for the profit system, for free enterprise, for management's right to manage, and for the corporate world's role of providing employment to workers. He then concluded that the only disagreement left between labor and management was a matter of what share workers should receive of the wealth produced by any particular company. He was confident, however, that both sides were intelligent enough to resolve that issue "in a fair, square

American way."[60] Sligh's remarks were less fulsome about unions than Meany was about free enterprise and management.[61] That is, he probably admired workers more than he did their getting organized. Nevertheless, he spoke cordially.

The Cold War

While the national bargain lasted, America's disdain for China and the Soviet Union provided a constant source of enthusiasm for consumerism. Americans regarded the United States as more free politically than Communist states were, with their scorn for individual rights, their ubiquitous secret police forces, their terrifying concentration camps, and their government control of mass media.[62] On this score, republican practices in America, although never perfect, were surely superior to communism. In addition, lower standards of living in all Communist countries seemed to indicate that free enterprise generated better material results than those produced by central planning. This point was widely publicized when, for example, Vice President Richard Nixon "debated" Premier Nikita Khrushchev among the kitchen appliances on display in America's exhibition at Moscow's World Fair in 1959.[63]

Godfrey Hodgson analyzed these and other points of faith in America's economy as a central theme in what he called "the ideology of the liberal consensus" that reigned in America during the Cold War.[64] Hodgson used the term *liberalism* not as a counterpoint to conservatism but to denote the shared belief of most Americans that, within the Western political tradition, a bourgeois, democratic society was better than monarchy or aristocracy on one side and communism or fascism on the other.

The liberal ideology had six assumptions, according to Hodgson. First, that American capitalism was no longer as brutal and exclusive as it had been in the nineteenth century, that it had become democratic and enjoyed

---

[60] George Meany, "What Organized Labor Expects of Management" (1956), in Leon Stein and Philip Taft (eds.), *The Management of Workers, Selected Arguments* (New York: Arno and the *New York Times*, 1971), pp. 10–11.

[61] Charles R. Sligh, "What Management Expects of Organized Labor" (1956), in ibid., pp. 12–19.

[62] In one of this era's typical textbooks, these were some of the classic characteristics of totalitarianism according to Carl J. Friedrich and Zbigniew K. Brzezinski, *Totalitarianism, Dictatorship and Autocracy* (New York: Praeger, 1956), pp. 3–13.

[63] The debate is described in Stephen E. Ambrose, *Nixon: The Education of a Politician, 1913–1962* (New York: Simon and Schuster, 1987), pp. 523–525.

[64] Godfrey Hodgson, *America in Our Time: From World War II to Nixon, What Happened and Why* (New York: Vintage, 1976), pp. 67–98.

the capacity for being socially just. Second, that the key to capitalist success was economic growth which permits wide distribution of products. Third, that a natural harmony of interests existed in America as workers had become more like middle-class people. Fourth, that social problems, were they to arise, could be solved by research and by the application of administrative expertise and public funding. Fifth, that the main threat to this "beneficent system" came from international Marxism. And sixth, that Americans saw themselves as charged with a moral mission in the world, to spread the gospel of a free enterprise system which they regarded as effective and equitable.[65]

It was an instructive list. Without Hodgson using the term, liberalism as he described it implied that Americans need not exercise much Citizenship III, because justice would flow mainly from letting the economy take its normal course. If a social problem were to arise, it could be solved chiefly by technical means, with research, expertise, and the appropriate funding. Again, the consensus assumed that little republican activism was required. And finally, the main threat to continued happiness was not located at home, say, in poverty or the denial of civil rights or gender discrimination or destruction of the environment. Instead, the main danger resided abroad, in faraway left-wing states that expressed doctrinaire hostility to the American way of life.

What Hodgson described, in short, was a set of beliefs which assumed that a society dedicated to consumerism worked well and would continue to do so almost automatically. This was the confidence that began to wear thin, for some people, as civil rights demonstrations and the Vietnam War ground on during the 1960s. And when, in the 1970s, the national bargain began to unravel for reasons, as we shall see, unrelated to communism and, to some commentators, beyond technical repair.

Republicanism and Consumerism

The multiplication in recent years of groups advocating environmental protection and constraints on globalization is an indication that the consensus on consumerism is less persuasive than it used to be. But before

---

[65] Ibid., p. 76. Leaders subscribed enthusiastically to this mission. For example, see the early statement of America's Cold War doctrine of containment in X [George F. Kennan], "The Sources of Soviet Conduct," *Foreign Affairs* (July 1947), pp. 566–582. In his closing paragraph, Kennan thanked Providence for the great challenge of Russian hostility, saying it would make Americans coalesce and accept "the responsibilities of moral and political leadership that history plainly intended them to bear."

considering why this is so, we should reflect on how the ideals of republicanism and consumerism coexisted uneasily after World War II. Both were present and both were acceptable during the national bargain's heyday. But the two were also, to some extent, incompatible, and there was the rub.

Being a Good Citizen

By 1950 or so, the republican story in America assumed that the social role of *good citizen* rested upon elements of Citizenship I, II, and III. The good citizen obeys his or her country's laws, participates politically when authorized to do so, and does so virtuously, when that is necessary, to create or maintain laws that characterize a good state. Presumably, people will feel comfortable about being citizens and will accept the responsibilities of that office when they see that they live in a country whose basic institutions permit freedom, reward effort, foster public well-being, and therefore deserve loyalty and support.

Throughout twentieth-century America, this sort of citizenship was a mainstream ideal. Thus even before Hodgson, Louis Hartz claimed that America had long fostered a *liberal tradition*.[66] What he meant was that Americans took from Europe mainly an admiration for middle-class, democratic values. At the same time, they mostly abandoned whatever devotion some of them, as immigrants, may have had to an earlier political life, to monarchy, aristocracy, socialism, communism, fascism, and exclusive nationalism. Here was Hartz's way of explaining what historians call American exceptionalism. In his case, it was an explanation for why, unlike in much of Europe, America's major parties agreed on cardinal principles such as support for the Constitution, for open and frequent elections, for natural rights, for political party competition, for private property, and for individualism rather than social ranks.

Although Hartz did not dwell on it, practicing the liberal tradition depends on good citizenship. First, because citizens, be they Republicans or Democrats, consent to obey the laws their representatives enact. Citizens thereby contribute to maintaining public order and stability. Second, because the same citizens are responsible for doing the work of democracy's smallest public office. Here, they must track the course of public affairs, and they must act virtuously so that the political process will produce good social results.

---

[66] See his *The Liberal Tradition in America* (New York: Harcourt, Brace, and World, 1955).

Louis Brandeis's oft-quoted Supreme Court dissent in *Olmstead v. United States* (1927).[71] It follows that low utilization of participation rights may indicate only that many of the inactive are satisfied with America as it is, in which case they may be endorsing the status quo when they stay home rather than join organizations or vote. Thus research shows that most Americans still believe in the "American Dream." That is, they believe their country rewards hard work and integrity, regardless of how government and politics may inspire citizens less than in the past.[72]

The point seems obvious from abroad, because immigrants continue to flock to America. Almost 28 million legal immigrants arrived between 1941 and 2000,[73] and 5 million "undocumented aliens" were present in 1996 according to estimates made by the Immigration and Naturalization Service.[74] The point is also obvious at home. As Richard Reeves remarked in 1982 after retracing Tocqueville's footsteps through America, "not a single person I met talked about leaving the United States."[75]

Two Sorts of Good People

By definition, it is the good person who will become a good citizen, who will use well the rights of Citizenship II to serve the goals of Citizenship III. Yet in modern America there are three ways of thinking about how to be a good person, and not all of them lead to civic activism. The first, and oldest, emphasizes righteousness. Thus most Americans say they believe in God and try to treat other people decently. On this score, Americans are more likely to join a church and more likely to attend prayer services than people in other industrialized nations.[76]

However, most theological considerations that animate Americans lead them to charitable rather than political works. This is partly because, due to separation of church and state in the First Amendment, the country tends to try not to let religious convictions fuel public controversies. Prohibition was an early twentieth-century exception to this rule; the civil

---

[71] 277 U.S. 438. "The makers of our Constitution undertook to secure conditions favorable to the pursuit of happiness.... They conferred, as against the Government, the right to be let alone" (p. 478).

[72] Lipset, *American Exceptionalism*, pp. 281–282.

[73] *Statistical Abstract of the United States* (Washington, D.C.: U.S. Census Bureau, 2002), p. 10.

[74] Ibid. (1997), p. 12.

[75] Richard Reeves, *American Journey: Travelling with Tocqueville in Search of Democracy in America* (New York: Touchstone, 1982), p. 239.

[76] See Lipset, *American Exceptionalism*, pp. 278–280.

Reality, however, is more ambiguous than all this. Americans have divided in their attitudes toward the ʃ zenship II. Native Americans, women, and African Ame been excluded from Citizenship II were included, by con̨ vention or by constitutional amendments, as the twentiet on. Today, those steps toward inclusion are widely regarde tice long denied. But many people now permitted to vote to do so, and some Americans worry that their absence o may constitute a dangerous dereliction of civic duty.

So, on the one hand, study groups such as the Nationɛ on Civic Renewal have complained that Americans have tion of spectators and should be encouraged to use their to vote and join civic organizations more frequently.[67]] tist Robert Putnam agreed and claimed that "civic engagen 1965 and 1985 dropped by 25 to 50 percent, especially in such as the Elks, the PTA, the League of Women Voters, the bor unions, bowling leagues, sports clubs, and professional Putnam held that enthusiasm for joining such groups ɣ because television keeps Americans at home and apar neighbors.[68] Sociologist Seymour Martin Lipset describ Americans as increasingly cynical with regard to public ins cording to his data, they voluntarily maintain more church than people do in other Western countries, but their confider ment has dropped steadily since the mid-1960s.[69] It cannot be that voting rates dropped too.[70]

On the other hand, must Americans get involved in comm by exercising the rights of Citizenship II? After all, one of t most precious rights is the right to be left alone, highlighte

[67] See the Commission's report, *Nation of Spectators: How Civic Disengag America and What We Can Do About It* (Washington, D.C.: The Nation on Civic Renewal, 1998).

[68] Robert D. Putnam, "Bowling Alone: America's Declining Social Capit *Democracy* (January 1995), pp. 65–78. Major themes in this article were eɔ basis of further research in Putnam, *Bowling Alone: The Collapse and Reviɔ Community* (New York: Simon and Schuster, 2000).

[69] Seymour Martin Lipset, *American Exceptionalism: A Double-Edged Swoɾ Norton, 1996), pp. 279, 282.

[70] As a percentage of the voting age population, turnouts for presidential elec 1976, and 1996 were 62.6 percent, 53.5 percent, and 49 percent respec House of Representatives in 1960, 1976, and 1996, the turnouts were 48.9 percent, and 45.8 percent. See *Statistical Abstract of the United States* D.C.: U.S. Census Bureau, 2000), p. 301.

rights movement after World War II was another; and now it is the debate over abortion that challenges the principle of separation.

Apart from righteousness, a second version of the good life in modern America revolves around each person's secular potential for personal happiness. Here, the point is to live well and get ahead. The main theme is consumerism or the same practice by any other name. One seeks to work honestly and soberly, to get paid well, to use one's income to buy commodities, and to enjoy them, either alone or with friends and family. A few will even work hard and earn so much that they will be excused from working further although continuing to consume indefinitely.

Work is often arduous and sometimes boring. It is worth noting, then, that Americans may so aspire to material happiness that they will seek more opportunity to work rather than less. One clue to this preference is found in productivity statistics. Productivity went up after World War II, justifying wage hikes that made it possible, in theory at least, for workers to receive a constant income while working fewer hours as time passed. Instead, during the same years, hours of leisure declined while people worked more.[77] Thus between 1969 and 1987, annual hours of paid employment per worker rose by close to 10 percent.

Part of this increase occurred because some employers asked employees to accept overtime work, which costs companies less than hiring additional people who need training.[78] But longer workdays were also caused by consumerism, by the ability of business to disseminate images that stimulate an endless progression of wants. To satisfy these wants, some people worked longer hours, and that led to real improvements in the material standard of American living, that is, to acquiring more washing machines, more microwave ovens, more air conditioners, more color televisions, and larger homes.[79]

So Americans pursue affluence as an acceptable form of living well. However, not just advertisements encourage citizens to think that buying and consuming constitute a good life. Leaders of all stripes have joined the chorus and praise a steadily rising gross national product (GNP) for its ability to solve almost every conceivable problem that might affect the American way of life. As John Kenneth Galbraith observed, "Republicans

---

[77] This is the point of departure for Juliet B. Schor, *The Overworked American: The Unexpected Decline of Leisure* (New York: Basic Books, 1992).

[78] The preference of employers for overtime work is explained in William Greider, *One World, Ready or Not: The Manic Logic of Global Capitalism* (New York: Touchstone, 1997), p. 302.

[79] Ibid., p. 111.

and Democrats, right or left...the Chairman of the Americans for
Democratic Action...[and] the President of the United States Chamber
of Commerce" all believe that a steady supply of things will ease unemployment, advance equality, help maintain tax revenues, and finance the
national defense.[80]

Of course, public policy aimed at increasing GNP can work only if
people will buy the goods that are made. And so citizens are constantly
reminded, by opinion leaders in every realm, that a passion for consuming
is not only patriotic but morally sound.[81] Such leaders know that if shopping were to falter, economic disaster would quickly follow. How convenient for consumerism, then, that in 1971 the federal government moved
Washington's Birthday, Memorial Day, Columbus Day, and Veterans'
Day to Mondays so that three-day weekends would permit Americans
to spend more time and money on shopping and leisure.[82]

The Good Republican Person

To complement the theological and economic versions of living well in
America, there is the republican vision of a life spent in spiritual and
material decency but punctuated on important occasions by using the
rights of Citizenship II to advance the public interest. In this vision, a good
person is entitled to promote goodness privately through religion and
economic enterprise. But he or she is also obliged to consider public issues
and, from time to time, come down politically on the side of fostering
well-being for all members of the community.

Here, finally, is the formula for Citizenship III. Economist Lester
Thurow had it in mind when he argued that "to be workable, a democracy [in America, at least] assumes that public decisions are made in
a framework where there is a substantial majority of concerned but
disinterested citizens who will prevent policies from being shaped by those

---

[80] Galbraith, *The Affluent Society* (New York: Mentor, 1958), pp. 101–102. Galbraith observed the passion for promoting GNP in the 1950s, but most political elites continued to
express the same enthusiasm even later. For example, see President Bill Clinton's secretary
of labor Robert Reich, *The Work of Nations*, passim.

[81] "Belt Tightening Seen as Threat to the Economy," *New York Times* (July 15, 2001), pp. A1,
20.

[82] The decision was made for Washington, D.C., and federal workers in 1968. It took effect
in 1971. Most states quickly followed suit. For consumerism's response, see "Johnson
Signs Bill Making 4 Holidays Fall on Mondays," *New York Times* (June 29, 1968), p. A29:
" 'This is the greatest thing that has happened to the travel industry since the invention of
the automobile,' said Clarence A. Arata, president of the National Association of Travel
Organizations."

with direct economic self-interests." In the circumstances, he continued, "Decisions in the interests of the general welfare are supposed to be produced by those concerned but disinterested citizens. They are to arbitrate and judge the disputes of the interested parties."[83]

Habits of the Heart

So Americans believe in several elements of good citizenship and in various components of a good life. The problem is that, admirable as these things may seem when considered separately, they do not, as social building blocks, fit together well. Their failure to do so is not simply a logical quandary, because the lack of fit produces tangible difficulties. Some of these were described in *Habits of the Heart* (1986), a sociological study which asked, as its central question, whether or not private motives in America encourage or discourage people from taking part in public life as citizens.[84]

The authors of *Habits* interviewed middle-class people, so the citizens they described did not suffer from exclusion and did not lack economic resources to practice what we have called Citizenship III. In this sense, the people studied in *Habits* could live lives of republican virtue. Furthermore, they said that they wanted to lead such lives. They wanted to live well and to serve others; they wanted to connect to neighbors, whose social differences they respected; and they wanted to work together with those neighbors to maintain decent communities. So why were they hardpressed to do so?

To tell this story simply, *Habits* recast the people its authors interviewed as a small number of composite figures, including a business manager, a public relations expert, a civic activist, and a therapist. Regardless of their different occupations, these characters all suffered the same inability to know exactly what they should do to realize their ideal of good citizenship.

---

[83] Lester Thurow, *The Zero-Sum Society: Distribution and the Possibilities for Economic Change* (New York: Basic Books, 1980), p. 16. See also historian Alan Brinkley, *Liberalism and Its Discontents* (Cambridge: Harvard Univ. Press, 1998), p. 162:

> An effective democracy requires more from its citizens and its leaders than pragmatic calculations of immediate self-interest. It requires reflection – a willingness to examine the world and one's place in it, an openness to knowledge of oneself and one's society, a capacity to evaluate the claims of leaders critically and to balance them against a moral compass of one's own.

[84] Robert N. Bellah, Richard Madsen, William M. Sullivan, Ann Suidler, and Steven M. Tipton, *Habits of the Heart: Individualism and Commitment in American Life* (New York: Harper and Row, 1986), pp. vii–viii.

The problem started from a belief that everyone is entitled to choose a lifestyle. This the people in *Habits* held to be the hallmark freedom of modern society. But they did not know which values to choose for themselves, and if they did choose, they could not be sure that other citizens would make similar choices. In which case, it was not clear to them that a modern community existed. After all, a community properly defined consists of people who share at least some values, yet in modern life one may be surrounded by neighbors with disparate lifestyles. Where that is so, if citizens would trouble themselves to act on behalf of people not animated by their values, it is not clear that those people would join the activists or even appreciate their efforts.

Habits claimed that this sort of modern uncertainty is rooted in the language by which its American subjects tried to make sense of their lives. This language consists of three historic strands of vocabulary, concepts, and values, originating in the Bible, in republicanism, and in individualism, where individualism has lately become problematic to the point of driving people apart.

Biblical terms have long prescribed respect for all people whom God creates, and republicanism has long encouraged the same consideration toward interests shared by the community. Rounding out the picture, said *Habits*, individualism was the commendable nineteenth-century lifestyle of citizens not assigned by their communities to some particular place or status. Here was an antifeudal element in American life that fostered social ties when individuals voluntarily joined a wide range of civic-minded organizations and churches.

Then came the rise of a twentieth-century sort of individualism that *Habits* called "bureaucratic consumer capitalism." Here was a set of practices so powerful as to encourage Americans to accept the shape of economic life as natural and try to adapt to it. Within this social setting, which we have called consumerism, the choice of lifestyles described by *Habits* takes place. Thus the economy of ceaseless production and marketing encourages men and women to be whatever they want to be. Marketeers hope, of course, that such people will regard individual happiness as chiefly the outcome of an infinite number of shopping permutations which are available from the enormous variety of goods and services thrown up by an affluent society. In this way, consumerism does not deny other values but mostly leaves them aside.

Yet to leave aside old values is not a painless matter of benign neglect but a major cause of acute anxiety. For the impulse of modern individualism leads men and women on the job to serve the needs of an economic system, making more widgets and more profits, before they can go home and try to infuse the remaining hours of their days with biblical and republican values. And at home, even when they dwell upon earlier values, they can never be sure that strong commitment to traditional habits of the heart will not cause them to miss out on some exciting and rewarding modern opportunity available only to those who, during the age of consumerism, strike out on their own.

A Dissent

In short, consumerism in America after World War II did not reject republican citizenship so much as it displaced that ideal with other values that were widely accepted as defining a good life. With those circumstances in mind, *Habits of the Heart* concluded that Americans should redress the balance between individualism and the languages of biblical morality and republican virtue. Not everyone agreed that such an imbalance existed. For example, some took the collapse of communism in Russia and Eastern Europe as proof that America's combination of politics and economics, as described by what Hodgson called the liberal consensus, was not only good for America but worth exporting to the rest of the world. As Francis Fukuyama proclaimed in "The End of History?" (1989), the Cold War's conclusion marked an American triumph in the sense that there remained on the world stage only one persuasive idea, which he called the Western idea.[85]

And what was that idea? That "liberal democracy in the political sphere" can be combined successfully with "easy access to VCRs and stereos in the economic." With this formulation, Fukuyama claimed that politics and economics in America were entirely compatible. *Habits of the Heart* argued instead that, in some respects, these two realms did not mesh well. Let us turn, then, to what *Habits of the Heart* regarded as a mismatch and see that what troubled the scholars who wrote that book can eventually suggest to us how to fashion a standard of Citizenship III fit for the twenty-first century.

[85] Francis Fukuyama, "The End of History?" *National Interest* (Summer 1989), p. 8. See also Francis Fukuyama, *The End of History and the Last Man* (New York: Free Press, 1992).

7

The Costs of Consumerism

During the twentieth century, consumerism became increasingly popular in America. Modern jobs and new products lifted many people out of hardship and some out of poverty. This progress encouraged Fukuyama to assume that democratic politics and capitalist economics fit together fairly comfortably and mainly automatically. However, while most people admired economic success, some saw it as generating social costs that made good citizenship hard to conceive and difficult to practice. Here was the clash of republican aims and consumerist realities that *Habits of the Heart* noticed, a matter of economic trends that frustrate at least some political expectations.

For our story, the civic shortfall emphasized in *Habits of the Heart* has important consequences that are worth considering now. Yet the subject is vast and the literature that explores it is endless. Moreover, many of the predicaments that flow from consumerism are familiar, in which case to describe them here is to risk repeating what readers know from elsewhere. Still, to see something of how many aspects of American life are now linked to modern ways of getting and spending, and to gain a sense of civic direction and urgency, let us use this chapter to review some of consumerism's costs. Insofar as these endanger individual and collective well-being, we will in Chapters 8 and 9 consider how, via Citizenship III, to avoid or minimize such dangers, or others like them.

Kinds of Issues

Many Americans worry little about consumerism's effects. Instead, they talk mainly about three kinds of political issues. The first finds most people standing in opposing camps on, for example, homosexuality, abortion, drugs, affirmative action, and the teaching of evolution. To reach broader agreement on such matters would require a great deal of education and persuasion, to the point where some people would change their minds and join their opponents. When the difficulty is for citizens to decide what is right or wrong, disagreements tend to persist.

A second kind of political issue evokes less disagreement, with preferences sometimes shared by parallel or overlapping majorities of Americans. Yet citizens who may largely agree on, say, wilderness preservation, gun control, and adequate access to medical care cannot easily achieve the public policies they want in a complicated society. Progress in such areas, as Martin Luther King, Jr., understood, requires not only education and persuasion but that some passive people will overcome their indifference to others in distress. Here the difficulty is not so much to calculate what is right or wrong, but to inspire a decisive number of citizens to rise at crucial moments and insist that government will do what they believe it should.

A third sort of issue involves the allocation of public resources to competing interest groups. Here representatives of the rich and the poor, the young and the old, the unions and the industrialists, and many more haggle endlessly over budgets and governmental regulations. Most participants in such skirmishes advance arguments about right and wrong as a way of justifying what they regard as their fair share of tax revenues or legal loopholes. Compromises based on moral half loaves in this realm are common and expected.

The Fourth Kind of Issue

Against a backdrop of such concern for public affairs, most Americans invent, produce, promote, sell, purchase, and consume as usual. That being so, various aspects of consumerism – including research and development, technological upgrading, superstores, fast-food restaurants, an active stock market, and rising gross national product – routinely characterize the American experience. In the quest for affluence, much of this seems praiseworthy. Yet consumerism as a way of life increasingly worries some people, who talk about dissonance between how citizens should build a good society and how the same people make and sell, get and spend.

From such talk there emerges a fourth kind of political issue. Percentage-wise, not many Americans take this type of issue seriously. Moreover, most major party candidates and officeholders prefer to discuss standard quandaries relating, for example, to Social Security, Medicare, education, national defense, and family values. Still, some citizens are convinced that seemingly commendable economic activity by individuals, be they workers or managers, engineers or financiers, can generate undesirable social results. This is especially likely to occur when many people do not understand that such results flow from everyone pursuing his or her business as usual.

Issues of the fourth kind are special, then, because they entail few differences of opinion. In fact, issues of the fourth kind challenge what happens when most Americans do what almost everyone thinks of as right, acting out economic roles which seem popularly justified. It follows that the problem for people who wish to raise such issues is to promote a wider understanding of how, even while consumerism gives Americans much to admire, it also produces disagreeable consequences. To appreciate the connection would encourage those in the know to use Citizenship III to avoid such consequences and thereby increase public well-being.

On the road to such an understanding, complacency is the chief cause for advancing slowly. There is plenty of evidence that consumerist behavior causes many difficulties in American life, in realms from family relations to leisure, from religion to education, from military service to professional ethics, from the quality of products to the conditions of work. In fact, one difficulty after another indicates that economic efforts and choices may produce short-term happiness for some but, at the same time, cause long-term damage to those same people, to others, and to the world they live in. If we will note now just some of the danger signals, as a sample of many which space does not permit us to discuss here, we may begin to appreciate the civic challenge they pose.

Economic Growth

Since the Great Depression, many economists, most citizens, and almost all successful politicians have agreed that America's well-being can best be served by government fostering economic growth. During World War II, federal statisticians began to portray such growth by an annual index called gross national product. GNP measures, roughly speaking, the income earned by all Americans together, on whatever goods and services they and their investments produce.[1] When GNP grows in one year faster

---

[1] Paul A. Samuelson and William D. Nordhaus, *Economics*, 13th ed. (New York: McGraw-Hill, 1989), pp. 77–81. Economists now speak of Gross Domestic Product (GDP) to refer

than the number of Americans rises, the nation is said to be better off than previously. As economist Paul Krugman says, "Depression, runaway inflation, or civil war can make a country poor, but only productivity growth can make it rich."[2]

Goods and Bads

In truth, however, as Krugman knows, an increase in GNP does not necessarily indicate a gain in social well-being. Of course, adding up the money values of goods and services in one index is workable and therefore tempting for economists, bureaucrats, and politicians. But doing so combines with good items those that are bad.[3] Some of these are obvious, like cigarettes.

What some economists understand, accordingly, is that policy makers may act unwisely if they seek to promote well-being by monitoring an index which suggests that people are better off whether money is spent on chocolates or on public libraries. For example, the purchase of one dollar's worth of chocolates will raise GNP by that amount and please someone in the short run. But it may also require the same person to pay another dollar for dental care, which is a spillover effect that increases GNP, adds nothing to previous well-being, and merely repairs the damage caused by eating chocolates in the first place.[4]

To explain the presence of "bads" such as tooth decay, economists sometimes speak of *externalities*. When someone purchases a car, for example, he or she apparently pays, from personal income, for the production and operating costs of that car. But using the car contributes to traffic congestion, in which case the original purchase creates discomfort and even danger for other drivers. Furthermore, the resolution of such external difficulties may require taxpayers to furnish public money for expensive road solutions. These expenditures, to cover goods and services supplied by private contractors, will register in GNP as signifying increased social

---

to that part of output produced within the United States and not including American income from activities and investments abroad. For example, David Begg, Stanley Fischer, and Roger Dornbusch, *Economics*, 2nd ed. (New York: McGraw-Hill, 1987), pp. 424–433.

[2] Paul Krugman, *Peddling Prosperity: Economic Sense and Nonsense in the Age of Diminished Expectations* (New York: Norton, 1994), p. 56.

[3] For a clear analysis of this inconsistency and its consequences, see Clifford Cobb, Ted Halstead, and Jonathan Rowe, "If the GDP Is Up, Why Is America Down?" *Atlantic Monthly* (October 1995), pp. 59–78.

[4] On spillover effects, see E. J. Mishan, *The Costs of Economic Growth*, rev. ed. (London: Weidenfeld and Nicolson, 1993), pp. 22–29.

well-being. They represent, however, only compensation for strain and hardship which private commodities force upon the community.

On this score, pollution costs are painful instances of externalities, such as when fertilizer runoff from private crop lands may contaminate public streams and compel government to pay for cleanup efforts which, although representing no net gain in social well-being, seem to represent as much when they enter GNP. In 1992, companies dealing with toxic-waste storage, water purification, air scrubbing, and other cleanup activities accounted for $86 billion worth of annual economic activity in America.[5] Their revenue was a boon to GNP but repaired only some of the damage caused mostly by private production and consumption.

Priceless Goods

So goods that are worth money are not necessarily good. GNP is also misleading, however, because it ignores some goods that are neither bought nor sold and therefore do not appear in a price-based index of growth.[6] Thus some items which are not priced but may contribute nonetheless to human well-being in a traditional society may disappear as people move on to money making.[7] For example, a middle-class mother who decides to work full time in an office will have less time to spend with her children than her homemaker mother did, thereby requiring the children to attend a day care center. In that case, the working mother may be happier for spending time outside the home, and her happiness deserves consideration as an enlargement of personal well-being. But her increased day care expenditures will count in GNP as an addition to national wealth whereas, in truth, they may represent no net gain, and perhaps even a loss, of well-being in the realm of child rearing.[8]

---

[5] Joshua Karliner, *The Corporate Planet: Ecology and Politics in the Age of Globalization* (San Francisco: Sierra Club Books, 1997), p. 35. On clean-up technology, see Curtis Moore and Alan Miller, *Green Gold: Japan, Germany, the United States, and the Race for Environmental Technology* (Boston: Beacon, 1994).

[6] See the discussion in Fred Block, *Postindustrial Possibilities: A Critique of Economic Discourse* (Berkeley: Univ. of California Press, 1990), pp. 156–168.

[7] See the examples in George P. Brockway, *The End of Economic Man*, 3rd ed. (New York: Norton, 1995), p. 99.

[8] This is a debatable example. Some day care centers may do more for their children than the children's own mothers (or fathers) can do. Furthermore, a woman (or man) who spends hour after hour with demanding children can become so miserable as to make them miserable also. On the other hand, if there is controversy here, it demonstrates the point that GNP adds up prices and cannot take into account what people think those prices may or may not represent for well-being.

Natural Resources

In the limited world that GNP describes, many people who make products and provide services do so by using resources such as fresh water, oil, iron, coal, old-growth timber, chromium, tin, nickel, and so forth. In a rational accounting system, we would subtract the value of natural resources used for such purposes from a nation's store of economic capital, indicating that they will cost something to replace or that they are gone forever.[9] Such accounting might help people to understand that these materials should be used more sparingly until required by future generations. Instead, the profits gained from resource extraction, use, and sale appear in GNP as an apparent increase in well-being. And so, in the language of commerce, billions of gallons of oil are "produced" each year in places like Texas and Kuwait whereas, in fact, when used as fuel the same gallons are destroyed.[10]

The New Economy

As an index, GNP does not register well-being but only the prices charged for one year's worth of goods and services. However, GNP also says nothing about how economic institutions, and especially great corporations, make goods and create prices over time. Yet since the 1970s, new production trends, often associated with what is called *globalization*, have seriously altered the shape of getting and spending for many Americans. We should consider, then, how no matter what level the sum total of prices will reach, those trends may cause such social turmoil as to diminish national well-being.

The World of Work

A New Economy appeared in America when foreign products came to undersell their domestic equivalents, thereby compelling American companies to compete more energetically than before on a global scale. Japanese products most obviously led the way. In 1960, Japan exported fewer than 40,000 cars across the world. But in 1980, Japan exported 6,000,000 cars, including 2,300,000 to the United States alone.[11] The trend was

---

[9] On some of the irreplaceable values lost when natural conditions are violated, see Bill McKibben, *The End of Nature* (New York: Doubleday, 1989).

[10] Garrett Hardin, *Living Within Limits: Ecology, Economics, and Population Taboos* (New York: Oxford Univ. Press, 1993), pp. 48–49.

[11] Barry Bluestone, "In Support of the Deindustrialization Thesis," in Paul D. Staudohar and Holly E. Brown (eds.), *Deindustrialization and Plant Closure* (Lexington, Mass.: D. R. Heath, 1987), p. 9.

clear. By 1979, imports into America as a percentage of all manufactured goods produced at home had reached 37.8 percent, as opposed to only 10.8 percent in 1959.[12]

Some scholars argue that foreign competitors caused a massive *deindustrialization* in America, by which they mean a closing down of many manufacturing facilities in basic industries.[13] For example, locally owned factories produced in 1965 all the color televisions sold in America. But as time passed, work in one such factory after another ceased, so that in 1992, Zenith transferred the last American production of color televisions from Springfield, Massachusetts, to Reynosa, Mexico.[14] Similarly, during the 1970s and 1980s, substantial portions of the nation's industrial capacity were lost in manufacturing sectors such as tires and inner tubes, household appliances, clothing, footwear, machine tools, motor vehicles and parts, and chemicals.[15]

Along these lines, American companies such as Whirlpool, General Electric, IBM, Ford, Motorola, Nike, and General Motors engaged in *downsizing* their workforce at home and *outsourcing* much of their production. Enormous savings accrued to corporate balance sheets. For example, when American electrical workers were earning $4.10 per hour in the mid-1970s, comparable workers were earning $.17 per hour in Indonesia, $.26 per hour in Thailand, and $.32 per hour in the Philippines.[16] Similarly, pay levels for 1984 in manufacturing abroad as a percentage of similar American wages in the same year were 9 percent in Brazil, 10 percent in South Korea, 13 percent in Mexico, and 15 percent in Taiwan.[17] By 1994, America's hourly labor costs in manufacturing averaged $16.40, as opposed to $1.80 in Hungary, $1.10 in the Czech Republic, and $.50 in China.[18]

---

[12] Barry Bluestone and Bennett Harrison, *The Great U-Turn: Corporate Restructuring and the Polarizing of America* (New York: Basic Books, 1988), p. 9.

[13] Barry Bluestone and Bennett Harrison, *The Deindustrialization of America: Plant Closings, Community Abandonment, and the Dismantling of Basic Industry* (New York: Basic Books, 1982), p. 6.

[14] Donald L. Barlett and James B. Steele, *America: What Went Wrong?* (Kansas City: Andrews and McMeel, 1992), p. 35.

[15] Robert B. Reich, *The Work of Nations: Preparing Ourselves for Twenty-First-Century Capitalism* (New York: Vintage, 1992), p. 72, n. 6.

[16] Paul Blumberg, *Inequality in an Age of Decline* (New York: Oxford Univ. Press, 1980), p. 156.

[17] "Introduction," in Staudohar and Brown (eds.), *Deindustrialization and Plant Closure*, p. xx.

[18] William Greider, *One World, Ready or Not: The Manic Logic of Global Capitalism* (New York: Touchstone, 1997), p. 477.

Optimists claimed that workers who got laid off in America soon managed to find other employment. After all, government statistics indicated that business was creating millions of jobs.[19] Pessimists observed that many of the new jobs, such as hamburger flipping at McDonald's, paid less than those lost in manufacturing, such as on automobile assembly lines.[20] Partly this was because the fastest growing areas of employment were service occupations such as cashier, janitor, truck driver, waiter and waitress, retail salesperson, kindergarten and elementary school teacher, nurse's aide and orderly.[21] Furthermore, critics pointed out that, to minimize production costs, employers assigned much of the new work to *contingent labor* who might be temporary or part-time workers, employees of subcontractors, and homeworkers. Because such workers lacked the assurance of long-term employment, they were unlikely to join unions, to bargain powerfully, to receive good wages, and to enjoy fringe benefits such as pensions and health insurance. As the millennium approached, roughly 10 percent of all American workers fell into this category.[22]

The Social Contract

Work conditions in the new economy challenged the tacit understanding between workers and corporations that earlier commentators had regarded as a *national bargain* or *social contract*.[23] As we have seen, a sense of loyalty and mutual responsibility evolved between leading American corporations and their employees after World War II. Corporations devised new products and managed much of the national economy privately; they provided decent pay and steady jobs to millions of workers; unions

---

[19] Civilian employment rose from 99,303,000 in 1980 to 126,708,000 in 1996. See *Statistical Abstract of the United States* (Washington, D.C.: U.S. Census Bureau, 1998), p. 403.

[20] The switch from "making things to selling things" is described in Donald L. Barlett and James B. Steele, *America: Who Stole the Dream?* (Kansas City: Andrews and McMeel, 1996), pp. 112–133.

[21] Bluestone and Harrison, *The Great U-Turn*, pp. 70–71. (When service jobs could be computerized, workers filling them were also laid off. Thus the Bank of America would eliminate some 34,000 out of 175,000 jobs in the bank between 1998 and 2001. See "Bank of America to Cut Up to 6.7% of Work Force, or 10,000 Jobs," *New York Times* [July 29, 2000], pp. B1, B14.) The difficulties of making a living while working at low-paying jobs are the central theme in Barbara Ehrenreich, *Nickel and Dimed: On (Not) Getting By in America* (New York: Metropolitan, 2001).

[22] David M. Gordon, *Fat and Mean: The Corporate Squeeze of Working Americans and The Myth of Managerial "Downsizing"* (New York: Free Press, 1996), pp. 223–228. The concept of "contingent labor" can be variously defined, in which case the number of workers in the contingent labor category will vary from one scholarly study to another.

[23] See the essays in Frances Fox Piven and Richard A. Cloward, *The Breaking of the American Social Compact* (New York: New Press, 1997).

representing many of those workers called strikes infrequently and therefore enhanced corporate profitability.

When global competition intensified, however, many of the same corporations discharged tens of thousands of American employees, moved much of their production abroad, and used the threat of plant closure to weaken unions and squeeze wage concessions from those employees who remained.[24] Such steps were possible because investment capital could move thousands of miles while workers, who were emotionally attached to homes, families, neighbors, and nation, could not. Under the circumstances, when corporate leaders decided that something drastic had to be done, mainly to workers, to insure good salaries for themselves and profits for their stockholders, the tactical weapons were at hand. In this sense, as Robert Kuttner pointed out, money markets are "exquisitely capitalist in their unsentimentality. They are the antithesis of social compacts."[25]

Critics argued that the new economy unfairly rewarded some people even while others slipped into deprivation. One indication was that many American workers lost income both absolutely and relatively. Thus the buying power of an average American worker's weekly earnings declined by 15.5 percent from 1973 to 1991.[26] Similarly, as a share of the national income, the lowest two-fifths of family incomes in America between 1973 and 1990 dropped 16.4 percent and 9.2 percent respectively, while the upper fifth rose 7.8 percent.[27] Many working and middle-class families managed to maintain or slightly increase their incomes only because, among married couples, more women went to work or worked longer hours than previously.[28]

---

[24] The perception that corporations violated the national bargain shows up in survey research. Thus a *New York Times* national poll in 1995 asked "Are companies more loyal or less loyal to their employees today than they were 10 years ago?" Seventy-five percent of the poll's respondents said "less." See the *New York Times, The Downsizing of America* (New York: Times Books, 1996), p. 55.

[25] Robert Kuttner, *Everything for Sale: The Virtues and Limits of Markets* (New York: Knopf, 1998), p. 160. See also Bluestone and Harrison, *The Great U-Turn*, p. 51, on the abrogation of the "social contract"; and Reich, *The Work of Nations*, p. 212, on the repeal of the "national bargain."

[26] Wallace C. Peterson, *Silent Depression: The Fate of the American Dream* (New York: Norton, 1994), p. 37.

[27] *Ibid.*, p. 59.

[28] Lawrence Mishel, Jared Bernstein, and John Schmitt, *The State of Working America: 1998–99* (Ithaca: Cornell Univ. Press, 1999), pp. 71–83. See earlier statistics and the general story in Katherine S. Newman, *Falling from Grace: The Experience of Downward Mobility in the American Middle Class* (New York: Vintage, 1989).

Meanwhile, CEOs paid themselves handsomely. Thus between 1975 and 1995, while many workers lost jobs and income, multimillion-dollar CEO salaries became commonplace and average income for top executives at Fortune 500 companies rose by more than 900 percent.[29] The increase helps to explain how in 1959 the top 4 percent of income earners in America made as much money as the lowest 35 percent, whereas in 1989, the top 4 percent earned as much as the bottom 51 percent.[30]

Such disparities might be regarded as manifestations of a *winner-take-all society* which, in some cases, assigns great rewards to those who exercise a small increment of relative rather than absolute talent.[31] For example, a successful CEO needs to be only slightly more competent than his or her competitors to get promoted. After all, someone has to move up. But each promotion will elicit a salary increment much larger than the immediate differences in talent, in which case enormous income gaps come to obtain between those who reach the top and those who do not. Thus the ratio of pay between CEOs and production workers went from 20.3 to 1 in 1965 to 115.7 to 1 in 1997.[32] While such conditions prevail, it strains political

[29] Barlett and Steele, *America: Who Stole the Dream?*, p. 8. See also Graef S. Crystal, *In Search of Excess: The Overcompensation of American Executives* (New York: Norton, 1992).

[30] Barlett and Steele, *America: What Went Wrong?*, p. ix.

[31] Robert H. Frank and Philip J. Cook, *The Winner-Take-All Society: Why the Few at the Top Get So Much More Than the Rest of Us* (New York: Penguin, 1996).

[32] Mishel, Bernstein, and Schmitt, *The State of Working America*, p. 212. These differentials are probably understated. Corporations like Nike, the Gap, Levi Strauss, Wal-Mart, and Kmart, now contract out most of their brand-name production to independent firms in countries like Indonesia, Thailand, China, and Malaysia. In reality, workers in those contract shops are working for the corporation but not listed on its books. In such cases, if we assume that a CEO earns $1,000,000 annually, and many make more, his or her hourly rate is $480 during fifty-two weeks at forty hours per week. This as opposed, in such countries, to sweatshop wages of less than $1.00 per hour. (For a similar calculation, see Naomi Klein, *No Logo: No Space, No Choice, No Jobs* [New York: Picador, 2002], p. 352.) Popular economic thought, at least before America's seventh largest company – Enron – declared bankruptcy on December 21, 2001, after commiting massive accounting deceptions, assumes that large wage disparities occur because extremely well-paid CEOs are more competent than their competitors in the business of making and selling commodities. That is, they are paid for an unusual contribution to their corporation's profitability. In truth, however, the disparities reflect mainly the degree of administrative control that each CEO wields over the corporation he or she runs. That is, CEOs are paid by corporate directors, who in many cases they appoint, as much as their bureaucratic power can secure for them. This reality is confirmed in Lucien Bebchuk, Jesse Fried, and David Walker, "Managerial Power and Rent Extraction in the Design of Executive Compensation," *University of Chicago Law Review*, Vol. 69 (2002), pp. 751–846.

imagination to see them as reflecting a harmony of interests between rank-and-file employees and corporation chiefs.[33]

The Ecological Downside

Most Americans believe that economic growth is good, and their conviction encourages elected officials to regard growth as electorally painless. Yet regardless of the well-being such growth may promote, it generates dangers to individuals and to the community as a whole. Among these, ecological degradation stands out because, if the Earth will not accommodate human life, people will not survive to complain about lesser sorts of damage caused by incessant production and consumption. The general problem, as Godfrey Hodgson pointed out, is an American penchant for believing that making and using more commodities is good for everyone.[34]

Hazardous Materials

Ecologists disagree. They warn that industry has created, and will continue to create, life-threatening materials whose danger may not be recognized immediately. An early case came to light in 1962, when Rachel Carson published *Silent Spring*.[35] Carson described the menace of insecticides. She especially condemned DDT (dichloro-diphenyl-trichloro-ethane), which was designed to control pests such as cockroaches and mosquitoes. DDT killed insects but unexpectedly accumulated in the bodies of the birds that ate them. The insecticide's unwanted chemicals weakened the egg shells that the birds laid and thereby caused the death of, among others, embryo robin redbreasts and bald eagles.

DDT's side effects demonstrated that materials such as pesticides, asbestos, phosphates, chemical fertilizers, and mercury may accumulate, in human bodies, in the food people eat, in the fields, in the air, and in the sea. In specific cases, such as leaded paint and asbestos insulation, some modern chemicals can be banned and replaced with others less harmful. An occasional ecological victory does not eliminate the larger problem,

---

[33] For example, after his nomination as the Republican vice presidential candidate in 2000, Richard Cheney resigned as CEO of the Halliburton Corporation and was awarded by that company severance compensation worth millions of dollars. See "Few Options on Cheney Option Problem," *New York Times* (August 26, 2000), pp. C1, C14.

[34] Godfrey Hodgson, *America in Our Time: From World War II to Nixon, What Happened and Why* (New York: Vintage, 1976), pp. 67–98.

[35] Rachel Carson, *Silent Spring* (Boston: Houghton Mifflin, 1962).

however, for as soon as one threat is discovered and overcome, another is sure to take its place from among the thousands of preservatives and isotopes, additives and catalysts, that are the very stuff of modern life.[36] Furthermore, even if such materials seem safe after rigorous testing, they may combine spontaneously after use, as in underground aquifers, to produce unanticipated concoctions that nature cannot neutralize.

Overpopulation

While modern industry produces pollutants, modern science causes overpopulation. In particular, medical technology, immunizations, and miracle drugs enable more children to survive than in the past. As a result, unless birth rates fall drastically, more people than ever grow to adulthood and reproduce themselves. The world supported perhaps 500 million people in 1650. This population doubled to 1 billion by 1850, doubled again to 2 billion by 1930, doubled again to 4 billion by 1970, and reached approximately 6 billion in the year 2000.[37]

Such populations ravage the earth by causing soil erosion, deforestation, urban congestion, and industrial pollution.[38] They cannot be housed, clothed, and fed adequately under present conditions of product distribution. If they migrate, they may spread environmental pressure to places where it did not exist previously.[39] Moreover, even if the rate of reproduction for fast growing communities could be reduced by foolproof contraception, the effort would not substantially affect world population growth for many years. This is because one pernicious result of lowering infant death rates is that in underdeveloped countries such as Kenya, Nigeria, Indonesia, and Costa Rica, up to 40 percent of local people are under

---

[36] Threats come almost daily. Thus recently the Environmental Protection Agency sought to ban or phase out the use of methyl tertiary butyl ether (MTBE). This widely used gasoline additive is designed to reduce air pollution but may accumulate in ground water which, if subsequently ingested, can cause cancer. See "EPA Seeks to End Use of Additive in Gasoline," *Washington Post* (March 21, 2000), pp. A1, 14.

[37] Paul Ehrlich, *The Population Bomb* (New York: Ballantine, 1968). The figure for 2000 is from *Statistical Abstract of the United States* (Washington, D.C.: U.S. Census Bureau, 2002), p. 823.

[38] On the effects of population pressure, see Paul Harrison, *The Third Revolution: Population, Environment, and a Sustainable World* (New York: Penguin, 1993).

[39] For example, America's population would barely grow were it not boosted by immigrants who tend to have large families. See Lindsey Grant (ed.), *Elephants in the Volkswagen: Facing the Tough Questions About Our Overcrowded Country* (New York: Freeman, 1992). See also Virginia D. Abernathy, *Population Politics* (New York: Plenum, 1993), pp. 206–209, which shows the U.S. rate of increase and how immigrants cause most of it.

fifteen years old. In such cases, even if young adults will begin to have smaller families, and even if reproduction rates will fall to 1 percent or 2 percent per year, total population will continue to grow. In fact, at a world reproduction rate of 1.7 percent per year, as in the 1990s, if no natural or social catastrophes will interfere to reduce surplus population, the number of human beings alive will take less than seven hundred years to reach the infamous number of 529 trillion, which amounts to standing room only, or three square feet of the Earth's surface per person.[40]

Relative to the danger it augurs, overpopulation is not widely debated in America. Partly this is because some religious traditions condemn abortion or birth control. Indifference is further encouraged, however, by reasoning that appeals especially to those who profit from production and sales. Thus many Americans believe that overpopulation can be solved by economic growth. Population decline, they say, can be fostered by raising living standards throughout the world to the point where more people will voluntarily chose, as in many developed countries today, to have small families so as to enjoy material comforts that can be acquired only if parents will have few offspring to support.[41] Unfortunately, this prescription for perpetual economic growth clashes with conclusions drawn elsewhere in the ecological debate and which insist that growth itself must be curtailed.[42]

---

[40] Hardin, *Living Within Limits*, p. 121. If Hardin's numbers seem incomprehensibly large, consider the following historical example described in Jared Diamond, *Guns, Germs, and Steel: A Short History of Everybody for the Last 13,000 Years* (London: Vintage, 1998), p. 45. People from Siberia long ago populated North and South America. Archeologists have dated their earliest habitation sites in Alaska to around 12,000 B.C. and believe that similar sites in Patagonia, Argentina, were founded around 11,000 B.C. For the later date, archeologists believe that the total population for both continents was around 10 million souls. Accordingly, we can assume that if 100 hunter-gatherers arrived from Siberia originally, they would have had to sustain a demographic increase of only 1.1 percent yearly in order to number 10 million people at the end of a thousand years. That is, the Western hemisphere's population rose from 100 to 10 million in a thousand years at a rate of increase smaller than the earth's population is now growing.

[41] This optimistic forecast is described by Abernathy, *Population Politics*, pp. 33–35, as the "demographic transition model." She also explains, pp. 35–46, why it is inaccurate.

[42] See Mancur Olson and Hans H. Landsberg (eds.), *The No-Growth Society* (New York: Norton, 1973), and Douglas E. Booth, *The Environmental Consequences of Growth: Steady-State Economics as an Alternative to Ecological Decline* (London: Routledge, 1998). On reasonable development, see Herman E. Daly and John B. Cobb, Jr., *For the Common Good: Redirecting the Economy Toward Community, the Environment, and a Sustainable Future* (Boston: Beacon, 1989), and Hazel Henderson, *Building a Win-Win World: Life Beyond Global Economic Warfare* (San Francisco: Berrett-Koehler, 1996).

The Global Greenhouse

For example, ecologists warn that life on Earth depends on what they describe as a greenhouse effect. First, heat in the form of radiant energy from sunlight penetrates the major atmospheric gases of nitrogen and oxygen to warm the Earth. Second, part of that heat gets trapped by so-called greenhouse gases, such as carbon dioxide, nitrous oxide, and methane, so that some of it remains in the Earth's environment in the form of invisible infrared radiation. Trapping more or less heat in this way has important results. Research indicates, for example, that small variations in average temperatures produced by the global greenhouse correlate with eras of different life forms and lifestyles, so that dinosaurs flourished when Earth was only four to five degrees centigrade warmer than today, and the last Ice Age peaked eighteen thousand years ago with temperatures only about four degrees centigrade colder than now.[43]

Research also shows that global temperatures in the twenty-first century will rise, relative to 1990, by 1.5 to 4.5 degrees centigrade, thereby causing coastal flooding, the spread of deserts, and potentially disastrous effects on world agriculture.[44] The culprits, not surprisingly, are modern production and consumption. Thus burning large quantities of gasoline, natural gas, oil, and coal, for mechanized transportation and for the generation of electrical power, increases the amount of atmospheric carbon dioxide and thereby boosts global temperatures. In addition, raising enormous numbers of livestock for human consumption increases the release of bovine methane, again trapping more infrared heat around the Earth.

Because affluent Americans consume more energy per capita than most people in the world, America contributes more than other countries to the atmospheric pollution that causes greenhouse problems.[45] In fact, America produces almost 25 percent of atmospheric carbon dioxide, while all northern industrialized countries together produce about 85 percent of the total. Some efforts to reduce this pollution have been made, as in state and federal requirements for fuel efficient cars. But enthusiasm for

[43] Michael Oppenheimer and Robert H. Boyle, *The Race Against the Greenhouse Effect* (New York: New Republic, 1990), p. 2.

[44] National Research Council, *Climate Change and Science: An Analysis of Some Key Questions* (Washington, D.C.: National Academy Press, 2001), p. 3. Indications of climactic change include early flowering due to rising temperatures. See, for example, the case of Washington's cherry blossoms in "Early Bloomers: On Average, Plants Flowering a Week Sooner," *The Washington Post* (March 22, 2000), pp. A1, A17.

[45] For a cross-national chart on greenhouse gas emissions, see Paul Kennedy, *Preparing for the Twenty-first Century* (New York: Random House, 1993), p. 117.

economic growth worldwide, supported strongly by American corporations involved in globalization, envisions third world economies emulating the West. If they will do so, temperatures will continue to rise along with increasing fossil fuel consumption. Indeed, if poor countries will succeed in attaining a Western standard of living, resource consumption and attendant pollution might rise two hundred times.[46]

Systemic Projections

Viewed separately, some of the ecological trends that flow from modern production and consumption may seem manageable. To combat complacency, ecologists describe such trends as likely to reinforce one another. In the early days of ecological awareness, such patterns of reinforcement were highlighted in *The Limits to Growth*, a computerized simulation study published in 1972.[47] The study assumed that, for political and ideological reasons, all modern countries seek to generate economic growth. This growth – and here are the related trends – will require stepping up food production, enlarging industry, and consuming more nonrenewable resources. But doing so will increase pollution, for example, from industry, transportation, power stations, and agriculture. Moreover, while growth takes place, population will continue to rise.

The Limits to Growth assumed that most countries, animated by modern expectations, aim at achieving economic growth of 3 percent annually. Rising geometrically over time, growth at that rate would double national incomes every twenty-five to thirty years. However, such increases cannot be sustained, because they will massively deplete natural resources and severely contaminate the Earth. Plentiful resources can occasionally replace those becoming scarce, such as when concrete is substituted for structural steel, or when glass cables are used instead of copper telephone wires. And technical innovations can sometimes retard expected rates of depletion and environmental degradation, such as when computers become smaller but more powerful over time.[48] But such improvements are quickly swallowed up by growth rates that increase geometrically, and efficiency innovations will only postpone shortly the day when famines,

---

[46] H. V. Hodson, *The Diseconomics of Growth* (London: Pan/Ballantine, 1972), p. 193.

[47] Donella H. Meadows, Dennis L. Meadows, Jørgen Randers, and William W. Behrens III, *The Limits to Growth: A Report for the Club of Rome's Project on the Predicament of Mankind* (New York: Universe Books, 1972).

[48] Computer chip databit power rose from sixty-four thousand in 1980 to 1 billion in 2001, while chip production costs dropped from $.17 to $.03 per million databits. See Greider, *One World, Ready or Not*, p. 484.

wars, plagues, or other social catastrophes will suspend growth sometime between 2050 and 2100.

The scenario projected by *The Limits to Growth* was complex and disputed by optimists.[49] So ecologists came to prefer general analogies which, through vivid images, conveyed similar messages of associated trends and inherent limitations. One image portrayed Earth as a spaceship, carrying an environment which, if used up or befouled, would no longer sustain life on board. To sharpen the analogy, economist Kenneth Boulding described irresponsible living under such circumstances as "cowboy" behavior, where producing and consuming proceed without regard for resource depletion and environmental contamination.[50]

Another image described Earth as a feudal village. If members of the community were separately to use the common pasture too intensively for grazing their cattle, grass on the commons would be unable to renew itself, whereupon all the village's cows, and their human owners, would perish.[51] Drawing an analogy between the environment and a village commons suggested that America's attitude to the physical world, summed up in Locke's vision of men endlessly mixing their labor with natural resources and appropriating the product as private property, helped to explain why people animated by consumerism so easily squander the world's resources without paying sufficient attention to future needs.[52]

Personal Dilemmas

The paradoxes of economic growth, what happens to work during globalization, undoing the national bargain, and various ecological predicaments: All these are general aspects of modern life that flow from

---

[49] For optimism, see Carl Kaysen, "The Computer That Printed Out W*O*L*F*," *Foreign Affairs* (July 1972); Wilfred Beckerman, *Two Cheers for the Affluent Society: A Spirited Defense of Economic Growth* (New York: St. Martin's, 1974); Julian L. Simon, *The Ultimate Resource* (Princeton: Princeton Univ. Press, 1981); and Bjorn Lomborg, *The Skeptical Environmentalist: Measuring the Real State of the World* (New York: Cambridge Univ. Press, 2001). For continued pessimism, see William Ophuls and A. Stephen Boyan, Jr., *Ecology and the Politics of Scarcity Revisited* (New York: W. H. Freeman, 1992), which updates the statistics on exponential natural resource consumption trends presented in *Limits to Growth*.

[50] Kenneth E. Boulding, "The Economics of the Coming Spaceship Earth," in H. Jarrett (ed.), *Environmental Quality in a Growing Economy* (Baltimore: Johns Hopkins Univ. Press, 1966), pp. 3–14.

[51] Garret Hardin, "The Tragedy of the Commons," *Science* (December 13, 1968), pp. 1243–1248.

[52] Ophuls and Boyan, *Ecology and the Politics of Scarcity Revisited*, pp. 190–192.

what people do when carrying out economic roles assigned to them by consumerism. Other consequences of the ceaseless quest for getting and spending may be described as more personal, having to do with how Americans regard themselves and the world around them.

Other-Directedness

Consumerism affects, for instance, what psychologists call self-images, which entail the ways that people see themselves, their responsibilities, and their chances for happiness. In *The Lonely Crowd* (1950), an early study of life under consumerism, David Riesman, Nathan Glazer, and Reuel Denney described many twentieth-century Americans as having acquired an other-directed personality.[53] This emerged, they said, from a series of three historical eras. First, tradition had ruled people's lives, mainly in small and static societies, where children grew up in families, clans, tribes, and castes, and where they learned to act out social roles based on stable patterns of expectation and behavior. Second, as on the American frontier, people moved around more frequently, often over large distances, and had to establish new communities under difficult conditions. Consequently, the authority of some traditions weakened, and innovative individuals responded to changing circumstances by evoking an inner sense of conscience derived from one or another of the great religions, for example, from the Protestant Ethic.

But third, when setting up new communities became unnecessary, when science weakened religious convictions, and when technology offered a multitude of things to buy and consume, Americans found that circumstances permitted them to devise and adopt personal lifestyles more freely than before. Since absolute freedom to do so was psychologically unsettling, though, they usually chose to live with some concern for what other people thought of them.

Here was the other-directed behavior which Riesman and his colleagues described as the hallmark of people dedicated to consuming rather than to tradition. It appeared when such people internalized not a code of behavior but the equipment of sensitivity, not a moral gyroscope but social radar. The new guides to emulation were compatible, of course, with industry's need to market many products, from automobiles to color televisions to automatic cameras. After all, staying on good terms with the Joneses usually entailed buying the same things that they did. And this

---

53 David Riesman, with Nathan Glazer and Reuel Denney, *The Lonely Crowd*, abr. ed. (New Haven: Yale Univ. Press, 1950).

sort of ceaseless catch-up kept industry going even though many of the items it fashioned and sold were not needed for a good life as defined by old-time consciences dedicated, in principle at least, more to good deeds than material success.

Core Values

One political implication of all this is that the conditions that provoke other-directedness may weaken commitment to core values that should endure from one generation to another and thereby foster stability in human affairs. On the one hand, ads tell Americans, subtly or not, that they should be like everyone else, that they should buy this or that product so as to conform to what other people expect them to be. There is the spur to other-directedness.[54] On the other hand, ads encourage everyone to focus on his or her own importance and to decide which combination, perhaps fleeting, of consumer goods is most worth buying and enjoying. There is an invitation to choose a personal lifestyle.

True, what we choose usually conforms to one of a finite number of lifestyles permitted by existing technology or shopping options. Still, even this limited range of lifestyles tends, in an important sense, to set people adrift. The sequence is as follows. Many Americans feel they are entitled to buy whatever they like and thereby decide how to live. They cannot be sure, however, that members of their community, who are equally entitled to buy and live as they like, will choose similarly from the range of practices and expectations that are available.[55] Some will and some won't. Yet when people suspect that neighbors have not made the same choices they did – that is, do not share their values – they are reluctant to invest time and energy in acting civically on behalf of people who, while honoring different values, may evince no appreciation for those who make such efforts.

In this sense, the individualism promoted so strongly in recent years militates against maintaining faith in standards that may be necessary for fostering public life. To demonstrate this point, *Habits of the Heart* noted that one of modern society's archetypical figures, the therapist, tends to reinforce moral pluralism by advising his or her client to adopt existing norms rather than to challenge social expectations by clinging to core

---

[54] On the effects of "consumption communities," see Daniel Boorstin, *The Americans: The Democratic Experience* (New York: Vintage, 1974), pp. 89–164.

[55] This is the general dilemma explored in Robert Bellah, Richard Madsen, William M. Sullivan, Ann Swidler, and Steven M. Tipton, *Habits of the Heart: Individualism and Commitment in American Life* (New York: Harper and Row, 1986).

values.[56] In the face of Northern acquiescence to Southern slavery, Henry David Thoreau long ago condemned such conformity by insisting that, when great issues are at stake, people must sometimes defy convention, insist on doing what is right, and act as if they are "a majority of one."[57]

The Financial Yardstick

When modern America offers a bewildering choice of identities, one possible response is for individuals to measure their worth by financial success. Historian Christopher Lasch has written about how the self-indulgence encouraged by consumerism combines with economic imperatives inherent in modern production.[58] From seventeenth-century New England primers to nineteenth-century McGuffey readers, Americans praised hard work. But the work they admired, even if it led to material success, was always tempered by a moral goal such as self-improvement. More recently, according to Lasch, many Americans have pursued accumulation as if it were absolutely justified, since other goals seemed, in modern society, to be interminably disputable.[59]

And so some Americans, but of course not all, have lately tended to regard economic victory as life's major goal.[60] This inclination is fostered, no doubt, by moral ambiguity in business, where law and circumstances provide parameters within which most decisions are made mainly with an eye to profit.[61] Wealthy alumni at Harvard, trying sincerely to promote virtue, may endow their alma mater with large sums for studying

---

[56] Ibid., esp. Ch. 5, "Reaching Out," pp. 113–141.

[57] Henry David Thoreau, "Civil Disobedience (1849)," in Carl Bode (ed.), *The Portable Thoreau* (New York: Viking, 1947), p. 120.

[58] Christopher Lasch, *The Culture of Narcissism: American Life in an Age of Diminishing Expectations* (New York: Warner, 1979).

[59] Ibid., p. 115.

[60] On frenetic security traders and other Wall Street high rollers in the 1980s, see the essays in Michael Lewis, *The Money Culture* (New York: Penguin, 1992), p. xiv: "The money was important, but mainly as a way of keeping score." See also Nicolaus Mills, "The Culture of Triumph and the Spirit of the Times," in Mills (ed.), *Culture in an Age of Money: The Legacy of the 1980s in America* (Chicago: Ivan Dee, 1990). This essay opens with Nancy Reagan buying 220 place settings of new dishes for the White House at a cost of $209,508, and then (p. 26) characterizes the Age of Money as "rooted in the belief that possession is the key to authenticity."

[61] In praise of profit as the *only* legitimate goal of business enterprise, see Milton Friedman, *Capitalism and Freedom* (Chicago: Univ. of Chicago Press, 1962), pp. 133–136. See also his "The Social Responsibility of Business Is to Increase Its Profits," *New York Times Magazine* (September 13, 1970), pp. 32–33, 122–126. Charles Dickens condemned this sort of thinking in *Hard Times* (orig., 1854; New York: Penguin, 1994), p. 103, where he described Bitzer, bank clerk in Coketown, as a young man of "steady" principle unswayed by "affections or passions," an "excellent economist," a son who put his widowed mother

"business ethics." But professors lecturing on that subject cannot easily ignore the fact that, according to ethics per se, "more" is not necessarily "better," in which case rising profits do not necessarily indicate that a company is doing good.[62] Or, as Charles Dickens observed in *Hard Times* (1854), his classic indictment of early industrialization, in a world ruled by business values "the Good Samaritan" may be "a bad Economist."[63]

The Pursuit of Happiness

Americans have more possessions than ever. In 1958, this prosperity led John Kenneth Galbraith to describe them as constituting an *affluent society*.[64] But more was still to come for, between 1958 and 1980, the number of American homes with air conditioners rose 484 percent, while those with freezers rose 134 percent, those with clothes dryers rose 356 percent, and those with dishwashers rose 743 percent.[65] Yet while such commodities made some aspects of life easier, there remained a question of whether they made Americans happier. The answer is that, in significant respects, they probably did not.[66]

For example, in a society dedicated to making and selling commodities, people will to some extent become commodities, since a person's worth to other people may be judged according to what he or she can contribute to their earnings or possessions.[67] Yet to feel like a commodity

in the poorhouse. Bitzer allowed this relative "half a pound of tea a year," but, as Dickens observed, this

> was weak in him ... because his only reasonable transaction in that commodity would have been to buy it for as little as he could possibly give, and sell it for as much as he could possibly get, it having been clearly ascertained by philosophers that in this is comprised the whole duty of man – not a part of man's duty, but the whole.

[62] Laurence Shames, *The Hunger for More: Searching for Values in an Age of Greed* (New York: Vintage, 1991), pp. 198–201.

[63] It is the coldly analytical Thomas Gradgrind who says this. See Dickens, *Hard Times*, p. 192.

[64] John Kenneth Galbraith, *The Affluent Society* (New York: Mentor, 1958).

[65] Paul L. Wachtel, *The Poverty of Affluence: A Psychological Portrait of the American Way of Life* (Philadelphia: New Society Publishers, 1989), p. 14.

[66] Happiness is subjective and therefore cannot be compared precisely from one person or era to another. But see Juliet B. Schor, *The Overspent American: Why We Want What We Don't Need* (New York: HarperCollins, 1998), which argues that Americans are not happier today even though they are buying more things than in the past. Robert Frank, *Luxury Forever: Why Money Fails to Satisfy in an Era of Excess* (New York: Free Press, 1999), explores the same situation and recommends a consumption tax to finance collective amenities that he believes *will* make people happier.

[67] Erich Fromm, *Man for Himself: An Inquiry into the Psychology of Ethics* (New York: Rinehart, 1947), pp. 69–70.

is to lose a sense of one's inviolate self, because a person's commercial value is determined not by the extent of inner worth but by how much one can serve, if only momentarily, the needs of a changing marketplace.[68] At worst, in such circumstances, even successful people will live in fear of being judged obsolete. Anxiety will especially thrive when many employers have abrogated the former national bargain and feel free to treat employees as disposable items, like Kleenex.

To people who are unhappy for whatever reason, market enthusiasts suggest that buying something they don't yet have will improve their mood or, as economists might say, provide utility. But here there lurks a *fallacy of the individual commodity*, in that to seek happiness in one commodity after another is to forego the things that make up the sum total of life, the social ties that bind people to each other, the emotional security afforded by pausing to enjoy what we already have.[69] To aspire to earn somewhat more in order to buy something else is willingly to move on in life, from one place to another, seeking the main chance but, in the process, sometimes leaving behind friends, family, neighborhood, and other vital human associations.

The dilemma is intractable. An endless quest for additional commodities forestalls the psychic satisfactions of community but cannot generate happiness on its own terms. For one thing, it tries to satisfy wants rather than needs.[70] Yet those wants are boundless, because they are incessantly created by the production system rather than by arising, in some limited way, from within the personality of consumers.[71] Then, too, many of those wants are relative rather than absolute. That is, Smith may seek goods of position such as housing in a prestigious suburb or education at an elite college. But the satisfaction that Smith derives from such goods cannot last long because, when Chang, O'Donnell, Goldberg, and Rodriguez attain similar housing or education, the value of Smith's holdings will decrease and he or she will feel driven to achieve more.[72]

In fact, even if having more goods and services does provide economic well-being, this is not the same as human well-being, which includes

[68] Jules Henry, *Culture Against Man* (New York: Vintage, 1963), p. 23.

[69] On the fallacy of the individual commodity, see Wachtel, *The Poverty of Affluence*, p. 39f.

[70] Henry, *Culture Against Man*, p. 19.

[71] Galbraith, *The Affluent Society*, Ch. 11: "The Dependence Effect," pp. 124–130. See also Richard Easterlin, who argues that economic growth does not increase happiness because wants expand along with income. In Easterlin, *Growth Triumphant: The Twenty-first Century in Historical Perspective* (Ann Arbor: Univ. of Michigan Press, 1996), pp. 152–153, he describes this process as a "hedonic treadmill."

[72] Fred Hirsh, *Social Limits to Growth* (Cambridge: Harvard Univ. Press, 1976), pp. 1–15.

qualities of stability, tranquility, introspection, and association with other people.[73] On this score, two problems arise. First, consumerism corrodes a long-standing American value, the Puritan concept of calling, the notion that people should aspire to fulfill some social role which will enable them to feel they are improving the quality of human life.[74] Yet if the definition of human life changes constantly according to the nature of new commodities that appear in the marketplace, who can say which social roles contribute vitally to happiness there?

Second, for all its talk about how consumption improves our existence, consumerism rarely fosters the capacity for truly effective consumption. Such consumption would enable people to appreciate deeply the useful or aesthetic qualities of commodities that modern science and technology make possible. But if people would learn to enjoy commodities in this sense, they might be satisfied with what they have and not crave the next available item.[75] That is, on the basis of finite ownership, citizens might enjoy true felicity, which is exactly what consumerism must avoid fostering in order to continue to sell the additional things it cannot stop producing.

Television

A major cause for all of the above is television. The machine is a technological miracle that can be used by authoritarian or democratic regimes to serve what they regard as public interests. One thinks here, for example, of the Jordanian Television Authority or the British Broadcasting System. In America, on the other hand, television stations are mainly owned by

---

73 Tibor Scitovsky, *The Joyless Economy: An Inquiry into Human Satisfaction and Consumer Dissatisfaction* (New York: Oxford Univ. Press, 1976), p. 145f.

74 Ibid., p. 207. See also Richard Sennett, *The Corrosion of Character: The Personal Consequences of Work in the New Capitalism* (New York: Norton, 1998), pp. 15–31, for a discussion of how people who have no long-term workplace in the modern economy feel they are unable to pass on to their children a traditional sense of commitment to other people via stable loyalties. Thus, p. 19: "Rico [a business consultant working from one short-term contract to another] has no fixed role that allows him to say to others 'This is what I do, this is what I am responsible for.' "

75 See Wachtel, *The Poverty of Affluence*, p. 106:

> Today our problem is not to produce more but to learn to enjoy what we have produced.... "A chicken in every pot" used to be a slogan that implied a satisfying abundance. Now, in a *New York Times* article on how Americans cope with inflation, we find quoted, with no apparent intent at irony, the plaint of a Long Island schoolteacher, grown used to steak and roast beef, that "if I see chicken or hamburger once more I'll scream."

individuals and used chiefly to stimulate desire and sell private goods. To this end, commercial television dominates American life. At least 98 percent of American homes have television sets;[76] on the average they are turned on for six or seven hours every day; in which case, counting vacations, children may watch more hours of television programming than they spend in school until age eighteen.[77]

Television Ads

By promoting consumption, commercial television fuels runaway economic growth. Additional costs flow from how the same television showcases advertisements that are really quite peculiar. For example, in the original competition between General Motors and Ford, we saw that ads have long cultivated a therapy factor in the sense that, by making people unhappy with what they have, ads encourage their audience to maintain a *culture of procurement*.[78] Television ads perpetuate this strategy, which helps to raise GNP but, at the same time, affects the ways in which viewers think, sometimes unrealistically, about the nature of commodities they see and buy.

Thus ads tend to portray America not as it truly is, with occasional imperfections, but to highlight what might be called the *plastic* rather than the *real*.[79] Plastic America is cleaner, friendlier, more exciting, and more colorful than reality, a sort of Disneyworld version of Main Street America or a *Sports Illustrated* image of swimsuits on the girl next door. Plastic is the telephone booth shown in an ad to suggest family intimacy even when real cities have stopped using booths for fear of vandalism.[80] Plastic

---

[76] This figure was reached by 1980 and leveled off afterward. See Lawrence W. Lichy, "Television in America" in Philip S. Cook, Douglas Gomery, and Lawrence W. Lichty (eds.), *American Media: The Woodrow Wilson Quarterly Reader* (Washington, D.C.: Wilson Quarterly Press, 1989), p. 164.

[77] Robert D. Putnam, *Bowling Alone: The Collapse and Revival of American Community* (New York: Simon and Schuster, 2000), pp. 222–223. On commercial television as an informal educational message, Neil Postman, *The End of Education: Redefining the Value of School* (New York: Knopf, 1996), p. 33, notes that between the ages of three and eighteen, average Americans will watch five hundred thousand television ads.

[78] Roland A. Delattre, "The Culture of Procurement: Reflections on Addiction and the Dynamics of American Culture," in Charles H. Reynolds and Ralph V. Norman (eds.), *Community in America: The Challenge of Habits of the Heart* (Berkeley: Univ. of California Press, 1988), pp. 57–58.

[79] These terms are from Peter Schrag, *The Decline of the WASP* (New York: Simon and Schuster, 1970), pp. 185–225.

[80] In Michael J. Arlen, *Thirty Seconds* (New York: Farrar, Straus and Giroux, 1980), pp. 103–108, there is an example of advertisers seeking emotional effect who, for lack of working examples, had to rent a stage-prop telephone booth.

is the sports utility vehicle seen on television gliding over a forest road rather than immobilized in commuter traffic. Plastic is the way advertisers present their products via images so attractive that the image becomes, for many consumers, the product itself which, as a matter of fact, may hardly be distinguishable from another car, soft drink, computer, lipstick, or tennis shoe.[81]

The sum total of plastic ads is an artistic fantasy that may be called *capitalist realism*. Just as *socialist realism* once reflected a vision of how socialist life should be lived, so capitalist realism shows life not as it is but as what we should aspire to.[82] For example, a study of five hundred American magazine ads discovered in them many couples playing games, expressing affection for each other, consuming commodities together, and so forth. But the same ads showed no old, poor, sick, or unattractive couples.[83] Their absence reflected not real life but some sort of consumerist mirage.

Reason

When images are detached from reality, the factual content of ads decreases. *Puffery* is one term used to describe what happens here.[84] Puffery takes place when an item is promoted with "subjective opinions, superlatives, or exaggerations...stating no specific facts."[85] Examples would include: "You Can Be Sure If It's Westinghouse," or "G.E. – We Bring Good Things to Life," or "When You Say Budweiser, You've Said It All."

Puffery provides consumers with a reason for buying products, but the reason is emotional impulse rather than explicit information. Thus puffery is attractive to corporations that use it because some of their products are so similar to competing products that there is nothing worth saying about them factually. Puffery is also attractive to marketeers because, if no facts are stipulated, none can be disproved as a liability against the seller.

On this last count, a term covering much the same ground describes many television ads as *nonrefutable*. Here the point is that where images rather than facts dominate an ad, the image does not promise a particular

---

[81] Eric Clark, *The Want Makers: Inside the World of Advertising* (Baltimore: Penguin, 1988), p. 23: "What is new is that advertising has now moved on from being the creator of the image that *helps* sell the product. Today, advertising *is* the product."

[82] The two terms are used by Michael Schudson, *Advertising, the Uneasy Persuasion: Its Dubious Impact on American Society* (New York: Basic Books, 1984), pp. 214–218.

[83] Ibid., p. 220.

[84] See Ivan L. Preston, *The Great American Blow-Up: Puffery in Advertising and Selling* (Madison: Univ. of Wisconsin Press, 1975).

[85] Ibid., p. 17.

performance but evokes an emotional disposition to regard the product sympathetically.[86] Perhaps the most famous example is the Man from Marlboro Country, whose rugged outdoor image needs no words to suggest that smoking Marlboro cigarettes will somehow enable the consumer to associate himself or herself with the cowboy. At that point, advertising becomes a message which is not, in fact, about what you are selling but about who you are selling to. Or, as Neil Postman observes, advertisers need to know not "what is right about the product but what is wrong about the buyer."[87] And there, of course, lies the nexus between ads and therapy.

More than a century ago, Thorstein Veblen's concept of *pecuniary truth* foreshadowed the modern perception that ads are designed not so much to convey objective truth as to evoke sales and profit.[88] But there is a larger point here, which is that, for an institution which constantly and powerfully tells people what to think of themselves and what to do with their lives, advertisers have little sense of social responsibility.[89] Churches, we may hope, preach virtue; universities, when effective, promote wisdom. But advertising, whose American budgets challenge those of religion and higher education,[90] does not seek to improve the individual or to

---

[86] See the example in Neil Postman, *Amusing Ourselves to Death: Public Discourse in the Age of Show Business* (New York: Penguin, 1985), p. 128:

> A McDonald's commercial... is not a series of testable, logically ordered assertions. It is a drama – a mythology, if you will – of handsome people selling, buying and eating hamburgers, and being driven to near ecstasy by their good fortune. No claims are made, except those the viewer projects onto or infers from the drama. One can like or dislike a television commercial, of course. But one cannot refute it.

[87] Ibid.

[88] Veblen did not use the term *pecuniary truth*, but his argument assumed that what we hold to be socially true is determined mainly by economic factors designed to achieve adequate profit rather than accurate insight. See especially his *The Theory of the Leisure Class: An Economic Study of Institutions* (orig., 1899; Amherst, N.Y.: Prometheus, 1998) and his *The Higher Learning in America* (orig., 1918; New Brunswick, N.J.: Transaction, 1993). Pecuniary truth is explicitly the hallmark of advertising according to Jules Henry, *Culture Against Man*, Ch. 3: "Advertising as a Philosophical System," pp. 45–99. See especially the three postulates of this system on p. 50: "Truth is what sells. Truth is what you want people to believe. Truth is that which is not legally false."

[89] This point is raised in David M. Potter, *People of Plenty: Economic Abundance and the American Character* (Chicago: Univ. of Chicago Press, 1954), pp. 176–177.

[90] In *Statistical Abstract of the United States* (Washington, D.C.: U.S. Census Bureau, 1990), pp. 129, 556, higher education for 1986 cost $107 billion while advertising in all media cost $102 billion. In Virginia A. Hodgkinson, Murray S. Weitzman, and Arthur D. Kirsch, *From Belief to Commitment: The Activities and Finances of Religious Congregations*

promote social usefulness. Advertising is, in fact, a peculiarly neutral instrument, operating, at best, within the bounds of common decency but no more.

Entertainment

Thus advertisers do not look for a socially redeeming quality in television shows but for programs, like *Survivor*, that interest viewers.[91] Commercial viability says it all. If a program does not assemble an audience of potential buyers, advertisers will not pay to address them. In which case the broadcasting station will fail to draw revenues, will cancel the program, and will replace it with one more likely to attract viewers.

The effect of this linkage is profound: A financial imperative requires American television producers to turn every sort of program into entertainment so that viewers will stay tuned in. The comparative ability of programs to entertain is then monitored by companies that provide ratings, whose findings are used to determine which programs are worth keeping from one season to the next.

The problem here is not that television offers "entertaining subject matter but that all subject matter is presented as entertaining."[92] But where every sort of broadcast seeks to entertain, a community and its members may lose their ability to relate effectively to vital dimensions of human life. Thus events such as a president's funeral, religious rites, university convocations, and the Persian Gulf War deserve intense and sober consideration rather than fleeting responses of diversion and amusement.[93]

---

in the United States (Washington, D.C.: Independent Sector, 1988), p. 48, expenditures for religion in 1986, *not including* schools and hospitals, are estimated at $49 billion.

[91] On this score, the structural difference between television, on the one hand, and schools and churches, on the other, is profound. Television programs are mostly composed to deliver what viewers want to see. After all, the goal is entertainment. Under the circumstances, such programs rarely inspire viewers to think beyond what they already believe. See James B. Twitchell, *For Shame: The Loss of Common Decency in American Culture* (New York: St. Martin's, 1997), pp. 61–64. But in schools and churches, children and congregants must consider stories – analogous to programs – fashioned by educators and theologians working from special knowledge and expertise. In which case the goal, although not always achieved, is enlightenment.

[92] Postman, *Amusing Ourselves to Death*, p. 87.

[93] On the Persian Gulf War as spectacle, see Leo Bogart, *Commercial Culture: The Media System and the Public Interest* (New York: Oxford Univ. Press, 1995), pp. 186–187, where Michael Gartner of NBC News is quoted as saying "It's unreal to be watching a war unfold like a football game. You get so wrapped up in covering it that you forget it's a war and you have to stand back sometimes and say 'My God, this is a war.'"

Fiction

Documentary channels and educational television make some effort to tell the truth. But beyond what they do, there begins what Newton Minow called the "vast wasteland" of commercial programs, a realm which, for the most part, projects not apparent reality but patent fiction.[94] Thus soap operas, sit-coms, westerns, and courtroom dramas are all freely fabricated to hold viewers firmly in front of broadcast advertisements.

Yet these programs, too, have important social consequences. First, they seem so real that viewers tend to believe the world resembles what they are looking at, even though the programs are known to be imaginative. Thus, after seeing police shows, audiences tend to think there is more violence in America than there is in fact.[95] Such a perception may translate into political support for law and order candidates, for unregulated gun sales, or for mandatory sentencing of minor offenders. Or, after seeing *The Cosby Show*, white viewers may conclude that African American families enjoy so many economic opportunities that those who remain poverty-stricken deserve to be poor.[96] This perception may militate against affirmative action programs.

Second, the sum of commercial programs, which are mainly fictional but which include, for example, talk shows, comes to constitute for many viewers a virtual community which they lack in real life.[97] Most people belong to networks of acquaintance based on family, religion, work, and neighborhood. Such networks link together people who share interests and expectations. The linkages are incomplete, however, for most members of such networks do not feel they are part of an overarching community which enlivens human existence by knitting together diverse inhabitants into geographical, social, and historical associations. And one result of this alienation is that television programs, which are shaped by mythmakers and storytellers, have the capacity for coming into separate

94 Newton Minow, then chairman of the Federal Communications Commission, first compared American television to a wasteland in 1961 while addressing the National Association of Broadcasters. See his remarks thirty years later in Newton Minow, *How Vast the Wasteland Now?* (New York: Gannett Foundation Media Center, 1991).

95 Marie Winn, *The Plug-in Drug: Television, Children, and the Family*, rev. ed. (New York: Peguin, 1985), pp. 103–105. According to Bogart, *Commercial Culture*, p. 160, the murder rate in prime-time American television is one thousand times that in real American life.

96 On white responses to *The Cosby Show*, see Sut Jhally and Justin Lewis, *Enlightened Racism: The Cosby Show, Audiences, and the Myth of the American Dream* (Boulder, Colo.: Westview, 1992), pp. 71–111.

97 Richard Schickel, *Intimate Strangers: The Culture of Celebrity* (New York: Fromm, 1986), pp. 356–360.

homes and affording their occupants a feeling that they can participate, if only passively, in the life of something large and inspiring.[98]

What may be called the *television community* can seem real for being populated by familiar faces such as Oprah Winfrey, the characters from Seinfeld, Jay Leno, Bill O'Reilly, Jackie Gleason, the people from JAG, the friends of Ally McBeal, Wolf Blitzer, Regis Philbin, Jerry Springer, Lucille Ball, Ted Koppel, the staff of *General Hospital*, the lifeguards of *Baywatch*, and more. At the flick of a switch, these characters come to share a reassuring moment with us at home and accompany us when we are visiting or working far away. Such characters seem to be our friends even though we know almost nothing about their real lives, about whether or not they are married, if they have children, where they live, what they do with their spare time, whether or not they speak a foreign language or tinker with cars.

On the whole, people from America's television neighborhood are celebrities, well known not for their accomplishments in real life but for how they appear in roles designed to hold our attention. That is, they are not classically famous people like Martin Luther King, Jr., or Albert Einstein, recognized for the remarkable quality of their deeds or discoveries. They are, instead, people who, by entertaining others successfully, evoke an emotional bond that causes them to be well known for being seen often and mentioned widely.[99]

One drawback here flows from the way in which celebrity status is attained, for in some cases television intentionally provides information about the offscreen life of celebrities who appear there. Much of this information is quite unimportant, such as whether an actress jogs, or what a diplomat had for breakfast, or how a banker has furnished her house. But the few available facts purport to take the viewer, in effect, to what might be called the *backstage* of public appearances, to glimpse various celebrities as they "truly" are rather than as they usually appear on *frontstage*, coiffed and coached for performances.[100]

To show celebrities on-screen as they might appear backstage in life, such as to invite Bill Clinton to play the saxophone while participating

[98] On television knitting together "fragmented communities," see James Oliver Robertson, *American Myth, American Reality* (New York: Hill and Wang, 1980), pp. 233–236.

[99] On the distinction between celebrity and fame, between being known for being known and being known for great deeds, see Schickel, *Intimate Strangers*, pp. 31–33.

[100] The terms *backstage* and *frontstage* are from Joshua Meyrowitz, *No Sense of Place: The Impact of Electronic Media on Social Behavior* (New York: Oxford Univ. Press, 1985), esp. pp. 35–51.

in a talk show, is to offer viewers the intimacy they crave from contact with the television neighborhood. Surely it keeps many people watching. It is, however, a practice that undermines authority, that makes celebrities seem like everyone else even though, in some cases, every society needs people of extraordinary stature to perform frontstage duties of unusual difficulty which require exceptional respect.[101] In this sense, Americans followed George Washington and Abraham Lincoln to great achievements precisely because no one cared what George or Abe ate for breakfast.

Television News

Television ads and fictional programs indirectly cause viewers to misunderstand the world, since the medium's primary intention is not to inform but to entertain and thereby solicit sales. Television newscasts, on the other hand, mislead viewers directly, while purporting to describe exactly what happens both nearby and far away. On this score, televised news programs participate in the general influence exercised by the entire press, including television, radio, newspapers, and news magazines. For the press, by reporting on some subjects and ignoring others, helps to determine which social problems and public policies the public will talk about.[102]

In the case of television news, this process is particularly significant because since 1963, when CBS and NBC increased their national newscasts at dinnertime from fifteen to thirty minutes, Americans have said that they receive more of their news from television than from any other source, such as newspapers.[103] Moreover, since 1961 television news has seemed more credible to Americans than reporting from other sources, a predictable response since broadcast pictures, as compared to printed words, convince many viewers they are looking at reality.

Story-Line Considerations
Even with pictures, television news does not portray reality accurately because, like other programming, it suffers from commercial and technical

---

[101] Ibid., pp. 167–169, on "Backstage Visibility and the Decline of Authority."

[102] Fay Lomax Cook, Tom R. Ryler, Edward G. Goetz, Margaret T. Gordon, David Protess, Donna R. Leff, and Harvey L. Molotch, "Media and Agenda Setting: Effects on the Public, Interest Group Leaders, Policy Makers and Policy," *Public Opinion Quarterly* (Spring 1983), pp. 16–35; and Shanto Iyengar and Donald R. Kinder, *News That Matters* (Chicago: Univ. of Chicago Press, 1987), pp. 16–33.

[103] "ABC Nightly News" went to half an hour in 1967, and CNN started reporting around the clock in 1980. On the most common news sources and on their respective degrees of credibility, see the figures in *Public Opinion* (August–September 1979), p. 30.

constraints. To begin with, news is a program with time slots that must be sold to advertisers. This means that thirty minutes of nightly news offers only twenty-two minutes of reporting, sliced up by eight minutes of commercials into perhaps twenty stories and announcements that rarely last even two minutes each. And what can be compressed into two minutes or less about the real world? No matter how dull the day, producers will choose to screen mainly exciting news items, because their program must entertain rather than bore its audience. These items will be described mainly via pictures, since viewers expect to see something when they tune in rather than read a newspaper. The result is that one half hour of televised news will convey no more exact information than what is contained in two and a half front page columns of print in the *New York Times*.[104]

There is, in addition, the peculiar nature of televised news reports. Because the program seeks to entertain its viewers, social processes and events are presented as stories, with some unfolding built into the action, starting somewhere and leading to somewhere else.[105] Stories, however, are usually an art form with specific protagonists, even though individuals rarely dominate events in the real world. And thus television news implicitly suggests that public affairs are more about personalities such as Saddam Hussein, Ralph Nader, and Slobodan Milosevic than about historical forces such as oil, environmentalism, and nationalism.

This sort of broadcasting portrays politics, like all other subjects, as an entertaining story. In the case of politics, it is usually a tale of actors whose efforts before the electorate become an exciting game full of impressive photo opportunities, where one dramatis persona struggles against another for power and personal gain. Such *horse race journalism* tends to slight the importance of political parties and social issues because they are less exciting, more difficult to film, and almost impossible to describe without more talk than television ordinarily cares to provide. In all, it is a view of reality that makes candidates seem more important than their parties, and that will penalize any potential candidate who, like Abraham Lincoln, might be competent but homely.

The Loss of Proportion

Just as ads corrupt the language of reason, so the news on television distorts the terms of proportion that citizens need to make sense of what they

---

[104] Frank Mankiewicz and Joel Swerdlow, *Remote Control: Television and the Manipulation of American Life* (New York: Ballantine, 1978), p. 97.

[105] On stories, see Edward Jay Epstein, *News from Nowhere: Television and the News* (New York: Vintage, 1974), pp. 153, 164–174.

see on the small screen. There are, for example, unwitting consequences to the standard broadcast format, which is the same from one anchorperson to another and which breaks up the real world into a series of items interspersed with "messages" about headache relievers, dental adhesives, and the like.

Some of these consequences arise from the "now . . . this" formula whereby announcers invite viewers to turn their attention from a murder, a beauty pageant, a catastrophic oil spill, a new bridge, or a coming war, and think instead about ads.[106] "Now . . . this" implies that reality is not very important, else why interrupt consideration of it so frequently on behalf of trivial matters? Or, to put the point another way, "now . . . this" indicates that reality is composed of unrelated events and people, with no overall significance to a broadcast series of items beyond the capacity for holding viewers' attention so they will stay tuned in for ads. Such a stream of news stories, framed by commercial glitz and jingles, will bombard viewers with conflicting emotional cues and do little to help them reflect on a world they should judge carefully for consistency and coherency.

Proportionality also gets lost when television presents all things as equal to all other things, which is the meaning of screening a thirty-second story on car bombs in Baghdad followed by a thirty-second "message" explaining why Tylenol is superior to Advil.[107] This lack of discrimination fails to help viewers gain historical perspective. Night after night the news flashes by as an outpouring of mainly unrelated and unranked events, products, candidates, criminals, athletes, refugees, and public policies. But where that is so, how can viewers exposed to such a hodgepodge formulate steadfast and long-range strategies toward a world that, unlike vaudeville, is composed of acts which persist and require patient and

---

[106] Postman, *Amusing Ourselves to Death*, 99–133.

[107] See Michael Sorkin, "Simulations: Faking It," in Todd Gilin (ed.), *Watching Television* (New York: Pantheon, 1986), p. 176: "From TV's perspective, the agenda is always to assert that any *thing* that can be represented is ultimately comparable to *anything* else that can be represented. This is the TV transference, the operation of reciprocal ennobling that makes a can of pop as consequential as a murder, that allows the cut from commercial to carnage." See also Lewis H. Lapham, *The Wish for Kings: Democracy at Bay* (New York: Grove, 1993), p. 162:

> Any statement [in the talk-show world of celebrities] is equal to every other statement, and the question of what Mikhail Gorbachev said to Ronald Reagan about thermonuclear war at a summit meeting in Iceland is of no more or less consequence than the question of what Madonna ordered for breakfast – raspberries or strawberries – in a suite at the Chateau Marmont on the morning after her marriage to Sean Penn.

intelligent treatment over time?[108] How, for example, can citizens focus on the remote dangers of global warming if the news features, without comment, candidates who promise to bring the price of gasoline down so consumption of it can stay up?

Political Theater

Public life in any era requires leaders to perform before audiences, whether Alexander the Great was inspiring his troops at Issus or Louis XIV was dazzling his courtiers at Versailles. Performances have changed, however, since technology permitted very large groups of people first to hear and then see the bearer of political tidings. Using only voice power, Abraham Lincoln and Stephen Douglas challenged each other before thousands of Illinois citizens in their famous debates between August 21 and October 15, 1858.[109] But radio enabled Franklin Delano Roosevelt to deliver fireside chats to millions of Americans across the land, and television later brought not just voices but also images of Richard Nixon and John F. Kennedy debating each other into the homes of even more millions.

The Two-Step Sequence

The advent of radio, and after that of television, transformed the relationship between American citizens and their leaders. The larger the electoral arena, the greater the change. For generations, political parties served to attract and organize a multitude of voters. Parties earned the allegiance of such voters by providing various services, some tangible and others symbolic, some pork and some platitudes. Under the circumstances, and with rudimentary technology, a potential candidate for public office would speak mainly to relatively small groups of party activists, asking for their support, and combining his or her ideas with their insights into what constituents might want or need. Here was a first step in political communications.

An understanding of what the candidate would do later, if elected, was then passed on to party loyalists in wards, precincts, and districts, mainly by local opinion leaders. These people were party activists, known in their towns or neighborhoods but not necessarily holding office there,

---

[108] By comparison, Charles Prestwich Scott, the late nineteenth-century editor of the *Manchester Guardian* in England, held that "the function of...a good journalist is to see life steady and see it whole." Quoted in James Fallows, *Breaking News: How the Media Undermine American Democracy* (New York: Vintage, 1997), p. 47.

[109] See Harold Holzer (ed.), *The Lincoln-Douglas Debates* (New York: HarperCollins, 1993).

who explained where the party stood and why loyalists should support candidates picked mainly by the activists to begin with. Here was a second step in political communications.[110]

Candidate-Centered Politics

Especially at the national level, the two-step process has largely disappeared, so that candidates are now more important than the parties they nominally represent. This happened because, starting with radio broadcasting, and continuing into the era of televised campaigning, presidential and congressional candidates took to speaking directly to more voters than ever and thereby created what may be called *candidate-centered politics*.[111]

Two developments encouraged this trend. First, it seemed increasingly necessary to communicate via electronic media, and especially via television, because those instruments obviously influenced how citizens perceived public affairs and what they might do in response. In 1952, for example, critics attacked Senator Richard Nixon for accepting gifts from his supporters. The *New York Times* even called upon him to withdraw as the Republican candidate for vice president. Then Nixon went on television and delivered his famous Checkers speech, named after a gift dog he refused to return. From an audience of almost half of America's television households, perhaps a million people wrote letters or telegrams supporting Nixon, and Dwight Eisenhower decided to keep him on the Republican national ticket.[112] In 1960, the Nixon-Kennedy presidential debates similarly demonstrated the power of television to sway voters. Of 4 million voters who watched these debates, perhaps 3 million voted for Kennedy in an election that he won by only 112,000 votes.[113]

The second reason for candidates to appeal directly to voters was a rise in the number of primary elections as opposed to party conventions

---

[110] See Elihu Katz and Paul F. Lazardfeld, *Personal Influence: The Part Played by People in the Flow of Mass Communications* (Glencoe, Ill.: Free Press, 1955), pp. 32–33. See also Elihu Katz, "The Two-Step Flow of Communications: An Up-to-Date Report of an Hypothesis," *Public Opinion Quarterly* (Spring 1957), pp. 61–78.

[111] For various components of the process, see Martin P. Wattenberg, *The Rise of Candidate-Centered Politics: Presidential Elections of the 1980s* (Cambridge: Harvard Univ. Press, 1991), and Barbara G. Salmore and Stephen A. Salmore, *Candidates, Parties, and Campaigns: Electoral Politics in America*, 2nd ed. (Washington, D.C.: Congressional Quarterly, 1989), Ch. 3, "The Rise of the Candidate-Centered Campaign," pp. 39–61.

[112] The Checkers speech and its effects are described in Edwin Diamond and Stephen Bates, *The Spot: The Rise of Political Advertising on Television*, rev. ed. (Cambridge: MIT Press, 1988), pp. 66–75.

[113] Larry Sabato, *The Rise of Political Consultants: New Ways of Winning Elections* (New York: Basic Books, 1981), p. 116.

and caucuses at the state level of American politics. In those primaries, candidates for every sort of public office turned increasingly to voters rather than intermediaries in order to evoke support for themselves as nominees.

Presidential campaigns revealed the logic of this process most clearly. In 1968, before reforms sparked by political assassinations and peace demonstrations in that year, there were seventeen Democratic primaries, which elected 37.5 percent of delegates to that party's national nominating convention, while the Republicans conducted sixteen primaries, which elected 34.3 percent of their delegates. But by 1976, after changing their party's nominating rules, the Democrats conducted thirty primaries and thereby elected 72.6 percent of their delegates, while the Republicans, following suit, used twenty-eight primaries to choose 67.9 percent of their delegates.[114]

Under these circumstances, why should anyone seeking the presidency wait for party activists to gather at his party's nominating convention and then try to persuade them to nominate him? Candidates in the 1970s, 1980s, and 1990s chose, instead, to assemble personal campaign teams, to spread out across the country, and speak directly to local voters. The aim was to acquire so many committed delegates during primary elections that the convention would turn into a coronation rather than a convocation run to find common ground among state delegations and locate a candidate ready to serve the party's will. Using this system, Vice President Al Gore and Texas governor George W. Bush secured a majority of Democratic and Republican convention delegates by March of 2000. It followed that their nominating conventions in August of 2000 were conducted as television spectaculars and that their parties would do mainly their bidding rather than vice versa.[115]

The Triumph of Marketing

While parties lost much of their power to enlist voters, candidates had to make themselves attractive to those same voters. To this end, they increasingly hired political consultants. In the age of television, such people offered advice on how to reach and move the public more effectively than

---

[114] These figures on primaries are from David E. Price, *Bringing Back the Parties* (Washington, D.C.: Congressional Quarterly, 1984), pp. 208–209.

[115] See Peter Marks, "The Republican Convention: A Plan to Accentuate the Positive and (at Least) Minimize the Negative," *New York Times* (July 25, 2000), p. A20. The article describes Andy Card as "general co-chairman and chief conceptualizer of the $63 million event" and quotes him as saying, "This convention is really about George [W.] Bush," and "I view this as a mini-series that has to be told over four nights."

old-time party bosses and neighborhood organizers could. Eventually, such consultants offered their clients package deals of advice on what positions would be popular with the voters, where to direct campaign messages for the greatest impact, how to frame those messages most effectively in the media, and how to budget for forms of persuasion ranging from personal appearances to bumper stickers, from broadcast time to visiting constituents at home.

In the broadest sense, consultants were experts in marketing their clients, in the business of using techniques already shown to have sold commercial products successfully. Their firms employed scores or hundreds of workers, from pollsters to telethon organizers, from market researchers to demographers, from makeup artists to voice coaches, from graphic designers to direct mail advertisers.[116]

In significant ways, the new work on behalf of nominations and elections differed from that done by political parties which had long promoted, at least intermittently, some vision of a good society in America. By contrast, consultants who advised candidates were not particularly concerned with the quality of their product but with how it might be sold. Like business marketeers, political consultants were less devoted to the well-being of the community than to the success of their client.[117]

To this end, they used techniques such as polling, pioneered by people who sell products to consumers. *Polling* helps candidates to know what potential supporters want, that is, what they are willing to "buy" with their votes. So polls taken before and during the campaign reveal what voters think about various issues, after which consultants package candidates so they will appear committed to what those voters were looking for all along. This packaging relies heavily on political advertisements that resemble their commercial counterparts, partly because the same creative people are often hired to produce both and partly because what works in selling Nescafé, Bufferin, and Kodak film will appeal to candidates looking for proven techniques. The result is that political ads are short, to

---

[116] On political consultants in general, see Sabato, *The Rise of Political Consultants*, and Frank I. Luntz, *Candidates, Consultants, and Campaigns: The Style and Substance of American Electioneering* (Oxford: Basil Blackwell, 1988).

[117] See F. Christopher Aterton, "The Persuasive Art of Politics: The Role of Paid Advertising in Presidential Campaigns," in Matthew D. McCubbins (ed.), *Under the Watchful Eye: Managing Presidential Campaigns in the Television Era* (Washington, D.C.: Congressional Quarterly, 1992), p. 105: "To quote Lee Atwater, who ran George Bush's 1988 campaign: 'We had only one goal, to help elect George Bush. That's the purpose of any political campaign. What other function should a campaign have?'"

discourage zapping, and are mostly nonrefutable, to evoke emotions but avoid criticism for inaccuracy and exaggeration.[118]

Polling results reveal the public to be not a unified entity but a congery of preference groups and categories, or what advertisers call *market segments*. A campaign designed by consultants begins, then, by acknowledging that the candidate will address various groups differently in accordance with their respective attitudes and aspirations. Nationwide television must be handled very carefully on this score. Many people watch it, and thus messages broadcast there tend to address large and general matters such as education, Social Security, family values, and crime. But local radio and television stations, and cable TV, specializing in country-and-western songs, classical music, talk shows, rock music videos, Spanish-language programming, and more, offer a variety of relatively homogeneous audiences. For them, political messages can be tailored more specifically and candidates can stake out positions more clearly.[119]

For targeting market segments even more precisely, consultants advise their clients to send out direct mail. Using techniques developed in commercial marketing, direct mail specialists identify those market segments most likely to respond favorably to a candidate's particular appeal for support, those people with special characteristics, such as, perhaps, the right-handed, heterosexual, Latino, liberal Honda owners living in suburbs of more than forty thousand people. Each group so identified then receives the appropriate message, often scathingly negative on opponents since, as in the world of commerce, ads that criticize a competitor tend to be remembered more often than those that praise a client.

The Effects of Consulting

Unfortunately, consultants do not aim at achieving the sort of civic result that political parties are supposed to provide, and their marketing techniques do not encourage citizens to think constructively and vote on behalf of public interests. Polling, for example, does not seek to inform but to ascertain preferences and even prejudices. Ads are then devised which are so short as to contain little information, so nonrefutable as to withhold facts deliberately, and, in many cases, so negative as to foster

---

[118] Montague Kern, *30-Second Politics: Political Advertising in the Eighties* (New York: Praeger, 1989); and Sig Mickelson, *From Whistle Stop to Sound Bite: Four Decades of Politics and Television* (New York: Praeger, 1989).

[119] On campaigning in different markets, see Paul West, "Is TV Losing Its Campaign Clout?" *Washington Journalism Review* (October 1986), pp. 14–16.

anger and alienation rather than solidarity and a willingness to promote common projects. Moreover, as a general practice, when consultants target marketing segments, different messages are sent to different people, speaking to what sets them apart rather than what might draw them together. On this score, instead of talking about shared hopes and values to encourage tolerance of others only marginally different, modern campaigning splinters the community and perpetuates disarray by reinforcing people's sense of their own distinctiveness.[120]

Campaigning Versus Governing

The qualities needed for candidate-centered *campaigning* are not necessarily those required for *governing*. The former include "dexterity, opportunism, volatility, expediency, and short-run manipulation," all of which can help candidates to project a personal image that captures voter attention and achieves the immediate goals of nomination and election. Governing, on the other hand, is a matter of patient, steady work based on farsighted strategies for improving the quality of community life, and it is best conducted by those who work well with others rather than radiate personal, but perhaps misleading, images of competence.[121]

In analogous terms, *running* is not the same as *ruling*.[122] The two diverged because of campaign strategies developed especially for marketing via television. When parties controlled the process by which they nominated presidents, power barons in each party – from state leaders to union activists, from elected officials to business executives – would choose a candidate for his ability to strike the deals necessary to serve their many and sometimes conflicting interests. In that sense, the nominating convention was a process for building an electoral coalition which the president-elect would lead during his years in the White House. But modern nominations are captured by the telegenic candidate who builds popularity rather than coalitions, who seizes the nomination rather than

---

[120] Elizabeth Drew, *Money and Politics: The New Road to Corruption* (New York: Macmillan, 1983), pp. 130–131. The term *wedge issues* refers to issues that are highlighted in order to drive voters apart. Classic cases include Republican talk about, say, crime or welfare, designed to encourage white Democrats to flee black Democrats by joining the Republican Party. See Thomas Byrne Edsall and Mary D. Edsall, *Chain Reaction: The Impact of Race, Rights, and Taxes on American Politics* (New York: Norton, 1992).

[121] On campaigning and governing qualities, see James MacGregor Burns, *The Power to Lead: The Crisis of the American Presidency* (New York: Touchstone, 1984), pp. 42–43.

[122] Hedrick Smith, *The Power Game* (New York: Random House, 1988), pp. 693–708, esp. 693–698.

heads the party, so that he or she arrives in Washington with an office but not necessarily the talent for doing its work.

There is, moreover, after election day a constant distraction caused by *the permanent campaign.*[123] As we have seen, candidates learned, in the age of television, that they must speak directly to voters rather than rely on their parties to bring voters to the polls. Therefore candidates turned to political consultants for help. These experts used polls to discover what voters wanted, after which they advised politicians what to say and do so they would seem to be what voters were looking for. And thus, for politicians seeking reelection, it became advisable to maintain a constantly favorable image so that when election day arrived, incumbents could cash in on whatever long-term popularity they had built up. As a result, campaigning now starts right after candidates win office, to the point where campaigning by incumbents becomes permanent.

The downside to permanent campaigning is that lawmakers tend to worry more about appearances than about governing. They therefore spend a great deal of time *positioning* themselves with regard to issues that polls discern in the electoral marketplace.[124] Such flexibility may help incumbents to win elections. But agility in moving from one immediate issue to the next, such as whether or not to unite Elian Gonzales with his Cuban father in 2000, does little to help politicians govern. Governing, after all, consists in responding to constituencies defined by fairly stable interests, in which case the goal of governing, properly speaking, is to serve a community of real needs rather than poll results based on temporary impressions. In fact, then, the strategy of constantly positioning candidates before audiences may fail to provide for governmental policy rooted in an intelligible conception of where communal life should move.

---

[123] Sidney Blumenthal, *The Permanent Campaign: Inside the World of Elite Political Operatives* (Boston: Beacon, 1980).

[124] See Meg Greenfield, *Washington* (New York: Public Affairs, 2001). On p. 8, Greenfield, former editorial page editor of the *Washington Post*, writes about bureaucrats, appointees, and elected officials in "the world of endless competitive image projection." As she describes them,

> the most common result is. . . . self-creation as a walking, talking, person-shaped but otherwise not very human amalgam of "positions," that familiar, tirelessly striving figure interviewed on the evening news who resoundingly tells you what he is thinking – and you keep wondering whether you should believe a word of it. These are people who don't seem to live in the world so much as to inhabit some point on graph paper, whose coordinates are (sideways) the political spectrum and (up and down) the latest overnight poll figures.

Republican Results

In short, consumerism increasingly dominated twentieth-century America. It rested on large producing organizations, on the flood of commodities they generated, and on the need to motivate people to consume those commodities constantly. From this modern condition there emerged predicaments that persist into the twenty-first century, such as other-directedness, nonrefutable advertising, environmental damage, economic insecurity, candidate-centered politics, and permanent campaigning. It remains to consider how, here and there, in the circumstances, consumerism directly affects the sort of republican citizenship that Americans have long idealized.

Two Kinds of Disengagement

To begin with, consumerism weakens ties that can bind citizens to their communities. In one sense, this happens because large corporations enhanced modern productivity but reduced the number of men and women who can afford to exercise independent judgment in public affairs. Working for wages became a normal way for most people to make a living in twentieth-century America. It followed that many citizens felt constrained to take into account, openly or tacitly, the interests of their employers on election day. Hence they became apprehensive, wary of retaliation, timid about advocating public policies which their employer might oppose. People in this situation may continue to vote, but they are unlikely to agitate, to inspire, and to lead their neighbors when controversial public issues are at stake.

Jefferson and Lincoln, among others, had long ago feared economic dependence and believed it would constrain hired hands from exercising full republican citizenship. Twentieth-century researchers concurred. From sociology, C. Wright Mills argued that many Americans who work for large organizations are wary of risking their livelihood by standing up against corporate interests.[125] Consequently, in his opinion, they lack detachment in judging public affairs. From political science, Andrew Hacker agreed. Moreover, he observed that, when small-scale property ownership facilitating independent thinking got replaced in America by a culture which promotes immediate gratification, many people became so

---

[125] C. Wright Mills, *White Collar: The American Middle Classes* (New York: Oxford Univ. Press, 1951), pp. xi–xii, 7–12, 54–59.

ego-centered that they lost their willingness to sacrifice the time and energy that good citizenship may require.[126]

So those who rely on whoever owns the means of production lose some of their capacity for political independence. Oddly enough, the context of getting and spending also encourages some highly successful people to move away from active citizenship. Here the problem is not so much those who feel constrained but others who, in whatever way, earn so much that they can afford to withdraw into private enclaves of privilege. Here are the parents who ignore public schools because they are wealthy enough to send their children to private academies; here are the CEOs who disregard creaky public transit because they get chauffeured to work; here are the New Economy pundits who belittle proposals for government regulation to protect Old Economy workers threatened with demotion to poorly paid service jobs; here are the gated communities which hire security guards and leave policing to tax-poor municipalities.[127] In short, here are people who, to some extent, regard themselves as linked only by limited liability toward the larger communities in which they live.

Christopher Lasch summed up this trend when he termed it a *revolt of the elites*, by which he meant that a considerable number of Americans who might provide leadership in public affairs have decided not to do so.[128] He and economist Robert Reich agreed that many middle-class people, sensing the breakdown of America's social contract under the strain of deindustrialization, downsizing, outsourcing, and globalization, are set on protecting themselves in a commercial world that seems indifferent to their fate.[129] In the shuffle some capacity, and certainly some enthusiasm, for good citizenship gets lost.

The Decline of Civil Society

Apart from income factors that may encourage civic disengagement, consumerism fosters a general loosening of social bonds which translates into reduced willingness to exercise active citizenship via political participation. This process unfolds in two stages. First, a declining number of people voluntarily join the social organizations of civil society with

---

[126] Andrew Hacker, *The End of the American Era* (New York: Atheneum, 1980), pp. 9–37.

[127] Edward J. Blakely and Mary G. Synder, *Fortress America: Gated Communities in the United States* (Washington, D.C.: Brookings, 1997).

[128] See Christopher Lasch, *The Revolt of the Elites and the Betrayal of Democracy* (New York: Norton, 1996).

[129] Reich, *The Work of Nations*, pp. 268–281.

their neighbors. Whereupon, second, fewer citizens than previously attach themselves to political society by joining political parties, attending political rallies, discussing public issues, voting, running for public office, and so forth.

Regarding the first step, political scientist Robert Putnam observes that, since the 1960s and 1970s, young to middle-aged Americans have joined familiar grassroots organizations at rates that are 10 percent, 20 percent, or even 30 percent lower than those registered by their parents and grandparents.[130] The result is that even where group membership numbers seem high, they are low in relation to the number of people who are available to join. This decline in social engagement, he notes, spreads out over bowling leagues, bridge clubs, labor unions, religious congregations, parent-teacher associations, professional societies, fraternal orders, and more.

According to Putnam, the culprits on this score are mainly trends that accompany the advanced materialism of a consumer society and use up time and energy that might otherwise be invested in social involvement. These trends include suburbanization, commuting, two-career families, high rates of divorce, and passivity bred by electronic entertainment. The main cause of broken social relations, however, is commercial television.[131]

Television is so fascinating, says Putnam, that it causes people to stay home rather than socialize with neighbors. This the small screen does by using up leisure time that earlier generations might have devoted to visiting friends or attending group activities of many sorts. Moreover, television keeps family members apart, as when several receivers in a single house are turned on simultaneously in different rooms to different programs. Here is a result of targeting market segments, which makes some programs appealing to part of the family while other programs speak to the rest. Furthermore, television impedes social intercourse even when family members are together. This happens, for example, when television is watched at mealtimes and interrupts family conversations.

As a second step in Putnam's tale, broken social relations, including those caused by television, get translated into civic disengagement when

---

[130] These paragraphs on civil society and social capital rely on facts and interpretations that appear in Putnam, *Bowling Alone.* See also the earlier discussion of social capital in Robert Putnam, with Robert Leonardi and Raffaela Y. Nanett, *Making Democracy Work: Civic Traditions in Modern Italy* (Princeton: Princeton Univ. Press, 1993), pp. 163–185.

[131] Putnam analyzes the impact of television in *Bowling Alone,* Ch. 13, "Technology and Mass Media," pp. 216–246.

what Putnam calls *social capital* fails to materialize in sufficient quantity. That is, by spending time together and working on common projects, people learn to get along with each other, learn to trust one another, and also learn that it is desirable to seek out each other's company for the pursuit of mutual interests. Along the way, the social skills and confidence acquired in voluntary relationships, which may be private or public, permit and inspire people to regard themselves as connected to other people, culminating in a concern for community as the larger framework that can fruitfully unite them all. In this sense, failing to join formal and informal organizations to the extent they did even as late as a generation ago, Americans are not creating enough of the wherewithal, or social capital, required for good citizenship.

The Decline of Voting

Researchers are not sure of the exact degree to which wage employment, commercial television, elite circumstances, and group memberships in a consumer society affect political behavior.[132] In our story, television is a major culprit because the small screen so obviously promotes shopping and uses up time that might be spent on other activities, some of them possibly relevant to good citizenship. However, there are studies that reveal more specifically political reasons which also discourage civic activism. For example, to gain freedom of maneuver to set public policy, government has, over the years, used automatic taxes rather than voluntary bonds to pay for war, even while the army that goes into combat is staffed by paid professionals rather than amateur

---

[132] For example, Putnam's concept of social capital has stimulated enormous scholarly interest, resulting in an academic debate far too complicated to be summed up here. For journal articles in that debate, by order of appearance rather than importance, see Charles Heying, "Civic Elites and Corporate Delocalization: An Alternative Explanation for Declining Civic Engagements," *American Behavioral Scientist* (March–April 1997), pp. 657–668; Eric Uslaner, "Social Capital, Television, and the 'Mean World': Trust, Optimism, and Civic Participation," *Political Psychology* (September 1998), pp. 441–467; Pamela Paxton, "Is Social Capital Declining in the United States? A Multiple Indicator Assessment," *American Journal of Sociology* (July 1999), pp. 88–127; Bob Edwards and Michael Foley, "Is It Time to Disinvest in Social Capital?" *Journal of Public Policy* (May–August 1999), pp. 141–174; Alan Ehrenhalt, "Appraising Social Capital," *Responsive Community* (Fall 2000), pp. 59–63; Theda Skocpol, "A Nation of Organizers: The Institutional Origins of Civic Voluntarism in the United States," *American Political Science Review* (September 2000), pp. 527–546; Carl Boggs, "Social Capital and Political Fantasy: Robert Putnam's *Bowling Alone*," *Theory and Society* (April 2001), pp. 281–297; and Kenneth Newton, "Trust, Social Capital, Civil Society, and Democracy," *International Political Science Review* (April 2001), pp. 201–214.

draftees.[133] In such cases, government "sidelines" many citizens and does not call on them to participate in great national decisions. It follows that some of them, no longer regarded by others as a public sharing common interests, respond by attending chiefly to private affairs.

For various reasons, then, something is seriously wrong with civic behavior in America today. One place where this shows up is when many citizens do not bother to vote. Turnout of the voting age population for the presidential election of 1960 was 62.8 percent. By 1972 it dropped to 55.2 percent and in 1996 reached 49.2 percent.[134] Figures for congressional elections sank even lower, trailing presidential voting by 4 to 5 percent in presidential election years and by 15 to 18 percent in midterm elections.[135] Declining trust in governmental institutions apparently accounts for at least some of the falling voter turnout.[136] On this score, the number of citizens expressing "a great deal of confidence" in Congress went down from 42 percent in 1966 to 11 percent in 1997, while similar expressions of high regard for the executive branch fell from 41 percent in 1966 to 12 percent in 1997.[137]

Voters as Consumers

Putnam would say that those who are less active in civil society will participate less in politics and trust other people less in public life. It also seems

---

[133] Matthew A. Crenson and Benjamin Ginsberg, *Downsizing Democracy: How America Sidelined Its Citizens and Privatized Its Public* (Baltimore: Johns Hopkins Univ. Press, 2002), pp. 29–46.

[134] The presidential vote rose to 51.2 percent in 2000. These figures are from Ruy A. Teixeira, *The Disappearing American Voter* (Washington, D.C.: Brookings Institution, 1992), p. 6; and *Statistical Abstract of the United States* (Washington, D.C.: U.S. Census Bureau, 2002), p. 254.

[135] *Statistical Abstract of the United States* (Washington, D.C.: U.S. Census Bureau, 2000), pp. 273, 276–277.

[136] Additional reasons cited by the voters include governmental inefficiency and waste, government spending on "the wrong things," politicians seen to lack integrity, and special interests openly exercising great power. See Frances Fox Piven and Richard A. Cloward, *Why Americans Still Don't Vote: And Why Politicians Want It That Way* (New York: Beacon, 2000); and Joseph S. Nye, Jr., Philip D. Zelikow, and David C. King (eds.), *Why People Don't Trust Government* (Cambridge: Harvard Univ. Press, 1997), pp. 210–215. See also Thomas E. Patterson, *The Vanishing Voter: Public Involvement in an Age of Uncertainty* (New York: Knopf, 2003), esp. pp. 23–145, on how attack politics, long campaigns, critical journalism, registration requirements, and other elements of the political process discourage voter turnout.

[137] See David M. Shribman, "Insiders with a Crisis from Outside," in Joseph Cooper (ed.), *Congress and the Decline of Public Trust* (Boulder, Colo.: Westview, 1999), p. 30. On the trend to political cynicism, see also Seymour Martin Lipset, *American Exceptionalism: A Double-Edged Sword* (New York: Norton, 1996), pp. 281–283.

probable, however, that an additional reason for such indicators is that many citizens are fed up with being treated like political consumers.[138] We may suspect as much from the way campaigns are now run. Some voters are still loyal Democrats and Republicans, in which case candidates for those parties can, in theory at least, talk to such voters openly and plainly about supporting their party as if it represents an intelligible view of how to attain public well-being. But since the 1970s, roughly a quarter to a third of Americans have considered themselves to be independent voters. Precisely because they lack loyalty to any party, such people become the swing voters who can provide a margin of victory between major party candidates.[139]

It follows that candidates will court independents not by proposing a sensible and coherent party platform but by offering bits and pieces of what independent voters seem to want momentarily. Yet in order to address such people, the same candidates will have to talk, via television, to everyone who is watching, since the medium is mostly nonselective. The result is that promises and images aimed at swing voters dominate election campaigns,[140] even while campaign messages are, as we have seen, guided by what consultants believe works best when marketing commercial products to fickle consumers. Under the circumstances, and via the techniques of polling and aiming at market segments, American campaigns have come to treat voters like their shopping counterparts, assuming that they are interested mainly in what a particular candidate, the political equivalent

---

[138] For a general explanation of how citizens came to be treated this way, see Robert B. Westbrook, "Politics as Consumption: Managing the Modern American Election," in Richard Wightman Fox and T. J. Jackson Lears (eds.), *The Culture of Consumption: Critical Essays in American History, 1880–1890* (New York: Pantheon, 1983), pp. 145–173. On soliciting voters via techniques more appropriate to commercial marketing than to politics, see Marshall Ganz, "Voters in the Crosshairs: How Technology and the Market Are Destroying Politics," *American Prospect* (Winter 1994), pp. 100–109.

[139] Ibid., p. 152: "Winning elections became less a matter of mobilizing the faithful and more a matter of attracting the undecided."

[140] On aiming at swing voters, see Bob Woodward, *The Choice: How Clinton Won* (New York: Touchstone, 1996), p. 437:

> Chaos, multiple and inconsistent daily messages had marred the first two years of . . . [Clinton's] presidency. . . . The new campaign message imposed a needed discipline. . . . The ads were carefully calibrated to appear in media markets rich with *undecided or persuadable voters*. The same ads or variations of them often appeared hundreds of times in key markets. . . . The Clinton television advertising ran for six months, from the fall of 1995 to the spring of 1996. . . . In retrospect, I would argue that Clinton won the 1996 elections in late 1995 and early 1996. He found his message, stuck to it and brought it into the homes of millions. [emphasis supplied]

of Microsoft or Chevrolet or Kodak, will promise to provide in order to make them happy.

For citizenship, one problem here is that people acting as consumers do not constitute a community.[141] That is, they do not choose commodities, or politicians, the way that republican citizens are supposed to choose leaders and policies. Watching television and going occasionally to vote, after all, cannot substitute for deciding how to vote by participating in a civic culture, by discussing issues with friends and neighbors, by lobbying, by attending public hearings, by marching in demonstrations, by writing letters to editors, by helping to create coalitions to promote this or that policy, and so forth.[142] On the contrary, whereas the behavior of citizens is supposed to flow from a mental process of deliberating, consumers are permitted, and even encouraged, to buy on impulse.[143] Thus citizens are expected to calculate their community's interest and act to promote it, whereas consumers are entitled to buy on behalf of private ends as if the sum total of those ends, although informed by no shared rationale, is somehow equivalent to what the public needs.

The Fourth Language

One cause for citizen anger at politics as consuming is the language of persuasion that consumerism created. *Habits of the Heart* claimed that

---

[141] Worse, aiming at undecided voters can weaken whatever attachment they do sense for an existing community. This happens when, in pursuit of such voters, political campaigns speak mainly to approximately 10 percent of adult Americans. Fifty percent of potential electors choose not to vote; 40 percent are loyalists about evenly divided between the two major parties; and thus 10 percent are the undecided segment of likely voters who are vigorously wooed by both Republicans and Democrats. See Aterton, "The Persuasive Art of Politics," pp. 88–90. Under the circumstances, many citizens grow alienated from politics because they feel that most candidates and elected officials, who campaign permanently, do not address them or their concerns. Unfortunately, the perception is accurate.

[142] Jean Bethke Elshtain, *Democracy on Trial* (New York: Basic Books, 1995), p. 29.

[143] This distinction is drawn in Joseph Tussman, *Obligation and the Body Politic* (New York: Oxford Univ. Press, 1960), pp. 104–121. The same distinction appears in the language of cultural studies used by some scholars to criticize great business firms. For example, see Henry A. Giroux, *The Mouse That Roared: Disney and the End of Innocence* (New York: Rowman and Littlefield, 1999). Giroux describes Walt Disney Enterprises as a powerful educational force in American life – as potent as nineteenth-century editions of *McGuffy's Reader* – pitching the virtues of consumerism every day to millions of people, mostly children, via films, compact disks, home videos, television programs, theme parks, toys, and clothing. In the Disney universe of fun, games, and uncomplicated narratives, the goal is profit but the effect is to train children to be consumers rather than citizens, to think of themselves as passive economic subjects rather than critical civic actors. See especially "Disney and the Politics of Public Culture," pp. 17–61.

modern America suffers from an imbalance among the three languages of republicanism, biblical morality, and individualism. Yet there is a *fourth language* in America, used mainly for advocacy, that finds expression in what is said publicly and what is not said, that underlies the ways in which things are described and the ways in which they go unremarked, that generates attractive images and ringing endorsements rather than tangible data and measured arguments.

This *language of persuasion* was designed largely by advertisers and other marketeers to stimulate the reflexive self-centeredness that links the pursuit of happiness with the acquisition of commodities. We can see it most clearly, then, in the realm of commercial television, which addresses people in a style designed to persuade them to buy more things than they need. After all, if viewers needed what they see promoted on television, sales would flourish unaided and corporations would not have to sponsor popular programs to peddle their wares powerfully.[144] Consequently, television broadcasts are fashioned not to inform citizens but to attract audiences of people who will stay tuned in to watch ads.

In the process, as we have noted, every sort of human activity, from religion to state funerals, from famines to wars, gets transformed into entertainment, thereby flattening out distinctions that citizens should make between things that are consequential and those that are not. Furthermore, television "news" describes what is happening in the world via a series of one- or two-minute "stories," thereby indicating that viewers are not supposed to think more deeply about one thing than another, or even to think deeply about anything.[145] Television also suggests that politicians, who must occasionally deal with serious affairs, should not themselves be taken seriously. This happens when anchorpersons debunk them with ironic closing remarks about how, after a politician has spoken, we will just have to wait and see what happens.[146]

And finally, television displays ads whose purpose, as a form of deliberate communication, is to "fix the attention but not to engage the

---

[144] It would also be unnecessary to hide television ads no one wants to see behind shifty phrases such as "Stay with us. We'll be right back after *this*."

[145] By constantly flitting from one thing or event or person to another, commercial television encourages witless viewer responses. See Mark Crispin Miller, *The Bush Dyslexicon: Observations on a National Disorder* (New York: Norton, 2002), pp. 63–76.

[146] James Fallows claims that journalists tend to irony in their closing remarks as a response to "spin-control" and outright deception practiced by politicians and their spokespeople. See his *Breaking News*, pp. 60–65, but esp. p. 63: "The reporter's remaining outlet is an all-purpose sneer, which vents his frustration and sends viewers a warning that politicians are trying to hoodwink them too."

mind."[147] To this end, it showcases products from companies which seek not to inform but to make viewers feel good with meaningless phrases like: "Toyota – for Everyday People," and "IBM – Solutions for a Small Planet," and "Panasonic – Just Slightly Ahead of Our Time."

Truth as Casualty

In sum, television rests on a language of persuasion that is not an instrument of truth but an idiom of effectiveness. Anthropologist Jules Henry described this language as dealing in *pecuniary pseudo-truth*.[148] That is, when a gasoline company says it is putting a tiger in your tank, neither you nor the company believes that the tiger is actually there. On the other hand, you know that the statement was not made to be believed but to sell the gasoline. In such cases, the proof of "truth" in a statement of commercial persuasion is simple: Does it do its job, which is to sell commodities?

Modern candidates, of course, learn to use the language of advocacy for speaking to voters, whom their consultants regard as political consumers in the sense that, if they will come to admire the candidate via exciting images and nonrefutable promises, they will "buy" him or her with a vote on election day. But what if, in addition to dominating political campaigns, this same language were to infect communications in public life which, according to republican expectations, are supposed to enable citizens to reason together?[149] That is what happened during the twentieth century, for the syntax and grammar, style and strategy, of commercial persuasion now pervade what politicians and government agencies tell the American people even between elections.[150]

In *The Federalist*, Alexander Hamilton, James Madison, and John Jay used historical analogies and analytic arguments to encourage voters in New York to elect state convention delegates who would favor ratification of the Constitution. Seeking to sway opinion today, they would

---

[147] Potter, *People of Plenty*, p. 182.

[148] Henry, *Culture Against Man*, p. 47.

[149] Lapham, *The Wish for Kings*, p. 41: "The energy of the American idea flows from the capacity of its citizens to speak and think without cant, from their willingness to defend their interest, argue their case, say what they mean."

[150] As always, we should not regard the past as better than it was. Thus the problem of irrationality in American public life today is a matter of degree, for democratic politics have never been entirely rational. On nineteenth-century voting, see Benjamin Disraeli, *Conigsby* (orig., 1844; New York: New American Library, 1962), pp. 110–111: " 'Pray what is the country?' inquired Mr. Rigby. 'The country is nothing; it is the constituency you have to deal with.' 'And to manage them you must have a good cry,' said Taper. 'All now depends on a good cry.' 'So much so for the science of politics,' said the Duke."

first meet with a campaign consultant who would advise them, on the basis of polls, how to make their message persuasive not on the merits of the case but in keeping with the sometimes uninformed opinions and narrow prejudices entertained by swing voters.[151] In the same vein, every politician in important public office now has a press secretary, while every bureaucracy has a spokesperson. And those people are constantly addressing the public but not speaking the truth, the whole truth, and nothing but the truth because, as in the commercial world, the point is not to tell the truth but to make one's client look good.

Sometimes plain lying gets plainly exposed, as when Ron Ziegler, press secretary to President Richard Nixon, famously admitted that his earlier statements describing Nixon as innocent in the Watergate Affair should be considered "inoperative."[152] Or when David Stockman, director of the Office of Management and Budgeting for President Ronald Reagan, confessed that the Great Communicator's budget looked balanced on paper only because it contained an asterisk in place of program cuts which the White House would never ask Congress to enact.[153]

Leading politicians, and not just their hired guns, are also seen to dissemble occasionally. Thus President Bill Clinton said he "never had sex" with Monica Lewinsky. Not at all. Well, not exactly. And thus Congressman Henry Hyde and Senator Trent Lott told America that Republicans sought to remove Clinton from office because he had lied about Lewinsky. No political motives there. Well, maybe a few.

Credibility suffers under such circumstances. And then, for good reason, credulity flags. After all, whether half-truths, equivocations, exaggerations, and outright lies are delivered by a paid spokesperson or principle actor, the public is treated to carefully measured phrases that insult more than they inform. The list of offending cases is endless. The Defense Department, after slight resistance to the 1983 American invasion of Grenada, awards 8,612 medals for an operation in which 19 Americans were killed and 115 wounded, some by friendly fire.[154] Is this not puffery?

---

[151] Concerning *The Federalist*, this point is made in Walter Truett Anderson, *Reality Isn't What It Used to Be: Theatrical Politics, Ready-to-Wear Religion, Global Myths, Primitive Chic, and Other Wonders of the Postmodern World* (New York: Harper and Row, 1990), pp. 157–158.

[152] Carl Bernstein and Bob Woodward, *All the President's Men* (New York: Warner, 1975), pp. 321–322.

[153] David A. Stockman, *The Triumph of Politics: The Inside Story of the Reagan Revolution* (New York: Avon, 1987), pp. 135, 145.

[154] Nicolaus Mills, "The Culture of Triumph and the Spirit of the Times," p. 14. For recent Pentagon puffery, see the case of Pfc. Jessica Lynch, who served courageously in Iraq

Evisceration of federal welfare programs gets described as "The Personal Responsibility and Work Opportunity Reconciliation Act" of 1996.[155] Are "crack babies" responsible for their plight? Should North Carolina textile workers follow their jobs to China? Presidential candidate George W. Bush proclaims that he is a "compassionate conservative." What does that mean?[156] "Intelligence sources" warn the press, which cautions the people, that North Korea "could" have missiles capable of striking the United States by 2005.[157] The assertion is grammatically empty, for the North Koreans could also invade California by then. No matter. Such double-talk is designed to justify spending $100 billion, or maybe more, of public money on the development and deployment of antimissile missiles that, so far, do not work.

The Republican Dilemma

What happens to a society in which business people, professionals, and politicians increasingly address citizens in messages that only the gullible can believe? Where, for example, the Government Employees Insurance Company (GEICO) advertises that "A fifteen-minute call could save you 15 percent or more on car insurance." *Could*?[158] Surely the pervasion of

---

and, like other American soldiers who served there, deserves her country's gratitude. Part of a six-hundred-truck convoy carrying Lynch, supply clerk in the 507th Maintenance Company, took a wrong turn during the war against Saddam Hussein and was attacked near An Nāsirīyah, Iraq, on March 23, 2003. Eleven Americans were killed and numerous others were wounded in the incident. Official reports of what happened were vague. Apparently Lynch's legs were badly injured when her vehicle, under enemy fire, crashed into another; it does not apear that she was able to fight back, and she has no recollection of exactly what occurred. Pfc. Lynch was awarded the Bronze Star (for heroism), the Purple Heart (for being wounded in combat), and the Prisoner of War (for being captured) medals on July 21 in Washington and returned home to Palestine, West Virginia, on July 22. See "Private Lynch Comes Back Home to a Celebration Fit for a Hero," *New York Times* (July 23, 2003), pp. A1, A11.

[155] On the terms of this act, see Michael B. Katz, *In the Shadow of the Poorhouse: A Social History of Welfare in America*, rev. ed. (New York: Basic, 1996), pp. 324–334.

[156] Some clues may be found in Marvin Olasky, *Compassionate Conservatism: What It Is, What It Does, and How It Can Transform America*, foreword by George W. Bush (New York: Free Press, 2000). There, "compassionate conservatism" appears as a slogan designed to justify using government money to finance what might be called, in plain English, sectarian social projects with a missionary bent. As befits the language of persuasion, "religion" is absent from the slogan, and the projects are described as administered by "faith-based" organizations.

[157] "Korea Accord Fails to Stall Missile Plan," *New York Times* (June 18, 2000), pp. A11, 16.

[158] The word *could* exemplifies the capacity of fourth-language communications for seeming to present facts without actually doing so. Thus when President George W. Bush encouraged Americans to support his plan for going to war against Saddam Hussein, he

public life by such slippery language is one cause for declining trust in major institutions over the last half century.[159] For example, corporations like Dow Chemical, Mobil, Philip Morris, Monsanto, and Ford sponsor organizations like "The National Wetlands Coalition," "Consumer Alert," the "National Right to Work Committee," and "Keep America Beautiful," where the name implies vigilance on behalf of public well-being even though the goal is to lobby against labor unions, environmental protection, and product safety laws.[160] How can citizens respect institutions that, intentionally misnamed, apparently do not respect them?[161]

For republicanism, the language of persuasion is especially toxic because, to the extent that it dominates political messages, it leaves the facts aside in favor of techniques like puffery and nonrefutable messages. The

informed them that "Iraq has a growing fleet of manned and unmanned aerial vehicles that *could* be used to disperse chemical or biological weapons across broad areas." Moreover, "Iraq *could* decide on any given day to provide a biological or chemical weapon to a terrorist group or individual terrorists. Alliance with terrorists *could* allow the Iraqi regime to attack America without leaving any fingerprints." Furthermore, "If the Iraqi regime is able to produce, buy, or steal an amount of highly enriched uranium a little larger than a single softball, it *could* have a nuclear weapon in less than a year." And finally, "we cannot wait for the final proof – the smoking gun – that *could* come in the form of a mushroom cloud" (emphases supplied). See "Transcript: Confronting Iraq Threat 'Is Crucial to Winning War on Terror,'" *New York Times* (October 7, 2002), p. A12. Technically, such allegations do not constitute falsehood because, grammatically, they make no falsifiable claim.

[159] See the charts in Gary Orren, "Fall From Grace: The Public's Loss of Faith in Government," in Nye, Jr., Zelikow, and King (eds.), *Why People Don't Trust Government*, pp. 81–87.

[160] Mark Megali and Andy Friedman, *Masks of Deception: Corporate Front Groups in America* (Washington, D.C.: Essential Information, 1991), analyze the groups cited above and dozens of additional groups funded by corporations, serving corporate interests, and bearing names such as Citizens for Sensible Control of Acid Rain, the American Tort Reform Association, Citizens Against Government Waste, the Coalition for American Energy Security, the Coalition for Vehicle Choice, and the National Institute for Chemical Studies.

[161] For example, see the ad entitled "Collaborating to Increase Chemical Knowledge," *New York Times* (August 22, 2002), p. A23, which tells readers that the American Chemistry Council (whatever that is) sponsors research on "the relationship between highly useful chemical products and their potential impacts on humans, wildlife and the environment." In this ad, displayed for high exposure on the *Times*'s op-ed page, ExxonMobil, presumably a financial supporter of the council, concludes that "armed with better knowledge, the public can be confident that chemicals, properly used, are unlikely to pose consequential risks." This is language designed to soothe but not inform. Why should the public be "confident" when it does not know which "chemicals" the ad's author has in mind, when it cannot be sure that they will be used "properly," when it does not know the exact nature of a "consequential" risk, and when the term *unlikely*, which does not refer to an absolute number of occurrences, is compatible with an occasional ecological disaster?

result is that when politicians speak on behalf of society's great interests – from women to workers, from agriculture to industry, from children to retirees – they often describe political issues and social problems in terms designed to evoke emotions rather than facilitate reason. At best, this tactic fails to provide citizens with information they need to make judgments they should. At worst, such discourse, which is inherently self-serving, promotes civic indifference by encouraging people to regard modern society "as an arena for rival frauds."[162]

And finally, by overloading everyday perceptions with a flood of attractive but trivial images, the fourth language disables and undermines cultural literacy which, by providing a shared sense of community, may help republicanism to function and survive.[163] Thus a warning signal is sounded for good citizenship when research shows that college students get bored when asked to identify items, all important to public life, such as federalism, Auschwitz, Shawnee Indians, Joseph and his brothers, the Reign of Terror, installment buying, and the National Guard. The same students respond enthusiastically, though, when given the opportunity to identify things of no public consequence, like the White Knight, the Jolly Green Giant, Tony the Tiger, We Try Harder, Aunt Jemima, Master the Moment, and That's Italian.[164] Here is a disparity which suggests, to worried republicans, that watching and listening too much to television, politicians, and official spokesmen may produce a nation of such civic dilettantes that freedom will be lost not because government bans books but because not enough citizens will want to read them.[165]

[162] The phrase "an arena for rival frauds" is from Robert Merton, *Mass Persuasion: The Social Psychology of a War Bond Drive* (New York: Harper, 1946), p. 143.

[163] This is the argument in E. E. Hirsh, *Cultural Literacy: What Every American Needs to Know* (Boston: Houghton Mifflin, 1987). See also Diane Ravitch and Chester E. Finn, *What Do Our 17-Year-Olds Know?: A Report on the First National Assessment of History and Literature* (New York: HarperCollins, 1989).

[164] These examples are from James B. Twitchell, *Adcult, USA : The Triumph of Advertising in American Culture* (New York: Columbia Univ. Press, 1996), pp. 6–7.

[165] Postman, *Amusing Ourselves to Death*, pp. 138–141. On this score, Aldous Huxley's *Brave New World* (1932) was more prescient than George Orwell's *1984* (1949).

PART IV

GOOD CITIZENSHIP

8

Constructive Thinking

Most adult Americans enjoy Citizenship II although, as the 2000 presidential election recount in Florida showed, they should exercise their civic rights very carefully. It follows that the same people are formally equipped to work together politically and resolve problems caused by consumerism. Before doing so, however, they must see what those problems are, understand how they arise, and appreciate their severity. The challenge, then, is to fashion an outlook that will lead Americans to use Citizenship II well, via Citizenship III. The goal should be mandates aimed at building a community that enjoys affluence, although less than that promised by consumerism, while reducing costs that consumerism imposes today.

Preliminary Concepts

Most Americans, including those wary of consumerism, do not intend to renounce prosperity, convenience, leisure, comfort, and good health. But perhaps the time has come to consider how far, in a rush to place consumption at the center of American life, the country has strayed from its original pursuit of happiness. In the words of one critic, the men who framed and adopted the Declaration of Independence hoped to build a free and prosperous society, a commonweal rooted in shared well-being, and "not a perpetual Victorian Christmas in the company of one's analyst."[1]

---

[1] John Ralston Saul, *Voltaire's Bastards: The Dictatorship of Reason in the West* (New York: Penguin, 1993), pp. 480–481.

Private Goods

The first step toward deciding how to rein in consumerism is to understand the difference between private goods and public goods. *Private goods* are those a person can acquire, say, by inheritance or purchase. Once acquired, no one else may use them without getting that person's permission. For example, if I buy a house, it belongs to me. Unless I invite other people to join me there, I alone am entitled to occupy it. In short, the fact that my house is private excludes, in most circumstances, the public from enjoying it as well.

Americans buy houses in a marketplace dominated by firms that own most of the modern means of production. That marketplace, which is created and safeguarded by law, exists to provide a context within which those firms may fashion private goods and sell them for profit. Thus American factories produce goods such as cars, washing machines, clothing, cosmetics, breakfast cereals, and a host of other items that individuals purchase mainly for private use.

In this marketplace, science, technology, organization, and hard work make and deliver the goods that consumerism promises to individuals who can afford to buy them. However, they also generate, under private auspices, many goods needed by Americans collectively. Federal, state, and local governments need various things for public rather than for private use. But they run very few factories, in accordance with a national reluctance to authorize government ownership of such facilities. And therefore most of what American governments need, from copy paper and schools to fire engines and nuclear submarines, they buy from private contractors.

Public Goods

One shortcoming of production in the marketplace is that private enterprise, unless instructed by government, does not usually create what economists call *public goods*.[2] These are not simply goods that seem public rather than private. For example, a toll road like the Ohio Turnpike serves many people and therefore seems public in nature. But it is not, technically speaking, a public good because it provides no passage to those unable to pay. And so, as economists see it, the defining characteristic of a public good is that it consists of items or circumstances from which the public cannot be excluded.

---

[2] A classic discussion of public goods is Paul Samuelson, "The Pure Theory of Public Expenditures," *The Review of Economics and Statistics* (November 1954), pp. 337–339.

In other words, public goods generate benefits that no owner controls in the same way that she controls whatever benefits flow from her private goods. But public goods have an even more characteristic quality, which is that, once they exist, everyone can enjoy them. A free highway, for example, is a public good in this sense, and so is national defense. Without paying a toll, everyone can travel on the highway after it is built. Similarly, everyone in the country, whether or not they pay taxes, will live safely after the federal government has recruited an army to defend it.

Once we understand the nature of public goods in this way, two things become clear. On the one hand, citizens could ease some modern problems by creating more public goods than they now enjoy. Water pollution, for example, occurs largely because farms and factories dump agricultural and industrial wastes into national rivers and lakes. Such pollution could be eliminated by enacting stringent laws to make fresh water clean and safe for all Americans. Generous and steady taxpayer support for public television would also enhance the quality of collective life. Without advertising, it would provide all viewers with an educational and recreational alternative to the powerful, and sometimes harmful, impact of commercial television in America.

On the other hand, public goods will not normally be produced in the marketplace. Most obviously, this is because goods like national defense, or a new urban park, or a state university, or clean air are almost impossible to price in such a way that they can be sold over the counter, so to speak, in separate pieces to individual customers. Of course, anyone can buy an air conditioner to filter the air in her home. But she will still breathe smog when she leaves the house. Then too, consumers think it is worthwhile to buy things in the marketplace for the very reason that those things will belong to them alone. The same people are not likely to want to pay for part of a public good that would confer on its buyer neither the advantage nor the satisfaction of private control.

Free Riders

A technical explanation for why markets do not provide public goods, appears in what economists call the *free-rider* phenomenon.[3] Generally speaking, this term refers to inaction driven by the reluctance of many people to pay for something they might get for nothing by waiting for others to pay first. That is, if my neighbors are determined to collect

---

[3] See Mancur Olson, *The Logic of Collective Action: Public Goods and the Theory of Groups* (Cambridge: Harvard Univ. Press, 1965), pp. 9–16.

money and create a park, why should I not decline to contribute to their efforts yet take a free ride on their enthusiasm by enjoying the park once it is built?

To use a specific example, most people prefer to let someone else pay membership dues in the Sierra Club. When the club is successful at lobbying for laws limiting destruction of wetlands and safeguarding wildlife there, even nonmembers of the club will enjoy the preservation of nature that results. A similar tendency accounts for why some workers refuse to join unions. The laggards know that, if their peers will pay union dues, all workers in a unionized factory or office will receive the good wages that collective bargaining can produce.

The Role of Governments

The concept of free-rider behavior suggests that governments, at least those called democratic today, are instituted in large part to provide public goods. The logic is clear. First, citizens can identify public goods that will generate well-being for their community as a whole. Second, the marketplace will not automatically provide those goods because, if someone would offer to sell such a good, many individuals would refuse to pay their share of its costs while hoping to receive its benefits for nothing.[4] Third, when citizens envision a project capable of creating a public good, most likely only government can bring that project into being. This government does when, for example, the people's representatives apportion the costs of such an undertaking by deciding to pay for it with taxes that no citizen can avoid paying.

The main reality here is that democratic citizens authorize their government to make free ridership difficult or impossible. In some areas, tax money is raised to create tangible goods that would not otherwise exist. These include schools, roads, parks, libraries, and reservoirs. On other occasions, the common weal may require throttling back undesirable behavior, such as drunken driving, adulteration of food, bribery, assault, or pollution. To prevent such acts, government can use its police power, funded also by taxes, to compel everyone to behave well without fearing that, while they do, others will be free to gain from behaving badly.

---

[4] The same behavior discourages many business people from befriending the environment. Thus William Ophuls and A. Stephen Boyan, Jr., *Ecology and the Politics of Scarcity Revisited* (New York: W. H. Freeman, 1992), Box 19, pp. 196–197, observes that even a "socially responsible" manufacturer will be afraid to add pollution control costs to the price of his product because consumers might purchase a similar but cheaper product made by less virtuous competitors.

In the history of political thought, the assumption that governments exist to provide public goods is an elementary principle. It is confirmed, although not always noticed as such, in the document that, together with the Declaration of Independence, defines America's commitment to national life. Thus the Constitution's Preamble speaks plainly of great public goods that Washington, Franklin, Madison, Adams, Hamilton, and their colleagues hoped to create when it says that "WE THE PEOPLE of the United States" ordain and establish the Constitution in order "to form a more perfect Union, establish Justice, insure domestic Tranquility, provide for the common defence, promote the general Welfare, and secure the Blessings of Liberty to ourselves and our Posterity."

The Office of Citizenship

In democratic countries, citizens are entitled to tell government which public goods to provide. This they can do by exercising their rights to vote, to speak freely, to consult with neighbors, to participate in demonstrations, to join political parties, to lobby elected representatives, to contribute money to campaigns, to promote watchdog agencies, to form public interest groups, and so forth. Thus to be a good citizen is to occupy the office of citizenship which, as we saw in Chapter 1, is the smallest public office in a democratic society and open to all who enjoy the rights of Citizenship I and Citizenship II.

This office does not oblige citizens to ignore personal interests.[5] It does require them, though, to occasionally promote the public interest, which is the community's well-being.[6] And that means, at a minimum, that good citizens should prefer what, in a technical sense, scholars call the *republican* as opposed to the *liberal* ideal.[7] The liberal ideal argues

---

[5] See "A Day in the Life of a Socialist Citizen," in Michael Walzer, *Obligations: Essays on Disobedience, War and Citizenship* (Cambridge: Harvard Univ. Press, 1970), pp. 229–238, for a reminder that some delegation of good citizenship to public officials via elections is necessary, since we cannot reasonably expect an ordinary person to sacrifice his or her normal life by spending most of every day on committee meetings and other adjuncts of civic activism.

[6] Terry L. Cooper, *An Ethic of Citizenship for Public Administration* (Englewood Cliffs, N.J.: Prentice Hall, 1991), pp. 137–138.

[7] *Liberal* and *republican* in this sense are terms of analytic convenience used by political philosophers. A leading example of liberalism is John Rawls, *A Theory of Justice* (New York: Oxford Univ. Press, 1971). See also Robert Nozick, *Anarchy, State and Utopia* (New York: Basic, 1974). A leading example of republicanism is Michael Sandel, *Liberalism and the Limits of Justice* (New York: Cambridge Univ. Press, 1982). See also Benjamin Barber, *Strong Democracy: Participatory Politics for a New Age* (Berkeley: Univ. of California Press, 1984). Other examples, equally excellent, are too numerous to cite here.

that citizens should possess political rights but are not necessarily obliged to exercise them. The republican ideal, alternatively, insists that citizens will use their rights constructively rather than stay at home. Indeed, it charges them to reject indifference in favor of political involvement when conditions warrant the practice of active virtue in public affairs.[8] And here, of course, we have arrived at Citizenship III.

Citizens and Consumers

Concepts such as private and public goods, free riders, and citizenship as public office will help us understand where to look for solutions to difficulties caused by consumerism. But first we should adjust, in our own minds, the chart of citizenship whose elements have evolved over more than two thousand years. To this end, let us begin by stipulating that, while democracy needs virtuous people to fill the office of citizenship, those people should not behave like consumers when they perform their civic duties, even though modern candidates and public officials will tempt them to do so.[9]

Citizenship as a Vocation

This injunction can be amplified in several ways. Consumers are often animated by *wants* rather than *needs*. They therefore respond more to short-term desires than to long-run necessities. Consumers are also likely to concentrate on the commercial *price* of a thing rather than its intrinsic *value*. Thus they are sensitive to changing fashions but tend to neglect enduring benefits. And finally, consumers tend to rely on *bargaining* rather than using their capacity for *deliberation*.[10] They therefore compute what they can afford based mainly on current resources rather than calculate what they need and then decide how to expand available means to pay for it.

---

[8] On various aspects of civic virtue, see Michael Walzer, *What It Means to Be an American: Essays on the American Experience* (New York: Masilio, 1992), pp. 82–95.

[9] On this score, see Albert Gore, *The Best Kept Secrets in Government: How the Clinton Administration Is Reinventing the Way Washington Works* (New York: Random House, 1996) – a reprint of the Fourth Report of the National Performance Review (Washington, D.C.: Government Printing Office, 1995) – which claimed that the Clinton administration was trying to reform government agencies so they would better serve their "customers," who might be individuals, business firms, or state and local communities.

[10] Such points are made in Joseph Tussman, *Obligation and the Body Politic* (New York: Oxford Univ. Press, 1960), pp. 104–121.

To restate the matter, people in their consumer mode tend not to notice that citizenship should be regarded as a *vocation*. A vocation such as law or medicine entails activity very different from that aimed at personal gratification. Of course, lawyers and doctors strive to earn a comfortable living. But making money does not define the nature of their work. Rather, every vocation embodies a special calling, as colonial Puritans would have said, which requires the practitioner, regardless of income, to implement standards that define how to do a job that serves other people and the community.[11]

The concept of vocation points our story back to Citizenship III. As we have seen, formal citizenship rights are the basis for Citizenship I and II, where Citizenship I makes me a member of the community, and where Citizenship II entitles me to participate in public affairs. What complicates the picture is how these two dimensions of citizenship are affected by two *social roles*, which have appeared century after century as the *good citizen* and the *good person*.

For much of Western history, political thinkers defined good citizens chiefly as those who obeyed existing laws and thereby helped preserve their communities by fostering public order. Thus Plato wrote about Socrates, who refused to break Athenian laws by fleeing his polis. But over many generations, political thinkers from Aristotle to Hannah Arendt have speculated that obedience is not enough, that citizens should some-times reject their community's laws to assure the quality of public life.[12] Thus during America's great civil rights demonstrations, good citizens were called to act also as good persons, perhaps disobeying bad laws and, if empowered, promoting better ones.[13] Here was where Citizenship II could be augmented by Citizenship III, which obliges citizens to act well.

Two Sorts of Good People
On this score, Americans think of being a *good person* in two ways. One of these evolved together with republicanism. In various historical eras, it called upon citizens to behave virtuously toward the communities in which

---

[11] On citizenship as a vocation, see Richard Dagger, "Metropolis, Memory, and Citizenship," *American Journal of Political Science* (November 1981), p. 718. Cited in Adrian Oldfield, *Citizenship and Community: Civic Republicanism and the Modern World* (New York: Routledge, 1990), p. 160.

[12] This point underlies Arendt, *Eichmann in Jerusalem: A Report on the Banality of Evil* (New York: Viking, 1963).

[13] The classic appeal along these lines came in "Letter from Birmingham Jail," in Martin Luther King, Jr., *Why We Can't Wait* (New York: Signet, 1964), pp. 76–95.

they lived. Especially after the Protestant Reformation, this tradition high-lighted civic as opposed to theological virtue. Consequently, it called for public acts aimed not at assuring individual salvation but at promoting collective happiness. To affirm this distinction, the Founders designed the First Amendment to forbid Congress from establishing any religion.

As described by historians such as J. G. A. Pocock, the main republican requirement for exercising civic virtue was a considerable but not absolute measure of detachment, an ability to step back from everyday stakes and advance the longer and more inclusive view of human well-being.[14] Of course, one did not have to be a citizen to be a good person. And thus, in Roman times, even the slave Epictetus strove to do good.[15] But if you were a citizen, said Pocock, the qualities required for being a good person should guide your exercise of citizenship.

In America, this republican ideal of being a good person must compete with the consumerist ideal of being a good person.[16] The latter says you are good if you work hard, if you avoid being burdensome to others, if you are diligent and prudent, if you deal openly and honestly with people you meet in the marketplace, if you earn there as much as your efforts are worth, and if you use your income to enjoy whatever private commodities you can afford to buy. Via this sort of behavior, Americans strive to succeed, to serve others while doing so, to provide food, clothing, shelter, health care, and leisure for themselves and their families, to increase production on the job, to raise the national standard of living, and to spend enthusiastically even if they must borrow to do so.

In the consumerist view of doing good, there is little cause for players to agonize over what all this activity is worth. Citizens and politicians

---

[14] Thus republicanism, sometimes called civic virtue, is the underlying theme in J. G. A. Pocock, *The Machiavellian Moment: Florentine Political Thought and the Atlantic Republican Tradition* (Princeton: Princeton Univ. Press, 1975).

[15] Epictetus (A.D. 55–135) advocated a philosophy of honorable behavior for all, including the politically unempowered. See Epictetus, *Moral Discourses, Encheiridion and Fragments*, trans. and introd. by Elizabeth Carter (New York: Dutton, 1910).

[16] History offers an ironic gloss on this score. The Charles F. Kettering Foundation of Dayton, Ohio, was established in 1927, is supported today by a $265 million endowment, and has all along hoped to make democracy work better by devising and testing "strategies that will strengthen the role of citizens in governing themselves." (See its home page at www.kettering.org.) As we saw in Chapter 6, Kettering was a businessman who epitomized consumerism by promoting planned obsolescence at General Motors in the struggle against Ford eighty years ago. How odd it is, then, that part of the fortune he made in that endeavor now finances a foundation whose employees seek to strengthen the very republicanism to which consumerism has always been, at best, indifferent. A grant from that foundation paid for the report cited in Ch. 1, n. 3.

TABLE 8.1. *Good Citizenship Today*

	Citizenship	Roles	Standards
State	I	Good citizen	Obey laws
	II	Good citizen	Participate
Society	III	Good person	Exercise virtue and economic conscience

set the rules for economic enterprise where they live together. Once that is done, a businesswoman, for example, is directed to work within those rules but only to make money, for which she is presumably qualified. She is discouraged from trying to confront ethical conundrums related to her work, such as whether or not she has a moral right to manufacture cigarettes because doing so is legal. The assumption is that such puzzles are matters which she is not especially competent to judge and which anyway provoke endless arguments in society at large.[17]

Economic Conscience

In truth, citizens are not always virtuous, and consumers often behave well toward their families, neighbors, and even strangers. The problem, however, is that, although republicanism recommends civic virtue, consumerism praises private gratification. Consequently consumerism does not urge that Americans will heed an other-regarding outlook that may be called economic conscience. This constraint appears in Table 8.1 to show that it properly belongs to any modern definition of what sort of virtue should guide a good person's acts.

Economic conscience is a term that can refer, in our story, to much of what Tocqueville had in mind when he talked about "self-interest rightly understood." It suggests that while modern people may work hard to succeed financially and live comfortably, they should not profit without contributing something to the community which enables them to work and then defends the fruits thereof. In this sense, economic conscience should oblige every citizen to think of how private actions produce larger consequences. Thus it should insist that she consider not just her personal

---

[17] The classic advice along these lines was given in Milton Friedman, *Capitalism and Freedom* (Chicago: Univ. of Chicago Press, 1962), pp. 133–136. See also the discussion in Robert L. Heilbroner, "Controlling the Corporation," in Heilbroner, Morton Mintz, Coleman McCarthy, Sanford J. Ungar, Kermit Vandivier, Saul Friedman, and James Boyd, *In the Name of Profit* (Garden City, N.Y.: Doubleday, 1972), pp. 236–245.

gains but also external costs, such as global warming and deforestation, which flow from producing and consuming too many goods, including her own.[18]

Economic conscience can remind us that citizens should not insist that government will permit them to consume whatever they desire even if it is unsafe and unwholesome. Two cases in point might be hard drugs and sports utility vehicles, both known to be exciting but also dangerous.[19] On this score, economic conscience should note that one of America's defining principles, of consumer sovereignty, is actually imperfect. It sounds right to say that ordinary people, by making or not making voluntary purchases, will shape the fate of giant corporations. But all of us know we are occasionally better off for not following our shopping instincts, for instead letting elected officials legislate a framework for rational behavior – including Social Security, lead-free paint, and mandatory automobile seat belts – that consumers, sometimes inattentive to larger consequences, might fail to promote.[20]

Then too, economic conscience should insist that the best things in life are not always free but sometimes expensively public. That being so, good citizens must refrain from believing that, to have money to buy alluring merchandise, they cannot afford to pay whatever taxes are necessary to finance vital public services. Economic conscience should also encourage us to think ahead, to forego immediate profits from, say, logging and whaling, in order to conserve natural resources that our children may need to sustain their happiness.[21] And finally, economic conscience should tell us that consumerism will not foster what economist John Kenneth Galbraith called *social balance*.[22] That is, while a welter of private goods piles up

[18] Described in somewhat different terms, the theme of economic conscience underlies Kalle Lasn, *Culture Jam: How to Reverse America's Suicidal Consumer Binge – and Why We Must* (New York: Quill, 2000).

[19] On SUVs, Detroit has admitted some culpability. See "Ford Is Conceding S.U.V. Drawbacks: Sees Health and Safety Issues, But Won't Stop Production," *New York Times* (May 12, 2000), pp. A1, C2. Automotive journalists are less skeptical. See "A Sport-Brute Takes a Civilized Turn," *Washington Post* (May 28, 2000), p. N1, where Warren Brown says that the 2001 Mitsubishi Montero Limited, costing "nearly $40,000," which he describes as "a motorized ode to hedonism," is "a rolling testament to ... freedom, and there is something inherently good in that."

[20] On the need to challenge the concept of consumer sovereignty, see Peter Donaldson, *Economics of the Real World*, 2nd ed. (Harmondsworth, England: Pelican, 1978), pp. 154–155.

[21] The almost complete destruction of the American buffalo constituted a glaring example of this sort of pitiless environmental waste. See Thomas Schelling, "On the Ecology of Micromotives," in Robin L. Marris (ed.), *The Corporate Society* (London: Macmillan, 1974), pp. 32–33.

[22] Galbraith, *The Affluent Society* (New York: Mentor, 1958), pp. 198–211, 240–249.

over time, markets will not automatically produce a parallel set of public works and services capable of bringing tolerable order to private life. Large airports, for example, which only governments provide, are public projects that America requires because they enable planes to fly and keep most of them from crashing when the number of private flights increases constantly and cannot be handled adequately by small and profit-oriented airports.

Where to Focus Attention

What we have seen so far suggests a general principle: The way to repair at least some of the damage caused by consumerism is to insist, via Citizenship III, on using government to create public goods that will mitigate or eliminate the unwelcome results of, for example, economic growth, globalization, contingent labor, advertising, environmental pollution, and commercial television. In a moment, I will expand on this principle. Before examining the preferred strategy more closely, however, we should consider a relevant aspect of political talk today.

Rights

If we subtract from what Americans say about mega-issues such as Social Security, Medicare, and federal tax rates, a good deal of their political talk refers to gender and distinction, to race and multiculturalism, to identity and respect. Concerning such matters, critics argue that those who are socially and economically deprived – say, women, Latinos, African Americans, Native Americans, gays, lesbians, the poor, and the handicapped – have difficulty translating the civic rights they possess into the sort of status they deserve. That is, most Americans are blessed with the formal opportunities of Citizenship II. But some groups include members who lack resources that would help them take advantage of those opportunities and succeed in life.[23]

Looking at inequality this way suggests that whenever access to the main chance is missing, some people of little means will be members of the community in theory but not in fact. It follows, in this view, that

---

[23] A great deal of scholarly literature treats such matters. For example, see Iris Marion Young, *Justice and the Politics of Difference* (Princeton: Princeton Univ. Press, 1990); Jeff Spinner, *The Boundaries of Citizenship: Race, Ethnicity and Nationality in the Liberal State* (Baltimore: Johns Hopkins Univ. Press, 1994); and Timothy J. Gaffaney, *Freedom for the Poor: Welfare and the Foundations of Democratic Citizenship* (Boulder, Colo.: Westview, 2000).

some Americans are only nominal instead of real citizens.[24] If that is so, lawmakers should enact affirmative action guidelines to assure the downtrodden and oppressed an entitlement to whatever assets of work, housing, education, health, and leisure will enable them to exercise their legal rights so successfully as to advance into the mainstream of American society.[25] At the highest level of social principles, philosopher John Rawls recommended this sort of thinking when he argued that inequality in the division of society's resources is morally acceptable only if it improves the situation of all, including the worst off.[26]

In the devastating case of racism, existing terminology labels the problem of difference instructively. Inspired by leaders like Martin Luther King, Jr., and Thurgood Marshall, demonstrators convinced white Americans to reverse or repeal laws that enforced separation of the races. In this sense, de jure segregation disappeared in America during the 1960s and 1970s. But de facto segregation persisted, based to some extent on racial antipathy that can preserve informal exclusions and disadvantages in work, housing, and education.

Some critics, like law professor Lani Guinier, are so frustrated by America's persistent inability to eliminate this intolerance and its results that they have recommended that African Americans as a group will receive weighted voting rights because no other device can improve their circumstances.[27] But such proposals offend the American tradition of one citizen, one vote.[28] The country is therefore as unlikely to adopt them as

---

[24] For example, unless they are independently wealthy, all citizens must have jobs that provide enough income for them to participate in the community as real citizens. If the requisite jobs do not exist, or if some citizens are unable to work at them, the slack must be taken up by welfare arrangements. See this line of analysis in Michael B. Katz, *The Price of Citizenship: Redefining the American Welfare State* (New York: Henry Holt, 2001).

[25] The literature is extensive. See Ronald Dworkin, *Taking Rights Seriously* (Cambridge: Harvard Univ. Press, 1977); and Ronald Beiner, "What Liberalism Means," *Social Philosophy and Policy* (Winter 1996), p. 191: "Considerable state intervention is required in order to distribute to every individual an equitable share of the total aggregate of social resources, in order to give each individual a fair opportunity to give play to his or her conception of his or her own personal good."

[26] Rawls, *A Theory of Justice*, pp. 60–71, 75f.

[27] See Lani Guinier, *The Tyranny of the Majority: Fundamental Fairness in Representative Democracy* (New York: Free Press, 1994).

[28] See Newt Gingrich, writing as Speaker of the House of Representatives in his *To Renew America* (New York: HarperCollins, 1995), pp. 153–154:

> The very concept of group rights contradicts the nature of America.... America is about a dynamic, shifting, mobile world of opportunity where everyone has a chance to build a better mousetrap or bake a bigger pie.... Group rights trap

when John C. Calhoun suggested constructing a concurrent majority veto in Congress to protect the slave-holding South.[29]

Acceptable or not, talk about liabilities flowing from difference is mainly talk about *rights*. Those who seek redress usually ask government to create social and economic entitlements that, for argument's sake, they call rights rather than privileges. These should be provided, they say, to citizens whose present circumstances do not enable them to fully utilize Citizenship II which, as we have seen, belongs to virtually all adult Americans.

Obligations

Talk about rights addresses situations that are immensely important to people who are affected by them. In many cases we should try to help those people in the give-and-take that characterizes democratic politics.[30]

us within our own group. Each association is measured by genes rather than by compatibility. Group rights would reconstitute America into a seething band of competing, legally defined groups maneuvering against one another for governmentally imposed special privileges.

[29] There can be no *substantive* comparison today between the views of Calhoun and Guinier. In the late 1840s, Senator Calhoun of South Carolina argued that important political decisions in America should be made only by a "concurrent majority," that is, by the consent of all sectional interests, including that of pro-slavery whites in the South. While favoring this special majority, which gave veto power to a minority of the entire population, he opposed in the Congress what he called rule by a "numerical majority," which in his era included mainly antislavery whites from the North and West. In *The Tyranny of the Majority*, Professor Guinier of course does not regard her proposals – like group representation, cumulative voting, supermajorities, and race-conscious districting – as analogous to those made by Calhoun. Neither do I. But she does address a situation which, in some respects, is *technically* similar to the circumstances that prompted him to write. Thus in her view (esp. pp. 1–20, but also passim), a specific American majority (white) repeatedly outvotes a specific American minority (black) and therefore makes the minority feel that the principle of majority rule serves, unjustly, to legitimate the routine rule of some citizens over others. As stated, the problem seems intractable. Moreover, one of racially weighted voting's severest critics is himself an African American, Supreme Court Justice Clarence Thomas. See his opinions in *Holder v. Hall* (1994) 114 S. Ct. 2581 and *Miller v. Johnson* (1995) 115 S. Ct. 2475. See also the five-to-four decision in *Abrams v. Johnson* (1997) 117 S. Ct. 1925, where Thomas joined the majority against drawing two majority-black congressional districts in Georgia. See also his dissent in *Hunt v. Cromartie* (2001) 121 S. Ct. 1452.

[30] To this end, people who do not suffer from racism may need to hear what historian Oscar Handlin called a "fire-bell in the night." (See Handlin's *Fire-Bell in the Night: The Crisis in Civil Rights* [Boston: Little, Brown, 1964].) For example, see Marc Mauer, *Race to Incarcerate* (New York: New Press, 1999). Mauer surveys some of the horrific statistics on black incarceration and voting rights. Black Americans are seven times as likely to be jailed as white Americans (p. 126), from which it follows that 13 percent of all black men in America, as felons and former felons, are disenfranchised (p. 186).

Indeed, a student of poverty and discrimination might well conclude that when haggling over public budgets takes place, public support and government assistance should go more to society's outcasts and less to corporate clients like DaimlerChrysler, Boeing, Dupont, and General Electric.[31]

Nevertheless, much of this talk does not touch on our story's major concern, which is *obligations* rather than *rights*. The reasoning is as follows. Many of today's disadvantaged will, like former immigrants, suffragettes, and other supplicants, improve their stations in life via political activism, lobbying, legislative bargaining, and individual economic enterprise. That is, after all, what America is about. Eventually, then, many of them will acquire passable resources and become socially acceptable to mainstream Americans, as have the Irish, the Italians, the Poles, the Jews, and many other people who came after the Mayflower. It seems clear, for example, that many Latinos and Asian Americans are already on their way.

Once such people have "arrived," however, they will become part of the larger problem, which was identified by Robert Bellah and his colleagues in *Habits of the Heart*, and which consists of not knowing how to exercise Citizenship III even when people who enjoy Citizenship II possess enough resources to act civically. Here is the problem of obligation, which applies to people already "included" in America. In a country which recognizes many rights, such people find little to guide them in the realm of obligations. And so our concern can be summed up in one sentence: Beyond obeying most laws and paying their fair share of taxes, what obligations do citizens owe to the community which assures their rights?[32]

---

[31] On government support for business, see Donald L. Barlett and James B. Steele, *America: Who Really Pays Taxes?* (New York: Touchstone, 1994).

[32] In slightly different terms, Rufus E. Miles suggests that America has enshrined in law a great many rights which are not accompanied by comparable responsibilities. See his *Awakening from the American Dream* (New York: Universe, 1976), Ch. 5, "The Chasm Between Rights and Responsibilities," pp. 76–88. See also Katherine S. Newman, *Declining Fortunes: The Withering of the American Dream* (New York: Basic Books, 1993), p. 221:

> Every great nation draws its strength from a social contract, an unspoken agreement to provide for one another, to reach across the narrow self-interests of generations, ethnic groups, races, classes, and genders toward some vision of the common good. Taxes and budgets...express this commitment, or lack of it.... Through these mechanistic devices, we are forced to confront some of the most searching philosophical questions that face any country: what do we owe one another as members of a society?

Implications

Two implications to this question are worth noting before proceeding to see how it might be answered. First, obligations are mainly a problem for democratic majorities. Such majorities are likely to dominate their societies and to utilize without fuss the rights they possess. It is minorities, on the other hand, who tend to succeed less in life, sometimes because of social discrimination. Not surprisingly, then, in their effort to join the majority, minorities are likely to try to overcome discrimination by agitating to acquire additional resources labeled as rights.

Is a scholarly apology in order here? Does centering our story on obligations pay too much attention to the strong and not enough to the weak? Well, yes. But other books focus on the weak,[33] and there is a sense in which civic problems of the majority are noteworthy precisely because they are more typical than minority concerns are of the national way of life. We can understand American citizenship best, then, if we will examine the lives of those who enjoy it most fully.[34]

Second, to focus on minority rights would risk making the mistake of appreciating specific parts of American society more than the whole. As political philosopher Michael Walzer says, to emphasize group rights and multiculturalism too strongly is to forget that every American, in whichever group, must act not just as a member of that group but also as a citizen in the civic community that provides safe space where all Americans live together. It follows, with regard to citizenship, that talk about group rights concentrates on what some people think those groups should receive but diverts attention from what they should give.[35]

---

[33] For example, Herbert J. Gans, *The War Against the Poor: The Underclass and Antipoverty Policy* (New York: Basic Books, 1995); William Julius Wilson, *When Work Disappears: The World of the New Urban Poor* (New York: Vintage, 1997); and Ruth Sidel, *Keeping Women and Children Last: America's War on the Poor* (New York: Penguin, 1998).

[34] For example, see Alan Wolfe, *One Nation, After All. What Middle-Class Americans Really Think About: God, Country, Family, Racism, Welfare, Immigration, Homosexuality, Work, the Right, the Left, and Each Other* (New York: Penguin, 1998).

[35] Walzer, *What It Means to Be an American*, pp. 9–11, 17. See also Jean Bethke Elshtain, *Democracy on Trial* (New York: Basic, 1995), p. 41, where she contends that in the debate over multiculturalism, some participants think that "difference" rules our thoughts so strongly that we cannot put it aside and think like citizens. In which case, as she says, "the category of 'citizen' is a matter of indifference at best, contempt at worst. Increasingly, we come to see ourselves exclusively along racial or gender or sexual-preference lines. If this is who I am, why should I care about the citizen? That is for dupes who actually believed their high school civics teacher."

Political scientist Terrance Ball draws a similar conclusion in somewhat different terms. The problem with what he calls "identity politics" is that it talks mostly about what groups are like rather than about what it means to be an American in the widest sense. As a result, people who focus too strongly on identity politics lack a "civic vision" of what common destiny all Americans should share.[36] They argue at length, and sometimes convincingly, about what society owes their groups. But they have little or nothing to say about what their groups owe society.[37]

Reshaping the Debate

The concepts noted so far reinforce one another. Private goods generate happiness for those who can afford to buy them. At the same time, the way those goods are created, marketed, and distributed can impose substantial costs on individuals and society, including a serious undermining of republican behavior. Some of these undesirable by-products of consumerism may be alleviated by collective action, which can curb excessive materialism and self-gratification on behalf of reasonable satisfactions. To do so would create public goods and therefore well-being for all members of the community. Contractors in the marketplace, however, cannot sell such systematic restraint, in which case it must be supplied by government. It follows that the essence of good citizenship, for those already empowered, is to analyze the results of consumerism, to consult their economic consciences, and to instruct government on what it must do to prevent or repair damages caused by that way of life.

From this syllogism, it appears that good citizens should support public policies designed to deal with where consumerism brings us. However, many Americans fail to see a connection between various social problems and consumerism because they perceive the world as ruled by individuals rather than systems. And this means that many important consumerist trends and patterns of behavior receive little attention in America's normal political conversation.

---

[36] Terrance Ball, "The Myth of Adam," in Ball, *Reappraising Political Theory: Revisionist Studies in the History of Political Thought* (Oxford: Clarendon, 1995), pp. 295–296f.

[37] See also Mary Ann Glendon, *Rights Talk: The Impoverishment of Political Discourse* (New York: Free Press, 1991), p. 17: "In recent years, we have made great progress in making the promise of rights a reality, but in doing so we have neglected another part of our inheritance – the vision of a republic where citizens actively take responsibility for maintaining a vital political life."

The Concept of Systems

Why do Americans tend to focus on individuals rather than systems? One reason is that thinking about systems may be regarded as somewhat undemocratic, as if special people trained to do it, such as the proverbial rocket scientist, will tell everyone else how to live. There is, after all, a long-standing American premise that, in principle at least, all people can be rational and therefore competent to hold political opinions and act on them. Thomas Paine championed this assumption in *Common Sense* when he encouraged American colonists to revolt against London because British officials believed that some men are superior and therefore entitled to rule others. Sixty years later, Tocqueville noticed that Americans were still generally indifferent to philosophers who presume to tell simpler souls how to live.[38]

More recently, systems are overlooked because Americans have typically regarded Marxism as preposterous. Marx and his followers described America as a capitalist society. By this they meant that the country was in thrall to a pattern of behavior or "system" which linked various economic institutions and practices undesirably. Most Americans condemned this view as dangerously misguided. But while dismissing what Marx, Engels, Lenin, and the rest said about America, they also tended to disparage the Marxian assumption that a systematic analysis of social life is possible. Cold War intellectuals led the way by rejecting such analysis as "ideology."[39] Then, when the Soviet Union collapsed, they argued that its ideology and, by extension, all ideologies must be unreliable guides to thinking accurately and constructively about public affairs.[40]

For whatever reasons, it is a fact that Americans tend to blame individuals for society's ills.[41] Examples come from every direction. Thus some Americans decry violence and profanity in Hollywood productions and demand that directors who make offensive movies clean up their act. But few critics admit that those directors are the rule rather than an exception,[42] even though the look of commercial products is, in the words of

---

[38] Alexis de Tocqueville, *Democracy in America*, 2 vols. (orig., 1835, 1840; New York: Vintage, 1954), Vol. II, pp. 3–8.

[39] See the essays collected in Chaim L. Waxman (ed.), *The End of Ideology Debate* (New York: Simon and Schuster, 1969).

[40] Francis Fukuyama, "The End of History?" *National Interest* (Summer 1989), pp. 3–18.

[41] Television strengthens this tendency when it tells stories where protagonists like Alan Greenspan, Bill Gates, or Kofi Anan are more important than historical trends and the interaction of great institutions, both of which are difficult to photograph and describe.

[42] For example, Michael Medved, *Hollywood vs. America* (New York: Harper Perennial, 1992). Medved favors boycotting films that offend what he calls traditional values. The

economist Robert Heilbroner, "a deeply rooted functional necessity" of making profits in a free market economy.[43]

Likewise, psychologist Barry Schwartz, referring to the explosion that killed thousands of people in and around a Union Carbide factory in Bhopal, India, in 1985, notes that he never met a person whose ambition was "to run a chemical company with unsafe plants in Third World countries." It happens nevertheless, he said, because corporate managers work to standards laid down by an economic system that cannot avoid, occasionally, producing such results.[44] Similarly, in the classic textbook example of how environmental disaster unfolds, ecologist Garrett Hardin warns that it is not the herdsman's greed, akin to personal sin, that destroys the village commons. Rather, disaster emerges inevitably from the system of common property that forces every herdsman to overgraze his cattle before other herdsmen will do the same.[45]

And finally, there are those who fault teachers for poor academic performance in American schools. They might assign blame elsewhere if they would consider what really shapes American education. Anthropologist Jules Henry observed that every society trains its children for whatever roles they will fill as adults.[46] This means that in America, which is committed to endless consumption, most children must be educated not to think. After all, if they would wise up, they might buy too little and thereby topple the economy. So advertising takes up the slack and deliberately encourages people to be "fuzzy-minded and

logical response to his position is that of James B. Twitchell, *Carnival Culture: The Trashing of Taste in America* (New York: Columbia Univ. Press, 1992), p. 250: "Why blame the messenger when so many of us seem to want the message?" For a nonpartisan view of the situation, see *Marketing Violent Entertainment to Children: A Review of Self-Regulation and Industry Practices in the Motion Picture, Music Recording and Electronic Game Industries: A Report of the Federal Trade Commission* (Washington, D.C.: Federal Trade Commission, September 2000). This report says that all these forms of entertainment are marketed to children younger than the advisory labels permit. For example, see p. iii: "Of the 44 movies rated R for violence the Commission selected for its study, the Commission found that 35, or 80 percent, were targeted to children under 17. Marketing plans for 28 of those 44, or 64 percent, contained express statements that the film's target audience included children under 17."

43 Robert L. Heilbroner, *The Limits of American Capitalism* (New York: Harper Torchbooks, 1967), p. 96.

44 Barry Schwartz, *The Costs of Living: How Market Freedom Erodes the Best Things in Life* (New York: Norton, 1994), p. 365.

45 Garrett Hardin, *Living Within Limits: Ecology, Economics, and Population Taboos* (New York: Oxford Univ. Press, 1993), p. 218.

46 Jules Henry, *Culture Against Man* (New York: Vintage, 1963), p. 70.

impulsive."[47] Against such competition, even teachers who try to promote reason and intelligence may fail.

The Logic of Capitalism

To make a long story on systems short, what happens economically is not a random outcome of individual acts and decisions, some more admirable and others less so. On the contrary, most people who make and sell things do so within a web of commercial relationships that looks complicated and sometimes even haphazard but derives logically from the way in which large corporations, based on great concentrations of capital, set the stage for most other economic actors by relating with some regularity to one another and the world around them.

One way of grasping the central element that orders this world is to consider the nature of capital itself. Unfortunately, nothing in American culture encourages ordinary people, or even economists, to do this. Indeed, as Heilbroner points out, "The best kept secret in [academic] economics is that economics is about the study of capitalism."[48]

While exploring this secret, Heilbroner points out that capital comes in two forms, either capital-as-money or capital-as-commodities. In the case of manufacturing, for example, there exists between the two forms of capital a connection which impels a capitalist to invest money in a factory, where it will be used to make commodities such as toothpaste, cars, or computers. These commodities will be sold for a profit to the public which, by paying the capitalist, will convert the commodities back into somewhat more money than he or she spent on production to begin with.

Heilbroner summed this all up in the formula of $M-C-M^1$, which he borrowed from Marx. The formula expresses this sequence: M is capital-as-money, which by financing the production of goods and services becomes C in capital-as-commodities, which then becomes M^1, which

---

[47] Ibid., p. 48:

> In order for our economy to continue in its present form people must learn to be fuzzy-minded and impulsive, for if they were clear-headed and deliberate they would rarely put their hands in their pockets; or, if they did, they would leave them there. If we were all logicians the economy could not survive, and herein lies a terrifying paradox, for *in order to exist economically as we are we must try by might and main to remain stupid.* [emphasis in the original]

[48] Heilbroner is quoted in Thomas I. Palley, *Plenty of Nothing: The Downsizing of the American Dream and the Case for Structural Keynesianism* (Princeton: Princeton Univ. Press, 1998), p. 15. The connection between economic analysis and capitalism is explained in Robert Heilbroner and William Milberg, *The Crisis of Vision in Modern Economic Thought* (New York: Cambridge Univ. Press, 1995), pp. 106–113.

includes the capitalist's production costs plus whatever profit he or she gained from selling the commodities represented by C.[49]

The logic of capitalism seems obvious thus far. One invests, makes, sells, and profits. But Heilbroner emphasized what many people overlook, that the process is inexorably dynamic, because the money of M^1 becomes a new M and, as such, must then be converted into a new C, which must be sold in order to generate a new M^1. The reason for endlessly repeating this cycle is that, contrary to popular belief, money at rest, say in a factory, has no intrinsic value. It cannot be eaten, for example, and if it remains embodied in unchanging machinery, the factory will eventually become obsolete and worthless. So it is not enough for capitalists to make a profit now. They must use their money to create commodities again and again, sell them for profit year after year, and thereby maintain the value of their capital over time.[50]

The upshot is that capitalists are constantly driven to change the world we live in. They continually search for ways to upgrade their productive facilities; they ceaselessly invent new commodities; and they relentlessly advertise what they make to assure that consumer demand will not flag. The point is to compete successfully against other capitalists who are also inviting shoppers to hand over some of their money. To this end, each capitalist will never stop looking for new customers, say, young smokers, for workers who will accept lower wages, say, in Bhopal, and for raw materials at lower prices than before, say, from strip mining.

In other words, capitalists work on a *treadmill* from which they cannot dismount,[51] and where they must cater to absentee stockholders before accommodating members of the community in which they work. Thus some managers and entrepreneurs, who at home are decent people and good neighbors, behave less admirably on the job.[52] There, they occasionally make defective tires, design books that encourage children to eat junk

---

[49] Robert L. Heilbroner, *The Nature and Logic of Capitalism* (New York: Norton, 1985), pp. 36–38, and passim. See the original formula in Karl Marx, *Capital: A Critique of Political Economy* (orig., 1867; New York: Modern Library, 1936), pp. 169–173.

[50] A capitalist might sell her factory, stop working, and retire to live off the money from that sale. But her exit would not change the system, because whoever buys the factory would then get caught up in converting M to C to M^1 again and again.

[51] On this treadmill, see Allan Schnaiberg and Kenneth Alan Gould, *Environment and Society: The Enduring Conflict* (New York: St. Martin's, 1994), pp. 46, 93, and passim.

[52] Ralph Estes, *Tyranny of the Bottom Line: Why Corporations Make Good People Do Bad Things* (San Francisco: Berrett-Johler, 1996); and Peter Schwartz and Blair Gibb, *When Good Companies Do Bad Things: Responsibility and Risk in an Age of Globalization* (New York: John Wiley, 1999).

food,[53] dispense free cigarettes to minors,[54] discharge thousands of workers on short notice, and resist environmental safety standards as an unacceptable cost in the struggle to prevail against other capitalists.[55] There, too, they may seek to replace durable products with disposable items that generate corporate profits but use up resources and clutter the garbage disposal system. Such was the classic case a century ago of Gillette razor blades, which – peddled under the slogan "Look Sharp! Feel Sharp! Be Sharp!" – displaced straight razors that could be used again and again.[56]

Jockeying

In the perpetual quest for profits, capitalists constantly maneuver for position among competing political jurisdictions. Sometimes this *jockeying* takes place within the United States, like when J. C. Stevens after World War II closed textile plants in the Northeast and reopened them in southern states where right-to-work laws made organizing unions difficult and kept labor costs down.[57] At other times, jockeying takes place on the world stage, as part of globalization, when corporations like General Motors, IBM, Zenith, and Motorola move assembly lines out of the United States and set them up again in low wage countries like Thailand, Bangladesh, Singapore, Indonesia, Mexico, and the Philippine Islands.[58]

The goal of jockeying is to increase profits by building factories in places where unions are weak, taxes are low, and environmental protection is feeble. Where these conditions obtain, business associations will say that the local jurisdiction, such as Indonesia or Texas, maintains a

---

[53] See "Snack Foods Become Stars of Books for Children," *New York Times* (September 21, 2000), pp. A1, C17.

[54] "Enticing Third World Youth: Big Tobacco Is Accused of Crossing an Age Line," *New York Times* (August 24, 2001), pp. C1, C4.

[55] Business resistence to environmental standards is noted in Schnaiberg and Gould, *Environment and Society*, p. 59.

[56] See the Gillette case in Susan Strasser, *Satisfaction Guaranteed: The Making of the American Mass Market* (Washington, D.C.: Smithsonian Institution Press, 1989), pp. 97–101. See it also in Phil Patton, *Made in USA: The Secret Histories of the Things That Made America* (New York: Penguin, 1992), pp. 321–324.

[57] See Jefferson R. Cowie, *Capital Moves: RCA's 70-Year Quest for Cheap Labor* (Ithaca: Cornell Univ. Press, 1999), which traces the relocation of Radio Corporation of America manufacturing lines from Camden, New Jersey, to Bloomington, Indiana, to Memphis, Tennessee, to Ciudad Juarez, Mexico. See also Barlett and Steele, *America: Who Really Pays Taxes?*, pp. 299–318, on cases such as BMW, Keebler, and Northwest Airlines jockeying between American states and cities.

[58] On corporations seeking lax environmental standards around the world, see Joshua Karliner, *The Corporate Planet: Ecology and Politics in the Age of Globalization* (San Franscisco: Sierra Club Books, 1997), pp. 148–167.

good business climate.[59] Community life in those places may suffer from poverty, potholes, smog, sweatshops, and a general lack of public amenities. But conditions favorable to business are likely to persist because the host government, in America or abroad, is afraid that if its tax and regulatory policies will offer business a setting for only modest profits, corporations will locate elsewhere.

Jockeying is a predictable and consistent part of corporate behavior because it pays off in two ways. First, in return for agreeing to build a plant in someplace new, or by threatening to close down operations in someplace old, the corporation may be awarded tax abatements and other subsidies. Such a response seems reasonable to the corporation, which is driven by M-C-M^1 to practice any legal tactic that will lower costs and raise profits. The same response also seems reasonable to government officials, who feel they should do whatever they can, within the law, to bring jobs to their communities. The downside is that, when corporations pay low taxes or receive subsidies in the form of, say, a municipal stadium for a professional baseball team,[60] less public money is available to pay for public services such as garbage removal, pollution control, roads, schools, airports, libraries, parks, and so forth.[61]

Jockeying is additionally profitable because it impairs the ability of unions and workers to bargain powerfully and successfully for good working conditions. Jockeying exerts downward pressure on wages and upward pressure on overtime because, while a corporation may be able to move its capital to someplace more profitable, workers with families and

[59] Barry Bluestone and Bennett Harrison, *The Deindustrialization of America: Plant Closings, Community Abandonment, and the Dismantling of Basic Industry* (New York: Basic Books, 1982), pp. 181–182.

[60] See Mark Rosenthal, *Major League Losers: The Real Cost of Sports and Who's Paying for It* (New York: Basic Books, 1997), for a description of how wealthy investors threaten to move their sports teams or do so, in order to get stadiums built largely at public expense. The stadium deal worked out in 1991 to keep the Texas Rangers in Arlington, Texas, is described on pp. 19–22. In that deal, George W. Bush appears as "a minority shareholder" in the Rangers franchise. "RBI: Revenue Brought In," *Washington Post* (July 31, 2000), p. A12, reported that Bush's investment of roughly $600,000, started in 1989, was worth $14.9 million when the team was sold in 1998.

[61] Former Michigan governor G. Mennen Williams noted that national highways were built after World War II only because the federal government gave states and municipalities money to do so. On their own, and in competition to attract people and industries, local governments would not have taxed their residents to build those roads. See Richard Reeves, *American Journey: Travelling with Tocqueville in Search of Democracy in America* (New York: Touchstone, 1982), p. 46.

neighborhood ties are less mobile.[62] In these circumstances, a corporation which is willing and able to relocate can insist that workers accept poor work conditions rather than none at all.[63]

Since the tactic is legal and profitable, we may expect corporations to use it repeatedly. Within America, at least, they will continue to jockey for so long as they are not nationally chartered and can therefore play one jurisdiction against another according to the strategy of divide and conquer. Only federal law, say, in the name of interstate commerce, would be capable of imposing on corporations operating in separate states a uniform standard limiting capital mobility and plant closures, and only federal law could compel corporations to carry with them wherever they go consistent obligations concerning local taxation and environmental protection.[64]

[62] The ability of some firms to move elsewhere is an example of "exit" from existing conditions. See Albert Hirschman, *Exit, Voice, and Loyalty: Responses to Decline in Firms, Organizations, and States* (Cambridge: Harvard Univ. Press, 1970). This connection is pointed out by Frances Fox Piven and Richard A. Cloward, *The Breaking of the American Social Compact* (New York: New Press, 1997), pp. 6–8. For an example of corporate exit, see Louis Uchitelle, "States Pay for Jobs, but It Doesn't Always Pay Off," *New York Times* (November 10, 2003), pp. 1, 17. In this case, Indianapolis and Indiana gave United Airlines $320 million to build and operate an aircraft maintenance center at Indianapolis International Airport. Ten years later, after September 11, 2001, United Airlines walked away from the subsidized facility, choosing to do its maintenance work in the American South, where private contractors serviced planes by using nonunion mechanics who earned a third of the wages and benefits that United had paid to unionized mechanics in Indianapolis.

[63] See "Cap Maker Is Assailed by Colleges: Big League Supplier Is Called Anti-Labor," *New York Times* (August 21, 2001), p. A15. In this case, the Workers Rights Consortium composed of 82 colleges and universities accused the New Era Cap Company of Derby, New York, which produces caps worn by Major League Baseball players, of running a dangerous workplace, transporting production to the South, and cutting workers' wages. On behalf of the company, CEO David Koch explained that New Era had to cut costs to compete with rivals like Nike and Reebok because it was paying workers $10 to $12 per hour while their Chinese workers were receiving 15 to 20 cents per hour. As for jobs transferred to the South, Robert Doren, the company's lawyer, explained that caps cost $2.80 to produce in Derby and $1.10 in New Era's Alabama factories.

[64] Federal incorporation is a policy proposal not actively promoted by any leading Republicans or Democrats. But it occasionally surfaces in works of political criticism. For example, see Donald L. Barlett and James B. Steele, *America: What Went Wrong?* (Kansas City: Andrews and McMeel, 1992), p. 218. See also the discussion in Lucien Bebchuk, "Federalism and the Corporation: The Desirable Limits on State Competition in Corporate Law," *Harvard Law Review*, Vol. 105 (1992), pp. 1435–1510. An example of why critics call for federal incorporation is the fact that many major American business firms – such as Marriot, Office Depot, Texaco, DuPont, Apple, Days Inn, Motorola, Coca-Cola, MacDonald's, and Merck – have chosen to incorporate in Delaware. These

Creative Destruction

Economist Joseph Schumpeter used the phrase *creative destruction* to describe what happens when capitalists seek to maintain the value of their
capital by producing old commodities more cheaply or by inventing new
ones to replace profitably the old.[65] In this process, valuable items and
skills are created. Ford's assembly line turned out cars more quickly than
before, Boeing 707s reduced long-distance travel costs, antibiotic drugs
replaced traditional remedies, and women all over the world left behind
some of their housework and started assembling televisions, toaster ovens,
and computers.[66]

In such instances, progress is made. But at the same time, Schumpeter
noted, the existing worth of once valuable properties and skills is destroyed.[67] For example, factories based on new techniques make old ones
obsolete and worthless. Thus abandoned steel mills in the Midwest help
to give that region its reputation as the "rust belt" of America. Other
factories may be blindsided by new products. Thus when plastic drinking
straws replaced paper straws, the machinery for making the latter became
useless. Some American workers get replaced by cheaper workers in the
South or abroad. And others, like bank clerks and business secretaries,
fall prey to automatic teller machines and networked computers.

In many cases, those who are ousted find no work at comparable rates
of pay. This is especially so because New Economy corporations like Microsoft and Intel, no matter how successful, employ fewer people than
Old Economy corporations like General Motors and Kodak. In 1995, for
example, 15,500 people worked for Microsoft, while 721,00 still worked
for General Motors. So Americans discharged from Old Economy jobs are
most likely to take new jobs at lower wages in service sector corporations

include about half of the Fortune 500 and about 40 percent of all companies listed
on the New York Stock Exchange. Incorporating in Delaware does not mean doing
much business there or running operations from that state. It means only that firms
pay Delaware a fee to establish a "headquarters" office there and then benefit from
the fact that Delaware's laws make it difficult for stockholders to sue a "local" company for mismanagement or for consumers to sue it for product defects. On Delaware's
attractiveness to corporations, see "Delaware Inc.," *Washington Post* (May 7, 2000),
pp. H1, H4.

[65] See his *Capitalism, Socialism, and Democracy*, 3rd ed. (New York: Harper and Row, 1962),
pp. 81–86.

[66] The term spinster denotes a person who operates a spinning wheel to make thread from,
say, cotton or wool, and reminds us of how few kinds of work were once considered
respectable for unmarried women.

[67] Schumpeter, *Capitalism, Socialism, and Democracy*, pp. 81–86.

like Wal-Mart and McDonald's, which in 1995 employed 434,000 and 177,000 people respectively.[68]

Like jockeying, creative destruction is not the fault of particular entrepreneurs and managers. Rather, it is an inevitable outcome of capitalism as a system, and for so long as creative destruction rewards successful corporations, it will continue. The problem, obviously, is that when some people gain, others will lose, in which case long-standing patterns of life may be destroyed at great personal cost.

Consider, for example, great American cities like Boston, New York, Detroit, Chicago, and San Francisco. Green and spacious suburbs were built in America when trains, trolleys, and automobiles became available for commuting. Taking advantage of these new devices, many successful people moved out of central cities and into a house of their dreams. Then forklift trucks made one-story factories more efficient than loft buildings downtown. So sprawling factories were built on empty land outside of crowded central cities, and additional successful people moved out to work in them and forgo commuting. At around the same time, rural Americans relocated to older housing in urban areas when new machinery such as mechanical cotton pickers made their labor unnecessary on farms. Central cities did not absorb those people easily, in part because many good jobs had already moved out.

From all of these comings and goings, some individuals did well, achieving more comfort and leisure than they had enjoyed before. In America's metropolitan areas, though, central cities were left with large numbers of poor people lacking modern skills, often unemployed, whose neighborhoods deteriorated in part because many taxable enterprises, which could support public services, had moved to suburbs. Here was a social imbalance caused in city after city by the destructive tendencies of dynamic capitalism, which can change long-standing patterns of life more dramatically than most political revolutions.[69]

A more recent American example of creative destruction, now spreading to many other countries, is the growth of large chain stores. Here, profits come from more effective marketing rather than from revised production. Wal-Mart was a pioneer in this trend. Sam Walton built large stores on cheap land near small towns. Such stores in effect paid lower

---

[68] These figures are from Edward Luttwak, *Turbo-Capitalism: Winners and Losers in the Global Economy* (New York: HarperCollins, 1999), Ch. 4, "The Microsoft Mirage," pp. 76–90.

[69] See Daniel Bell, *The Cultural Contradictions of Capitalism* (New York: Basic Books, 1976), pp. 66–72, on the far-reaching effects of, for example, automobiles and credit cards.

rents than stores on Main Street, they had ample parking lots where customers could arrive and depart conveniently, and they bought sale items in bulk directly from producers, sometimes abroad.[70]

On all three accounts, Wal-Mart could undersell Main Street merchants, which it proceeded to do, followed with some variation by Home Depot, Target, Staples, and more. The result was to drive out of business mom-and-pop grocery stores, small pharmacies, gift shops, hardware stores, and family haberdasheries on Main Streets all over America.[71] Ronald Reagan built a political career by claiming that governments destroy small-town values. If his supporters had paid more attention to the nature of capitalism as a system, they might have concluded that creative destruction was the real culprit, that free enterprise and stable communities are in some respects incompatible.[72]

Socialism and Free Enterprise

In the long run, creative destruction should be praised because it improves some aspects of life even while it generates social turmoil. Thus middle-class people today are healthier and live more comfortably than kings and queens in eighteenth-century Europe.[73] There is a capitalist tendency which has less to recommend it, however, and which led Michael Harrington to speak of "socialism for the rich and free enterprise for the poor."[74] What prompted Harrington to use this phrase was that affluent people manage to get together, lobby, and obtain government help of

[70] On the Wal-Mart way of doing business, see Bob Ortega, *In Sam We Trust* (New York: Times Books, 2000).

[71] Elements of the case against Wal-Mart, for undermining community in America, are noted by Michael L. Sandel, *Democracy's Discontent: American in Search of a Public Philosophy* (Cambridge: Harvard Univ. Press, 1996), pp. 334–335.

[72] See Bluestone and Harrison, *The Deindustrialization of America*, "Introduction: Capital vs. Community," pp. 3–21. See also John Ralston Saul, *The Unconscious Civilization* (Toronto: Anasi, 1995), p. 42:

> Believers [in the market ideology] preach two contradictory visions: (1) a return to the American small-town ideal; (2) the achievement of a magic balance that will be created by the freeing of the capitalist mechanism. Most sensible people would be surprised by the suggestion of such a strange cohabitation. The global economy and the small-town ideal are not simply nonsequiturs. They are direct enemies.

[73] This is because, by one estimate, per capita income in "presently developed countries" increased eightfold between 1750 and 1980, from $180 in 1750 to $3000 in 1980. See Paul Bairoch in Just Faaland (ed.), *Population and the World Economy in the Twenty-first Century* (Oxford: Basil Blackwell, 1982), p. 162.

[74] Michael Harrington, *The Other America: Poverty in the United States* (Baltimore: Penguin, 1963), p. 157.

various kinds while the poor join few organizations, remain unorganized, and compete against one another with little assistance.

At work here is a systematic but underrated element of capitalist behavior. Economists often assume that business firms oppose one another in a marketplace defined by laws and public opinion. That is, they assume that there exists a stable playing field where capitalist competitors struggle for advantage in a game controlled by neutral referees. In truth, however, firms work hard at persuading politicians to fashion an economic arena whose boundaries will befriend capitalists and within which the game they play will have rules designed to boost profits. Therefore both the playing field and the game it offers are not fixed like the Rock of Gibraltar but constantly changing to the extent that capitalists can cause lawmakers to mold a marketplace more useful to themselves.[75] Thus Washington is home to an enormous collection of well-heeled lobbyists, corporate-financed think tanks, and business-oriented political action committees, all trying to influence government policy and almost none speaking for the poor.[76]

Cases of economic advantage gained by political means abound. In the federal budget, for example, affluent people and corporations enjoy direct subsidies in the form of tax breaks and government expenditures. These include accelerated depreciation, the savings and loan bailout,[77] the homeowner's deduction for mortgage interest, tax-free municipal bonds for wealthy investors, nuclear subsidies for utility companies, airport construction for those who can afford to fly, tax breaks for business meals and entertainment, and military waste, duplication, and fraud in contracts with corporate suppliers. Against such interventions poor people

[75] A recent example is deregulation of markets for electric power in states such as New York and California. Under New York regulation, power companies were obliged to reduce demand for power, say, by installing more efficient equipment, if doing so would be cheaper than building a new generating plant. The result was ecologically sound. But with deregulation, companies that want to sell more power, for more profits, can do so by building more generating plants. See Kirk Johnson, "Why Cost of Power Hasn't Dropped," *New York Times* (September 26, 2000), p. A23: "On the new playing field . . . the incentives are all one-sided. Power generating companies have no motive to encourage people to use less energy or to use it more efficiently because the most money is to be made when demand is at its peak. And electricity delivery companies make more money by sending more electricity through their wires."

[76] See Kay Lehman Schlozman, "What Accent the Heavenly Chorus? Political Equality and the American Pressure System," *Journal of Politics* (November 1984), 1011–1017; and Robert H. Salisbury, "Interest Representation: The Dominance of Institutions," *American Political Science Review* (March 1984), pp. 64–76.

[77] See Stephen Pizzo, Mary Fricker, and Paul Muolo, *Inside Job: The Looting of America's Savings and Loans* (New York: HarperCollins, 1991).

are helped, but not as much, by Social Security, welfare, Medicaid, food stamps, aid to single mothers, and various programs directed at rural and urban poverty. By one estimate of the value of such items in fiscal 1996, the rich got $448 billion in annual subsidies while the poor, including proverbial "welfare queens," got $130 billion.[78]

Monetary Policy

The political impact of capitalism, then, does not flow merely from individual impulses but is collective, massive, widespread, and persistent. It is not, however, always obvious. For example, the Federal Reserve Board adjusts interest rates across the land in a way that pits some people against others while pursuing an ostensibly neutral policy of dampening inflation on behalf of "sound" economic growth.[79] The rationale for this policy, apart from class interests that usually go unmentioned, is related to an economic theory derived from the Phillips Curve.[80]

The Phillips Curve describes a direct relationship between inflation and employment, that is, when one goes up or down, so usually does the other. When economists tried to understand why this was so, they concluded that, when more people are employed, they are able to buy more goods and thereby drive up the price of those goods. Thus demand pulls inflation. At the same time, when more people are employed, their ability to bargain for higher wages in a tight labor market drives up production costs and, once again, increases commodity prices. Thus cost pushes inflation.

Prices that rise too far can lead to social chaos. This happened most famously when Germany's mark fell from 8.9 per U.S. dollar in January of 1919, to 64.9 marks per dollar in January of 1921, to 17,972 marks per dollar in January of 1923, to 4,200,000,000,000 marks per dollar on

---

[78] Mark Zepezauer and Arthur Naiman, *Take the Rich Off Welfare* (Tucson, Ariz.: Odonian, 1996). Subsidies for the rich are tallied in pp. 6–114; subsidies for the poor are listed in pp. 157–162. Information about much of the military waste described in this book was first collected in Christopher Cerf and Henry Beard, *The Pentagon Catalog* (New York: Workman, 1986). Zepezauer and Naiman, p. 16, describe this source as "the greatest bargain in history. To quote its cover copy: 'Buy this catalog for only $4.95 and get this $2,043 nut for *free*.' Attached to each book was a small metal nut, the kind that costs a few cents at the hardware store – and that McDonnell Douglas sold to the Navy for $2,043 each."

[79] For a detailed account of how this began and how it continues, see William Greider, *Secrets of the Temple: How the Federal Reserve Runs the Country* (New York: Simon and Schuster, 1987).

[80] See A. W. Phillips, "The Relation Between Unemployment and the Rate of Change of Money Wage Rates in the U.K.," in *Economica* (November 1958), pp. 283–299. See also the discussion of Phillips's theory in Peter Donaldson, *Economics of the Real World*, pp. 86–89.

November 15, 1923.[81] In light of such cases, many American economists have argued that government must restrain inflation. This can be done, they say, by setting interest rates high enough to rein in "irrational" economic "exuberance,"[82] limit the number of jobs available, and thereby assure the normal rate of unemployment.

Economists define the *normal rate of unemployment* as roughly the rate that obtains when whoever wants a job will be able to find one. The trouble is that "normal" in this case implies some sort of natural order in human affairs when, in truth, social life is shaped by expectations and aspirations that vary from one time and place to another. Thus a normal unemployment rate has no particular numerical value. It could be 3 percent, 5 percent, or 8 percent, depending on how many people, including married mothers and teenaged children, are looking for work and how many, including college graduates and former steelworkers, are so discouraged by wages offered at MacDonald's that they will stay home.

Moreover, the concept of a normal unemployment level, presumably set by forces beyond human control, obscures the fact that, in several ways, deflation helps the affluent whereas inflation helps the poor.[83] For example, wealthy people, who invest in fixed-income bonds, will lose more from rising prices than people of small means, whose mortgages will become easier to pay when their wages go up in an inflated economy. Furthermore, the practice of hiking interest rates to reduce inflation means that, from a distance but with implacable force, the Federal Reserve Board knowingly punishes people who have acted responsibly by finding and holding jobs, for whatever pay. In the name of reining in the economy to prevent inflation, the board raises interest rates so that some business activity cannot be financed. When that happens, some employees will be discharged, for no fault of their own, and the labor market will loosen up. After which, circumstances will compel those still at work to accept lower wages, which will contribute to deflation.[84]

---

[81] These figures are from Fritz K. Ringer (ed.), *The German Inflation of 1923* (New York: Oxford Univ. Press, 1969), p. 79.

[82] The term *irrational exuberance* was used by Federal Reserve Board Chairman Alan Greenspan in his Francis Boyer Lecture at the American Enterprise Institute for Public Policy Research, in Washington, D.C., on December 5, 1996. See "Greenspan Asks a Question and Global Markets Wobble," *New York Times* (December 7, 1996), pp. A1, 36. For an extended discussion, see Robert Shiller, *Irrational Exuberance* (Princeton: Princeton Univ. Press, 2000).

[83] See the chapter on inflation in George P. Brockway, *The End of Economic Man*, 3rd. ed. (New York: Norton, 1995), pp. 200–218.

[84] On checking inflation in order to maintain a "normal" rate of unemployment, see ibid., pp. 219–228; and Robert Lekachman, *Greed Is Not Enough: Reaganomics* (New York:

The political paradox here is striking. Congress and the president are elected to increase GNP and thereby put people to work. At the same time, the Federal Reserve Board, consisting of seven governors including the chairman, and insulated from voters by overlapping fourteen-year terms of office, insures that, if Congress and the president succeed "too well," employers will discharge millions of employees.[85] In fact, to attack inflation by assaulting workers is to implement a perverse axiom in the social theory of modern capitalism. The board assumes that a wide array of clerks, drivers, bricklayers, nurses, pilots, stockbrokers, and more, no matter how conscientiously they work, *must* lose the jobs they hold, else the economy will overheat and crash. Yet to say as much and to act accordingly is to renege on President Franklin D. Roosevelt's promise of a decent job for all Americans willing to work.[86]

Pantheon, 1982), pp. 200–202. See also Alan Greenspan, chairman of the Federal Reserve Board, quoted in William Greider, *One World, Ready or Not: The Manic Logic of Global Capitalism* (New York: Touchstone, 1997), p. 303: "Unfortunately, even when the economy is producing at its 'potential' [2.5 percent annual economic growth according to Greenspan] many people are still unemployed. But attempts to run at lower levels of unemployment [more people working].... would in the end do more harm than good." These remarks do not tell us who might suffer harm rather than good if more people could find jobs in the world according to Alan Greenspan. However, for a powerful account of the privations visited on involuntarily idle people when government promotes a "normal unemployment rate" of, say, 6 percent, see Leslie Dunbar, *Common Interest: How Our Social Welfare Policies Don't Work and What We Can Do About Them* (New York: Pantheon, 1988).

[85] Decisions on the federal fund rate are made by the Federal Open Market Committee, which consists of the seven Reserve Board members plus five out of twelve of the regional Reserve Bank presidents. Decisions on the discount rate are made by the seven board members. Steady contraction of the nation's money supply by the Federal Reserve Board caused a recession in 1981–1982 and raised official unemployment in December of 1982 to 12 million people, with an additional 4 or 5 million not actively seeking work through employment offices. The Urban Institute estimated that 4.3 million people slipped below the poverty line. See Greider, *Secrets of the Temple*, pp. 454–455f.

[86] This retreat is described in Richard DuBoff, "Full Employment: The History of a Receding Target," *Politics and Society*, No. 1 (1977), pp. 1–25. For one explanation of why relevant political forces line up as they do, see Benjamin R. Barber, *Jihad vs. McWorld: How Globalism and Tribalism Are Reshaping the World* (New York: Ballantine, 1996), p. 27: "Although full employment is a *public good* it is not a *corporate good*" (emphasis supplied).

9

The Primacy of Politics

Credit should be given where it is due. By blending an abundance of natural resources with powerful elements of science, technology, managerial innovation, individual freedom, entrepreneurial speculation, hard work, and personal profits, America's modern economy has outproduced all other forms of economic enterprise in history. As a result, many Americans are equipped to sustain a level of health and comfort that few are inclined to relinquish. Not surprisingly, poorer states around the world hope to achieve a similar measure of material success.

On the other hand, the tale of citizenship highlights predicaments that will not go away. First, that consumerist aspirations, and the economy which makes, promotes, and sells commodities, create a wide range of social and economic problems. Second, that addressing such matters is difficult, because Americans tend to overlook the systematic practices which generate them and therefore lack motivation to pull together in a republican fashion to improve the quality of community life.

The Eight-Hundred-Pound Gorilla
All this suggests that only a *paradigm shift* can energize citizens and direct them to where political action should take place. Americans usually regard civil society as benign and even beneficial.[1] Before the Revolution, they came to believe that religious pluralism does not threaten the general welfare. Later, they decided that the realm of work is harmless and

---

[1] See Daniel Bell, "The 'Hegelian Secret': Civil Society and American Exceptionalism," in Byron E. Shafer (ed.), *Is America Different? A New Look at American Exceptionalism* (Oxford: Clarendon, 1991), pp. 46–70.

fruitful. And finally, they all along tended to accept immigrants who would adopt republican values. Cultural dissonance caused social friction between old-timers and newcomers. But the country never succumbed to ethnic tensions as severe as those that plagued Europe. Instead, Americans came to regard ethnicity, in most cases, as a harmless aspect of civil society, often expressed pleasantly in exotic foods and colorful parades.

Taking these beliefs into account, here is the present paradigm: With exceptions from time to time, Americans have traditionally regarded religion, the economy, and national origin as matters that require little, if any, government control. It follows that few Americans believe a strong state is needed to preserve public order and promote shared well-being. Instead, they assume that, for the most part, voluntary organizations can serve their collective needs.

In the history of political thought, Old Worlders were more cautious. Georg Hegel, for example, teaching early in the nineteenth century, argued that strong states in Europe served to suppress dangerous antagonisms arising from religious intolerance, economic inequality, and ethnic feuds like those that wracked the old Austro-Hungarian Empire and still plague what used to be Yugoslavia.[2] In the European view, therefore, strong governments may be commendable, provided they are reasonable, precisely because they can reach into civil society and restrain there forces that, uncurbed, might cause extensive damage to society at large.

The European approach to civil society, although not rooted in New World experiences, offers a clue to how Americans should redirect their thinking. What they confront is a modern version of capitalism, which fabricates commodities relentlessly, which is expanding by globalization, and which generates a vision of consumerism that complements capitalism's endless production, promotion, sales, and profits. Output continues to rise. At the same time, this economic system, without malice, imposes sizable costs on America, to say nothing of the world at large. Moreover, it will not voluntarily provide unprofitable public goods that can enhance collective well-being.

In a new paradigm, the capitalist economy must be seen for what it is, an eight-hundred-pound gorilla born in civil society.[3] Sometimes this

---

[2] On Hegel, civil society, and the state, see Shlomo Avineri, *Hegel's Theory of the Modern State* (Cambridge: Cambridge Univ. Press, 1972).

[3] This sentence locates capitalism in the realm of (1) civil society as opposed to the realm of (2) politics or the state. On this score, I agree with Adam B. Seligman who, following the examples of Adam Smith and Georg Hegel, assumes that economic activity, often problematical, belongs to civil society. See his *The Idea of Civil Society* (Princeton: Princeton Univ. Press, 1992). Many scholars today would disagree. They use the term *civil society* to

giant behaves well, but sometimes he threatens the happiness of people who live there. That being the case, government must restrain capitalists, since only government can confine economic enterprise to civilized limits. Or, to put the matter bluntly, in a society where people agree that checks and balances must restrain government to prevent tyranny, an economic system of such private power has arisen, and is so likely to dominate the shape of public life, that it must be checked and restrained by government itself, instructed by voter mandates. Is that not what many Americans already have in mind when they call for campaign finance reform designed to prevent large-scale political contributions?[4]

Prescriptions

The objective is to use government, reasonably and democratically, to redress the balance between consumerist outcomes and the republican vision of a good life.[5] Whatever solutions that end may require specifically,

refer to personal relations while leaving (3) the marketplace economy as a realm standing somewhere between or beside (a) civil society and (b) the state. For example, see Jean Cohen and Andrew Arato, *Civil Society and Political Theory* (Cambridge: MIT Press, 1992), p. ix, where civil society is defined as "a sphere of social interaction between economy and state, composed of the intimate sphere (especially the family), the sphere of associations (especially voluntary associations), social movements, and forms of public communication." Or see Larry Diamond, "Rethinking Civil Society: Toward Democratic Consolidation," *Journal of Democracy* (July 1994), p. 5: "Civil society is an intermediary entity, standing between the private sphere and the state. Thus it excludes individual and family life, inward-looking group activity (e.g., for recreation, entertainment, or spirituality), the profitmaking enterprise of individual business firms, and political efforts to take control of the state." I disagree with Cohen, Arato, and Diamond, for to speak of the economy as standing outside of civil society implies that its present shape is as natural and as inviolate as the better part of personal relations. On the contrary, I regard the marketplace as a human artifact, defined by law, which could be constructed differently and more beneficially to the community. For various definitions of civil society and for their political implications, see John Ehrenberg, *Civil Society: The Critical History of an Idea* (New York: New York Univ. Press, 1999), esp. pp. 233–250.

4 For an academic analysis of the money problem in party politics, see Thomas Ferguson, *Golden Rule: The Investment Theory of Party Competition and the Logic of Money-Driven Political Systems* (Chicago: Univ. of Chicago Press, 1995).

5 On this point, it is worth recalling what John Maynard Keynes said about reforming capitalism. See his *The General Theory of Employment, Interest, and Money* (London: Macmillan, 1936), where Keynes offered a theory of effective demand that justified government action to create full employment if unregulated markets failed to do so. Especially in Ch. 24, "Concluding Notes on the Social Philosophy Towards Which the General Theory Might Lead," pp. 372–384, Keynes argued that capitalism had to be fixed *somewhat* (to overcome some problems it creates) but *mostly* retained (because it effectively allocates some resources and helps to preserve many freedoms). For a recent exploration of considerations that might bear on the project of modifying capitalism without destroying

it is generally true that they should be implemented within a framework of *structural reforms*. That is, new regulations and oversight must change the way in which individuals and groups, who might be corporations, are permitted to behave, so that they will interact more reasonably with one another and with more regard for collective well-being.[6]

The general prescription for structural reform cannot be avoided because, when confronted by a defect of consumerism fueled by capitalism, a "just say no" appeal for better individual behavior will not work. *Moral exhortation* may improve human relations somewhat.[7] But it cannot thoroughly restrain systematic impulses, which are driven by an internal logic that promises compelling rewards. Indeed, from whatever pulpit, moral exhortation must be repeated constantly because individuals, such as miscreant corporate managers, when behaving badly but systematically, are unlikely to desist for long.[8] And if they do, they will probably be replaced by people who, bound by whichever imperatives caused the problem to begin with, will backslide into similar misbehavior.[9]

markets entirely, see Claudio J. Katz, "Private Property Versus Markets: Democratic and Communitarian Critiques of Capitalism," *American Political Science Review* (June 1997), pp. 279–289.

[6] See Thomas I. Palley, *Plenty of Nothing: The Downsizing of the American Dream and the Case for Structural Keynesianism* (Princeton: Princeton Univ. Press, 1998). The prescription for structural reform is not popular today, partly because it is frequently denounced by economic conservatism, which I will describe later. Charles Derber, *Corporation Nation: How Corporations Are Taking Over Our Lives and What We Can Do About It* (New York: St. Martin's, 2000), explains how a "corporation mystique," promoted vigorously by business and conservative spokespeople, hides the fact that corporate forms and market-place behavior are *not* natural and therefore sacrosanct, but evolve within boundaries set by legislation and regulation.

[7] I have in mind books such as William Bennett, *The Book of Virtues: A Treasury of Great Moral Stories* (New York: Simon and Schuster, 1993).

[8] This point is familiar to democratic socialists, but their writings are not read widely in America. For example, see the Fabian socialist George Bernard Shaw, "Preface on the Prospects of Christianity," which is the introduction to Shaw's *Androcles and the Lion*, in Shaw, *Collected Plays with Their Prefaces*, 7 vols. (New York: Dodd, Mead, 1970), Vol. IV, pp. 455–584. On p. 518, Shaw says:

> Whereas . . . in the commercial night of the nineteenth century, it was believed that you could not make men good by Act of Parliament, we now know that you cannot make them good in any other way. . . . The [Christian] disciple cannot have his bread without money until there is bread for everyone without money; and that requires an elaborate municipal organization of the food supply, rate [tax] supported.

[9] Bad behavior is not always illegal. But on corporate crime, see Paul Blumberg, *The Predatory Society* (New York: Oxford Univ. Press, 1989); and Irwin Ross, *Shady Business: Confronting Corporate Corruption* (New York: Twentieth-Century Fund, 1992).

Social Value

Within a commitment to structural reform, the concept of *economic conscience* suggests several prescriptions for what should be done. First, citizens must understand that their appraisal of whatever they want to purchase must take into account how that thing affects other people. That is, a private item should not be judged by its market price but for its *social value*, which consists of the market price of that item minus the external costs that it generates.[10]

Looked at this way, a new car, no matter how much it will delight me, may have little social value. Instead, it may greatly burden the community, for its true value embraces not only what I pay for it and the happiness it provides me but also the environmental damage which producing it caused at iron mines and oil refineries, plus the money for building and maintaining roads where it will travel, plus the social dislocations caused by urban sprawl and suburban strip development, plus the extra air pollution and global warming generated by commuters using cars rather than public transport, plus the trash disposal costs of getting rid of old cars, and so forth.[11] The same is true, with various external costs, for many other private goods. For example, if I buy air conditioners for my house, using them will increase air and water pollution from generating electricity.

Public Goods

Making calculations based on social value leads to a second prescription, which is that when citizens decide wherein that value exists, they should promote it by authorizing government to create new *public goods*. Some of these will contribute more to well-being than private goods whose social value is low, and others can help to neutralize externalities caused by affluence based mainly on owning private goods.

Some public goods are easy to create because many citizens agree, more or less, that they are beneficial in the widest sense. When we decide to promote such items, the main problem is generating the political will to impose taxes sufficient to pay for them.[12] Public goods of this sort include national defense, scientific research, Medicare, education, public

---

[10] On external costs and social value, see E. J. Mishan, *The Costs of Economic Growth* (Baltimore: Penguin, 1967), pp. 82–142.

[11] Estimates of the "true costs" for cars vary and may go as high as $100,000 for their purchase price and $250 for a tank of gasoline. See Kalle Lasn, *Culture Jam: How to Reverse America's Suicidal Consumer Binge – and Why We Must* (New York: Quill, 2000), pp. 180–181.

[12] To overcome the difficulty of repeatedly evoking the necessary political will, Robert Frank, *Luxury Fever: Why Money Fails to Satisfy in an Era of Excess* (New York: Free Press,

housing, libraries, roads, parks, bridges, Social Security, post offices, soil conservation, and so forth.

It will be difficult, however, to gain the collective well-being afforded by controlled economic growth, which can preserve what ecologists call *the commons*. On this score, we should concede the obvious: No one knows exactly how to rein in economic growth selectively rather than slashing all investments, good and bad, like the Federal Reserve Board does when it raises interest rates. After all, we do not agree on where cuts should be made. For example, whether to enrich school programs and subsidize public transit or to upgrade lawn mowers and multiply disposable diapers are today regarded as matters of choice rather than necessity. This is because in industry, commerce, agriculture, and other realms of production and consumption, science does not always tell us unequivocally what to do. Instead, when trying to assess complex situations and forecast the future, even scientists may disagree on which economic practices are ecologically sound and which will trigger disaster.

Furthermore, we know that reduced growth will probably require some measure of coercion, for two reasons. First, because capitalists work according to impulses that do not yield voluntarily, such as the drive to exploit natural resources, the search for distracting media themes, and the tendency to skimp on antipollution devices. So management of economic growth must be at least partly Hobbesian, enforcing order on those who, in an endless economic war of all against all, would destroy the commons.[13] And second because even men and women who are not capitalists seek constantly to improve their material circumstances. They too, therefore, are unlikely to forgo voluntarily and separately the gains they might make from an economic tide that raises many boats, if only unequally.

If force will be necessary, the need to compel economic prudence will raise a serious issue for American democracy, since ordinary citizens may understand the consequences of economic growth even less than scientists. It follows that voters may not know enough to decide satisfactorily which proposals for government regulation should be enacted and which should be rejected. On this score, we must recognize that a great attraction of mainly unchecked growth is that it is mostly democratic. That is,

---

1999), pp. 211–226, recommends a consumption tax which will automatically increase government revenues when spending rises for private goods.

[13] On coercion and the Hobbesian solution, see William Ophuls and A. Stephen Boyan, Jr., *Ecology and the Politics of Scarcity Revisited* (New York: W. H. Freeman, 1992), pp. 195–206, and passim.

citizens are free to act economically while, for most of the time, no one in government has to justify forbidding new techniques or inventions unless they are patently dangerous.[14]

On the other hand, while elected officials should exercise power cautiously, they need not abjure it in principle. American government already acts decisively on large matters, for example, with regard to taxes, the right of eminent domain, and military drafts when necessary. Such power is acceptable, but why dwell on it unnecessarily? Prudence suggests, instead, conducting the debate over checking growth not in terms of essential coercion but as a discussion over improving existing rules of the economic game, of occasionally moving the goalposts to benefit the spectators. This can be done by asking voters to recognize that marketplace results are not always beneficial but may be pushed in that direction by familiar devices such as minimum wage laws, equal opportunity laws, child labor laws, maternity leave laws, workplace safety laws, truth-in-lending laws, environmental protection laws, fugitive capital laws, insider trading laws, and other undramatic but cumulative regulations.

Industrial Policy

Here, the second prescription gives rise to a third, which may be called an *industrial policy*. Although it is strikingly productive, the New Economy can be cruel to working Americans. Sometimes it transports their jobs away or downgrades them via jockeying, and sometimes it eliminates places of work through creative destruction. The social costs are enormous, as individuals lose their livelihoods and as towns and cities lose taxable resources when increased public services are needed for those not earning enough to help themselves.[15]

---

[14] Thus there are writers who recommend economic growth because the public wants it and will vote for politicians who promote it. The same writers say little or nothing about the difficulties of changing the public's mind and inspiring the civic will to rein in growth's long-term consequences. For example, Jeffrey Madrick, *The End of Affluence: The Causes and Consequences of America's Economic Dilemma* (New York: Random House, 1995); and Stanley B. Greenberg, *Middle-Class Dreams: The Politics and Power of the New American Majority*, rev. ed. (New Haven: Yale Univ. Press, 1996).

[15] One problem is that many Americans who work hard and responsibly do not earn enough in the New Economy to live comfortably and safely. A discussion of this situation appears in Michael Massing, "Ending Poverty as We Know It," in Robert Kuttner (ed.), *Making Work Pay: America After Welfare* (New York: New Press, 2002). See esp. p. 25, where Washington is described as a state in which 37 percent of jobs pay less per hour than a single adult needs to survive without public assistance, and where 73 percent of jobs pay less per hour than a single parent needs to support two children.

An industrial policy, which some might regard as a new *social contract*,[16] would have two faces. First, it would pursue enactment of laws designed to reduce dislocations caused by jockeying and creative destruction in America. For example, it might insist on federal charters for corporations, impose a slowdown on plant relocations, require corporate compensation for workers who lose their jobs, fund public works to maintain employment in bad times, and so forth.

Second, an industrial policy would demand wholesome behavior from America's trading partners.[17] Business leaders often claim that to improve economic rules at home, for example, by protecting workers and nature more than today, would weaken American firms in their struggle against foreign rivals who are free from such costs and restraints. Because this claim is sometimes valid, Washington should insist that other countries will raise their standards in tandem with those of America. Getting them to do so will entail making trade conditional on environmental protection laws, helping foreign workers to form unions, slowing the movement of plants and capital from one country to another, promoting universal political rights, protecting especially women in the workplace, regulating global securities markets, forcing financial disclosure on corporations in all countries, abolishing bank havens and overseas tax shelters,[18] and so forth.

[16] The right of every country to protect its citizens economically is noted by Joseph E. Stiglitz, *Globalization and Its Discontents* (New York: Norton, 2002), esp. pp. 208–209. Various countries might devise different policies to achieve this protection, but the point worth noting here is that Stiglitz regards the sum total of those policies in any particular country as a social contract.

[17] This is not enough the case today. Thus Washington has implemented the North American Free Trade Agreement without making serious attempts to enforce environmental and civil rights standards in Mexico. See *Deals for NAFTA Votes II: Bait and Switch* (Washington, D.C.: Public Citizen, 1997), pp. 1–23, and John P. MacArthur, *The Selling of 'Free Trade': NAFTA, Washington and the Subversion of American Democracy* (New York: Hill and Wang, 2000).

[18] See Joint Committee on Taxation, *Report of Investigation of Enron Corporation and Related Entities Regarding Federal Tax and Compensation Issues, and Policy Recommendations* (Washington, D.C.: Government Printing Office, 2003), p. 11:

> Enron had a total of approximately 1,300 different foreign entities.... Approximately 80 percent of Enron's foreign entities were inactive shells that did not hold and were not engaged in or associated with any ongoing business and that were therefore largely irrelevant for [real] tax purposes. Enron created many entities in jurisdictions that do not impose a tax on such entities. In particular, as of December 31, 2001, the Enron ownership structure included 441 entities formed in the Cayman Islands, a country that has never imposed a corporate income tax. Most of these entities were inactive shells not associated with any ongoing business.

The aim of an industrial policy propelled by republican aspirations is not necessarily to channel investment in particular directions, for example, by using government money to finance research leading to flatter and more profitable television screens. The goal, instead, is to foster healthy economies everywhere, so they cannot undermine American workplaces shaped by economic conscience and good citizenship. In technical terms, an industrial policy should encourage a shift away from "export-led growth" and a drive to create in poor countries conditions that will enable people there, unlike today, to buy American products based on reasonable and ecologically sound labor costs. The target should be, via social and political pressures, to raise real wages worldwide so that, as in first world countries, ordinary people elsewhere can afford modern amenities, can educate themselves and their children, and can create a decent public life. At that point, good American jobs will stop hemorrhaging away.[19]

The Primacy of Politics

Mandating government intervention into civil society, appreciating social value, creating public goods, and implementing an industrial policy are imperatives that call for political decisions to establish safe parameters for economic activity. Citizens will disagree here and there on which aspects of American life are problematic and which need repair. Such is rightfully the nature of democratic politics. As members of a civic community, however, they should understand that the ideal of good citizenship presumes they are free to make whatever repairs seem warranted. That is, *political freedom*, for citizens serving their public office, is a necessary condition for taking steps to improve the quality of collective life. Without political freedom, republican men and women cannot proceed as circumstances may require.

Of this freedom, more in a moment. Meanwhile, since we have broadly concluded that good citizenship, informed by economic conscience, should inspire political decisions on behalf of public interests, let us note that our tale of citizenship has returned to where it started, to the Greeks and their great teacher Aristotle.[20] Today's vocabulary is new.

---

[19] Walter Russell Mead, *Mortal Splendor: The American Empire in Transition* (Boston: Houghton Mifflin, 1987), pp. 306–317. On the need to balance imports against exports, see William Greider, *One World, Ready or Not: The Manic Logic of Global Capitalism* (New York: Touchstone, 1997), pp. 192–223.

[20] A qualification is necessary. My argument here comes close to what historians call "the Whig interpretation of history," whereby people tend to highlight, and somewhat distort, ideas from other eras that seem particularly important to their time and age. See Herbert

But the primacy of politics, which assumes that political considerations may rule over lesser interests, is a timeless concept.[21]

Aristotle spoke of happiness and well-being. At the outset, he defined *economics* as the art of household management, where *oikos* was the Greek word for household.[22] In Aristotle's version of economics, Greek households included extended families plus their servants, craftsmen, apprentices, and slaves, and made mainly goods of food, clothing, and shelter for themselves. However, they also made some goods for trade, where money might be earned. And since money could accumulate indefinitely, Aristotle feared that the desire for profit from trade was insatiable, thereby threatening to undermine well-being based on leisure and contemplation. It followed, in his view, that household management should promote a reasonable output of necessary goods and shun acquisition without limit.

From all this it followed that *politics*, which was the science of running the polis well, is the right sort of economics writ large. That is, politics entails promoting the well-being of many households together, in the

---

Butterfield, *The Whig Interpretation of History* (orig., 1931; London: G. Bell, 1963). Thus I say in the text above that our tale of citizenship "has returned to where it started." This is not to claim that, because some Greek terms inform our civic conversation today, we understand those terms exactly as the Greeks understood them. The truth is that words used by Plato, Aristotle, et al. to talk about politics may be instructive and useful to us, when understood approximately, *even though* the people who invented them created and maintained a sort of politics very different from ours. On some of the differences, see Paul H. Rahe, "The Primacy of Politics in Classical Greece," *American Historical Review* (April 1984), pp. 265–293.

21 As used in the text above, the phrase "primacy of politics" refers to the right of citizens to regard political decisions, democratically derived, as a force which, in most cases, may legitimately be employed to give desirable shape to community life. The emphasis here is on a moral assumption to the effect that making laws properly, although not in every case and not at every moment, is the correct way to live together. Another approach to the primacy of politics, which I will not elaborate in the text, speaks more of facts than of morality. It says that, intentionally or not, politics shapes community life in the real world, so why not do politics *well*? For example, various scholars have pointed out that the "free market" did not arise naturally, that it was framed by laws in Western society over hundreds of years, and that it will not thrive in other countries until their leaders take political steps to enforce contracts, define private property, establish limited liability, and so forth. For this second approach, which claims that much of economic life, in modern societies at least, is in fact shaped by political decisions, see Douglas C. North and R. P. Thomas, *The Rise of the Western World* (Cambridge: Cambridge Univ. Press, 1973); Hernando de Soto, *The Mystery of Capitalism: Why Capitalism Triumphs in the West and Fails Everywhere Else* (New York: Basic Books, 2000); and Niall Ferguson, *The Cash Nexus: Money and Power in the Modern World, 1700–2000* (New York: Basic Books, 2001).

22 Aristotle, *The Politics of Aristotle*, trans. and ed. Ernest Barker (New York: Oxford Univ. Press, 1946), Bk. I, Chs. 3–13, pp. 8–38.

larger and civic community which Greeks knew as the polis, and which later political thinkers, using Latin terminology, referred to as the *republic*, or the public thing.

Whoever studies Economics 101 knows that Aristotle's view is not popular with economists today, who when they talk about economics refer mainly to a cash-nexus activity which The Philosopher regarded as capable of contributing no more than partially to well-being. Aristotle would have said that what many economists today regard as *economic* is actually only *commercial*. It should not be confused with the truly economical, since what is commercial consists of only one aspect of a good life that should be defined according to standards of social value set by human volition rather than the capricious forces that dominate modern marketplaces.[23]

In this view, we should look to *true economics*, which can be expressed in democratic politics, to help us achieve not only material things but a safe environment, productive and meaningful work, knowledge and autonomy, and close social relations.[24] Many political scientists share this view. A. D. Lindsay, for example, writing on the modern democratic state under fire during World War II, defined politics as the "conscious control of common life. That is what ruling, properly conceived, is."[25] David Easton, speaking to a scholarly generation more attuned to professional jargon, said what amounted to the same thing in 1953 when he defined politics as "the authoritative allocation of values."[26]

Free Riders and Narratives

The primacy of politics is a fitting capstone to the tale of good citizenship. It indicates a connection between early ideas of who should belong to the civic community, and to what end, and later ideas about what members of that community should do and why. Yet in public life today, the degree of civic engagement that is required for authorizing fundamental, rather than routine, political decisions is sometimes difficult to evoke for at least

---

[23] On the commercial versus the economic in this sense, see Peter Donaldson, *Economics of the Real World*, 2nd ed. (Harmondsworth, England: Pelican, 1978), pp. 209–210.

[24] Some of these items come from Barry Schwartz, *The Costs of Living: How Market Freedom Erodes the Best Things in Life* (New York: Norton, 1994), p. 150.

[25] A. D. Lindsay, *The Modern Democratic State* (orig., 1943; New York: Oxford Univ. Press, 1962), p. 55.

[26] See his *The Political System: An Inquiry into the State of Political Science*, 2nd ed. (orig., 1953; New York: Knopf, 1971), pp. 143–144.

two important reasons, one very general and the other more specific to our day and age.

The general difficulty resides in what we have called the free-rider problem, a logical situation that challenges each citizen every day. On this score, whoever suggests that citizens should pay more attention to public needs and act accordingly, must admit that for many people it is cheaper and less bothersome to let others take up the slack. Earning a living and maintaining good relationships with friends and family are complicated matters that use up much of our time and emotional energy. Yet if, while we attend to such matters, we will let other people work at good citizenship and improve the quality of public life, we know that everyone will benefit, including ourselves. In the circumstances, it may seem quite reasonable – some people would even say rational – to abstain from public affairs on the grounds that one more vote or activist would make no difference.

Since Mancur Olson defined the free-rider problem, political scientists have conceded that this difficulty exists.[27] Unfortunately, they have not resolved it. That is, they have not managed to fashion for modern society a technical fix to free-rider situations in public life.[28] For instance, no one who cherishes personal independence would suggest that the state should require everyone to join political parties or attend street demonstrations. Moreover, to make voting compulsory, as in countries like Australia and Belgium today, cannot assure that those who cast ballots will inform themselves properly about what is at stake on election day.

Of course, all is not lost. We know that some Americans practice citizenship conscientiously. Accordingly, the country's problem is not so much that good citizenship has disappeared but that there should be more of it. To promote the notion that politics, in a democratic mode to be sure, should shape community life is to assume that, from time to time, the community as a whole should consider its condition and then decide how to proceed. As we have seen from mediocre rates of voting, however, many Americans do not participate in this stocktaking. Where that is the case,

---

[27] For example, Samuel Popkin, *The Reasoning Voter* (Chicago: Univ. of Chicago Press, 1991), pp. 10–11.

[28] Here is one reason, I think, for scholarly interest in Robert Putnam's idea that if something can be done to encourage more people to join social groups voluntarily – that is, to frame American life so that group membership will become more attractive to them – their interaction with other people in such groups will lead to more satisfactory rates of political participation. See his *Bowling Alone: The Collapse and Revival of American Community* (New York: Simon and Schuster, 2000).

the insights and information they might bring to politics are missing in the final equation, perhaps fatefully so.

Now when we ask why, despite free-rider temptations, so much as the current level of good citizenship practice is maintained, a likely answer lies in the realm of messages that one generation passes on to the next. These messages may be transmitted with little conscious coordination in school lessons, presidential speeches, judicial decisions, talk shows, family memoirs, commercial advertisements, and more. Yet even where a degree of cacophony reigns, we know that every society tells stories that define its character, stories about heroes and villains, about victories and defeats, about achievements and failures, about what sort of behavior citizens should admire and what sort they should shun.[29] In America's case these stories are, among others, about George Washington admitting that he chopped down the cherry tree, about Abraham Lincoln being born in a log cabin, about Elizabeth Cady Stanton and Susan B. Anthony campaigning tirelessly for women's rights, and about Martin Luther King cut down before he could realize his dream.[30]

By affecting citizens in ways we cannot fully analyze, such stories help them to understand what it means to be, for example, French, Mexican, English, Chinese, Pakistani, or American. In this sense it seems clear, but not in any precise degree, that civic behavior is inspired by shared narratives, some going back all the way to Athens and Sparta. And in this sense, the chronicle of good citizenship in America, built upon many smaller stories, emerges from the realm of such narratives.

What all this means is that, (1) so long as we know of no technical solution to the problem of free ridership, then (2) the amount of civic activism

[29] The importance of civically relevant stories is noted by political theorist Ronald Beiner in his *What's the Matter with Liberalism?* (Berkeley: Univ. of California Press, 1992), pp. 10–14: "Prologue: The Theorist as Storyteller." A sample of such stories is analyzed by Rogers M. Smith, *Stories of Peoplehood: The Politics and Morals of Political Memberships* (Cambridge: Cambridge Univ. Press, 2003). The original notion can be traced back to ancient Greece. See Aristotle, *The Politics*, Bk. V, Ch. 9, p. 233: "The greatest . . . of all means . . . for ensuring the stability of constitutions . . . is the education of citizens in the spirit of their constitution."

[30] See Michael Frisch, "American History and the Structures of Collective Memory: A Modest Exercise in Empirical Iconography," *Journal of American History* (March 1989), pp. 1130–1155. To discover what students about to start an American history survey course knew about their country's past, Frisch asked them to list famous people who lived in America until the Civil War. Along with patent heroes like George Washington, Thomas Jefferson, and Andrew Jackson, they also listed obvious villains like Benedict Arnold and John Wilkes Booth. They also listed Betsy Ross who, although widely regarded as heroic, does not seem, as a matter of historical fact, to have made the first American flag.

capable of providing adequate mandates for great political projects can probably be evoked only by inspiring stories. Potentially, at least, the tale of good citizenship is such a story, not because I have told it particularly well but because, given its parameters, that story may speak powerfully to Americans about profoundly important aspects of their national experience. To this end, as I noted several times in earlier chapters, what I have written does not dwell upon many difficulties in American life. Instead, it highlights the best parts of American experience, drawing attention to lofty expectations and generous ideals, expressed frequently over many years, and linking them analytically so as to offer readers a sense of belonging to an admirable project that is larger than themselves.[31] To speak of good citizenship in this way, at least sometimes, seems to me worthwhile because, in America today, it is exactly this sense of belonging that seems weaker than it was, say, half a century ago.[32]

The Dangers of Conservatism

Free ridership is a general force that limits the practice of good citizenship defined as public-minded activism. But there exists also a specific force that inhibits the same good citizenship. It may be seen in the fact that,

[31] In a world of economic globalization, many Americans feel no connection to such a project. Instead, they regard themselves as Schumpeterian men and women, constantly buffeted by impersonal forces that unpredictably steamroller ordinary people on behalf of, at best, what Schumpeter called "creative destruction." See the discussion in Richard Sennett, *The Corrosion of Character: The Personal Consequences of Work in the New Capitalism* (New York: Norton, 1998), pp. 30–31.

[32] Since the 1950s, roughly speaking, research projects have produced many books that describe how a wide range of groups in American life – women, homosexuals, African Americans, Hispanics, Asian Americans, migrant workers, and more – have suffered from various sorts of exclusion and discrimination. Such books are welcome for providing a wealth of information long neglected by the public transcript. At the same time, they have made it difficult to fashion a replacement for the national narrative that, even while it was inaccurate, did have a capacity for inspiring, on occasion, many Americans to act on behalf of public ends. Some of the paradoxes in this situation are explored in Frances FitzGerald, *America Revised* (New York: Vintage, 1980), a study of American history textbooks that shows how they increasingly fail to agree on answers to vital questions such as (p. 73) "Is there such a thing as an American identity? What kind of society does the United States have? What are American values? What position does the United States occupy in the world?" As FitzGerald observes, p. 8: "Poor Columbus! He is a minor character now, a walk-on in the middle of American history." For the longer view, suggesting that contemporary confusion over history education is, in some respects, the latest version of a perennial difficulty, see Joseph Moreau, *School Book Nation: Conflicts over American History Textbooks from the Civil War to the Present* (Ann Arbor: Univ. of Michigan Press, 2003).

since the 1970s, a significant number of American politicians have claimed that, in some respects, civic activism is either undesirable or untenable. From both major parties they favor extensively distributing the rights of Citizenship II. At the same time, however, in important cases, they hope to dissuade people who possess those rights from exercising them in order to call, via Citizenship III, for such activism.[33]

I will say something about where Democrats fit into this picture in a moment. But first let us consider the greater threat to good citizenship, which comes mainly from Republicans because so many of them are economic conservatives.[34] *Conservatism* in this sense is, to some extent, hostile to Citizenship III practices because, by telling people they should not call for some kinds of government regulation, it explicitly denies the primacy of politics. Or, as Edward Luttwak says, conservatism recommends a "hollowing-out of democratic governance over the economy."[35]

Economic and Social Conservatism

There are many nuances to American conservatism, as befitting a civic temperament rather than a political party. For our purposes, though, conservatism rests mainly upon two themes.[36] One is strong support for

---

33 I am about to discuss the views of conservative leaders, activists, and publicists who play the political game but often complain that when politics leads to political action, that action is somewhat or entirely suspect. In addition to such critics, many scholars have commented on the subject of whether or not large-scale political activity is as desirable as or less desirable than small-scale civic practices. One academic book that favors more politics and also discusses scholarly works that agree or disagree with such a recommendation is Christopher Beem, *The Necessity of Politics: Reclaiming American Public Life* (Chicago: Univ. of Chicago Press, 1999), esp. pp. 197–259.

34 I am about to argue that American conservatives have defined the limits of republican policies in ways that discourage some elements of good citizenship. Here is the place to note that Theodore J. Lowi, *The End of the Republican Era* (Norman: Univ. of Oklahoma Press, 1995), describes the tension between conservative ideas, mainly Republican, and what I call republican politics in somewhat different but complementary terms. For example, see p. 208: "The theory and policies of [Republican] negation amount to rejection of representative government [disdain for Congress] and [rejection of] democratic pluralism [insistence on Christian faith rather than religious tolerance as the basis for American democratic behavior]."

35 See his *Turbo-Capitalism: Winners and Losers in the Global Economy* (New York: HarperCollins, 1999), p. 187.

36 One must bear in mind how fuzzy the subject of modern American conservatism is. Conservatism is not a formal creed, set forth in a catechism and expounded by certified practitioners. Moreover, it is not the written platform of a national party with card carrying members who can be asked how firmly they believe in the principles of that platform. All that being so, scholars have no conclusive technique that can reveal exactly what

consumerism, and we may call this the theme of *economic conservatism*. During the 1930s, unemployment and bankruptcies made consumerist ideas somewhat irrelevant to Americans confronting scarcity. But after World War II, a growing economy spurred the entrenchment of consumerism as an ideal and financed the rise of conservative prophets in think tanks, research centers, universities, and the mass media. These people – such as Milton Friedman,[37] Irving Kristol,[38] and Jude Wanniski[39] – praised capitalism for making an abundance of things possible, where the prior assumption, already instilled by consumerism, was that steady consumption of those things, in comparison with other possible social goals, is highly desirable. Eventually, some politicians joined the conservative thinkers, some voters joined the politicians, and Barry Goldwater's failure of 1964 turned into the electoral success of Ronald Reagan and his heirs.[40]

Less important to our story, but often accompanying the support for consumerism, is a conservative theme of praise for long-standing values. We may call this the theme of *social conservatism*. On this score, conservative thinkers and politicians criticize people they call liberals for promoting lifestyles that conservatives believe are hostile to patriotism, private initiative, durable families, small towns, religious commitment, crime-free cities, hard work, personal responsibility, and so forth.[41]

American conservatism is. In fact, we cannot even say for sure who is a conservative and who is not, since many political thinkers, elected officials, and everyday activists, no matter how conservative they may look to you or me, insist that they do not belong to any ideological camp. It follows that what I offer in the text above, accompanied by supporting evidence, is my interpretation of the subject. Although I think that interpretation is reasonably accurate and moderately useful, I do not necessarily object to different interpretations of conservatism that other scholars might suggest. For example, see Charles W. Dunn and J. David Woodward, *The Conservative Tradition in America* (Lanham, Md.: Rowman and Littlefield, 1996), Ch. 2, "The Problem of Defining Conservatism," pp. 21–43.

[37] *Capitalism and Freedom* (Chicago: Univ. of Chicago Press, 1962).

[38] *Two Cheers for Capitalism* (New York: Basic Books, 1978).

[39] *The Way the World Works* (New York: Touchstone, 1978).

[40] Some of this story is told in Thomas Ferguson and Joel Rogers, *Right Turn: The Decline of the Democrats and the Future of American Politics* (New York: Hill and Wang, 1986). See also Paul Gottfried and Thomas Fleming, *The Conservative Movement* (Boston: Twayne, 1988); and Godfrey Hodgson, *The World Turned Right Side Up: A History of the Conservative Ascendancy in America* (Boston: Houghton Mifflin, 1996).

[41] For example, William J. Bennett, *The Devaluing of America: The Fight for Our Culture and Our Children* (New York: Touchstone, 1992); Jerry Falwell, *The New American Family: The Rebirth of the American Dream* (Dallas: Word, 1992); Gertrude Himmelfarb, *The Demoralization of Society: From Victorian Virtues to Modern Values* (New York: Knopf, 1995); and Dick DeVos, *Rediscovering American Values: The Foundations of Our Freedom*

The Republican Element

In a moment, we will examine the economic theme in conservatism and see how, promoted energetically by politicians and publicists, it can inhibit good citizenship. But to be fair to conservatism in toto, let us first note how social conservatism evokes a good deal of republican behavior in support of public projects that conservatives believe will enhance the quality of community life.

Especially since the 1960s, many Americans have agonized over how they might promote virtue in a society plagued by widespread images of violence and sex, an increasing incidence of divorce, extensive drug abuse, rising crime rates, social fragmentation encouraged by multiculturalism, a considerable waning of patriotism, expensive but sometimes ineffective schools, and the ubiquitous presence of commercial television in America life. With varying degrees of intensity, such matters worry both conservatives and liberals as they go about making a living and connecting morally and emotionally with family, friends, and neighbors.[42] Accordingly, when social issues are at stake, activists from the right and left encourage civic engagement based on acquiring information, getting organized, and expressing preferences for public policies designed to make America a better place to live.

In this age of transition leading to no one knows what, social conservatives are inclined to fear that Washington politicians and bureaucrats are indifferent to local virtues. They therefore tend to recommend that lawmakers will address social problems at the state rather than federal level of government. An inclination in this direction explains why, in party politics, social conservatives are likely to join forces with economic conservatives – of whom, more in a moment – for the latter, with an eye on safeguarding the marketplace, prefer that Washington, except for national defense, will maintain a low public policy profile.[43]

---

for the Twenty-first Century (New York: Dutton, 1997). For an analysis of the conservative approach to values, see George Lakoff, *Moral Politics: What Conservatives Know That Liberals Don't* (Chicago: Univ. of Chicago Press, 1996).

[42] See Alan Wolfe, *One Nation, After All. What Middle-Class Americans Really Think About: God, Country, Family, Racism, Welfare, Immigration, Homosexuality, Work, the Right, the Left, and Each Other* (New York: Penguin, 1998).

[43] Good examples of how social and economic ideas combine in conservatism to support hostility to Washington, appear in President Ronald Reagan's "Acceptance Speech" (August 15, 1980) and his first "Inaugural Address" (January 20, 1981). Both speeches are available in *A Time for Choosing: The Speeches of Ronald Reagan, 1961–1982* (Chicago: Regnery Gateway, 1983), pp. 217–235, 237–247. See esp. p. 240, where on Inaugural Day in 1981 Reagan said that "in the present crisis, government is not the solution to our

And thus in the world of conservative people and ideas, candidates and publicists, one finds frequent alliances of big business firms and small-town enthusiasts, the common ground for neoconservatives and ordinary workers, the ties that bind the *Wall Street Journal* to the Christian Right.[44]

Here, though, is a brake on what we have defined as good citizenship. Social conservatives encourage a considerable amount of republican behavior outside of Washington's Beltway. It follows that they deserve two cheers in our story.[45] But economic conservatives are almost characteristically suspicious of government activity. Consequently, as we shall see, they work hard to dissuade citizens from calling, within the framework of Citizenship III, on government to fashion the sort of structural reforms that economic conscience might suggest. The bottom line is that, to the extent economic conservatism impacts on American politics, it tends to inhibit republican practices.[46]

---

problem; government *is* the problem." A more recent expression of similar sentiments was offered in the 1990s by Don Fierce, then director of strategic planning at the Republican National Committee. See him quoted in Dan Balz and Ronald Brownstein, *Storming the Gates: Protest Politics and the Republican Revival* (Boston: Little, Brown, 1996), p. 15: "Washington has replaced communism as the glue for conservatives. . . . [It] is financially and morally bankrupt and because of that it is the glue that binds *economic and social conservatives*. These are people that love their country but hate their federal government" (emphasis supplied).

[44] Such alliances lead Michael Lind to describe the "Conservative Movement" as a "triangular trade" that rests upon "the grass-roots right, the corporate right, and the brain trust right." Less formally, he suggests that the alignments which underlie modern American conservatism may be described, with some exaggeration, as "midwestern foundations paying Jewish and Catholic intellectuals in the Northeast to tell Southern Baptists why they should vote for Sunbelt politicians (Nixon, Reagan, Bush)." See Lind, *Up from Conservatism: Why the Right Is Wrong for America* (New York: Free Press, 1996), pp. 75–76.

[45] I am not socially conservative and do not endorse much that social conservatives propose. Nevertheless, their civic activity in state and local politics is republican and therefore, in principle, deserves two cheers. The third cheer I withhold because, as I will point out in the text, social conservatives ally themselves to economic conservatives who advocate limiting republican practices in Washington. Some scholars will probably feel I should not offer even two cheers if I disagree with policies advocated by various groups which, in this formulation, I describe as republican. An argument along such lines, but not against me personally, may be found in Simone Chambers and Jeffrey Kopstein, "Bad Civil Society," *Political Theory* (December 2001), pp. 837–865. Chambers and Kopstein argue that among American groups, all assuredly "civil," some are good and some are bad, because some support democracy and others endanger it. I believe that in our story of good citizenship, such a distinction among "republican" groups is not necessary.

[46] A social conservative might discern a dilemma here. Thus while Gertrude Himmelfarb criticizes most federal activism, she also warns that by "denigrating the state, we risk

Measurement Problems

This impact cannot be gauged exactly. On the one hand, the term *conservatism* sometimes labels a collection of ideas promulgated by thinkers and activists such as George Will,[47] Charles Murray,[48] George Gilder,[49] and Burton Pines.[50] Yet no one knows how many American voters are familiar with the ideas of such writers or animated by them.[51] So the realm of political thought is not necessarily correlated with the world of political practice in America.

On the other hand, conservatism sometimes refers to the sort of governmental policies advocated by elected officials such as Senator Trent Lott and Congressman Dick Armey, who claim to serve a conservative mandate based on election results.[52] There are two measurement problems here.

---

attenuating the idea of citizenship." See her *One Nation, Two Cultures: A Searching Examination of American Society in the Aftermath of Our Cultural Revolution* (New York: Knopf, 1999), pp. 79–84.

[47] For example, Will, *The Morning After: American Successes and Excesses, 1981–1986* (New York: Collier Macmillan, 1986); and *Suddenly: The American Idea Abroad and at Home, 1986–1990* (New York: Free Press, 1990).

[48] For example, Murray, *Losing Ground: American Social Policy, 1950–1980* (New York: Basic Books, 1984).

[49] For example, Gilder, *Wealth and Poverty* (New York: Basic, 1981).

[50] For example, Pines, *Back to Basics: The Traditionalist Movement That Is Sweeping Grass-Roots America* (New York: William Morrow, 1982).

[51] Social science research suggests that so-and-so many Americans are "conservative," while a certain number of others are "liberal" or "undecided." But no one knows what such research results are worth, since they usually flow from asking respondents to define themselves. Such respondents may know little or nothing about the ideas they say characterize their own thinking. For example, in Arthur Sanders, "The Meaning of Liberalism and Conservatism," *Polity* (Fall 1986), 40 percent of survey respondents could offer no definition of liberalism or conservatism (p. 128), and among those who did have some definition in mind, "there is no [significant level of] agreement as to what liberalism or conservatism mean" (p. 134). The limited usefulness of such polls was noted by Neil Postman, *Technopoly: The Surrender of Culture to Technology* (New York: Vintage, 1993), p. 136:

> Let us imagine what we would think of opinion polls if the questions came in pairs, indicating what people "believe" and what they "know" about the subject. If I may make up some figures, let us suppose we read the following: "The latest poll indicates that 72 percent of the American public believes we should withdraw economic aid from Nicaragua. Of those who expressed this opinion, 28 percent thought Nicaragua was in central Asia, 18 percent thought it was an island near New Zealand, and 27.4 percent believed that 'Africans should help themselves,' obviously confusing Nicaragua with Nigeria. Moreover, of those polled, 61.8 percent did not know that we give economic aid to Nicaragua, and 23 percent did not know what 'economic aid' means."

[52] For example, Newt Gingrich and Dick Armey, *Contract with America* (New York: Times Books, 1994).

First, the American voting public is smaller than the number of adults who could vote if they would register properly and cast ballots. Thus a Republican president such as Ronald Reagan, or a Republican majority in the House of Representatives, formerly led by Newt Gingrich, even after winning a majority of votes cast on election day, does not necessarily represent a conservative consensus in the nation.[53]

Second, even those Americans who vote do not always like the policy preferences of candidates they support.[54] For one thing, candidates may camouflage those preferences with deceptive campaign advertising.[55] For another thing, the commitment of some individuals to conservative principles of laissez-faire and small government may not overcome their enthusiasm for Social Security, Medicare, environmental protection, public subsidies for child care, and many other government programs.[56] Thus sincerity may trump consistency, as when some John or Mary Q. Public will insist that Washington should stay away from his or her Social Security checks.[57]

---

[53] In the Republican congressional "landslide" of 1994, the G.O.P. received 52 percent of the national vote and gained fifty-four seats in the House of Representatives. See Gerald M. Pomper, Walter Dean Burnham, Anthony Corrado, Marjorie Randon Hershey, Marion R. Just, Scott Keeter, Wilson Carey McWilliams, and William G. Mayer, *The Election of 1996: Reports and Interpretations* (Chatham, N.J.: Chatham House, 1997), p. 205. However, because many people did not vote, only 21 percent of potential voters supported that party in the same elections, which makes all claims to a mandate suspect. See W. Lance Bennett, *The Governing Crisis: Media, Money, and Marketing in American Elections*, 2nd ed. (New York: St. Martin's, 1996), p. 115. A related phenomenon is the sometimes unrepresentative tendency of the Republican Party to nominate conservative candidates. For example, Republican national convention delegates tend to be more conservative than Republican voters. [Democratic national convention delegates tend to be more liberal than Democratic voters. D.R.] On the conservatism of Republican delegates in the 1992 national convention, see Lowi, *The End of the Republican Era*, pp. 211–212: "47 percent of the Republican delegates were 'born-again Christians' and ... 79 percent of the delegates defined their ideologies as ranging from conservative to very conservative."

[54] For an analysis of this disparity, see Larry M. Schwab, "The Myth of the Conservative Shift in American Politics: A Research Note," *Western Political Quarterly* (December 1988), pp. 817–823.

[55] Kathleen Jamieson, *Dirty Politics: Deception, Distraction, and Democracy* (New York: Oxford Univ. Press, 1992), esp. pp. 43–101.

[56] In the terms used by Lloyd A. Free and Hadley Cantril, *The Political Beliefs of Americans: A Study of Public Opinion* (New York: Clarion Books, 1968), pp. 15–32, some "ideological conservatives" are "operational liberals."

[57] For example, see Haynes Johnson and David S. Broder, *The System: The American War of Politics at the Breaking Point* (Boston: Little, Brown, 1996–1997), p. 588: "[Senator John Breaux of Louisiana] ... was walking through the New Orleans airport, returning home, when an elderly female constituent approached him. 'Senator, Senator,' she said, plucking emotionally at his sleeve. 'Now don't you let the government get hold of my Medicare.'" See also Mark Crispin Miller, *The Bush Dyslexicon: Observations on a National Disorder*

In short, one cannot say for sure how conservative America has become. There can be little doubt, however, that right-wing talk about values attaching to individuals, families, communities, work, and the marketplace took center stage in America's political discourse during the 1970s. In this sense, for a generation now, conservative ideas have made considerable headway in American public life. Many politicians who might formerly have endorsed liberalism moved to what they called the political center for fear of appearing too liberal, and some conservative preferences – less welfare, less government regulation, lower federal income taxes – were enacted into law even though the public is not wholeheartedly conservative.

The Locus of Danger

Although we cannot know for sure how strongly conservatism as a whole affects American politics, we can suspect that some elements of desirable civic behavior are especially difficult to achieve because of pressure from the economic side of conservative sentiments. Consumerism, which economic conservatives admire, does not deny the worth of civic virtue even though it commends a pursuit of commercial goods. Accordingly, it happens frequently that conservatives today advocate consumerism and, like everyone else, praise good citizenship. To recommend two ends does not guarantee, though, that they can be achieved together. And so, while conservative pundits like George Will and William Bennett encourage good citizenship,[58] they also defend practices that, on occasion, make that citizenship difficult to exercise. Thus conservatives tend to support an amalgam of consumerism, laissez-faire, and small government, all the while arguing that an economy shaped by such parameters encourages behavior which Americans admire.

For our story, the point to remember is that a recipe for civic inhibition lies in that part of conservatism, not necessarily promoted by Christian

---

(New York: Norton, 2002), p. 216, where George W. Bush is quoted, from *USA Today*, November 3, 2000: "They [liberals? Democrats? D.R.] want the federal government controlling Social Security like it's some kind of federal program."

[58] See George Will, *Statecraft as Soulcraft: What Government Does* (London: Weidenfeld and Nicolson, 1984), p. 134: "By virtue I mean nothing arcane or obscure. I mean good citizenship, whose principal components are moderation, social sympathy, and willingness to sacrifice private desires for public ends." See also William Bennett, *The Death of Outrage: Bill Clinton and the Assault on American Values* (New York: Simon and Schuster, 1998), passim, but esp. pp. 9, 133–134. Bennett called upon American citizens to be more virtuous, that is, to favor impeaching Bill Clinton for violating what Bennett regarded as basic values in American public life.

Rightists like Pat Robertson[59] or Ralph Reed,[60] which insists that individual happiness (1) lies mostly in the realm of tangible goods and (2) can be achieved mostly without government action. That is, economic conservatives argue that good lives are based mainly on personal consumption, and they hold that, if people will work hard, a maximum amount of that consumption and happiness can be assured by a minimal amount of government activity.

Some Americans are familiar with this view from claims promoted by conservative thinkers and politicians.[61] However, the same view is also driven home daily, to all Americans, by the forces of consumerism itself, by countless advertisements for every sort of personal product, from toothpaste to lipstick, from digital cameras to snowmobiles, and by a barrage of public relations talk sponsored by business people who oppose government regulation of their particular enterprises. In what amounts to a serious imbalance in national talk, the private sector generates no similar quantity of advocacy for public goods.[62]

Agenda Setting

Conservatism is not the only force turning America into "a nation of spectators."[63] Liberalism can also disable good citizenship, by promoting the exercise of rights and not always demanding the fulfillment of duties.[64]

---

[59] For example, Pat Robertson, *The Turning Tide: The Fall of Liberalism and the Rise of Common Sense* (Dallas: Word Publishing, 1993).

[60] For example, Ralph Reed, *Politically Incorrect: the Emerging Faith Factor in American Politics* (Dallas: Word Publishing, 1994).

[61] For example, see Jack Kemp, *An American Renaissance: A Strategy for the 1980s* (Lake Wylie, S.C.: Hopper and Associates, 1979); Charles Murray, *In Pursuit of Happiness and Good Government* (New York: Touchstone, 1988); and Dinesh D'Souza, *The Virtue of Prosperity: Finding Values in an Age of Techno-affluence* (New York: Basic, 2000).

[62] This imbalance was highlighted by Galbraith, *The Affluent Society*, Ch. 8, "The Theory of Social Balance," pp. 198–211.

[63] See *A Nation of Spectators: How Civic Disengagement Weakens America and What We Can Do About It* (Washington, D.C.: The National Commission on Civic Renewal, 1998). The Commission was co-chaired by Sam Nunn and William Bennett, and the report was paid for by the Pew Charitable Trusts.

[64] For example, see the many civic duties that David Selbourne regards as belonging to good citizenship in his *The Principle of Duty: An Essay on the Foundations of the Civic Order* (London: Abacus, 1997). See also the argument that people who are passionately committed to rights may overlook the importance of obligations, in Mary Ann Glendon, *Rights Talk: The Impoverishment of Political Discourse* (New York: Free Press, 1991), p. 17: "In recent years, we have made great progress in making the promise of rights a reality,

And the rise of "professionally run advocacy groups and nonprofit institutions" has discouraged many people from joining the kind of large, sometimes nationwide organizations that once provided an outlet for civic enthusiasm and activism.[65] Furthermore, government practices that yield unintended consequences, like the move to replace draftees with paid volunteer soldiers in 1973, can turn many citizens into onlookers rather than participants in great affairs of state.[66] Moreover, technical devices of no particular bent, such as television, can powerfully and unfavorably affect American attitudes and behavior toward public life.[67] And when state or county bureaucrats make it difficult for potential voters to register, the elected officials who can pass laws to make registration easier often refrain from doing so, apparently preferring small electorates whose behavior is fairly predictable.[68]

Fortunately, even together with other inhibiting forces, conservatism does not throttle citizenship entirely, for many Americans still vote, campaign, attend political meetings, and support, for example, the League of Women Voters and the American Civil Liberties Union.[69] Nevertheless, economic conservatism does impede good citizenship, in the sense that it forestalls some policy options via what John Kingdon calls *agenda setting*.[70] Thus when conservative ideas bear on individual and collective expectations, they tend to limit the scope of public debate to an agenda

but in doing so we have neglected another part of our inheritance – the vision of a republic where citizens actively take responsibility for maintaining a vital political life."

[65] Theda Skocpol, *Diminished Democracy: From Membership to Management in American Civic Life* (Norman: Univ. of Oklahoma Press, 2003), pp. 127–174.

[66] See Matthew A. Crenson and Benjamin Ginsberg, *Downsizing Democracy: How America Sidelined Its Citizens and Privatized Its Public* (Baltimore: Johns Hopkins Univ. Press, 2002), pp. 38–45.

[67] For example, see Robert M. Entman, *Democracy Without Citizens: Media and the Decay of American Politics* (New York: Oxford Univ. Press, 1989); Douglas Kellner, *Television and the Crisis of Democracy* (Boulder, Colo.: Westview, 1990); and Joseph N. Cappella and Kathleen Hall Jamieson, *Spiral of Cynicism: The Press and the Public Good* (New York: Oxford Univ. Press, 1997).

[68] This is a main theme in Frances Fox Piven and Richard A. Cloward, *Why Americans Still Don't Vote: And Why Politicians Want It That Way* (Boston: Beacon, 2000).

[69] See the cross-national comparisons of various forms of political participation in Sidney Verba, Kay Lehman Schlozman, and Henry E. Brady, *Voice and Equality: Civic Voluntarism in American Politics* (Cambridge: Harvard Univ. Press, 1995), pp. 69–74. Here, Americans lag behind other industrialized democracies in voting but lead in "campaign work" and "community work."

[70] John Kingdon, *Agendas, Alternatives, and Public Policy*, 2nd ed. (New York: HarperCollins, 1995), pp. 1–20. A complementary view of how some policy options never get contested publicly is offered, but without using Kingdon's descriptive terms, by Nina Eliasoph,

of acceptable topics and respectable solutions which, in their totality, advantage those who prefer that, when political issues are considered, some possible goals for good citizenship will seem off-limits.[71] The lines of cause and effect in this equation cannot be traced precisely, but two areas where difficulties appear are in the expression of political attitudes and in the scope of public policies.

Political Attitudes

How does conservatism foster political attitudes which militate against good citizenship? Americans are encouraged by consumerism, and also by economic conservatives, to pursue personal happiness in the marketplace. Thus shopping has become a major leisure time activity, and we cannot doubt that citizens are impelled to buy more than they truly need. The problem is not that people should sacrifice what they want but that to promote happiness mainly via acquisition is to upset a useful balance between individual and collective interests.[72]

Avoiding Politics: How Americans Produce Apathy in Everyday Life (New York: Cambridge Univ. Press, 1998). See p. 244:

> Important institutions surrounding the groups I studied propagated an image of community that helped vaporize debate. Social service workers, commercial culture, corporations, and politicians favored an image of "community" that excluded disagreement, discussion of justice and power, social analysis, and a sociological imagination.... Power worked through political etiquette, as citizens cooperated with dominant institutions by defining community gatherings in ways that rarely opened up public space for questioning and debate.

[71] On deliberate efforts at agenda setting by a leading conservative, see Elizabeth Drew, *Showdown: The Struggle Between the Gingrich Congress and the Clinton White House* (New York: Touchstone, 1997), p. 14. In January 1995, Drew asked Newt Gingrich (R-Georgia), newly elected speaker of the House of Representatives, what he expected to accomplish by the end of the legislative session (December 1996). The Speaker replied:

> We may have a more limited success in terms of bills, but the whole language of politics will be in the midst of transformation. We'll be building a bow-wave of change.... The real breaking point is when you find yourself having a whole new debate, with new terms. That's more important than legislative achievements.... We'll know in six months whether we have accomplished that.... [President Ronald] Reagan didn't quite pull it off.

[72] The stakes here are discussed in Robert E. Calvert, "Political 'Realism' and the Progressive Degradation of Citizenship: A Quiet Constitutional Crisis," in Calvert (ed.), *"The Constitution of the People": Reflections on Citizens and Civil Society* (Lawrence: Univ. of Kansas Press, 1991), pp. 127–157. Calvert describes a sequence of campaign statements by vice presidential candidates George Bush and Geraldine Ferraro in 1984. Bush announced

For example, the conservative insistence on cutting taxes whenever possible[73] derives much of its electoral appeal from the fact that, after spending much of their income on sometimes trivial consumer goods, many Americans feel they cannot "afford" to pay enough in taxes to underwrite a full range of public amenities.[74] And so taxation rates in America are consistently lower than those in other modern democracies,[75] which suggests that a cultural preference for spending privately rather than a national passion for frugality encourages America to underspend

that the election would be won by the party that put something into voters' wallets, while it would be lost by the party that would take something out. Ferraro replied that to describe American politics in wallet terms was an indication that the Bush-Reagan administration promoted selfishness in public life. Bush came back to argue that

> the opposition talks as if it were immoral to want to take care of your own family, loved ones, and work toward the good life and maybe buy a new car or get a mortgage on a house or save up for your children's education. We've got news for them – that is the American dream. There's nothing wrong about it [at] all; freedom, opportunity, family, faith, fair play – that's what America is all about.

Calvert concludes that by defining voter behavior as politics-by-wallet, Bush "reduced American citizenship, a complex political and moral status with a rich history, to a single, material, individualistic, and self-regarding dimension."

73 For an extended argument to this effect, see Gilder, *Wealth and Poverty*. For a realization of the argument in practice, see Republican President George W. Bush's tax cut proposal which, slightly amended, passed Congress on May 26, 2001, by a vote of 240–154 in the House and 58–33 in the Senate. No Republicans in the House opposed the bill and only two Republicans voted against it in the Senate. See "Congress Passes $1.35 Trillion Tax Cut," *Washington Post* (May 27, 2001), p. A1.

74 See Jules Henry, *On Education* (New York: Vintage, 1972), p. 21: "After we have calculated expenditures for food, drink, entertainment . . . , fishing tackle, guns, high-fi sets . . . , outboard motor boats, two cars . . . , a summer vacation, a barbecue pit . . . , mouthwashes, cosmetics, cigarettes, bowling, movies and repairs on the car . . . , we are willing to give our children the best education to be bought with the money that's left over." See also Juliet B. Schor, *The Overspent American: Why We Want What We Don't Need* (New York: HarperCollins, 1998), p. 108: "Americans increasingly resent paying taxes to buy public goods like parks, schools, the arts, or support for the poor because taxes are perceived as subtracting from the private consumption they deem absolutely necessary. We find ourselves skimping on invisibles such as insurance, college funds, and retirement savings as the visible commodities somehow become indispensable."

75 See Seymour Martin Lipset, *American Exceptionalism: A Double-Edged Sword* (New York: Norton, 1996), p. 73: "While America collected 31 percent of its GDP in tax revenues in 1991, other countries such as Sweden (52%), Holland (48%), Belgium (40%), France (40%), and the United Kingdom (36%) were taxed at higher levels." See also tax rates for different countries in Louis A. Ferleger and Jay R. Mandel, *No Pain, No Gain: Taxes, Productivity, and Economic Growth* (New York: Twentieth-Century Fund, 1992), p. 13.

on public education, roads, parks, low-income housing, child care, and other public services.[76]

On this score, a heightened sense of self-interest can overwhelm the republican capacity for practicing self-control on behalf of public interests. Where that is so, we may expect to find that, among citizens who are politically alert, some will turn to activism in hope of attaining a material or ideological reward there. Mancur Olson predicted this sort of political behavior,[77] and it may be said to characterize much of the recent activism of unions, fundamentalists, ethnic groups, and feminists.[78]

For the most part, political talk initiated by such people focuses on their needs rather than on the larger nature of American society, as it is being industrialized, computerized, bureaucratized, marketized, advertised, and televised. To some extent, indifference to larger realities may reflect a sense that the world of work, production, leisure, and consumption is running satisfactorily and needs no repair. Surely corporations seek to induce this impression when they encourage Americans to believe that the economy embraces no conflict of interests – say, between capital and labor, or chemicals and the environment – but only harmonious elements, as projected by reassuring advertising slogans such as "You're in Good Hands at Allstate."

Some political scientists believe that a structural difficulty has developed around this point.[79] Research suggests that danger arises not because some Americans will join pressure groups from self-interest. Rather, the larger task of reconciling those interests on behalf of the public weal will be difficult to perform now that party brokers, more than in the past, are

---

[76] Conservatives sometimes argue exactly the opposite, that American government tends to *overspend* because bureaucrats want higher budgets and politicians seek to "buy" voter support. The argument to this end is described in Desmond S. King, *The New Right: Politics, Markets, and Citizenship* (Chicago: Dorsey, 1987), pp. 100–104.

[77] *The Logic of Collective Action: Public Goods and the Theory of Groups* (Cambridge: Harvard Univ. Press, 1965), esp. pp. 9–52.

[78] On the increasing power of what are sometimes called single-interest groups, see Allan J. Cigler and Burdett A. Loomis (eds.), *Interest Group Politics*, 4th ed. (Washington, D.C.: Congressional Quarterly, 1995). See also Mark J. Rozell and Clyde Wilcox, *Interest Groups in American Campaigns: The New Face of Electioneering* (Washington, D.C.: Congressional Quarterly, 1998).

[79] See Clifton McClesky, "The De-Institutionalization of American Politics," in Ellis Sandoz and Cecil V. Crabb, Jr. (eds.), *A Tide of Discontent: The 1980 Elections and Their Meaning* (Washington, D.C.: Congressional Quarterly, 1981), pp. 113–138. See also Gerald Pomper, "The Decline of Party in American Elections," *Political Science Quarterly* (Spring 1977), pp. 21–41; and Morris Fiorina, "The Decline of Collective Responsibility in American Politics," *Daedalus* (Spring 1980), pp. 25–45.

in thrall to money and votes delivered by single interest groups and their Political Action Committees.[80]

Public Policies

What difficulties does conservatism cause for citizenship in the realm of public policies? Here, the conservative doctrine of communal restraint, focusing more on economic than on social affairs, tends to restrict the number of issues that citizens will debate publicly.[81] There are, for example, three powerful economic practices which, by conservative standards, citizens should leave alone.

In the first case, as we have seen, corporations inside America play state and local governments against each other, seeking low business taxes, weak pollution standards, and other costly subsidies in return for a willingness to set up shop within any particular jurisdiction.[82] If all jurisdictions could resist this sort of economic haggling, environmental quality would improve and tax revenues gained might be used for schools, parks, roads, and so forth. Yet little talk is heard of how setting national rules, such as federal charter requirements, might prevent corporations from gaining locally at public expense, and popular indifference to this option seems reasonable according to conservative ideas of how maximal

---

[80] On political contributions and PACs, see Larry J. Sabato, *PAC Power: Inside the World of Political Action Committees* (New York: Norton, 1984). See also Brooks Jackson, *Honest Graft: Big Money and the American Political Process* (Washington, D.C.: Farragut, 1990); and Dan Clawson, Alan Neustadtl, and Denise Scott, *Money Talks: Corporate PACs and Political Influence* (New York: Basic Books, 1992). On the general influence of money in American politics, see William Greider, *Who Will Tell the People: The Betrayal of American Democracy* (New York: Touchstone, 1992).

[81] Herbert McClosky and John Zaller, *The American Ethos* (Cambridge: Harvard Univ. Press, 1984), p. 169: "While democracy asserts the right of the people to rule, capitalism in effect limits this right by removing economic affairs from popular control."

[82] The ubiquity of public relations "spin" may mask the authentic flavor of jockeying both inside and outside of the United States. But see how Lee Iacocca, as president of the Chrysler Corporation in 1980, described his participation in this practice. Iacocca is quoted in Jeanie Wylie, *Poletown: Community Betrayed* (Urbana: Univ. of Illinois Press, 1989), p. 36:

> Ford, when I was there, General Motors, Chrysler, all over the world, we would pit Ohio versus Michigan. We'd pit Canada versus the U.S. We'd get outright grants and subsidies in Spain, in Mexico, in Brazil – all kinds of grants. With my former employer (Ford), one of the last things I did was, on the threat of losing 2,000 jobs in Windsor [Canada], I got $73 million outright to convert an engine plant.... I've had great experience in this. I have played Spain versus France and England so long I'm tired of it, and I have played the states against each other over here.

corporate freedom is desirable because it leads eventually to increased efficiency and enlarging the gross national product.

To this end, as we have noted, economic conservatism goes hand in hand with social conservatism. Thus those who object to economic regulation from Washington are natural electoral allies of those who praise state governments for promoting neighborliness, voluntarism, direct participation, and local initiatives, even while such governments are unable, coincidentally, to resist corporate jockeying for public subsidies of one kind or another. Curiously, as Michael Lind notes, the outlook here resembles an earlier Confederate devotion to states' rights and therefore recommends a sort of constitutional theory which many Americans assume the country rejected when Northerners won the Civil War.[83]

In the second case, unfolding in a larger arena, American corporations are allowed to move much of their production abroad, into the global economy. Here too they jockey between different political jurisdictions in order to obtain minimal taxation and weak pollution controls. Most important for its effect at home, as we have seen, they can hire foreign workers at wages lower than those in America, thereby exporting good jobs and depriving many Americans of decent pay.

In these circumstances, citizens sensible of a common destiny might seek to improve their national quality of life by promoting terms of trade designed to protect them, at least somewhat, from dislocations caused by international jockeying.[84] Instead, Republicans led by President George Bush proposed expanding *free trade* by creating the North Atlantic Free Trade Association (NAFTA). NAFTA encourages cheap manufacturing in Mexico and sets low tariffs on entry into the United States of goods produced there, under whatever conditions, the former drawing jobs out of the United States and the latter prompting importation of goods priced to undersell those made by American workers.[85] Complaining about

---

[83] See Lind, *Up from Conservatism*, Ch. 9, "The Confederate Theory of the Constitution," pp. 208–234.

[84] Against free trade, and therefore in favor of industrial policies, see Jeremy Seabrook, *The Myth of the Market: Promises and Illusions* (New York: Black Rose Books, 1991); Ravi Batra, *The Pooring of America: Competition and the Myth of Free Trade* (New York: Collier, 1993); and Tim Lang and Colin Hines, *The New Protectionism: Protecting the Future Against Free Trade* (New York: New Press, 1993). Against industrial policies, see Richard B. McKenzie, *Competing Visions: The Political Conflict over America's Economic Future* (Washington, D.C.: Cato Institute, 1985).

[85] On some of the drawbacks of NAFTA and other arrangements encouraging free trade, see Ralph Nader and Lori Wallach, "Gatt, NAFTA, and the Subversion of the Democratic

the social costs that NAFTA would impose on America, Ross Perot and Pat Buchanan, both former Republicans, ran unsuccessfully for president in 1992 and 1996.

In a third case of political scope, faith in free markets justifies a serious restraint on republican decision making when conservatives favor permitting America's Federal Reserve Board to create unemployment by raising interest rates to hold down inflation. Economists rarely criticize this practice because they tend to define inflation as a threat to legitimate business profits.[86] Moreover, unless they worry about falling stock prices or rising mortgage payments, most Americans probably pay little attention to monetary decisions of the Federal Reserve Board. Still, tight money and unemployment cause suffering not shared by all, and one result of tolerating the intentional creation of such suffering is that, by not reacting, citizens passively accept a somewhat blinkered public discourse.[87] Strongly influenced by conservative ideas, that discourse fails to promote debate over whether such matters should be handled by elected representatives or by an agency headed mainly by former bankers and business executives appointed rather than elected to their jobs.[88]

Modified Liberalism

Ergo, mostly from within the Republican Party, conservatives undermine good citizenship in economic affairs. In smaller measure, people who used to call themselves liberal, and who are mainly Democrats, are not always far behind. Of course, deciding what liberalism is, and who liberals are, is a complicated business. On the one hand liberalism, like conservatism, has

---

Process," in Jerry Mander and Edward Goldsmith (eds.), *The Case against the Global Economy and for a Turn Toward the Local* (San Francisco: Sierra Club Books, 1996), pp. 92–107.

[86] On the economists, see George P. Brockway, *The End of Economic Man*, 3rd ed. (New York: Norton, 1995), Ch. 13, "Inflation," pp. 200–218.

[87] See James K. Galbraith, "The Surrender of Economic Policy," in Robert Kuttner (ed.), *Ticking Time Bombs: The New Conservative Assaults on Democracy* (New York: New Press, 1996), p. 102: "To accept . . . the unchallenged monetary judgment of the Federal Reserve is, by definition, to remove macroeconomics from the political sphere."

[88] Scholars occasionally write about how central bankers work and what considerations, beyond the strictly technical, come into play when those men and women make decisions affecting the price and supply of money. For example, see Jonathan Kirshner (ed.), *Monetary Orders: Ambiguous Economics, Ubiquitous Politics* (Ithaca: Cornell Univ. Press, 2003).

no party that bears its name and therefore cannot be located in any group of people or formal platform. On the other hand, since conservatives have strongly criticized liberalism for several decades, and since some of these conservatives have succeeded electorally, politicians who might have run for office as liberal Democrats in previous generations are not always ready to identify themselves as such today.[89]

Notwithstanding these difficulties, it is reasonable to describe modern liberalism as situated on the political spectrum at a point where practitioners and publicists endorse two particular principles. The first of these says, as Progressives did a century ago, that social and economic forces do not always interact automatically to produce public well-being. In that case, government may arbitrate among groups with different interests to produce more satisfactory outcomes. Secondly, as during the New Deal, when government decides to act, liberals believe it may devise structural remedies to public problems. The prescription here is for specific programs and regulations rather than tax reductions or abatements that will change only the existing ratio between private and public expenditures.

On both grounds, some people who might have been liberal in the past are less so now. In this sense, conservative ideas have significantly sapped the willingness of their opponents, who are mostly Democrats, to advocate policies that require the full practice of good citizenship. The move rightward within the naturally liberal camp shows up both in thinking about public problems and in fashioning relevant legislation.

Mickey Kaus

There is, for example, a willingness among modified liberals to accept the conservative notion that economic affairs are ruled by inexorable laws leading to desirable outcomes. Thus Mickey Kaus, an editor for the *New Republic*, in *An End to Equality* (1992), writes of the need to reconstruct liberalism to make it more realistic.[90] By realism he means that Democrats

---

[89] From public statements, it is hard to know what many Democrats believe. Few of them openly champion liberalism, but they may be less sympathetic to the validity than to the effectiveness of conservative ideas. For example, Thomas Byrne Edsall and Mary D. Edsall, *Chain Reaction: The Impact of Race, Rights, and Taxes on American Politics* (New York: Norton, 1992), argue that conservative ideas were used to drive white Democrats away from black Democrats and into the Republican Party, which suggests that those ideas "worked" whether or not they were intellectually persuasive. Michael Lind, *Up from Conservatism*, pp. 15–44, 121–155, tells much the same story.

[90] (New York: Basic Books, 1992), pp. 4–5.

like Senator Edward Kennedy should concede that capitalism, which leads to affluence, "depends on *vast* inequality as the spur to risk-taking."[91] This Kaus regards as unquestionably true even though there are thriving modern societies, from Germany to Italy to Canada to the United States, which hedge in capitalism with varying degrees of taxation and therefore maintain greater and lesser degrees of inequality.[92]

It follows, according to Kaus, that people who advocate funding a substantial public sector, based on taxation high enough to provide a wide range of public goods and services, "must be prepared to give up the sort of material prosperity that only capitalist nations seem able to achieve."[93] Again, Kaus assumes economic inevitability even though adequate prosperity obtains in modern states which, like Sweden and Israel, France and Japan, mix capitalism and socialism in varying proportions and therefore specify different levels of incentives and personal rewards.

Since Kaus assumes that capitalism requires inequality, and that inequality causes poverty, he is not surprised that public spaces such as parks, playgrounds, and libraries are often occupied in America by poor people, many of them unemployed. In fact, as he notes, an *underclass* of such people clutters the social landscape and discomforts the middle class.[94] The solution, for modified liberalism, is to suspend welfare payments to those who make a nuisance of themselves and put them to work instead. This can be done, says Kaus, by government offering to the poor jobs similar to those created by Franklin Roosevelt's Works Progress Administration (WPA) in 1935. Such jobs, scattered across the country, would pay minimum wages to get done things that, for low pay, no one will do today. First, poor people would sign up to work wherever the new jobs would be available. Then, to show its sense of social responsibility, the government would use an Earned Income Tax Credit to bring workers on those jobs up to the official poverty line, say of $10,857 in 1991 for a family of three.[95]

Kaus argues that work of this sort would improve America's creaky public infrastructure by hiring trash collectors, nurses' aides, floor sweepers, public gardeners, bridge painters, office clerks, road repair workers,

---

[91] Ibid., p. 9. The *italics* in the passage cited are in the original.
[92] Some country comparisons are made in Edward W. Wolff, *Top Heavy: A Study of the Increasing Inequality of Wealth in America and What Can Be Done About It* (New York: Twentieth-Century Fund, 1995), pp. 21–25.
[93] Kaus, *An End to Equality*, p. 11. [94] Ibid., p. 55f. [95] Ibid., pp. 127–128.

and so forth, in addition to those already engaged in such work.[96] Union leaders might complain that forcing poor people to work for low pay in those jobs would drive down the income of employees who do such work today for higher wages. Kaus responds that those who work for government now are overpaid, that they should no longer be protected by their unions, and that they should compete as individuals for whatever employment the marketplace will offer, at any price.[97]

The general idea is clear: People should do whatever work the New Economy or government may generate; they should accept whatever wages private or public sector employers may offer; and they should move to wherever modern jobs are, of whatever sort. A citizen guided by what we have called economic conscience will sense here no enthusiasm for enabling Americans, whether current or potential workers, to protect their lives or society against corrosive market forces. Nevertheless, Kaus goes on to link his proposals directly, if inadvertently, to our story by saying that liberals should "make work the prerequisite for full citizenship."[98] This under whatever circumstances, regardless of how many jobs are exported by globalization, regardless of how corporations force wages down by threatening to relocate in America or abroad, and regardless of how the Federal Reserve Board forces unemployment even on Americans willing to work.

To praise capitalism for its material success and to criticize those caught in its backwash is to assume that government cannot or should not channel market forces to produce more desirable social outcomes. This Kaus does even though, like other modified liberals, he favors some government activism that will not affect capitalism's overall shape. Thus he proposes subsidizing day care centers to take in the children of poor working mothers and building orphanages for children whose parents will not work at whatever jobs Kaus wants government to offer them.[99]

---

[96] Ibid., pp. 132–135.   [97] Against labor unions, see ibid., pp. 97–98, 133–134.
[98] Ibid., p. 140.
[99] When he wrote *An End to Equality*, Kaus probably believed that enacting only part of his prescription for ending poverty would be neither fair nor wise. That is, however, what happened in 1996. Modified liberals including Bill Clinton joined with Republican members of Congress and senators to end federal assistance to families with dependent children, replace AFDC with block grants to states, and place time limits on welfare benefits. The same coalition did not, however, authorize federal funding for minimum wage jobs, day care centers, and orphanages. See Michael B. Katz, *In the Shadow of the Poorhouse: A Social History of Welfare in America*, rev. ed. (New York: Basic Books, 1996), Ch. 11, "Redefining the Welfare State [1996]," pp. 300–334.

Robert Reich

What Kaus abandons, together with economic conservatives, is liberal support for the primacy of politics. That is, he posits a state of economic affairs that he regards as inevitable. And then, since nothing citizens might do can improve that situation, he advises them to leave it alone and accept its results.

The primacy of politics is equally absent from another version of modified liberalism offered by Robert Reich, professor of social and economic policy who was secretary of labor during President Clinton's first term of office. In *The Work of Nations* (1992), Reich declares that the law of supply and demand is "ubiquitous and irrepressible."[100] That is, he regards globalization as unfolding in accordance with laws like those of physics and therefore immune to political control. It follows, in Reich's view, that national economies will soon disappear[101] and that trying to maintain them, on behalf of social solidarity, is impossible and would endanger "global economic prosperity."[102]

Having stipulated irrevocable economic laws, Reich concludes that Americans should conform to the international marketplace rather than compel it to adapt to their needs. He then proceeds, like Kaus, to advocate government projects that will leave untouched the basic structure of capitalism. In Reich's case, he proposes a substantial program of government support for education. The main point would be to train what Reich calls "symbolic analysts."[103] These are the research scientists, design engineers, financial consultants, computer programmers, and so forth, who have a marketable ability to handle ideas and information and thereby can "participate in the new global economy."[104]

Reich says that to invest in symbolic analysts would be an act of "positive economic nationalism."[105] On the surface, this sounds like an endorsement of the principle of structural reform, maybe even to the point of recommending an industrial policy. But what Reich actually has in mind is not to make America more livable – that is, to overhaul capitalism – but

---

[100] Robert B. Reich, *The Work of Nations: Preparing Ourselves for Twenty-First-Century Capitalism* (New York: Vintage, 1992), p. 244. Reich's fatalism here is similar to that of nineteenth-century Social Darwinists like William Graham Sumner. For example, see Sumner, *What Social Classes Owe to Each Other* (orig., 1883; Caldwell, Idaho: Caxton, 1961), p. 14: "God and Nature have ordained the chances and conditions of life on earth once for all. The case cannot be reopened. We cannot get a revision of the laws of human life."

[101] Reich, *The Work of Nations*, p. 3.   [102] Ibid., p. 307.   [103] Ibid., pp. 177–180.

[104] Ibid., p. 9.   [105] Ibid., pp. 311–312.

to promote a national effort to make American workers more commercially viable.[106] Indeed, capitalism in its present form seems satisfactory because Reich is confident that commercial worth reflects social value. And so he says that skilled and knowledgeable workers will develop a "virtuous relationship" with the world economy because they will add "greater and greater value" to it.[107] Not for Reich the idea that Americans are entitled to decide for themselves what is virtuous and what is not. And not for him the corollary, that citizens may pull together to design a better economy rather than ask workers to accept trade relations which already exist and which, all too often, foster severe human and environmental exploitation.[108]

---

[106] Reich's emphasis on utilitarian rather than republican consequences of education, resembles a major thrust of the report on American education issued by a committee appointed by Terrell H. Bell, Ronald Reagan's conservative secretary of education. See *A Nation at Risk: The Imperative for Educational Reform* (Washington, D.C.: The National Commission on Excellence in Education, 1983), pp. 6–7:

> We live among determined, well-educated, and strongly motivated competitors. We compete with them for international standing and markets, not only with products but also with the ideas of our laboratories and neighborhood workshops.... Knowledge, learning, information, and skilled intelligence are the new raw materials of international commerce.... Learning is the indispensable investment required for success in the "information age" we are entering.

For a more republican view of education, see John Adams, who recommended the following passage for inclusion in the Massachusetts Constitution of 1780:

> Wisdom and knowledge, as well as virtue, diffused generally among the body of the people, being necessary for the preservation of their rights and liberties, and as these depend on spreading the opportunities and advantages of education in the various parts of the country, and among the different orders of the people, it shall be the duty of legislators and magistrates, in all future periods of this commonwealth, to cherish the interests of literature and the sciences, and all seminaries of them; especially the university [Harvard] at Cambridge, public schools and grammar schools in the towns; to encourage private societies and public institutions, rewards and immunities for the promotion of agriculture, arts, sciences, commerce, trades, manufactures, and a natural history of the country; to countenance and inculcate the principles of humanity and general benevolence, public and private charity, industry and frugality, honesty and punctuality in their dealings, sincerity, good humor, and all social affections and generous sentiments among the people. (*The Works of John Adams, Second President of the United States*, 10 vols. [Boston: Little, Brown, 1850–1856], Vol. IV, "The Report of a Constitution, or Form of Government, for the Commonwealth of Massachusetts" [September, 1779], p. 259)

[107] Reich, *The Work of Nations*, pp. 264–265.

[108] On human exploitation, see Greider, *One World, Ready or Not*, p. 390, for an estimate that Michael Jordan, who in 1992 received from Nike $20 million in promotional

It is no wonder that Reich's boss, the somewhat liberal President Bill Clinton, moving rightward into the political center, embraced conservative enthusiasm for free markets and led Democratic members of Congress in 1993 to join Republicans in enacting George Bush's NAFTA proposal. Similarly, Clinton opposed applying civil rights and environmental standards to American-Chinese commerce but supported, instead, extending trading privileges unconditionally to Beijing in 2000, thereby encouraging the sort of globalization exemplified in NAFTA.[109] The immediate result was that Green candidate Ralph Nader, campaigning against globalization, free trade, and environmental destruction, received enough popular votes in 2000 to deny victory to Democrat Al Gore and propel Republican George W. Bush, an avowed "compassionate conservative," into the White House.

Then and Now

To sum up, the economic side of American conservatism favors private satisfactions and faults a wide range of efforts to deal with modern life collectively.[110] Or, to put the matter another way, conservative ideas, in

---

fees, earned from the company in that year more than all of the twenty-five thousand production workers in Indonesia's shoe industry who were employed by Nike, Adidas, Reebok, L.A. Gear, and other well-known brands. Similar figures appear in Walter LaFeber, *Michael Jordan and the New Global Capitalism* (New York: Norton, 1999), pp. 107, 126, 147.

[109] The issue was whether or not to end the practice of renewing American-Chinese trade relations every year, at which time demands for civil rights and environmental safeguards in China might be advanced as a condition for continued trade. In May of 2000, House members voted 237–197 to end the annual review. One hundred sixty-four Republicans and 73 Democrats voted for; 57 Republicans, 138 Democrats, and 2 Independents voted against. See "House, in 237–197 Vote, Approves Normal Trade Rights for China," *New York Times* (May 25, 2000), pp. A1, A10. The Senate vote in September of 2000 was 83–15. Forty-six Republicans and 37 Democrats voted for; 8 Republicans and 7 Democrats voted against. See "Senate Votes to Remove Curbs on U.S. Trade with China: Bipartisan Support Is Strong," *New York Times* (September 20, 2000), pp. A1, A16. No civil rights or environmental demands were approved, even though China's constitution forbids strikes. On the Chinese failure to permit effective unionization, see also "Workers' Rights Suffering as China Goes Capitalist," *New York Times* (August 22, 2001), pp. A1, A8. This article points out that Ms. Feng, in Dongguan, China, aged twenty, "said she made $36 a month at her electronics plant if she worked 12 hours, seven days a week." When asked about unions, she and her companion replied, "Trade union?...What's that?"

[110] This stance is not new. The essays in J. Peter Euben, John R. Wallach, and Josiah Ober (eds.), *Athenian Political Thought and the Reconstruction of American Democracy* (Ithaca: Cornell Univ. Press, 1994), explain how classical critics of Athenian democracy, via the

certain circumstances, discourage political participation and disparage politics, even though good citizens should regard both as commendable for enabling empowered people to act civically.[111]

The stakes here can be clarified by linking modern warnings against economic activism to conservatism in other eras. It seems clear, for example, that a significant number of Americans are encouraged by conservatism to believe they should wall off capitalism from the state as securely as the Constitution already separates state and religion.[112] In this regard, there is a difference but also a similarity between American support for uninhibited free enterprise and the traditional conservatism of someone like Edmund Burke. Burke spoke for wealthy members of his society and, economically at least, American conservatives do the same now. But whereas Burke sided with eighteenth-century England's landed aristocrats,[113] who were little responsible for leading commercial trends of their day, American conservatives have joined forces with capitalists and corporations, who are constantly and sometimes inconveniently altering the conditions of American life.

This difference suggests that Burke had the easier job of advocacy. He could criticize citizens promoting the French Revolution because he

---

fears they bolstered in Founders such as Madison, Hamilton, and Adams, have long exercised some influence over American politics. Thus there has always been a strand in American thought that regards popular sovereignty as self-centered, irrational, impulsive, fickle, and therefore dangerous enough to warrant reining in by terms and concepts, such as "limited" or "responsible" government, that, as interpreted by economic conservatives, have the capacity to place certain matters off-limits to civic action. See the essay by Ellen Meiksins Wood, "Democracy: An Idea of Ambiguous Ancestry," pp. 59–80, but esp. pp. 59–61 and 70–71.

[111] Thus for some Republicans, but not republicans, it may have sounded natural to say, in a 1998 campaign ad, that Charles Schumer, the Democratic candidate for senator of New York, "prefers politics to people." Citizens might wonder why any American would delegitimize part of republicanism by denigrating the activity which enables free people to shape public life.

[112] For example, see Clyde N. Wilson, "Citizens or Subjects?" in Robert W. Whitaker (ed.), *The New Right Papers* (New York: St. Martin's, 1982), p. 109: "The key to republicanism . . . is the precedence of the community over the government." From this juxtaposition of civil society versus government, Wilson concludes that government should not meddle with the people's right of free enterprise, because "the republic passes over into empire when political activity . . . [becomes] a mechanism for managing . . . [the people] for the benefit of their rulers."

[113] See his *Reflections on the Revolution in France*, ed. Thomas H. D. Mahoney (orig., 1790; New York: Liberal Arts, 1955), p. 58, where he describes England's "large proprietors" as "the ballast in the vessel of the commonwealth," and p. 160, where he describes England's nobility as "a graceful ornament to the civil order. It is the Corinthian capital of polished society."

wanted to preserve the status quo. But American conservatives have a more difficult assignment. They must distract attention from the fact that they are not criticizing but defending the greatest revolutionaries of all, those people most responsible for unremitting social flux and the painful effects of creative destruction.[114] That is why, even though conservatives in history were sometimes called "the party of order," there is a sense in which people who champion free markets today can no longer assure other people, or even themselves, that they will safeguard such an order.[115]

We have seen the solution. Modern conservatives extol capitalism by arguing that, in many cases, a republican sense of civic duty is misplaced. In this view, almost any national or local decision to restrain free market operations, no matter how democratic it may be, will be more costly than beneficial to society. Thus Phil Gramm, Trent Lott, Tom Delay, and their colleagues on Capitol Hill would scorn an hereditary nobility and rotten boroughs. Nevertheless, they join Burke and other historical conservatives by defending the existing balance of social power, which flows chiefly from the market, which favors their allies, and which makes politically inspired repair seem to them "perverse."[116]

Here, then, is the similarity. Conservatives in all eras reject the republican notion that a nation's citizens may decide for themselves how to live together. And so Burke argued that most people should stay away from public affairs because the status quo embodies an accumulation of wisdom unavailable to any group of ordinary people.[117] That is, "the people" must err. Changing the vocabulary, American conservatives argue that voters should leave economic affairs largely alone because market forces are more rational than people seeking to suggest an economic policy to their elected representatives.[118] In short, "the people" must err.

---

[114] On creative destruction, see Joseph Schumpeter, *Capitalism, Socialism, and Democracy*, 3rd ed. (New York: Harper and Row, 1962), pp. 81–86.

[115] This point is made by Alan Wolfe, "Introduction: Change from the Bottom Up," in Wolfe (ed.), *America at Century's End* (Berkeley: Univ. of California Press, 1991). p. 2.

[116] On the conservative "perversity" thesis, see Albert Hirschman, *The Rhetoric of Reaction: Perversity, Futility, and Jeopardy* (Cambridge: Belknap, 1991), pp. 11–42.

[117] See his *Reflections on the Revolution in France*, p. 99: "We are afraid to put men to live and trade each on his own private stock of reason, because we suspect that this stock in each man is small, and that the individuals would do better to avail themselves of the general bank and capital of nations and of ages."

[118] This thought was expressed colloquially by House Majority Leader Dick Armey in his *The Freedom Revolution* (Washington, D.C.: Regnery, 1995), p. 316: "The market is rational and the government is dumb." In a democratic society, scorning the government is politically safer than criticizing the people who elect it.

Of course, American conservatives are now more enthusiastic about democracy than most European conservatives were in the past.[119] For example, they favor allocating Citizenship II widely. The Americans may even be regarded, in some respects, as populists, seeking electoral support by promising to serve the will of "the people."[120]

Burke was never that democratic.[121] The point, though, is not who was or is more nominally democratic, for on substance, which is a matter of Citizenship III, the general thrust of economic conservatism bears a strong family resemblance to what conservatism has always been. Thus conservatives today, like their predecessors, believe that, regardless of what most people might want, some realms of success and privilege should be "conserved," or placed off limits to civic meddling by those less successful or less privileged. And that is where, to some extent, good citizenship flags.

Citizenship and Freedom

We observed above that good citizenship is possible only where citizens are free to exercise it, so let us return to *political freedom* and close with two observations.[122] First, it is a measure of conservative influence that certain

---

[119] In the classic literature of political science, Robert Michels pointed out that, in countries that hold elections, conservative parties will adopt a democratic style even though they believe in privilege and distrust popular tastes. See Michels, *Political Parties: A Sociological Study of the Oligarchical Tendencies of Modern Democracy* (orig., 1915; New York: Free Press, 1966), pp. 43–51. Thus, p. 44: "The political party [of all kinds] is founded in most cases on the principle of the majority.... [Therefore while] remaining essentially anti-democratic in nature... [advocates of the conservative view] find themselves compelled... to make profession of the democratic faith, or at least to assume the democratic mask."

[120] On this score, recent conservative activists know they are more populist than earlier American conservatives such as Russell Kirk, James Burnham, and William Kendall. See Paul M. Weyrich, "Blue Collar or Blue Blood? The New Right Compared with the Old Right," in Whitaker (ed.), *The New Right Papers*, pp. 49–62, and Gottfried and Fleming, *The Conservative Movement*, "Populist Rebellion: The New Right," pp. 77–95. See also Richard A. Viguerie, *The Establishment Vs. the People: Is a New Populist Revolt on the Way?* (Chicago: Regnery, 1983).

[121] See his speech in Bristol, November 3, 1774, where he promised the voters to exercise his best judgment but not necessarily to serve theirs. The speech is excerpted in Ross J. S. Hoffman and Paul Levack (eds.), *Burke's Politics: Selected Writings and Speeches of Edmund Burke on Reform, Revolution, and War* (New York: Knopf, 1959), pp. 114–117.

[122] I am about to claim that conservatism opposes certain elements of political freedom. Conservatives may say that I am wrong, that they are actually strong advocates of political freedom, but that they define it mainly as the right of citizens to act without government permission. Thus, for example, William Simon, *A Time for Truth* (New

items rarely show up on America's public agenda today, as if citizens are not free to act on them. Thus conservatives, even though they encourage political initiative in some local affairs, have succeeded in almost banning the sort of nationwide political discourse that would celebrate a thorough-going republic of free men and women, a great community of active and resourceful citizens, a nation which chooses to live together with common hopes and aspirations, an electorate that proudly fashions public policies designed to generate shared well-being.[123]

If such images of togetherness were widely entertained, they might inspire citizens to prompt Washington to create an *industrial policy*. Animating such a policy would be an assumption that Americans constitute a responsible society rather than a fortuitous collection of individuals living mainly between Canada and Mexico. Or, as Neil Postman observed, what needs saying again and again, and what should be embodied in public policy now more than ever, is that America is a culture rather than simply an economy.[124]

York: Berkeley, 1979), p. 21: "Freedom is difficult to understand because it isn't a *presence* but an *absence* – an absence of government constraint." For another example, see Martin Olasky, *The Tragedy of American Compassion* (Chicago: Regnery, 1992), p. 111, who defines freedom as "the opportunity to work and worship without governmental restriction." The conservative approach to freedom is described in Eric Foner, *The Story of American Freedom* (New York: Norton, 1998), Ch. 13, "Conservative Freedom," pp. 307–332.

123 For example, the "compassionate conservative" President George W. Bush recommended good citizenship several times in his inaugural address on January 20, 2001. But Bush certainly did *not* suggest and did *not* intend to imply that Americans should exercise citizenship by promoting great public projects capable of reshaping national life. For example:

> What you do is as important as anything government does. I ask you to seek a common good beyond your comfort, to defend needed reforms against easy attacks, to serve your nation, beginning with your neighbor. I ask you to be citizens. Citizens, not spectators. Citizens, not subjects. Responsible citizens, building communities of service and a nation of character. . . . When this spirit of citizenship is missing, no government program can replace it. When this spirit is present, no wrong can stand against it. ("President: 'I Ask You to Be Citizens,'" *New York Times* [January 21, 2001], p. A15)

In this speech, Bush rejected the primacy of politics by not calling for great public projects. For a more theoretical argument against various sorts of civic activism, see Irving Kristol, who offers a conservative explanation for why the marketplace rather than politics should "shape our civilization." See his "Business and the New Class," in Irving Kristol (ed.), *Neo-Conservatism: The Autobiography of an Idea* (New York: Free Press, 1995), pp. 205–210.

124 Postman, *Technopoly*, p. 174. See also James Fallows, "What Is an Economy For?" *The Atlantic Monthly* (January 1994), pp. 76–92.

Second, the conservative aversion to political activism in economic affairs reflects the uneasy dialectic between *consumerism* and *republicanism* that we have noted at length, where the former's aspirations may outweigh the latter's needs. Therefore we should remind ourselves that the will to act politically has not always been weak in America. Rather, it was strongly present when republicanism dominated public philosophy. It was vigorously expressed, for example, when the country confronted economic hardship at the end of the nineteenth century and the beginning of the twentieth. Consumerism at that time had not yet challenged republicanism as strongly as it would in later decades. Consequently, Populists, Progressives, many Democrats, and many Republicans understood that they were entitled, and even privileged, to act politically in defense of social values and collective well-being.

A proper grasp of American politics must emphasize the long-standing centrality of this conviction. It is a fact, after all, that many Americans a century ago believed that the right of citizens to use politics constructively, that is, to exercise political freedom, was a great moral achievement of their civilization.[125] Indeed, it was exactly this belief that sustained their forerunners during the two great defining events in early American history. Thus colonists seeking political freedom resolved to fight and, if necessary, to die in the Revolution. The objective then, as expressed in the Declaration of Independence, was to create and maintain a government that would safeguard their rights and serve their interests. To this end Lincoln later believed, and told Unionists in his Gettysburg Address, that Northern soldiers who died in that battle fought the Civil War to preserve political freedom. This he defined as a condition inherent in government of the people, by the people, and for the people.

Freedom, in short, as recommended by the republican vision, was the hallmark of American life, proudly commemorated on the Fourth of July and solemnly invoked on Memorial Day when honoring those who died to preserve it. From freedom other things might follow, including prosperity and happiness. But most importantly, Americans long understood freedom to mean a citizen's ability to join others, when necessary, in creating decent conditions for social life rather than a consumer's capacity, on occasion, to buy either a blue or pink cellular phone.[126]

---

[125] This is one reason why they created and maintained nationwide voluntary groups during the nineteenth and early twentieth centuries. On the political importance of those groups, see Skocpol, *Diminished Democracy*, esp. pp. 20–73.

[126] Scholars assume that such understandings are passed from generation to generation via shared stories which praise the right sort of behavior and condemn the rest. Some

I have noted several times that to cherish freedom in the republican sense is not the same as knowing what to do with it. As if to prove this point, Populists and Progressives did not always agree on exactly how to overcome America's economic difficulties. But many of them shared a firm conviction, based on what they regarded as common sense, that they were entitled to confront those difficulties together. As Theodore Roosevelt said: "The citizens of the United States must effectively control the mighty commercial forces which they themselves have called into being."[127] Woodrow Wilson reached the same conclusion: "Gentlemen say... that the particular kind of combinations that are now controlling our economic development came into existence naturally and were inevitable; and that, therefore, we have to accept them as unavoidable and administer our development through them." Not so, said Wilson: "Without the watchful interference... of the government, there can be no fair play between individuals and such powerful institutions as... trusts. Freedom today is something more than being let alone. The program of a government of freedom must in these days be positive, not negative merely."[128]

Confident of their right to act democratically to improve economic circumstances, Roosevelt, Wilson, and their contemporaries proposed many new projects in public life, from government offices such as the Department of Labor and the Federal Trade Commission, to government regulations in the Pure Food and Drug Act, the Clayton Anti-Trust Act, and the Child Labor Act. Elected officials turned some of these proposals into laws and agencies. Not all of them worked as planned, and changing conditions have made some early reforms obsolete. Nevertheless, the public record

---

of those stories, going back to Socrates, we have touched upon in the text above. Many of them are less persuasive than they used to be, and Neil Postman, *The End of Education: Redefining the Value of School* (New York: Knopf, 1996), notes one reason why this is so. Thus on p. 25, Postman deplores the capacity of consumerism to drain America's sacred symbols of their narrative power:

> There is, for example, the story of our origins, summarized so eloquently in Abraham Lincoln's Gettysburg Address. It tells of a nation "brought forth" through revolution, destined to serve as an example to the rest of the world. This is the same Abraham Lincoln whose face is used to announce linen sales in February. Emma Lazarus's poem celebrating an immigrant culture is lodged at the base of the Statue of Liberty. This is the same Statue of Liberty used by an airline to persuade potential customers to fly to Miami.

[127] Theodore Roosevelt, *The New Nationalism*, intro. by William E. Leuchtenburg (orig., 1910; Englewood Cliffs, N.J.: Prentice-Hall, 1961), p. 27.

[128] Woodrow Wilson, *The New Freedom*, intro. by William E. Leuchtenburg (orig., 1913; Englewood Cliffs, N.J.: Prentice-Hall, 1961), pp. 101, 164.

of those years clearly indicates that a great many voters and politicians were determined to exercise their political freedom whenever social costs became intolerable.

On this score, we may close by recalling the republicanism of William Jennings Bryan. As a Democrat, Bryan ran for president in 1896, 1900, and 1908. He never won the White House. But most of his opponents differed from him more by what they proposed to do for the country than by rejecting in principle the use of government to promote public well-being.[129] Listen to Bryan, then, as he delivers his "Cross of Gold" speech to the Democratic nominating convention in 1896. First, he insists that America need not yield to international pressure, coming then especially from Great Britain, to maintain a gold standard. That is, he assumes that Americans may resist decisions made elsewhere, in the global marketplace, when they think those decisions debase life in their country. Then he reminds his audience that the right to set their own course is a precious national heritage. As Bryan put it,

This nation is able to legislate for its own people on every question, without waiting for the aid or consent of any other nation on earth.... It is the issue of 1776 over again. Our ancestors ... had the courage to declare their political independence of every other nation; shall we, their descendants ... declare that we are less independent than our forefathers?[130]

---

[129] Gabriel Kolko, *The Triumph of Conservatism: A Reinterpretaton of American History, 1900–1918* (Glencoe, Ill.: Free Press, 1963), describes many corporate leaders during the Progressive Era as supporting government regulation of railroads, drugs, meat, banking, national forests [conservation], and more, if only to protect their market position against competitors. Thus, pp. 57–58, "the dominant fact of American political life at the beginning of this [the twentieth] century was that big business led the struggle for federal regulation." And, p. 60, "It was never a question of regulation or no regulation among businessmen during the Progressive Era, or of federal control versus laissez-faire; there was, rather, the question of what type of legislation at what time."

[130] William Jennings Bryan, "You Shall Not Crucify Mankind upon a Cross of Gold," in Ari Hoogenboom and Olive Hoogenboom (eds.), *The Gilded Age* (Englewood Cliffs, N.J.: Prentice-Hall, 1967), p. 176.

Index of Names

Subject Index